Public Relations Writing

As a global academic publisher, Sage is driven by the belief that research and education are critical in shaping society. Our mission is building bridges to knowledge—supporting the development of ideas into scholarship that is certified, taught, and applied in the real world.

Sage's founder, Sara Miller McCune, transferred control of the company to an independent trust, which guarantees our independence indefinitely. This enables us to support an equitable academic future over the long term by building lasting relationships, championing diverse perspectives, and co-creating social and behavioral science resources that transform teaching and learning.

Public Relations Writing

Essential Tools for Effective Storytelling

Valerie "VK" Fields

The University of North Carolina at Chapel Hill

 Sage

FOR INFORMATION:

2455 Teller Road
Thousand Oaks, California 91320
E-mail: order@sagepub.com

1 Oliver's Yard
55 City Road
London, EC1Y 1SP
United Kingdom

Unit No 323-333, Third Floor, F-Block
International Trade Tower Nehru Place
New Delhi – 110 019
India

18 Cross Street #10-10/11/12
China Square Central
Singapore 048423

Printed in the United States of America

Library of Congress Cataloging-in-Publication Number: 2024038050

ISBN: 978-1-0718-5646-8

This book is printed on acid-free paper.

FSC
www.fsc.org
100%
Paper from well-managed forests

Acquisitions Editor: Charles Lee

Editorial Assistant: Hannah Padua

Production Editor: Vijayakumar

Copy Editors: Eve Henningsen and Diane DiMura

Typesetter: TNQ Tech Pvt. Ltd.

Indexer: TNQ Tech Pvt. Ltd.

Cover Designer: Gail Buschman

Marketing Manager: Victoria Velasquez

24 25 26 27 28 10 9 8 7 6 5 4 3 2 1

BRIEF CONTENTS

DETAILED CONTENTS

PREFACE

At the core of every effective communications-focused campaign is quality content that connects and resonates with its target audience. With the introduction of every new product or innovation, community relations campaign, newsworthy story idea, organizational or corporate cause, and multimedia platform comes the need for compelling content and effective storytelling—a skillset that is honed in a public relations writing course. This PR writing textbook will serve as an invaluable resource that equips students well beyond their classroom learning—and into their roles as young professionals who are sufficiently prepared to become strong writers and versatile storytellers within the PR profession.

This new textbook, *Public Relations Writing*, is a step-by-step instructional "how to" guide that provides basic and straightforward approaches to writing PR documents—as opposed to a theoretical analysis of public relations history and the evolution of various tools of the trade. The book is organized such that a PR student or professional student of the industry can simply turn to any chapter and learn how to complete a specific writing task. Additional features include PR Tool Kits, PR Planning Checklists, and Tips for Beginners to reinforce important concepts.

To further comprehension, the textbook provides an in-depth overview of how and why specific PR documents are created — explaining and demonstrating the entire life cycle of documents from creation to implementation, to publication in various media outlets and communication channels. Additionally, the textbook addresses tough (but relevant) issues on Diversity, Equity and Inclusion and socially conscious content that students and young professionals will encounter as PR professionals. Effective and relevant PR Writing must address the realities of diversity, equity, inclusion, conflict, and controversy across the nation and around the world, and understand the significant impact that communicators (and the words they use) can have. Words matter. The consequences of using the right or wrong words can be significant. In the process of developing discourse, there is great value and importance in making students aware of the awesome responsibility that comes with influencing audiences through the power of the written word.

Practically speaking, employers are seeking entry-level workers and recent graduates who know how to produce quality content on Day 1. This book presents basic instruction and techniques with an emphasis on practical skills that allow new professionals to instantly become valuable contributors to the workplace team. Beginning with Associated Press style and PR Ethics, this textbook shapes the framework and explains the standards of professional conduct for PR practitioners and defines the parameters for how industry professionals communicate with the media and the public. Next, the book transitions from content development with media in mind to operational communications with clients at the forefront. From there, the book addresses consumer audiences and focuses on communication through social media, digital media, and visual storytelling, outlining the various tools and tactics used to create compelling copy. This thorough writing guide will train and prepare students to effectively and efficiently learn the skill of quality PR writing.

ACKNOWLEDGMENTS

Thank you to my wonderful husband Shelton for your never-ending support and encouragement from Day 1 — ideation to creation, through completion.

To my father, Leroy Fields Jr., your love, support, dedication and powerful example for our family paved the way for me, and I'm forever grateful.

Special thanks and gratitude to my colleague and dear friend Dr. Lois Boynton, at the University of North Carolina at Chapel Hill, for your expert introduction to ethics in this textbook; and for your amazing and tireless advocacy work.

Thank you to my two research assistants Peggy and Ginny for helping me get off to a strong start; and thank you to my graphic designer Billy for transforming my words and ideas into beautiful images.

Much love and appreciation to my friends and family for championing me throughout this journey: to the Fields, Garner, Minkins, and Russell families . . . I'm truly thankful.

Thank you to the *Public Relations Writing* reviewers whose comments, compliments, and critiques encouraged and inspired me throughout this journey:

- Alisa Agozzino, Ohio Northern University

- Arshia Anwer, Ph.D., Manhattan College

- Bonnie P. Riechert, Ph.D., APR, Fellow PRSA, Belmont University

- Braden Hale Bagley, Southern Utah University

- Heather Paige Preston, Appalachian State University

- Jeffrey D. Brand, University of Northern Iowa

- Jennie Donohue, Senior Lecturer and Director of the Public Relations Concentration, UMass Amherst

- Jill Alexander, APR, Fellow PRSA, University of Missouri–St. Louis

- Jill Wurm, Wayne State University

- Kristyn Hunt Cathey, Lamar University Adjunct Instructor of Communication

- Marcia Gomez, University of Miami

- Michael Babcock, University of Utah Department of Communication

- Ming (Bryan) Wang, University of Nebraska-Lincoln

- Miriam Hernandez, CSU Dominguez Hills

- Paula I. Otto, APR Virginia Commonwealth University

- Robin Street, Adjunct Instructional Assistant Professor of Integrated Marketing Communications

- Ryan Eanes, Klein College of Media & Communication, Temple University

- Sarah G. Hall, Illinois State University

- Vivien V. Angelus, California State University, Fullerton

- Xu Song, Stockton University

- Yang Cheng, North Carolina State University

- Yuchen Liu, Cleveland State University

"In every thing give thanks" —Thessalonians 5:18, KJV

ABOUT THE AUTHOR

Valerie "VK" Fields has a degree in journalism and mass communication, specializing in public relations, from the University of North Carolina at Chapel Hill. She also earned a bachelor's, master's, and doctoral degree in theology from New Covenant Bible Institute in North Carolina. Fields has worked in PR for some of the world's most well-known organizations including Walt Disney World Resort, McDonald's Corporation, and the Ronald McDonald Children's Charities of North Carolina.

Fields (known to her students as Professor VK) has taught Public Relations Writing, Introduction to Public Relations, and Crisis Communication courses over 18 years as a faculty member in the School of Journalism and Media at the University of North Carolina at Chapel Hill.

In May 2016, she received the university's Edward Vick Prize for Innovation in Teaching, honoring unique content and engaging instruction for undergraduate students. In 2018, she received the Michael L. Herman Excellence in Mentoring Award from the North Carolina Public Relations Society of America (PRSA) chapter. In 2019, she completed a certification program in crisis communication presented by the Public Relations Society of America.

Fields is also the founder and chief executive at PR PROS, LLC, an award-winning public relations and content creation agency in Raleigh, North Carolina. In 2023, Black Business Ink honored her with the Power 100 Award, recognizing Fields as one of the Top 100 most influential business leaders in North Carolina. In their spare time, Valerie and her husband Shelton enjoy photography and international travel.

1 INTRODUCTION TO PUBLIC RELATIONS WRITING

LEARNING OBJECTIVES

1.1 Learn how PR industry practitioners define public relations as a profession and what role PR writing plays.

1.2 Describe how the Public Relations Society of America (PRSA) defines public relations.

1.3 Identify what public relations writing is and what public relations writing is not.

1.4 Understand how public relations writing is used in PR campaigns to communicate with audiences.

1.5 Use proven approaches to create quality content for PR writing.

INTRODUCTION

Public relations writing is different from many other literary forms, because creating content and advocating for a client or a cause challenge the writer to be more creative, intentional, innovative and persuasive with their words absent of the journalistic parameters in news writing and reporting, which are carried out solely through the lens of objectivity. As a matter of practice, public relations writing often demands subjectivity because it is fueled by an agenda — for a client, for a campaign, for the greater public good.

Make no mistake, public relations writing needs to be well researched, accurate and written with high standards for spelling, grammar and style — but also with purpose and passion! Public relations writing is exhilarating, and content creation is fulfilling because the process, like every story, begins with a blank page, then results in copy that informs and inspires or motivates and mobilizes people to take action.

Public relations writing comes in many forms and sizes, from international messaging campaigns for global health organizations to social media posts for local nonprofit community outreach events and everything in between.

1.1 — DEFINING PR

To get a solid grasp on understanding public relations writing, it is important to know first what public relations is and how industry experts and professionals define the term. **Public relations** is the art and science of managing relationships and communicating specific messages to target audiences to achieve desired, measurable outcomes using multimedia platforms (V. K. Fields, PR PROS, LLC). This hybrid definition of public relations blends the theoretical and practical aspects of the industry and also defines the process and results often sought by PR practitioners. What follows is a breakdown of the PR definition to explain how each phrase fulfils the overall definition.

Art and Science

Representing both the creative and formulaic aspects of the industry, the art of public relations derives from innovative and imaginative storytelling that uses words and imagery to convey messages. The science of the industry relies on tools, data, statistics, metrics and replicable processes that offer quantitative measures of performance and results.

Managing Relationships

Whether it is client to agency, client to audience, or media to client, managing relationships is a core function of public relations work, which focuses on building and maintaining trust to establish and reinforce communication between all parties. In every definition of public relations, the role of managing relationships is an essential function and priority within the industry.

Communicating Specific Messages

A lot of public relations research and planning is driven by strategy, the "how" and intentional approach for getting things accomplished within a PR campaign. Communicating specific messages means understanding who the audience is and what is important to them and then developing and delivering messages in a meaningful way.

Target Audiences

Every message is not the same for every audience, because the needs and wants of the publics within target audiences are different. Understanding the priorities and motivations of target audiences will help the PR practitioner develop key messages that resonate with the receivers.

Desired, Measurable Outcomes

Depending upon the PR campaign goals and objectives, the process of measuring outcomes may vary. What matters is that every objective, goal and strategy has a built-in metric that allows progress to be monitored and success to be measured during the evaluation phase of the campaign.

Multimedia Platforms

Historically, traditional public relations relied primarily on press releases, press conferences, wire services and media impressions that measured the number of people exposed to a message. Now public relations utilizes traditional media, digital media and social media platforms with back-end metrics for insights and analytics that also incorporate media contacts and media relations efforts and leverage the power of direct-to-consumer messaging, hence streamlining the communication process. Most PR campaigns use a blend of every relevant and accessible outlet in order to extend audience reach and amplify messages to the largest target audiences possible.

1.2 — PR IN PRACTICE

The following section describes how the Public Relations Society of America (PRSA), a trade and advocacy organization for the PR industry, introduces and defines public relations to its membership.

PRSA DEFINES PUBLIC RELATIONS

The formal practice of what is now commonly referred to as "public relations" dates to the early 20th century. Since that time, public relations has been defined in myriad ways, the definition often evolving alongside public relations' changing roles and advances in technology. The earliest definitions emphasized press agentry and publicity, while more modern definitions incorporate the concepts of "engagement" and "relationship building." In 1982, PRSA adopted the following definition: "Public relations helps an organization and its publics adapt mutually to each other."

A more modern definition of public relations was drafted several decades later, a definition that still stands today: "Public relations is a strategic communication process that builds mutually beneficial relationships between organizations and their publics."

At its core, public relations is about influencing, engaging and building a relationship with key stakeholders across numerous platforms in order to shape and frame the public perception of an organization. Public relations also encompasses the following:

- Anticipating, analyzing and interpreting public opinion, attitudes and issues that might have an impact, for good or ill, on the operations and plans of the organization.
- Counseling management at all levels in the organization with regard to policy decisions, courses of action and communications — including crisis communications — taking into account their public ramifications and the organization's social or citizenship responsibilities.
- Protecting the reputation of an organization.
- Researching, conducting and evaluating, on a continuing basis, programs of action and communications to achieve the informed public understanding necessary to the success of an organization's aims. These may include marketing; financial; fundraising; employee, community or government relations; and other programs.
- Planning and implementing the organization's efforts to influence or change public policy.

- Setting objectives, planning, budgeting, recruiting and training staff, developing facilities — in short, managing the resources needed to perform all of the above.
- Overseeing the creation of content to drive customer engagement and generate leads.

Below are some of the disciplines/functions within PR:
- Corporate Communications
- Crisis Communications
- Executive Communications
- Internal Communications
- Investor Relations Communications
- Marketing Communications
- Integrated Marketing/Integrated Marketing Communications
- Media Relations
- Content Creation
- Events
- Social Media
- Multimedia
- Reputation Management
- Speechwriting
- Brand Journalism

Source: Public Relations Society of America. (n.d.). *About public relations.* https://www.prsa.org/about/all-about-pr

1.3 — REALITIES OF PR

This section will highlight what public relations writing is but also what public relations writing is not. At the core of every quality PR campaign is good content, which relies on a skilled and talented writer. Even brief social media posts and article headlines need to be well written in order to effectively capture and keep the reader's attention.

Public relations writing is not singular in its purpose, meaning that the creation of content that is shared with target audiences is not a one-dimensional endeavor. Rather, public relations writing can be layered and complex, as strategic messaging is used to hone and fine-tune communications to key publics using a variety of media vehicles. Even straightforward campaigns that seek to produce a specific outcome can be nuanced in how the goals and objectives are accomplished. PR professionals may utilize words, imagery, repetition and persuasive tactics to compel the end user to feel, think or act in a certain manner. Public relations writing is multifaceted in its approach to generating results and desirable outcomes on behalf of causes and clients.

In addition to its multifaceted nature, the realities of public relations writing also underscore the significance of adaptability and responsiveness. On a daily basis, PR professionals navigate a dynamic landscape where public opinions, media trends and communication platforms are constantly evolving. As such, effective PR writing requires the ability to pivot swiftly, adjusting strategies and messaging to leverage emerging opportunities or address unexpected challenges. This adaptability extends beyond content creation; it encompasses a strategic agility that enables PR practitioners to capitalize on current events, industry shifts or online trends, morphing their communication approach to maintain relevance.

Another reality in PR focuses on the ethical considerations that play a pivotal role in public relations writing. The content created should not only be compelling but also adhere to a set of moral and professional standards. Ethical dilemmas may arise in crafting persuasive messages, and PR professionals need to balance the interests of clients or causes with a commitment to honesty, transparency and respect for diverse perspectives. Negotiating this ethical terrain is an ongoing responsibility, as the public relations field continually grapples with issues such as misinformation, authenticity and the impact of persuasive communication on society. In reality, understanding and navigating the ethical dimensions of PR writing is crucial for practitioners in building and maintaining trust with their audiences over the long term.

What PR Writing Is Not

Now that there is a clearer understanding of what public relations writing is and what it can accomplish, it is also necessary to clarify what public relations writing is not. With so many misconceptions and misunderstandings about the PR industry overall, there is a lot of value in acknowledging and correcting some of the assumptions often connected with the profession. Public relations writing is not:

- hype
- publicity stunts
- lying, spin and misdirection
- promotions and publicity
- marketing
- advertising
- singular in purpose

Hype

There is a reason the phrase "Don't believe the hype" became commonly linked with the public relations industry. Hype is a form of extreme and exaggerated publicity for an individual, product or service, often leading people to believe that the subject of the promotion is better than it is in reality. Hype generates a lot of conversation in the media and a lot of buzz on social media but is often more sizzle than substance. PR cannot rely just on hype for success, because an engaged audience eventually will see through the smokescreen.

Publicity Stunts

A publicity stunt is an event orchestrated solely for the purpose of attracting attention to a person or an organization. The stunt is often designed with over-the-top elements as part of its construction to generate interest and media coverage. Another common saying associated with the PR industry is "There is no such thing as bad publicity, as long as they spell your name right." However, anyone who has worked in PR knows that bad publicity for the sake of publicity is a losing proposition, because stunts ultimately erode public trust along with the credibility of the PR practitioners who are orchestrating them.

Lying, Spin and Misdirection

Lying, spin and misdirection are different words for the same act, which is deception. Unfortunately, it is not uncommon for people outside the PR industry to associate public relations with misinformation and disinformation — terms distinguished by the intent to distribute inaccurate information unintentionally versus intentionally. The history of dishonest PR representatives traces back to the industry's origination, when PR work was synonymous with hype and press coverage at any cost. Fortunately, the industry has grown and progressed beyond those narrow and negative perceptions.

Promotions and Publicity

Promotions and publicity are very much a part of what public relations offers to the communications profession overall; however, limiting PR writing to simply pitching products and ideas for the sake of publicity in the media understates the power of PR to influence policy, legislation and public opinion on matters of concern ranging from free speech to climate change, medical and health standards and safety regulations, school board educational priorities and policies, and more.

Marketing

Rapidly changing technologies and ubiquitous accessibility to online content, along with innovative software applications, changed how PR practitioners develop and distribute content and how audiences access information. Long gone are the siloed days of advertising in one bucket and public relations in another bucket. PR clients and agencies are consistently and simultaneously using multiple communication channels to engage with audiences, which also introduced strategic communication and integrated marketing to the process. While marketing used to be generally defined as the process of bringing a product or service to consumers based on product, price, placement, promotion and one-way communication that simply pushed out messages to audiences, it is now more dynamic and interactive and uses elements from marketing, advertising, public relations and user-generated content for two-way conversations and engagement to effectively introduce and establish a presence in the marketplace. While all of these strategic options can be used by PR professionals, none of them wholly encompasses PR writing.

Advertising

Traditional advertising focused on paid placements in print publications or on radio or television stations. Now advertising is part of overarching strategic communication practices and integrated marketing processes. As advertising has expanded to include paid or "sponsored" social media content and paid promotional placements in quasi-editorial content, its distinction from public relations is based on the fact that advertising professionals pay to acquire space and guarantee visibility in front of target audiences. While public relations campaigns may sometimes incorporate paid or sponsored content into a larger campaign, this tactic is one spoke in a larger wheel of activities that fulfill the public relations role of managing relationships and reputations.

Singular in Purpose

As previously stated, public relations is not singular in purpose. However, early definitions of PR relegated its role mostly to publicity, then eventually expanded to include press agentry. Though the industry continues to evolve, it is clear that PR is multifaceted and multilayered in terms of the scope and scale of what can be accomplished. Public relations writing also showcases a multipronged approach to securing desired outcomes and measurable results. PR writing can be used for persuasion in political campaigns, promotions on social media, educating audiences using position papers and other research documents, reassuring the public in crisis communication, informing investors in financial releases, engaging with customers using digital storytelling, and countless more undertakings. Public relations doesn't simply accomplish one thing; it can be used to achieve corporate and community objectives and to fulfill important campaign goals, reaching millions around the globe, connecting a niche online community, or targeting a neighborhood in the suburbs—based solely on what is needed to manage the respective relationships for effective communication.

1.4 — WRITING FOR PR CAMPAIGNS

This segment explores some of the essential skills required to craft compelling content that forms the backbone of successful public relations campaigns. From shaping strategic narratives to deploying persuasive tactics, this chapter unveils the key principles and techniques that transform words into powerful instruments for achieving organizational goals in comprehensive PR campaigns.

Announce New Products, Services and Upcoming Events

Whether a company or brand plans to introduce a new product or announce a special event, PR writing documents help facilitate the process of publishing and distributing news to the media and to target audiences. Documents such as news releases, media advisories, fact sheets and infographics can concisely answer questions and share pertinent information that is of interest to reporters and consumers.

Consolidate Multiple Perspectives Into a Concise, Cohesive Message

One of the tenets of messaging strategy within the PR specialized area of crisis communication is referred to as "one voice," meaning that the authorized spokespeople and company representatives all say the same thing in response to public or media inquiries. In essence, they all respond the same way and stick to an approved script or "talk track" to present a united front and to speak as though the company has only one voice, for consistency and credibility purposes.

Define a Corporate Position on Important Issues

Whether through a white paper, position statement or company backgrounder, PR writing can be used to clearly articulate how a corporation has responded in the past or will react or respond in the future to major issues using well-written research documents to define stances about topics related to general business operations.

Direct a Public Relations Campaign

A public relations plan is one of the basic documents used to outline and guide campaign implementation and timelines. Simple in construction, the PR plan — used along with other tools explained in following chapters, such as Venn diagrams, organizational charts and spreadsheets, SWOT analysis (an assessment tool to identify Strengths, Weaknesses, Opportunities and Threats) and Gantt charts to plan campaign roll-outs — are utilized to guide the course of PR campaigns and messaging strategies.

Elevate Brand Awareness

PR writing can be used to amplify messages and extend audience reach to connect with the maximum number of people possible for a targeted campaign. Print, broadcast and online media outlets all support the work of PR writing to get the word out about a company or organization and its newsworthy announcements.

Explain or Simplify Complex Data or Statistics

In some instances, PR writing can be used to help audiences better comprehend information. Documents such as one sheets and infographics use clear, concise writing along with visually engaging graphics to condense a lot of data or statistics into digestible amounts of information for reader or viewer consumption.

Influence Public Opinion

Persuasive writing is the bedrock of influence campaigns, where the objective is to change the opinions, perspective and actions of the target audience. Using logic, reason and emotional appeals, PR writing professionals present information and make compelling arguments to advocate for clients and causes with the end goal of swaying opinions and potentially influencing outcomes.

Reassure the Public During a Crisis Situation

Crisis communication is a niche sector of public relations that helps to orchestrate communication and inform audiences during an emergency or crisis situation. Carefully chosen words — delivered in a timely fashion — that are offered in a composed, confident and empathetic manner can reassure the public and also rebuild trust and credibility for companies experiencing a crisis.

Shift the Media Narrative

For the most part, PR writing does not tell people what to think, but it can tell people what to think about. Sometimes introducing a new topic into the conversation is a simple and effective way of getting people to talk about something else. PR practitioners often have a direct line of communication to editors and producers who determine what gets printed and published or aired on the radio or television. A savvy PR professional armed with an interesting story idea can pitch a story to journalists or media outlets and shift the media narrative and audience focus to a new topic.

Tell the Client's Story

At the heart of public relations writing is good storytelling, which is often the reason brands hire PR agencies — to help tell their story. Through media relations, content creation, social media engagement and generating original, owned content, PR writing develops and distributes information that introduces and reinforces individual and corporate client stories to their target audiences.

Essential PR Writing

Several key characteristics of quality PR writing are consistent regardless of which type of document is being created. At a minimum, writing needs to be honest, transparent, clear, concise and inclusive. As the professional roles taken on by public relations practitioners continue to adapt and expand due to industry innovations and technology and as they continue to evolve with changing times, expectations and societal norms, what will not change is the need to quickly absorb new ideas and information and to develop compelling content that meets stakeholder groups where they are and appropriately addresses the needs and wants of target audiences through strategic communication.

As the demand for more and more quality content continues to increase, the need for skilled PR writers who are adept at writing anything and everything will become even more prevalent. Being equipped with a diverse repertoire for content development, ranging from press releases and media kits to social media posts, long-form narrative, executive speeches, researched white papers, intriguing media pitches and more, will serve the practitioner well.

It is easy to see online and elsewhere that quality, well-written content is becoming a lost art. Those who become proficient in this skill can do well; however, those who excel will find that the doors of opportunity will swing wide open to welcome them and at the same time help meet the demand for content.

1.5 — PROVEN WRITING TECHNIQUES

There is a common saying often borrowed and paraphrased from authors and songwriters that states, "If you don't know where you're going, any road will take you there." For the purposes of PR writing, this means if the communications professional does not begin the writing process with a purpose, goal, plan and strategy in place, then the destination will be uncertain and the outcome likely will be unsuccessful.

Prior to writing content, a beneficial step is to map out the purpose, plan and desired outcome to determine the documents that need to be written. Basic questions that inform the planning process revolve around knowing who the target audience is, what desired action the audience should take, which key messages should be conveyed, and which options are the best channels and outlets to deliver messages to the appropriate individuals and to achieve the stated goals and objectives.

Though many documents are written on behalf of a client and their respective campaign with the goal of elevating brand awareness or announcing important news, the materials still need to be written with consideration of what's in it for the recipient. Ultimately, audiences want to know what's in it for them. Answering that particular question during the research and planning process is what infuses value and purpose into the content and makes it useful to members of the media and the desired target audiences. Providing journalists with newsworthy content that aligns with their readers' and viewers' needs helps them do their jobs more effectively and efficiently. Presenting content that informs or entertains readers by offering useful information or addressing their interests is what makes the content worth reading or watching. PR writing is a strategic and intentional process, and becoming successful as a content creator is more likely to occur if the PR professional starts the writing process by beginning with the end in mind.

"RACE" Model

Countless PR writing and PR-industry-related textbooks tout the "RACE" model of PR as the foundational basis for approaching and implementing a PR campaign and the requisite PR writing that supports the campaign agenda. The acronym stands for Research, Action, Communication and Evaluation.

(R) Research

This first step sets the stage and helps to answer the question "Why?" before launching into the strategic "How?" of a PR campaign where PR writing and other content creation is required. Research facilitates a look back, reflects on what brought about the current situation facing an organization, and often includes a situation analysis that details the circumstances that led up to the current problem or opportunity to address. Primary and secondary research often provide data and other statistical information that inform the PR practitioner with quantitative metrics and anecdotal qualitative insights, which help guide the direction of PR planning and campaign implementation.

(A) Action

In the "RACE" PR model, the Action step employs the research findings to plot, plan and finalize the best course of activities to implement a campaign. Action in PR writing is bordered by planning and communicating — the background and foreground of public-facing PR practices. Action is all about getting things done, which is reflected in a PR plan that highlights and details objectives, goals, strategies, tactics, timelines, deadlines and budgets.

(C) Communication

This step in PR practice is what creates messaging content for interaction and engagement with the media and with the public. As indicated earlier in the chapter, PR is defined as *communicating specific messages to target audiences to achieve desired, measurable outcomes using multimedia platforms*. PR communication efforts leverage any and all relevant and accessible media outlets and communication channels to reach the right audiences.

(E) Evaluation

Almost every PR practice model ends with evaluation, which allows PR professionals to assess, review and measure what worked well or not so well within a campaign. Evaluation is not a final step but rather a transitional step from which practitioners can learn lessons and then apply them to ongoing or future campaigns. Evaluation should be used as part of growth and development for communication professionals to better serve clients, stakeholder groups, target audiences and key publics, as findings can be used to update and adapt future planning and to launch the entire process again for the next campaign.

Tips for Quality PR Writing

Nothing connects with people like stories. Any student desiring to learn how to write well for the PR industry needs to endeavor to learn how to tell a good story. Weaving together words and images that motivate, inspire and connect with people on both practical and emotional levels is a winning formula for successful communication campaigns. Of all the lessons, principles and concepts shared in this textbook, the common theme found throughout these pages is related to the ability to tell a good story in writing. The following pointers and tips in this section explain various resources, practices and habits that strong, versatile writers use to create quality content.

Start Writing Based on What Is Known and Confirmed

PR writing usually is not reliant on the creative muscles of fictitious narrative; rather, there is a client, cause or campaign with built-in details that need to be conveyed simply and clearly to an audience. Sometimes starting the writing process can be difficult because there are many competing messages in the marketplace that challenge writers who may struggle with making original copy stand out. A simple tip to kick-start the process is to start writing based on what information is confirmed and approved for publication. Even if the artistic writing juices are not yet flowing, putting words on a blank screen or sheet of paper can fuel momentum to keep writing. As an example, if the assignment is a feature profile that ultimately will be published on the client's blog and social media sites, begin writing what is known — even if it ends up being deleted. Describe who or what is known about the feature subject. What is the mission of the organization or the purpose for profiling a specific individual? When and where will an impact be made by the person or company at the core of the article? Why will the audience care about learning this information, and what will the audience gain by investing the time to read the content that was created?

Simply put, writing inspires more writing. Begin with short, declarative sentences. Use sentence fragments, if needed, to add variety. Write something, and then keep writing something else until the thoughts and ideas begin to gel. Write more than is needed so there is room to cut for clarity and conciseness.

Write Clearly and Concisely

Clear and concise content is not just a guide for the writer but also a gift to the reader. The easier it is to understand, the more widespread the content will become, based on its accessibility to people of all educational and skill levels. Unnecessary technical jargon or run-on sentences with an excess of polysyllabic words will definitely deter audiences and make readers less likely to return for more in the future. Shorter sentences and shorter paragraphs that focus on one topic at a time are easier to read and help the reader get through the information faster with higher levels of understanding.

Answer the Basic Questions First

PR writing content should focus on what the audience needs and wants to know. Oftentimes, a key public is the media, which serves as a conduit to reach end-user consumer audiences. Producing content that answers or addresses the basic questions and concerns that a journalist will have usually covers all the bases and ensures that no pertinent details are omitted that might potentially mislead the audience or create confusion for the recipient. At a minimum, answering the 5Ws and the H, "Who?" "What?" "When?" "Where?" "Why?" and "How?" — plus "Who Cares?" — will provide enough information to make a story complete.

In PR Writing, Less Is More

There are a few reasons why long-form content is less common than in previous years. The proliferation of platforms that limit words and character counts is a big reason that writing in short snippets became an elevated practice. Also, the massive volumes of content that inundate readers make it less likely that they will spend more time reading more information; rather, they will spend less time scanning or scrolling through many different types of information presented in various formats, such as audiobooks and podcasts, webcasts or social media video posts. PR practitioners need to be well versed in writing pieces of any and every length and for every platform, because fluency in writing at every level of the industry can propel a professional toward greater success within the industry.

Know and Understand the Audience

Great content that does not resonate with the audience is not great content. One of the primary rules of PR writing is to know and understand who the audience is. Based on the intended audience, certain words, terms or phrases may not make the cut because of education, cultural references, age-related contexts or other considerations. Additionally, knowing the audience and understanding their motivations to take action help assist the writer in developing useful and meaningful content.

Check Content for Authenticity

The concept of "fake news" is nothing new; however, with more and more publishers and distributors of content arriving on cable "news" stations and online media platforms, there are very few standards of accountability in place to ensure that the information being shared is accurate. Even some traditional news outlets are outnumbered by analysts, pundits and entertainers versus trained, professional journalists who are bound by journalistic standards of truth, honesty, objectivity, fairness, balance, ethics and independence in reporting. Just because there is a lot of noise in the marketplace does not grant PR practitioners permission to divulge themselves of their responsibility to truth telling, honesty, integrity and transparency in communication. Whether creating original content or referencing and citing existing content, PR writing requires research and fact-checking for accuracy and confirming that what is being shared is reliable information that can be trusted.

Review for Inclusion and Offensive Content

PR audiences have always been diverse; however, PR writing has not always been inclusive and written with diverse audiences in mind. Before posting or publishing content for the world to see and react to, it is worth a review to check for inflammatory or offensive content. A good rule of thumb (especially for larger teams) is to request editing and proofing from a diverse group of readers or reviewers to look for aspects within the content that might be harmful or offensive to underrepresented groups. During the review process, it also can be helpful to read the content aloud as though preparing for a speech to a real or imagined audience that reflects a diverse mix of the population, to include various ages, races, genders, ethnicities, income and educational levels, etc., just to make sure that the words, phrases and references used are not inflammatory, offensive or exclusionary to potential recipients.

Use the AP Stylebook

The Associated Press stylebook is not just for journalists; it is also a useful tool for PR professionals who create content for media audiences. The AP stylebook outlines basic rules and guidelines for writers related to spelling, grammar, punctuation, usage and inclusive language. Additionally, the stylebook shares explanations and recommendations for writing conventions that aid in accurately and consistently communicating with diverse audiences and in developing inclusive content. The stylebook is a practical resource that is organized into several sections and categories and provides guidance for accurate and consistent writing related to business, health and science law, religion, social media, sports, and other relevant topics likely to be covered in the media. The book is filled with terms, phrases and titles in alphabetical order and lists fundamental rules, recommendations and guidelines for spelling, abbreviations, capitalization, grammar, style, industry-specific verbiage, inclusive language, punctuation, technical terminology and general word usage for effective communication to standardize professional writing.

Keep a Dictionary and Thesaurus Handy

Sometimes it can be difficult to find just the right word or phrase. Every PR writing professional needs an online version or up-to-date hard copy of the dictionary nearby that can be used to keep content clear by helping to ensure that the correct words are being used and that they are being used accurately to reflect the intended meaning. Though repetition is common in PR writing as a result of "repurposed" content, approved messaging strategies and talking points, and frequent media responses that repeat the same information, the process of content development still presents opportunities for creativity — and the dictionary and thesaurus are copywriting and editing resources that help elevate and refine the craft.

Review, Edit, Proof, Repeat

Accuracy is nonnegotiable in PR writing and is just as important to PR practitioners as it is to reporters and media professionals. Names need to be spelled correctly. Titles should be accurate. Dates have to be correct. Facts and figures matter. A lot of damage can be done when a name has one incorrect letter or an age, date or dollar amount includes an incorrect numeral. With so many in-person and online resources available, there is no excuse for not checking and double-checking to make sure all the facts and figures are accurate. PR writing should be reviewed for spelling, grammar, substance, appropriate language and inclusion, as well as Associated Press style for documents developed for the media. In addition to using word-processing software to check spelling and grammar, reviews by a quality editor or proofreader are invaluable for checking proper nouns that may not be familiar to online apps. Two quick tips for catching errors are reading the content aloud and reviewing the content backward from the end to the beginning to easily check for spelling and capitalization errors. Once the editing and proofing are done, there is no harm in repeating the process . . . just to be sure.

In the following chapters, this textbook will prepare students to accurately, effectively and efficiently create content for various types of PR writing, including media relations and writing for journalists; virtual storytelling for online platforms, audiences and social media sites; writing socially conscious and inclusive content; strategic communication for business-related and corporate clients with internal and external audiences; writing for business development to secure new opportunities; broadcast writing for radio, television and online podcasts or webcasts; developing creative content for branding and marketing collateral materials; and persuasive writing to inform, educate and advocate various causes or community relations efforts or to influence public opinion.

CHAPTER SUMMARY

Effective public relations writing is honest, transparent, clear, concise and inclusive.

Honesty and transparency in communications reflect two of the ethical guidelines and professional standards that industry professionals commit to practice upon entering the field. Clear and concise content is easier and faster to read, making the information more likely to be used by media contacts or end-user consumers and target audience members. Inclusion and equity in content creation continue to be priorities as PR work becomes more global in nature and increasingly diverse audiences collaborate in business and community-related endeavors.

Understanding what public relations writing is and what public relations writing is not is a good starting point for developing effective skills within the practice. PR writing is used to announce new products and services, direct PR campaign strategy, increase awareness and elevate brands, influence public opinion and public policy, and motivate target audiences to take action. Public relations writing appears in many different forms and formats across various types of communication channels, allowing the PR practitioner to be creative, expressive, informative, persuasive and engaging on a daily basis.

KEY TERMS

Associated Press stylebook
hype
public relations

publicity stunt
spin

DISCUSSION QUESTIONS

1. How does public relations writing differ from other types of writing, such as news writing, advertising copy, literary narrative or prose?

2. How does using the Associated Press stylebook assist in PR writing?

3. What does it mean to say that PR writing is not singular in purpose?

4. How can the RACE (Research, Action, Communication, Evaluation) PR model help guide the planning and writing process?

WRITING EXERCISES

1. Write two paragraphs explaining the role of PR writing in a public relations professional's daily activities.

2. Write a brief overview explaining the importance of ethics in PR writing.

2 PUBLIC RELATIONS INDUSTRY STANDARDS AND ETHICS

LEARNING OBJECTIVES

2.1   Learn basic definitions for ethics, morals and values within the PR profession.

2.2   Understand the role and relevance of ethics in public relations.

2.3   Apply ethical standards to a scenario that presents a moral and/or ethical dilemma.

This chapter's introduction was written by Dr. Lois Boynton, associate professor in the School of Journalism and Media at the University of North Carolina at Chapel Hill. Her teaching and writing focus on ethics and professionalism in public relations and media. Prior to academia, she worked 14 years as a journalist and public relations/advertising practitioner.

INTRODUCTION: THE ETHICAL WRITER

Dr. Lois Boynton

Trust is the public relations writer's currency. Ethical practices can build and nurture trust. But violating basic ethical tenets can quickly erode the faith stakeholders have in your brand and organization.

Key messages take many forms on multiple platforms to help organizations build relationships with investors/donors, customers, employees, communities, policymakers, influencers and reporters. Professional organizations such as the Public Relations Society of America and International Association of Business Communicators have developed member ethics codes to guide practitioners, and the vast majority of large companies have formalized ethics codes. Provisions are pragmatic: Be honest and transparent, respect client confidentiality and avoid real or perceived conflicts of interest.

Some of the ethical challenges PR writers face include:

Advocating Ethically

Public relations is an advocacy function, but advocacy does not mean lacking in factual information. On the contrary, PR writers should ensure information they provide is accurate and not intended to deceive stakeholders. As humans, we may make an occasional error; we are ethically obligated to take responsibility and correct erroneous information.

Speed

Our 24/7, hurry-up culture is a breeding ground for shortcuts and errors. It's embarrassing to discover a typo in a fact sheet. But consequences multiply if you lift a passage from another source and neglect to cite it, resulting in (hopefully) unintentional plagiarism. In a rush to complete a task, a writer might employ patchwriting. As ethicist Kelly McBride (2012) explains, "Rather than copying a statement word for word, the writer is rearranging phrases and changing tenses, but is relying too heavily on the [original] vocabulary and syntax." Such carelessness is a breach of hard-earned stakeholder trust.

Transparency

Transparency can create ethical challenges for PR writers. Intentional deception — also called lying by omission — deliberately misleads stakeholders into making uninformed decisions that benefit the organization. However, not all information is for public consumption. There are ethical reasons for maintaining confidentiality of proprietary information such as trade secrets, inventions, passwords, marketing data, some personnel records, and client contracts.

Ghostwriting

According to ghostwriter Teena Lyons (n.d.), "[A] ghost is simply helping an author voice what they want to say in a clear, engaging way. The knowledge/ideas/memories belong 100% to the person who has the name on the cover . . . and all I am doing is helping get it on the page." The client-ghostwriter relationship must be grounded in ethics, from the strategic intent of the message to the platform on which it is presented. Transparency is essential: Does the audience understand who created or contributed to a speech, tweet, blog, brochure or other materials? Speechwriting is perhaps the most accepted ghosting practice. We don't really expect the president to stand at a podium and announce, "I'm now going to read a speech that Fred wrote for me . . ." But do we have different expectations for social media posts, blogs or even quotes? An executive may ask you to "make up" her quote for a news release. At minimum, any statement you draft should accurately reflect the executive's beliefs; ensure this by getting the executive's approval.

Working With News Media

Working with news media may involve some tensions, since journalists espouse objectivity. However, it's a symbiotic relationship — reporters cannot cover everything that's newsworthy; they rely on ethical public relations practitioners to keep them informed and help them access subject matter experts (SME) within their organizations. When writing materials for news media — releases, pitches, FAQs, backgrounders, etc. — practitioners should understand news values and routines, which can help engender trust with reporters and avoid unintentional misfires such as gift giving, for example. Although the PRSA Code of Ethics (Public Relations Society of America, n.d.) permits "nominal, legal, and infrequent" gifts, the Society of Professional Journalists (2014) Code of Ethics advises reporters to decline gifts, which might be perceived as attempts to influence news coverage.

Diversity, Equity and Inclusion

In PR, you'll hear one message over and over — know your stakeholders. Learning about the richness of communities and cultures is a lifelong process; it starts by knowing your own biases and assumptions. PR writers must be cognizant of word usage, which affects how we portray or frame issues and individuals. But as editors of "Conscious Style Guide" (n.d.) state, "the goal is not to be nice, inoffensive, or politically correct; even language intended to be inclusive and considerate might offend. If you're interested in using language consciously, then clarify your intentions and evoke and provoke skillfully" ("About," n.d.).

These are just a few of the ethical issues you'll confront in your career. Welcome to PR writing!

2.1 — STANDARDS FOR PR

The Institute for Public Relations defines ethics within the discipline to include values such as honesty, openness, loyalty, fair-mindedness, respect, integrity and forthright communication. Every PR trade association or advocacy organization also has its own statement that offers additional guidance to practitioners about the expectations and boundaries of professional conduct.

Establishing industry standards serves to level the playing field for all participants — whether experienced executives, freelance consultants or entry-level novices — and to protect the interests of those who are served by the profession.

As a point of reference, the Associated Press publishes a statement of news values and principles in each of its stylebook hard-copy and online editions. Some of the highlights include:

- We abhor inaccuracies, carelessness, bias or distortions. We will not knowingly introduce rumor or false information into material intended for publication or broadcast; nor will we distort visual content.

- We always strive to identify all the sources of our information.

- We avoid behavior or activities that could be perceived as a conflict of interest.

- We don't misidentify or misrepresent ourselves to get a story.

- When mistakes are made, they must be corrected.

- The policies set forth in these pages are central to the AP's mission. Any failure to abide by them could result in disciplinary action, up to and including dismissal, depending on the gravity of the infraction.

Source: The Associated Press Stylebook 2020-2022 (55th ed.). (2020). Associated Press, pp. 498-499.

Several professional association codes of conduct and ethics codes are included in the Chapter 2 Appendix (in their original, unedited form) to familiarize future PR professionals with the range of ethical standards and guidance created for individuals whose employment derives from communication-focused industries. Included are statements published by the International Public Relations Association, Public Relations Society of America, International Association of Business Communicators, and American Marketing Association. Finally, a Public Relations Student Society of America (PRSSA) pledge with a signature line and date line is also included for students who are planning career paths in public relations. See Figure 2.1 for a visual about ethics, morals, values and integrity.

2.2 — ETHICS IN PUBLIC RELATIONS

In public relations, the increasing demand to deliver results and outperform the competition also fuels the ethical challenges that confront PR professionals who pledge to operate in an ethical and honest way. The very nature of public relations and its ubiquitous moral gray areas makes it necessary to address the importance of ethics within the practice.

FIGURE 2.1 ■ Four-Way Sign With Ethics, Morals, Values and Integrity

Persistent and not-so-secret negative perceptions about PR representatives and their oft-times questionable relationship with the truth must be confronted and overcome by consistent and observable ethical behavior by all members of the public relations community. There is no justifiable reason that difficult clients, complex campaigns and impending deadlines should upend communicators' ability to create and promote content, manage strategic relationships and messaging, and advocate for client causes in a way that is honest and infused with integrity.

Certainly, every individual enters a PR career or professional journey with their own set of beliefs or values. The next step is to ensure those guiding principles align with the professional standards and codes of conduct for this desired profession. Three pillars of industry expectations and standards in public relations shape the narrative and the spirit of how PR professionals should conduct themselves. They are ethics, morals and values — each of which will be defined and explained in this chapter.

Ethics

Throughout this section, the term *ethics* is referenced as a standardized code or system that has collective implications on entire industries or groups of people. In general, ethics offer guidance for understanding and acting in ways that are perceived to be right versus wrong, whereas morals lend more toward perceptions of good versus bad. Ethical conduct is expected and required in countless professions, especially industries that have strict rules or regulations, where violating them can result in criminal liability and other severe consequences that may include fines, penalties, disbarment, etc.

For all intents and purposes, public relations is an unregulated industry. Compliance with the professional standards and codes of conduct is voluntary, with minimal consequences for misbehavior or noncompliance. With few rules and countless competing interests, the PR industry is ripe for potential corruption and misconduct. However, self-governance and shared accountability are frequently used to support a system of checks and balances to keep members of the professional community operating in accordance with generally accepted standards and practices within the industry. See Figure 2.2 for a visual about ethics.

Morals

Does working in PR with less-than-scrupulous clients make someone a bad person? Is telling a partial truth — while omitting a small but damaging detail — considered lying? Is framing content in a way that positively impacts a client but negatively affects their competition wrong? Is "borrowing" a colleague's winning pitch idea to advance a personal career move considered cheating if the colleague is thanked or acknowledged during the presentation? The morals someone applies to their life and decision-making process are often influenced by a personal and evolving moral code that informs their view of the world and their role in society. The opening questions in this section might have completely different responses and rationales depending on the moral codes of the individuals being asked.

Morals come into play when making determinations about behavior that is considered good or bad. Though morality is difficult to legislate or manage, these individual and often intensely personal guiding principles help people operate effectively within greater society by conforming

FIGURE 2.2 ■ PR Ethics Graphic

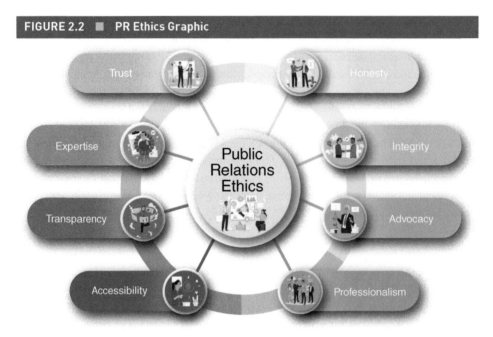

to standards and norms that the majority of people deem acceptable and appropriate. Morals often align with upbringing, as these core principles and values are often embedded during the early formative years and then shape the way individuals see and process the world around them.

Values

The term *values* can best be explained as a self-defining concept that reflects what an individual deems as having worth or significance in their decision-making process. What do they think is the most important factor that influences and shapes their behavior, thoughts and actions? What do they care about? What motivates them to take action in one direction versus another? What do they "value"?

A practitioner's unique set of values may influence decisions when it comes to, for instance, elevating money over life purpose in selecting a career path. If money is the primary motivating factor, it is easy to anticipate and understand how someone will view a situation or make a determination about the appropriate actions to take. In contrast, if fairness is the motivating value for a PR professional, that might lead them to focus more on doing quality and meaningful work for less money, because providing excellent service at a fair price — versus an immense profit — is more important. Many PR agencies, organizations and corporations publish a values statement to reaffirm their commitment to principles that influence the entity's priorities and practices.

Honesty and Integrity

Built on the bedrocks of ethics, morals and values are the principles of honesty and integrity, which become evident through actions and practical application. Honesty and integrity are two metaphorical sides of the same coin, which, when spent within the realm of professional conduct, purchase a lot of goodwill and credibility in professional development. At its essence, honesty is about telling the truth in a straightforward and forthright manner, not grudgingly or as a last resort. In a proactive sense, honesty is about truth, but it also reflects the absence of dishonesty; it is thus not built solely on random or sporadic truth but also devoid of misrepresentation and falsity — elements that breed distrust. Honest communication in public relations means honoring words that are spoken and following through on commitments made. In addition to spoken words, honesty is about interpersonal dealings and conducting oneself in a way that is free from deception or misrepresentation. Honesty at its optimal level also lends itself to building a reputation of being trustworthy enough to hold client confidentiality and keep it at the forefront as a standard operating procedure.

Within ethical considerations, public relations and communications professionals may be asked if facts and the truth are the same thing. The answer is no, because the framing, skewing or misrepresentation of facts can result in dishonest communication. Even if information is technically factual, it can be generally dishonest; thus, it is the communicator's responsibility to make sure the presentation and distribution of information is done in such a way that it maintains and reflects honest and ethical standards of practice.

Integrity is a way of life and doing business, built on unwavering and resolute principles of honesty, morality, ethics and consistent adherence to strong personal values that are applied without question or coercion. Professionals who operate with integrity often gain the trust and admiration of others because they are reliable in their approach and steadfast in their professional conduct. It is often said that integrity is what someone does when no one is watching. Furthermore, integrity is on full display when people act in a virtuous and upright manner regardless of the situation or the circumstances — and regardless of whether acting or responding in a different way might be more beneficial. For them, integrity is not negotiable, and it serves as its own reward.

2.3 — NAVIGATING ETHICAL DILEMMAS

Ethical challenges permeate public relations because there are so many temptations and high-stake opportunities at hand. As purveyors of information, PR practitioners often have advance access to valuable details that can put them at risk of insider trading if used inappropriately. Additionally, the prevalence of special events as an aspect of creative campaigns presents access to premiums, gifts, tickets and high-dollar incentives that are easily accessible and subject to abuse. Unfortunately, leveraging access to celebrity clients for personal gain, taking advantage of client-funded expense accounts, and utilizing confidential content for professional advancement are not unusual occurrences within the PR world. The ongoing responsibility for PR professionals is to maintain their standards of ethics, morals and values and to conduct themselves in a way that elevates the status of the profession as a whole.

Why the Industry Needs Ethical PR Practitioners

Without ethical standards, the public relations industry becomes a freewheeling circus of misinformation, disinformation and fraudulent claims, where anything goes and self-serving opportunists can corrupt communications at will. A large swath of PR responsibility rests with advocacy work for clients and elevating perspectives or voices that are often overlooked or ignored. A commitment to honesty, transparency, loyalty, fairness and expertise serves as the guardrails that keep the PR train on track and prevent it from swerving too far off the path or crashing altogether.

The PR industry is better when practitioners and clients experience and express mutual respect, trust and commitment to getting a job done well. The ability to set a high standard and then meet it is a powerful example for other professionals and industries to follow. Ethics in PR are not optional; they are mandatory and necessary.

CHAPTER SUMMARY

Ethics, morals and values are the foundational principles for effective public relations activities, and they also establish clear standards for professional conduct, which helps to provide a level of security and protection for clients who entrust confidential information to PR practitioners. Ethical systems guide right or wrong behavior, while morals help individuals act in ways that are inherently good or bad based on societal standards. Values are motivating factors that determine how individuals make decisions, based on their priorities and desired outcomes. Together these guiding principles provide a framework that instills confidence for individuals in the PR profession and those they serve. Most communications and PR trade organizations or professional associations have a written code of ethics or code of conduct to help guide how practitioners operate within that profession. There may be penalties or negative consequences for professionals who do not adhere to these standards. With emerging technology and constant innovation — along with faster and newer ways to create and disseminate information — it is important that professional ethical codes be reviewed and updated frequently to remain relevant as safeguards for the industry.

KEY TERMS

codes of conduct   ethics codes

ethics   integrity

DISCUSSION QUESTIONS

1. Why do communications organizations need to publish codes of conduct?

2. What type of ethical dilemma do you find most challenging?

3. What are some potential results or consequences when ethical standards are not followed?

WRITING EXERCISES

1. You and your roommate are both interning at different PR agencies for the summer. Both companies are competing for a new account and both made the short-list of finalists to make an in-person presentation. Both of you have been assigned to assist on the pitch

teams at your respective agencies. The roommate's agency is favored to win because of their successful track record and innovative approaches. After work, you happen to notice that your roommate left their laptop open while they stepped out to take a dinner break, and a draft version of the pitch presentation is within view. What decision do you make next? Do you close the laptop and walk away? Do you take a quick look, just to size up the competition? Do you take a deep dive and give your team an advantage — because your roommate shouldn't be so careless with important information? Finally, is your decision influenced at all if the contract is worth $1 million versus $20,000?

2. Create your own code of ethics for a small PR agency with nine employees.

- What are the leading ethical principles you want to incorporate into the policy?
- How will the code of ethics be enforced?
- What are the penalties for violating the code of ethics?
- How and where will you communicate the code of ethics to existing and new employees?
- How can you encourage adherence to the code of ethics?

APPENDIX: CODES OF CONDUCT AND CODES OF ETHICS FOR PROFESSIONAL COMMUNICATIONS ORGANIZATIONS

The following guidelines delve into many of the ethical considerations that anchor the PR profession. While exploring the varied landscape of professional and organizational codes of ethics in the public relations industry, these codes and standards also emphasize the moral compass that guides strategic decisions and communication practices, ensuring integrity and trustworthiness within the profession.

International Public Relations Association Code of Conduct

Launched in 2011 the IPRA Code of Conduct is an affirmation of professional and ethical conduct by members of the International Public Relations Association and recommended to public relations practitioners worldwide.

In the conduct of public relations practitioners shall:

1. Observance
    Observe the principles of the UN Charter and the Universal Declaration of Human Rights;

2. Integrity
    Act with honesty and integrity at all times so as to secure and retain the confidence of those with whom the practitioner comes into contact;

3. Dialogue
    Seek to establish the moral, cultural and intellectual conditions for dialogue, and recognise the rights of all parties involved to state their case and express their views;

4. Transparency
    Be open and transparent in declaring their name, organisation and the interest they represent;

5. Conflict
    Avoid any professional conflicts of interest and to disclose such conflicts to affected parties when they occur;

6. Confidentiality
    Honour confidential information provided to them;

7. Accuracy
    Take all reasonable steps to ensure the truth and accuracy of all information provided;

8. Falsehood
    Make every effort to not intentionally disseminate false or misleading information, exercise proper care to avoid doing so unintentionally and correct any such act promptly;

9. Deception
    Not obtain information by deceptive or dishonest means;

10. Disclosure
    Not create or use any organisation to serve an announced cause but which actually serves an undisclosed interest;

11. Profit
    Not sell for profit to third parties copies of documents obtained from public authorities;

12. Remuneration
    Whilst providing professional services, not accept any form of payment in connection with those services from anyone other than the principal;

13. Inducement
    Neither directly nor indirectly offer nor give any financial or other inducement to public representatives or the media, or other stakeholders;

14. Influence
    Neither propose nor undertake any action which would constitute an improper influence on public representatives, the media, or other stakeholders;

15. Competitors
    Not intentionally injure the professional reputation of another practitioner;

16. Poaching
    Not seek to secure another practitioner's client by deceptive means;

17. Employment

When employing personnel from public authorities or competitors take care to follow the rules and confidentiality requirements of those organisations;

18. Colleagues
Observe this Code with respect to fellow IPRA members and public relations practitioners worldwide.

IPRA members shall, in upholding this Code, agree to abide by and help enforce the disciplinary procedures of the International Public Relations Association in regard to any breach of this Code.

This code was formally adopted by the IPRA Board 5 November 2010 and launched in 2011.

Source: International Public Relations Association. (n.d.). *IPRA codes.* https://www.ipra.org/member-services/code-of-conduct/

PRSA Code of Ethics

The PRSA Code of Ethics applies to PRSA members. The Code is designed to be a useful guide for PRSA members as they carry out their ethical responsibilities. This document is designed to anticipate and accommodate, by precedent, ethical challenges that may arise. The scenarios outlined in the Code provision are actual examples of misconduct. More will be added as experience with the Code occurs.

PRSA is committed to ethical practices. The level of public trust PRSA members seek, as we serve the public good, means we have taken on a special obligation to operate ethically.

The value of member reputation depends upon the ethical conduct of everyone affiliated with the PRSA. Each of us sets an example for each other — as well as other professionals — by our pursuit of excellence with powerful standards of performance, professionalism and ethical conduct.

Emphasis on enforcement of the Code has been eliminated. But, the PRSA Board of Directors retains the right to bar from membership or expel from the Society any individual who has been or is sanctioned by a government agency or convicted in a court of law of an action that fails to comply with the Code.

Ethical practice is the most important obligation of a PRSA member. We view the Member Code of Ethics as a model for other professions, organizations and professionals.

PRSA MEMBER STATEMENT OF PROFESSIONAL VALUES

This statement presents the core values of PRSA members and, more broadly, of the public relations profession. These values provide the foundation for the Code of Ethics and set the industry standard for the professional practice of public relations. These values are the fundamental beliefs that guide our behaviors and decision-making process. We believe our professional values are vital to the integrity of the profession as a whole.

Advocacy. We serve the public interest by acting as responsible advocates for those we represent. We provide a voice in the marketplace of ideas, facts, and viewpoints to aid informed public debate.

Honesty. We adhere to the highest standards of accuracy and truth in advancing the interests of those we represent and in communicating with the public.

Expertise. We acquire and responsibly use specialized knowledge and experience. We advance the profession through continued professional development, research, and education. We build mutual understanding, credibility, and relationships among a wide array of institutions and audiences.

Independence. We provide objective counsel to those we represent. We are accountable for our actions.

Loyalty. We are faithful to those we represent, while honoring our obligation to serve the public interest.

Fairness. We deal fairly with clients, employers, competitors, peers, vendors, the media, and the general public. We respect all opinions and support the right of free expression.

PRSA CODE PROVISIONS OF CONDUCT

Free Flow of Information

Core Principle Protecting and advancing the free flow of accurate and truthful information is essential to serving the public interest and contributing to informed decision making in a democratic society.

Intent:

- To maintain the integrity of relationships with the media, government officials, and the public.

- To aid informed decision-making.

Guidelines:

A member shall:

- Preserve the integrity of the process of communication.

- Be honest and accurate in all communications.

- Act promptly to correct erroneous communications for which the practitioner is responsible.

- Preserve the free flow of unprejudiced information when giving or receiving gifts by ensuring that gifts are nominal, legal, and infrequent.

Examples of Improper Conduct Under This Provision:

- A member representing a ski manufacturer gives a pair of expensive racing skis to a sports magazine columnist, to influence the columnist to write favorable articles about the product.

- A member entertains a government official beyond legal limits and/or in violation of government reporting requirements.

Competition

Core Principle Promoting healthy and fair competition among professionals preserves an ethical climate while fostering a robust business environment.

Intent:
- To promote respect and fair competition among public relations professionals.

- To serve the public interest by providing the widest choice of practitioner options.

Guidelines:

A member shall:
- Follow ethical hiring practices designed to respect free and open competition without deliberately undermining a competitor.

- Preserve intellectual property rights in the marketplace.

Examples of Improper Conduct Under This Provision:
- A member employed by a "client organization" shares helpful information with a counseling firm that is competing with others for the organization's business.

- A member spreads malicious and unfounded rumors about a competitor in order to alienate the competitor's clients and employees in a ploy to recruit people and business.

Disclosure of Information

Core Principle Open communication fosters informed decision making in a democratic society.

Intent:
- To build trust with the public by revealing all information needed for responsible decision making.

Guidelines:

A member shall:
- Be honest and accurate in all communications.

- Act promptly to correct erroneous communications for which the member is responsible.

- Investigate the truthfulness and accuracy of information released on behalf of those represented.

- Reveal the sponsors for causes and interests represented.

- Disclose financial interest (such as stock ownership) in a client's organization.

- Avoid deceptive practices.

Examples of Improper Conduct Under This Provision:

- Front groups: A member implements "grass roots" campaigns or letter-writing campaigns to legislators on behalf of undisclosed interest groups.

- Lying by omission: A practitioner for a corporation knowingly fails to release financial information, giving a misleading impression of the corporation's performance.

- A member discovers inaccurate information disseminated via a website or media kit and does not correct the information.

- A member deceives the public by employing people to pose as volunteers to speak at public hearings and participate in "grass roots" campaigns.

Safeguarding Confidences

Core Principle Client trust requires appropriate protection of confidential and private information.

Intent:

- To protect the privacy rights of clients, organizations, and individuals by safeguarding confidential information.

Guidelines:

A member shall:

- Safeguard the confidences and privacy rights of present, former, and prospective clients and employees.

- Protect privileged, confidential, or insider information gained from a client or organization.

- Immediately advise an appropriate authority if a member discovers that confidential information is being divulged by an employee of a client company or organization.

Examples of Improper Conduct Under This Provision:

- A member changes jobs, takes confidential information, and uses that information in the new position to the detriment of the former employer.

- A member intentionally leaks proprietary information to the detriment of some other party.

Conflicts of Interest

Core Principle Avoiding real, potential or perceived conflicts of interest builds the trust of clients, employers, and the publics.

Intent:

- To earn trust and mutual respect with clients or employers.

- To build trust with the public by avoiding or ending situations that put one's personal or professional interests in conflict with society's interests.

Guidelines:

A member shall:

- Act in the best interests of the client or employer, even subordinating the member's personal interests.

- Avoid actions and circumstances that may appear to compromise good business judgment or create a conflict between personal and professional interests.

- Disclose promptly any existing or potential conflict of interest to affected clients or organizations.

- Encourage clients and customers to determine if a conflict exists after notifying all affected parties.

Examples of Improper Conduct Under This Provision:

- The member fails to disclose that he or she has a strong financial interest in a client's chief competitor.

- The member represents a "competitor company" or a "conflicting interest" without informing a prospective client.

Enhancing the Profession

Core Principle Public relations professionals work constantly to strengthen the public's trust in the profession.

Intent:

- To build respect and credibility with the public for the profession of public relations.

- To improve, adapt and expand professional practices.

Guidelines:

A member shall:

- Acknowledge that there is an obligation to protect and enhance the profession.

- Keep informed and educated about practices in the profession to ensure ethical conduct.

- Actively pursue personal professional development.

- Decline representation of clients or organizations that urge or require actions contrary to this Code.

- Accurately define what public relations activities can accomplish.

- Counsel subordinates in proper ethical decision making.

- Require that subordinates adhere to the ethical requirements of the Code.

- Report practices that fail to comply with the Code, whether committed by PRSA members or not, to the appropriate authority.

Examples of Improper Conduct Under This Provision:

- A PRSA member declares publicly that a product the client sells is safe, without disclosing evidence to the contrary.

- A member initially assigns some questionable client work to a non-member practitioner to avoid the ethical obligation of PRSA membership.

Access the online PRSA Code of Ethics and Statement of Professional Values at PRSA Code of Ethics, https://www.prsa.org/about/ethics/prsa-code-of-ethics.

Source: Public Relations Society of America. (n.d.). *PRSA code of ethics.* https://www.prsa.org/about/ethics/prsa-code-of-ethics.

PRSSA Conduct Pledge

I pledge to conduct myself professionally, with truth, accuracy, fairness and responsibility to the public, fellow members and to the Society; to improve my individual competence and advance the knowledge and proficiency of the field of public relations; and to adhere to the articles of the Member Code of Ethics and Conduct by the PRSSA National Committee.

I understand and accept that there are consequences for member misconduct, up to and including membership revocation.

I understand that members in violation of the PRSSA Code of Ethics and Conduct may be further barred from PRSA membership.

Source: (n.d.). PRSSA code of ethics and conduct. https://www.prsa.org/prssa/about-prssa/ethical-principles.

International Association of Business Communicators

As a professional communicator, you have the potential to influence economies and affect lives. This power carries with it significant responsibilities.

The International Association of Business Communicators requires its members to agree to the IABC Code of Ethics. This code serves as a guide to making consistent, responsible, ethical and legal choices in all of our communications.

IABC's Code of Ethics

1. **I am honest.** My actions bring respect for and trust in the communication profession.

2. **I communicate accurate information** and promptly correct any errors.

3. **I obey laws and public policies**; if I violate any law or public policy, I act promptly to correct the situation.

4. **I protect confidential information** while acting within the law.

5. **I support the ideals of free speech**, freedom of assembly, and access to an open marketplace of ideas.

6. **I am sensitive to others** cultural values and beliefs.

7. **I give credit to others for their work** and cite my sources.

8. **I do not use confidential information** for personal benefit.

9. **I do not represent conflicting or competing interests** without full disclosure and the written consent of those involved.

10. **I do not accept undisclosed gifts or payments** for professional services from anyone other than a client or employer.

11. **I do not guarantee results** that are beyond my power to deliver.

IABC's Code of Ethics in practice

IABC requires its members to embrace these ethical guidelines in their work and to sign the following statement as part of the application and renewal processes: I have reviewed and understand the IABC Code of Ethics.

Access the online International Association of Business Communicators Code of Ethics for Professional Communicators at https://www.iabc.com/About/Purpose/Code-of-Ethics.

Source: International Association of Business Communicators. (n.d.). *IABC code of ethics for professional communicators.* https://www.iabc.com/About/Purpose/Code-of-Ethics.

AMA Statement of Ethics

The American Marketing Association commits to the highest standards of ethical norms and values. We recognize that the marketing community not only serves organizations but also acts as a steward of society in creating and facilitating the transactions and experiences that drive the greater economy. In this role, all stakeholders of the community are expected to embrace the highest ethical norms and values implied by our responsibility to society.

Ethical Norms

As Marketers, we must:

1. Do no harm. This means not only consciously avoiding harmful actions or omissions but also striving to benefit all stakeholders and society at large. We must embody high ethical standards and, at a minimum, adhere to all applicable laws and regulations in the choices we make.

2. Foster and maintain integrity. This means striving for transparency and fairness in all aspects of the marketing ecosystem.

3. Embrace ethical values. Foster and maintain integrity. This means striving for transparency and fairness in all aspects of the marketing ecosystem.

ETHICAL VALUES

Values represent the collective understanding of what the community finds appropriate, desirable, and morally acceptable. Values also serve as the criteria for evaluating our own personal actions and the actions of others.

Honesty

- Be truthful in all situations, at all times, and with all stakeholders, rejecting any manipulation, coercion, or approaches that negatively affect trust.

- Offer valuable solutions that reflect the intentions stated in communications and interactions.

- Honor explicit and implicit commitments and promises.

Responsibility

- Acknowledge the social obligations to stakeholders that come with increased marketing and economic power.

- Consider environmental and societal stewardship in our decision-making.

- Strive to exceed industry or legal standards in the protection of private or sensitive information of customers, employees, and partners.

- Recognize and accept the consequences of our marketing decisions and strategies.

Equity

- Build a diverse marketing workforce and support inclusive marketing practices by valuing and embracing individual, cultural, and ethnic differences.

- Recognize the needs of, and commitments to, vulnerable market segments as well as those individuals not familiar with marketing and others who may be historically disadvantaged.

- Never stereotype anyone or depict any group (e.g., gender, race, sexual orientation, religious beliefs, etc.) in a negative or dehumanizing way.

- Make every effort to understand and respectfully treat buyers, suppliers, intermediaries, and distributors from all cultures.

Transparency

- Strive for a spirit of openness in all aspects of the marketing profession.

- Communicate clearly with all constituencies.

- Accept and acknowledge feedback from customers, colleagues, and other stakeholders.

- Take appropriate action to explain and mitigate potential significant risks or other foreseeable outcomes that will or could impact any stakeholder.

- Fully disclose any information that might affect interactions or decisions within the processes or protocols related to marketing.

- Avoid participation in conflicts of interest.

- Appropriately recognize the contributions of others to marketing endeavors, such as consultants, employees, and coworkers.

Citizenship

- Fulfill the economic, legal, philanthropic, and societal responsibilities that serve stakeholders.

- Value the role that marketing plays in business and society.

- Strive to protect the ecological environment and communicate sustainability efforts and aspirations honestly and transparently.

- Give back to the community through volunteerism and charitable donations.

- Contribute to the overall betterment of marketing and its reputation.

- Compel all partners to ensure that trade and production is fair for all participants in the marketing ecosystem.

IMPLEMENTATION

We expect those associated with the AMA and the marketing community at large to be courageous and proactive in the fulfillment of the explicit and implicit promises contained in this Statement of Ethics.

This Statement of Ethics is part of a broader AMA Code of Conduct that contains Behavior Expectations for anyone who interacts with or within the AMA community. The AMA upholds compliance with the Behavior Expectations through the reporting mechanisms and disciplinary procedures contained in the Code of Conduct.

However, the AMA does not have the resources to adjudicate compliance with the Statement of Ethics in all areas within the marketing community. Thus, it is intended as an aspirational statement to motivate and inspire the marketing community to commit to upholding the highest standards of ethical norms and values.

Source: American Marketing Association. (n.d.). *AMA statement of ethics.* Retrieved May 31, 2024, from https://myama .my.site.com/s/article/AMA-Statement-of-Ethics.

THE RELEVANCE OF ASSOCIATED PRESS (AP) STYLE

LEARNING OBJECTIVES

3.1 Understand the importance of AP style standards and how to effectively use the AP stylebook.

3.2 Recognize the types of errors and common writing mistakes that the AP stylebook corrects.

3.3 Become familiar with how the AP stylebook is organized and where to find classifications for entries to improve writing.

3.4 Learn how to correctly write, edit and proof documents or content using common usage guidelines and AP style exercises.

INTRODUCTION

This chapter on AP style is included to emphasize the importance of relying on generally accepted journalistic writing standards when creating content for the media and the public. The chapter includes a brief overview about the Associated Press and its mission in newsgathering, along with some important principles that guide the writing and reporting process.

Information is included about how to use the stylebook and when to use the stylebook for effective PR writing. It is highly recommended that PR writing students invest in updated hardcopy or online versions of the AP stylebook to remain up to date with new verbiage, inclusive language guidelines, and appropriate usage in writing.

3.1 — USING THE AP STYLEBOOK

The Associated Press nonprofit organization is known for much more than the reference book it publishes. The AP is a global conglomerate entity that dispatches journalists, digital storytellers and creatives alike to gather, report and distribute news content to media outlets and platforms around the world. According to the 55th edition of the AP stylebook, "the AP's mission is to get it first but first get it right, and to be the first choice for news, by providing the fastest, most accurate reporting from every corner of the globe across all media types and platforms" (Associated Press, 2022, p. 1115).

Though the stylebook was initially created for traditional journalists — and is a staple in newsrooms across the country — it was and still is a necessity for public relations professionals who endeavor to deliver quality content to their audiences, which usually includes journalists. The expressed writing standard by which reporters, editors and content creators will measure the quality and appropriateness of language in material received from PR professionals is the AP stylebook.

In 2022, the Associated Press stylebook published its 56th edition, marking almost 70 years of being in publication and guiding the content development process for professional writers in the media industry. The stylebook is renowned for its robust guidance for writers, offering fundamental rules, recommendations and guidelines for spelling, abbreviations, capitalization, grammar, style, industry-specific verbiage, inclusive language, punctuation, technical terminology and general word usage. Additionally, the stylebook establishes and expounds on accepted writing conventions and adaptations in response to a changing society. Throughout its pages, the AP stylebook serves as a tutorial and effectively demonstrates correct and incorrect usage through examples in the text, providing writers a frame of reference within the pages for seeing how and when to use specific instances of words or phrases to write clear and unambiguous content.

Additional resources for improving professional writing styles and standards include:

- "The Chicago Manual of Style"

- "Publication Manual of the American Psychological Association" (APA style)

- "The New York Times Manual of Style and Usage"

- AP Stylebook Online (online resource that also includes bonus features such as Ask the Editor, Topical Guides, and a Pronunciation Guide)

3.2 — COMMON AP STYLE ERRORS

Without the appropriate context, the AP stylebook might appear to be just a lot of random words and phrases that most people don't use very often. In reality, the stylebook is organized into practical sections based on how journalists and media professionals prepare to develop accurate, objective and clear content related to news and society.

The stylebook is organized into several sections that are filled with terms, phrases and titles in alphabetical order. The best way to get familiar with the stylebook and how to find what is needed is to peruse various entries and get an understanding of how the information is presented. Though it is not practical to simply read the entire stylebook at once, it is helpful to review random entries and become familiar with the content so it becomes intuitive when it comes time to find what is needed.

In general, entry words or phrases are listed in boldface type and represent the accepted or recommended word form, unless otherwise indicated. A single listing of the word or phrase in bold is meant to provide the correct spelling, usage in text, hyphenation or capitalization. Any additional text following the bolded entry word represents an explanation of why the preferred usage is in place. Examples of correct or incorrect usages are included in italicized text for demonstration purposes only — as there are no italics used in AP style. Oftentimes, if an entry has a common abbreviation, it also is indicated in italics. Any related topics or similar entries may be referenced in bold, such as:

times = See **midnight**, **noon**; **numerals**, **time zones**.

As an example, if a writer is seeking to learn how to accurately represent the name of a new creative piece of work, it is unlikely that they will find the exact name of the new production in the stylebook. However, a search under the "composition titles" entry will provide the AP stylebook rules and regulations on appropriate usage or representation of the name. The entry clearly explains how to apply the guidelines to titles of albums, books, lectures, movies, plays, poems, speeches, works of art and more. As another example, if a PR writing professional is working on a news release that mentions several cities and states, there are corresponding stylebook entries for "datelines," "city" and "state names." Additionally, there are numerous explanations of when and how to write about prominent individuals; how and when to use the correct punctuation; when to write out or capitalize geographic locations; how to use numerals and figures accurately; how to write out formal titles and when to use acronyms or abbreviations instead; and how to introduce an organization or topic within the first reference.

Entries featuring recommendations and preferences are included as well, comparing and contrasting similar words and then demonstrating their appropriate usage, such as the entry listing "stanch, staunch." The stylebook entry reads:

Stanch is a verb: *He stanched the flow of blood.*

Staunch is an adjective: *She is a staunch supporter of equality.*

The stylebook also includes references to phrases and terminology that should be avoided because they are considered to be slang, offensive, outdated or inappropriate. As an example, the stylebook entry for "gyp" reads:

gyp (n. and v.). Fraud or swindle or to cheat someone. Avoid use. Offensive to Gypsies, also known as Roma.

AP style also clarifies correct grammar usage with common words such as *who* or *whom*. The stylebook entry "who, whom" (Associated Press, 2022, p. 700) reads:

Who is the pronoun used for references to human beings and to animals with a name. Write *the person who is in charge*, not *the person that is in charge.*

Who is grammatically the subject (never the object) of a sentence, clause or phrase: *The woman who rented the room left the window open. Who is there?*

Whom is used when someone is the object of a verb or preposition: *The woman to whom to room was rented left the window open. Whom do you wish to see?*

The goal of the AP stylebook throughout its many iterations is to assist communicators in being accurate, relevant, fair and concise in their reporting or sharing of the news about and among a diverse global population.

When to Use the AP Stylebook

Because there are so many entries and so much information in the stylebook, it can be overwhelming. Here are 10 situations to keep in mind as a reminder of when to pick up the AP stylebook.

1. When the content being created is going to be distributed to the media and it needs to be aligned with traditional journalistic standards, which utilize the AP stylebook as a guide.

2. When government officials or institutions are mentioned in the content and the writer needs to clearly and accurately identify the individuals and institutions being referenced.

3. When writing about or referring to marginalized groups or historically underrepresented populations, where certain terms or phrases may be considered offensive.

4. When there are a lot of numerical figures and/or percentages that can easily confuse the reader — and AP style applies uniformity and consistency to the content.

5. When there are individual names, roles, titles and designations that require clarity and consistency.

6. When there are cities, states, regions and other geographic locations that need to be clearly and consistently identified in the text.

7. When there is a question about how to correctly punctuate text.

8. When industry-specific terms or corporate jargon may confuse readers without clarification.

9. When reporting on corporate earnings or filings with government regulatory bodies that need to ensure conformity with industry standards.

10. When the correct terminology, spelling or word choice is needed to accurately convey content.

3.3 — UNDERSTANDING THE AP STYLEBOOK LAYOUT

As stated, the stylebook outlines basic rules and guidelines for writers related to spelling, grammar, punctuation, usage and inclusive language. As part of an annual update to reflect the latest changes in accepted usage, punctuation, style and grammar, the 55th edition was introduced with the following announcement about inclusive language:

> Inclusive storytelling seeks to truly represent all people around the globe. It gives voice and visibility to those who have been missing or misrepresented in traditional narratives

of both history and daily journalism. It helps readers and viewers both to recognize themselves in our stories, and to better understand people who differ from them in race, age, gender, class and many other ways.

It makes our work immeasurably stronger, more relevant, more compelling, more trustworthy. It is essential to accuracy and fairness. It is not a "topic" to be siloed or explored here and there.

Inclusive storytelling should be part of everyday conversations, decision-making and coverage. That means integrating these goals in all aspects of conversations, from the beginning of the story idea to garnering reaction (and more story ideas) after publication.

One of the primary reasons that AP style is included in this textbook is to underscore the importance of good writing for PR professionals. The proliferation of social media as an instant tool for delivering information directly to the masses has simultaneously eroded the quality of good writing due to relaxed standards, limited space and socially accepted acronyms and emojis (visual icons for feelings and emotions) that diminish the quality of long-form content.

Though there are countless platforms and digital spaces where PR practitioners can speak directly to key publics, a major audience is still journalists and media representatives, who traditionally rely on a journalistic writing standard that is provided by the AP stylebook. To be taken seriously as a professional in the practice of PR, it is necessary to understand the role and importance of AP in effectively communicating with this audience. Basically, mastering AP style allows PR professionals to "speak the language" of the journalists to whom they are pitching story ideas.

One of the most significant reasons for PR writing professionals to rely on AP style is for the consistency it creates. Utilizing a standard that addresses and regulates content across connected and interrelated industries sets up the parameters and rules for everyone who is participating — and dispels the need to guess, speculate or "re-create the wheel" when style, form and content are in question.

To be clear, the stylebook does not answer every question or clarify every concern about writing clearly; however, it is comprehensive enough to be considered the gold-standard reference manual for agreed-upon writing rules. Hence, it is the go-to resource guide for both newsrooms and PR agencies to help shorten the distance between the two professional worlds and bridge the communication gap in how professionals respectfully develop and distribute content to the world.

This mandatory resource guide has evolved over the decades and now includes individual sections on old and new topics that are frequently part of daily news coverage and topics or causes that PR agencies represent. This next section will discuss the importance of AP style standards within these specific areas and their relevance to PR writing.

Punctuation

Clear and correctly placed punctuation marks can elevate writing to a higher standard. Punctuation in PR writing is an essential tool for clarity in communication and helps the reader navigate smoothly through the content. Quotation marks make it clear that an individual's actual words are being shared; exclamation points indicate energy and excitement in language; the presence of commas, semicolons and colons can speed up or slow down a sentence and influence the manner in which a thought is being conveyed. Metaphorically speaking, punctuation marks are the literary road signs that tell readers when to stop, go or turn. Incorrect, inconsistent or misplaced punctuation marks can change the meaning of a sentence and undermine the integrity of a story. The role of punctuation is to make written communication clear. When it comes to punctuation marks, less is more.

Business

With great frequency, PR practitioners write about news and stories that business clients want to tell. However, the various stakeholder groups who will receive the communications are not always business savvy or well versed in business or industry jargon. Guidelines on business writing provided by the stylebook help writers avoid unnecessary jargon and communicate complex data or financial information in a way that is easy to understand. PR professionals can reference the stylebook to better understand requirements for content related to financial disclosures and quarterly earnings reports, which are often published through business and public relations wire distribution companies.

Data Journalism

As a rapidly evolving area, data journalism is filled with a lot of facts and figures and innumerable data points that must be further analyzed to extract trends, patterns and information that is relevant to the reader. Data journalism also includes a lot of financial and numerical data (revenue, stock prices, profit and loss, year-over-year growth/loss percentages, etc.), so using the stylebook will standardize the use of formulas and figures to ensure that the information is accurately and consistently presented. Since so much of storytelling involves a visual component, effective leveraging of data journalism relies on the PR writer's ability to summarize comprehensive content and present it in an appealing manner and in a clear, manageable format.

Polls and Surveys

Whether conducted by phone, in person or online, polls and surveys are ubiquitous in the marketplace — collecting data and opinions and measuring consumer sentiments on every topic imaginable. Because polls and surveys are reflective of real people, the results are often of great interest and often can be used to gain traction in securing media coverage. The results generated from taking polls and surveys produce a lot of statistical and numerical data that need to be analyzed and shared in a manner that is easy to understand. The PR professional needs to understand and clearly communicate the purpose and parameters of the poll or survey, what the limitations are, which methods were used in collecting information and how the findings are relevant to the audiences.

Health and Science

Stories about health and science are universal to all audiences, so it is advantageous for PR professionals working in health care, the medical industry or any scientific field to understand how to make complicated jargon more digestible to the average reader. PR practitioners writing about these issues will find the AP stylebook to be helpful with guidelines regarding reporting on research, medical breakthroughs, commercial claims and medical privacy concerns. The stylebook also addresses medical claims regarding contagions and cures and the associated liabilities of such language, along with the importance of using third-party or independent subject matter experts who can confirm and validate content.

Social Media

To some, it might seem as though there are absolutely no guidelines for social media and that anything goes. However, behind the scenes, for those who are obligated to write with a level of accountability, the AP stylebook offers guidance about sourcing online content, protecting online privacy, avoiding copyright violations and accurately using the countless abbreviations and "webspeak" terms that have arisen from the ascension of social media as a platform for public discourse. In essence, anything a PR professional writes and publishes online is likely to find its way onto social media sites, so it is imperative that writing professionals commit to communicating in a manner that is consistent with the voice and brand of the client(s) being represented — and not in a way that puts the organization or company in legal, financial or reputational jeopardy.

Digital Security

Addressing the topic of digital security is fairly new for the AP stylebook, a result of increasing online phishing and hacking attempts related to cybercrimes. Guidelines on digital security mainly address online safety and using extra precautions to protect passwords and confidential information and to prevent costly data breaches. PR professionals are often privy to private information before it goes public, so using multistep authenticators in security as an added measure of protection is worthwhile to protect clients' sensitive data or information. Other important points to consider are data transmission and data retention, being mindful of how and where data is shared or stored and how to protect the PR agency or client(s) from cybersecurity threats.

Religion

It is often said that discussing religion and politics should be off-limits in mixed company, with people in your family and with people outside your family. The fact that professional writers tackle the topic of religion every day explains why there is a standalone section about it in the AP stylebook. Religion is a topic where offense can easily and quickly occur, so it is imperative to do the research before writing and publishing content to make sure that the language being used is nonoffensive and that it does not violate the religious rights or offend the religious beliefs of any particular group. Entries in the religion section of the stylebook offer guidance on correct terminology for religious leaders, titles of religious books and texts, names of religious rituals and designations, times and observances for religious ceremonies, official titles and roles of religious leaders, and spellings and definitions related to religious symbols and holidays. All of the entries are written to make sure that information on religious topics is presented in a fair and unbiased manner.

Sports

At every level of sports, there must be a realization that the industry is as much about exercise, fun and recreation for some as it is about business for others. The sports arena is also a financial juggernaut, so any individuals creating content about sports must be mindful of the terminology, jargon, rules and legal ramifications that accompany sports reporting, sports marketing and promotions. The AP stylebook is particularly adept at explaining the rules and scoring for individual sporting events and activities, equipping the journalist or PR writing professional with accurate language that correctly communicates about the sport. On its opening pages, the Sports section of the stylebook includes a list of sports identification codes along with common abbreviations for popular sports franchises. There are multiple charts and tables that demonstrate how specific sporting events are scored to ensure accurate and uniform reporting by the media. The guide also includes a list of major sports conferences, listing their headquarters and affiliations. As an example, there are separate entries for "baseball," "basketball," "football" and "soccer" that include specific moves or plays germane to each particular sport:

- Sample baseball terms and positions: backstop, bullpen, fastball, home run, outfielder, pinch hit, slugger, strike zone, triple play, walk-off

- Sample basketball terms and plays: air ball, alley-oop, foul line, free throw, goaltending, half-court pass, jump ball, layup, man-to-man, tipoff

- Sample football terms and positions: blitz, end zone, goal line, linebacker, line of scrimmage, onside kick, pick six, quarterback, split end, touchdown

- Sample soccer terms, plays and positions: backpass, corner, defender, free kick, goalkeeper, offside, penalty, red card, throw-in, wall

Media Law

The media law section of the AP stylebook is geared toward regulating and protecting the news-gathering process and clarifying the parameters of First Amendment rights in the process of reporting and sharing information. Here is a list of guidance for common legal issues that the AP stylebook is designed to prevent:

- Copyright violations

- Defamation, libel and slander

- False and misleading claims

- Insider trading

- Invasion of privacy

- Trademark infringement

- Violation of Securities and Exchange Commission (SEC) regulations

Though the majority of the guidance in the AP stylebook section on media law is geared toward working journalists and the constitutional protections afforded by the First Amendment, there are several areas with direct implications for PR professionals who frequently publish content on the internet and social media and must address concerns about copyright violations.

News Values and News Principles

The AP stylebook expounds on the importance of news values and news principles in newsgathering. Though public relations is less about newsgathering and more about storytelling, it is important for PR professionals to understand and appreciate the value system of traditional media outlets so they can respect and align with them in the daily operations of work. Some of the topics discussed in the news values section of the stylebook include anonymous sources, attribution, conflicts of interest, corrections, plagiarism, propaganda, privacy, quotations and social networks/social media.

Broadcast

The 55th edition of the stylebook comments on the straightforward writing structure that frames broadcast content — Lead→Backup→Details→Background — and includes numerous broadcast terms that are helpful for the PR professional in proficiently working on campaigns with an audio/video (A/V) component. Some broadcast terms and definitions highlighted in this section are *actuality, cut, fade, nonlinear editing, rough cut, sound bite* and *wall-to-wall coverage*. Here is a list of 10 principles used by AP broadcast writers that are helpful tips and reminders for PR writing students also (Associated Press, 2020, p. 513):

1. Lead with the news.

2. In leads, use forms of the present or future verb tenses.

3. Keep leads short and to the point.

4. Favor the active voice.

5. Attribute at the beginning of sentences.

6. Identify newsmakers before naming them.

7. Omit needless words.

8. Prefer the simple to the complex.

9. Simplify numbers.

10. Use a variety of sentence lengths, but keep most of them short.

Editing and Proofing Marks

The ease and accessibility of quality word-processing software with editing features is decreasing the need for and knowledge of AP-style proofreading marks. However, in the event of a technology failure, it is good to have a working knowledge of how to manually edit or proof a document for corrections. Common editing or proofreader marks are used to adjust spacing, correct spelling errors, insert punctuation, realign text, alter capitalizations, and insert or delete content. See Figure 3.1 for examples of AP stylebook editing symbols.

FIGURE 3.1 ■   Sample AP Style Proofreaders' Marks

SAMPLE AP STYLE PROOFREADERS' MARKS

Symbol	Meaning	Example
ℰ or ૪ or ૭	delete word	take it out
ℂ	close up space	print as o ne word
ℰ	delete letter and close up space	close up
∧ or ＞ or ⋀	caret; used to insert	insert here (something
⋀	insert a comma	Red, white and blue are the colors.
⋁	insert an apostrophe	Books on the teachers' desks are new.
⊙	period	Periods and commas go inside quote marks.
ⓈⓅ	spell out	set (5 lbs) as five pounds
¶	begin a new paragraph	That's all, folks. ¶ In conclusion,
#	insert a space	put one here
eq#	space evenly	space evenly ⋀ where indicated
stet	let stand	let marked told stand as set
tr	transpose letters or words	change order the
[	set farther to the left	L too far to the right
]	set farther to the right	too far to the left
cap	set in CAPITALS	set nato as NATO
lc	type in lowercase letters	set South as south
ital	change font to italics	set oeuvre as oeuvre
bf	set in boldface	set important as important
= or -/ or ⌢ or /H/	hyphen	Ex. It is a self-titled biography.
⌐/M or em or /M/	dash (two hyphens)	Now – finally – we can get started.
≪≫ or ⌣⌣	quotation marks	"Sunset" is my favorite song.
OK/?	query to author: is this correct or OK as printed?	

3.4 — AP STYLE APPLICATIONS

From meticulous spelling and grammar considerations to nuanced guidelines on titles, numerals, datelines, state names, usage, abbreviations and more, these AP style reminders serve as a guardrail to hone the accuracy and consistency vital to effective written communication in the field of public relations:

- Spelling: Spell-checker does NOT reliably catch errors in ALL CAPS

- Datelines (city) should be written in ALL CAPS; state names should be abbreviated/spelled out or written in upper/lowercase as indicated by AP style

- Check AP style for state names or abbreviations in datelines; U.S. Postal Service and AP style often differ

- Review address abbreviations (e.g., "1234 Main St." vs. "Main Street")

- Study "that, which" entry for correct usage

- Capitalize formal or official titles (e.g., "President" or "Vice President") prior to names; lowercase following names

- Review correct usage for "its"/"it's"; "their"/"there"/"they're"; "your"/"you're"

- Remember, no final comma is needed before "and" in a series

- Check abbreviations guidelines for months in dates

- Place a comma after the year when used with a specific, full date (e.g., "Jan. 1, 2028, is a holiday")

- No "00" is needed for top-of-the-hour times (e.g., "4 p.m.," not "4:00 p.m.")

- Use "noon" or "midnight," not "12:00 a.m." or "12:00 p.m."

- Double-check use of numerals one through 10; write out one through nine and use numerals for numbers over 10; always represent ages and metrics with numerals

- Read copy aloud and/or backward to catch common errors

- Double-check facts and spelling, then check again!

The more a student writes, the better a writer the student will become. Though there is a lot of information in the AP stylebook to absorb, a lot of common errors in PR writing show up in the same areas, because generally, public-facing content is used more often than specialized, industry-specific jargon. Take a look at the examples shown here to get acclimated to some of the more prevalent rules and usages outlined in the stylebook.

Rule and Common Usage: Numerals Used for Ages

This section highlights basic principles of AP style, focusing on ages.

- The 8-year-old girl sang a solo in the school's talent show.

- The girl who sang a solo in the school's talent show is 8 years old.

- She will be 9 years old on her birthday next month.

- The man in his 30s has a son 6 months old.

- The man in his 30s has a 6-month-old son. (compound modifier)

- The couple in their 40s have twin daughters, 10, and a teenage son who is 14. (When the terms or phrases "years" and "years old" are not used, the default for age-related figures is years.)

Rule and Common Usage: Time and Day Parts

This section highlights basic principles of AP style, focusing on time and day parts.

- Use figures to indicate times except noon and midnight to avoid confusion.

- The meeting will begin promptly at 9 a.m.

- The break for lunch is scheduled for 11:45 a.m.

- The guest speaker will begin her presentation at noon.

- The workshop will last from 2-4 p.m.

- The firework display will end at midnight.

Rule and Common Usage: Cardinal and Ordinal Numerals

This section highlights basic principles of AP style, focused on numerals. Generally speaking, spell out numerals one through nine and use figures for 10 and above, with the exception of ages and units of measure. Spell out numerals at the start of a sentence.

- There are four puppies in the basket.

- There are 17 golf balls on the course.

- The children are in the fifth grade.

- Twenty people were standing in line at midnight.

- There were countless technological advancements in the 21st century.

- The city experienced a 4-inch snowfall in early spring.

- The walking trail distance totals 2 miles.

Spelling Matters

Spelling errors and proper noun errors may be among the most egregious types of mistakes for PR professionals to make, because they are obvious to most readers. Even with spelling and grammar apps and countless word-processing software programs on various devices, spelling errors are quite common. The stylebook entries list correct spellings of commonly misspelled words. When in doubt, check the AP stylebook; if the term is not listed there, check the dictionary. According to online editors and grammar experts, here are some of the most frequently misspelled words (Table 3.1).

TABLE 3.1 ■ Commonly Misspelled Words	
Correct Spelling	**Common Misspelling**
accommodate	accomodate
achieve	acheive
acknowledgment	acknowledgement (acceptable British spelling)
acquire	aquire
all right	alright
a lot	alot
apparent	aparent
believe	beleive
calendar	calender
camaraderie	comraderie
colleague	collegue
collectible	collectable
conscience	consience
conscientious	consciencious
consensus	concensus
definitely	definately
embarrassment	embarassment
entrepreneur	entrepeneur
fulfill	fulfil
gauge	gage (variant spelling; not preferred)
government	goverment

(Continued)

TABLE 3.1 ■ Commonly Misspelled Words *(Continued)*	
Correct Spelling	**Common Misspelling**
grateful	greatful
guarantee	garauntee
harass	harrass
inoculate	innoculate
judgment	judgement (acceptable British spelling)
liaison	liasion
license	licence
millennium	milennium
mischievous	mischeivous
misspelling	mispelling
necessary	neccessary
occasion	occassion
occurrence	occurence
pastime	pasttime
personnel	personnal
privilege	priviledge
pronunciation	pronounciation
publicly	publically
receipt	reciept
receive	recieve
recurrence	recurence
referred	refered
relevant	relevent
rhythm	ryhthm
separate	seperate
successful	sucessful
terrific	terriffic
vacuum	vaccum
weird	wierd

CHAPTER SUMMARY

Understanding AP style standards and how to use the AP stylebook will significantly improve writing skills and the quality of content developed for distribution to the media. AP style is used to correct common errors in spelling, punctuation, grammar, style, language and usage. Major categories included in the stylebook for reference are punctuation, business, storytelling, data journalism, polls and surveys, health and science, social media, digital security, religion, sports, media law, news values, and editing/proofing marks.

In writing as in anything else, practice creates improvement, and better writing comes from writing more. Becoming familiar with the stylebook's contents and also understanding the types of guidelines provided for writing will make the book a more useful reference tool.

KEY TERM

Associated Press

DISCUSSION QUESTIONS

1. Why is the AP stylebook relevant to the PR profession?

2. Which sections of the AP stylebook do you find most helpful for improving your writing?

3. What additional updates or suggestions do you have for inclusion in the next edition of the AP stylebook?

WRITING EXERCISES

1. Write an AP-style headline announcing $1 hamburgers, hotdogs and fries for a celebration at the house located at 1600 Pennsylvania Avenue NW, in the nation's capital, one minute after 11:59 p.m. on the last day of the year.

2. Craft an AP-style announcement for a charitable fundraising event scheduled on the fourth day of the seventh month, highlighting the donation of ten thousand dollars, to twenty high school students and four teachers for their extraordinary volunteer work cleaning up a local park at the intersection of 5th Avenue and Maple Boulevard in Salt Lake City, Utah.

SAMPLE AP STYLE QUIZ QUESTIONS

This AP style quiz section measures basic knowledge of common AP style guidelines.

1. Which of the following sentences is correct AP style?
   A. The ten-year old boy invited 8 friends to his birthday party.
   B. The 10-year-old boy invited eight friends to his birthday party.
   C. The 10-year-old boy invited 8 friends to his birthday party.
   D. The ten-year-old boy invited eight friends to his birthday party.
       Answer: B | AP style rule is to always use numerals for ages and write out numerals one through nine.
   A. The ten-year old boy invited 8 friends to his birthday party.
   B. The 10-year-old boy invited eight friends to his birthday party.
   C. The 10-year-old boy invited 8 friends to his birthday party.
   D. The ten-year-old boy invited eight friends to his birthday party.

2. Which time reference is correct?
   A. The lunchtime show will begin promptly at 12:00 p.m.
   B. The lunchtime show will begin promptly at 12 pm.
   C. The lunchtime show will begin promptly at 12 noon.
   D. The lunchtime show will begin promptly at noon.
       Answer: D | AP style rule is to write out noon and midnight.
   A. The lunchtime show will begin promptly at 12:00 p.m.
   B. The lunchtime show will begin promptly at 12 pm.
   C. The lunchtime show will begin promptly at 12 noon.
   D. The lunchtime show will begin promptly at noon.

3. Which of the following is correct AP style?
   A. There will be an AP style quiz on Wednesday, January 26, 2028, and the quiz will be given on Sakai.
   B. There will be an AP style quiz on Wednesday, Jan. 26, 2028, and the quiz will be given on Sakai.
   C. There will be an AP style quiz on Wed., Jan. 26, 2028 and the quiz will be given on Sakai.
   D. There will be an AP style quiz on Wed., January 26, 2028, and the quiz will be given on Sakai.
       Answer: B | AP style rule is to abbreviate the month in AP style and insert a comma after the year when the complete month, day and year are listed.
   A. There will be an AP style quiz on Wednesday, January 26, 2028, and the quiz will be given on Sakai.
   B. There will be an AP style quiz on Wednesday, Jan. 26, 2028, and the quiz will be given on Sakai.
   C. There will be an AP style quiz on Wed., Jan. 26, 2028 and the quiz will be given on Sakai.

D. There will be an AP style quiz on Wed., January 26, 2028, and the quiz will be given on Sakai.

4. Which of the following is correct AP style?
   A. "I cannot believe it's almost time to go," Mary said.
   B. "I can not believe its almost time to go." Mary said.
   C. "I can not believe its' almost time to go," Mary said.
   D. "I cannot believe its almost time to go." Mary said.

   Answer: A | AP style rule is to write "cannot" as one word, and "it's" is a contraction for "it is." Periods and commas go inside quotation marks.

   A. **"I cannot believe it's almost time to go," Mary said.**
   B. "I can not believe its almost time to go." Mary said.
   C. "I can not believe its' almost time to go," Mary said.
   D. "I cannot believe its almost time to go." Mary said.

5. Select the correct AP style usage.
   A. Authorities reported that all 15 families and their four pets were okay after the hurricane.
   B. Authorities reported that all 15 families and their 4 pets were okay after the hurricane.
   C. Authorities reported that all 15 families and their four pets were OK after the hurricane.
   D. Authorities reported that all fifteen families and their four pets were okay after the hurricane.

   Answer: C | AP style rule is to write out numerals less than 10 and abbreviate OK.

   A. Authorities reported that all 15 families and their four pets were okay after the hurricane.
   B. Authorities reported that all 15 families and their 4 pets were okay after the hurricane.
   C. **Authorities reported that all 15 families and their four pets were OK after the hurricane.**
   D. Authorities reported that all fifteen families and their four pets were okay after the hurricane.

6. Which of the following states should be abbreviated in AP style datelines and text?
   A. New Mexico
   B. Iowa
   C. Maine
   D. Hawaii

   Answer: A | AP style rule is that eight state names are not abbreviated; Alaska, Hawaii, and the six states with five letters or fewer (Idaho, Iowa, Maine, Ohio, Texas and Utah).

   A. **New Mexico**

    B. Iowa

    C. Maine

    D. Hawaii

7. Which of the following is correct AP style?

    A. The grizzly-bear was running towards the campsite at full speed.

    B. The grizzly bear was running toward the campsite at full speed.

    C. The grisly bear was running towards the campsite at full-speed.

    D. The grizzly bear was running towards the campsite at full speed.

        Answer: B | AP style rule is to omit an "s" on "toward." "Grizzly bear" does not need a hyphen, as it identifies a specific type of animal.

    A. The grizzly-bear was running towards the campsite at full speed.

    B. **The grizzly bear was running toward the campsite at full speed.**

    C. The grisly bear was running towards the campsite at full-speed.

    D. The grizzly bear was running towards the campsite at full speed.

8. Select the sentence that is correctly written in AP style.

    A. The contestant with more than 50 percent of the votes will be announced at 4:00 p.m. during a press conference from the office located at the intersection of Belmont and Ridgeline Avenues.

    B. The contestant with more than 50% of the votes will be announced at 4:00 p.m. during a press conference from the office located at the intersection of Belmont and Ridgeline Avenues.

    C. The contestant with more than 50 percent of the votes will be announced at 4 p.m. during a press conference from the office located at the intersection of Belmont and Ridgeline avenues.

    D. The contestant with more than 50% of the votes will be announced at 4 p.m. during a press conference from the office located at the intersection of Belmont and Ridgeline avenues.

        Answer: D | AP style rule is to use the % sign after the numeral, omit the double zeros at the top of the hour, and lowercase road designations for multiple street names.

    A. The contestant with more than 50 percent of the votes will be announced at 4:00 p.m. during a press conference from the office located at the intersection of Belmont and Ridgeline Avenues.

    B. The contestant with more than 50% of the votes will be announced at 4:00 p.m. during a press conference from the office located at the intersection of Belmont and Ridgeline Avenues.

    C. The contestant with more than 50 percent of the votes will be announced at 4 p.m. during a press conference from the office located at the intersection of Belmont and Ridgeline avenues.

    D. **The contestant with more than 50% of the votes will be announced at 4 p.m. during a press conference from the office located at the intersection of Belmont and Ridgeline avenues.**

9. Which of the following is correct AP style?
   A. Even though temperatures are in the 50's, its still fun to enjoy outside activities such as walking, biking, hiking and running.
   B. Even though temperatures are in the 50s, its still fun to enjoy outside activities such as walking, biking, hiking, and running.
   C. Even though temperatures are in the 50's, it's still fun to enjoy outside activities such as walking, biking, hiking, and running.
   D. Even though temperatures are in the 50s, it's still fun to enjoy outside activities such as walking, biking, hiking and running.

   Answer: D | AP style rule is to omit an apostrophe when referring to a specific decade and omit the final comma (also referred to as an Oxford comma) in an "and" series.

   A. Even though temperatures are in the 50's, its still fun to enjoy activities outside, such as walking, biking, hiking and running.
   B. Even though temperatures are in the 50s, its still fun to enjoy activities outside, such as walking, biking, hiking, and running.
   C. Even though temperatures are in the 50's, it's still fun to enjoy activities outside, such as walking, biking, hiking, and running.
   D. Even though temperatures are in the 50s, it's still fun to enjoy activities outside, such as walking, biking, hiking and running.

10. Select the sentence that is correctly written in AP style.
    A. A chef from the television show Slice & Dice sang the Star-Spangled Banner before unveiling a red, white, and blue cake for independence day.
    B. A chef from the television show Slice & Dice sang "the Star Spangled Banner" before unveiling a red, white and blue cake for Independence day.
    C. A chef from the television show "Slice & Dice" sang "The Star-Spangled Banner" before unveiling a red, white and blue cake for Independence Day.
    D. A chef from the television show Slice & Dice sang The Star Spangled Banner before unveiling a red-white and blue cake for Independence Day.

    Answer: C | AP style rule is to place song titles and television show titles in quotation marks and capitalize Independence Day as a holiday.

    A. A chef from the television show Slice & Dice sang the Star-Spangled Banner before unveiling a red, white, and blue cake for independence day.
    B. A chef from the television show Slice & Dice sang "the Star Spangled Banner" before unveiling a red, white and blue cake for Independence day.
    C. A chef from the television show "Slice & Dice" sang "The Star-Spangled Banner" before unveiling a red, white and blue cake for Independence Day.
    D. A chef from the television show Slice & Dice sang The Star Spangled Banner before unveiling a red-white and blue cake for Independence Day.

4 CREATING NEWSWORTHY CONTENT THAT GETS COVERAGE

LEARNING OBJECTIVES

4.1 Learn the meaning of "newsworthy" and what makes up newsworthy content.

4.2 Review approaches to writing attention-grabbing headlines and quality content.

4.3 Explore different elements of newsworthiness and why they resonate with audiences.

4.4 Understand how newsrooms and news cycles work.

4.5 Learn how to craft a strong media pitch that highlights newsworthy content.

INTRODUCTION

The ability to create newsworthy content truly pays off for the PR professional once that content is picked up by media outlets and shared with the desired audiences. Knowing how to create newsworthy content comes first from understanding how newsrooms work and comprehending what makes information useful or interesting to those who consume it. Whether or not content is deemed newsworthy is often based on a list of criteria that shape and influence the selection of information as being worthy of publication, broadcast or distribution.

One of the most frustrating aspects of working in public relations is continually pitching to media outlets without getting the desired results of quality, positive coverage on behalf of a PR client. Developing newsworthy content goes beyond answering the basic questions of "Who?" "What?" "When?" "Where?" "Why?" "How?" and — don't forget — "Who cares?" Newsworthy content that gets coverage also must connect with audiences in a way that makes them want to know more.

4.1 — CREATING NEWSWORTHY CONTENT

Although it is fairly easy to teach students how to craft newsworthy content in the classroom setting, the art of pitching (presenting story ideas to journalists) is usually not put to the test until a student is working as an intern or getting real-world experience at their first entry-level position. Essentially, pitching to the media becomes an on-the-job training and learning experience. The key to successful pitching is knowing how to recognize multiple story angles and newsworthy elements (ones that won't get lost in translation) and craft a vision for how to tell a good story across different media platforms and to different audiences.

Whether it involves politics, business, education, health care or celebrity-related topics, the common denominator is that the media outlets want "news" — as in "new" information to inform, educate, persuade or entertain the reading, listening, scrolling or viewing audiences that tune in throughout the day.

4 .2 — WRITING ATTENTION-GRABBING HEADLINES

Most stories in print, broadcast or online begin with a headline that summarizes the story and captures the readers' or viewers' attention. It is safe to say that countless stories still go unread, even as individuals reliably scan the headlines to see if there is something of interest to read, watch or share with others. A great headline can make all the difference.

In PR writing, a headline or title — depending upon the document being written — is the hook that catches the reader's interest and encourages them to read more. Here is a list of tips for writing accurate, effective, concise headlines:

- *Summarize* — The headline should briefly explain the story content.

- *State the obvious* — Headlines should not be misleading or misrepresent the content; they should reflect the information included in the article.

- *Present tense and action* — Headlines need to include a verb to represent current and active language.

- *Short and concise* — PR headlines are usually six to eight words in length, with a little flexibility to include the client's name in the header.

- *Keep it simple* — Readers make split-second decisions about which content to consume, so the simpler and easier a headline is to understand, the better it will be received.

- *Use numerals* — Metrics, data and statistics provide a sense of certainty and credibility, which builds trust with the reader.

- *Replace "and" with a comma* — Removing unnecessary conjunctions and articles allows headlines to be short, concise and informative.

- *Include key words* — Because many headlines end up appearing in online publications, be sure to include relevant search terms and to consider the importance of search engine optimization (SEO).

- *Include the client's name* — Journalists scan headlines looking for story ideas, and one of the responsibilities of PR writing is to increase awareness about the client. An easy way to elevate exposure is to introduce the client's name early in the headline and lead paragraph.

- *Avoid clickbait and hyperbole* — Writing for attention without providing any real substance or content only goes so far. PR professionals need to think long term about writing with integrity to establish professional credibility, so it is important to resist the urge to create sensational or misleading headlines simply for the sake of more views.

- *Check for accuracy* — Witty creativity is a plus, but it is not more important than being correct; be sure to fact-check, review, edit and proof for spelling and grammar.

Sometimes it is helpful to write several headline options during the creative process and test them with small groups to see which resonates with them. Between advertising, public relations, and marketing content creation analysis reports, there is no question there are several proven approaches to writing attention-grabbing headlines. Though much content in PR writing is solely directed toward the media, there are times when PR professionals are creating content for owned platforms such as blogs, websites and social media — which allows them to speak directly to the customer or consumer. Here are some headline-writing examples to review for a company named Clutter Cleaners, which manufactures and distributes home organization supplies:

- *Emotional headline* — How removing clutter can improve your mood

- *Question headline* — Is clutter making you age faster?

- *Standard headline* — Removing clutter from homes saves time and space

- *How-to headline* — How to give your home a clutter-free makeover in 24 hours

- *User-friendly/Shareable headline* — Ways decluttering your home improves relationships

- *Data/Statistical headline* — 12 ways to organize and declutter your home and life

- *News headline* — Local company offers products to organize living spaces (objective and factual)

- *PR headline* — Clutter Cleaners' products use gravity to double home storage space (includes client name, piques readers' interest, addresses what the product does)

It is not uncommon or unusual for random, meaningless content to go viral online, capturing the eyes and ears of millions of people through posts, pins, likes and shares among family, friends and influencer circles. However, there is a difference between posting content for general audiences and pitching ideas to working journalists, who are held to a different standard of research, fact-checking, accuracy, objectivity and accountability for the content they publish or broadcast.

Though readers and viewers of traditional media outlets are a mixture of demographic and psychographic publics, they often share some commonality — whether it be geographic location, political ideology, attitudes and lifestyles, or recreational hobbies. Finding the common interests within journalists' audiences is the key to identifying relevant angle(s) for pitching newsworthy content or story ideas.

A surefire way for information to be overlooked or ignored is pushing content pitches that are purely self-serving or promotional for the brand issuing the information. No matter how exciting or interesting PR clients believe their "news" is, it is the job of the PR professional to ensure that credible content is at the forefront and that shameless PR stunts and promotional publicity are not the tools and tactics used to get media coverage.

TIPS FOR BEGINNERS — GETTING FAMILIAR WITH NEWSROOMS AND TV ASSIGNMENT DESKS

The best way to understand and appreciate how newsrooms and assignment desks work is to observe the process up close. Here are some tips and recommendations for novice PR professionals on gaining hands-on experience related to how news stories come together and make it into publications or onto the airwaves:

- *Intern in a newsroom* — Working in a newsroom is a guaranteed way to learn and understand what goes into developing quality long-form content. The environment also presents an opportunity to network with seasoned professionals and inquire about their professional journeys and to solicit career advice. Contributing to the news-writing process also will help develop a healthy respect for the tight deadlines that journalists have to meet and an appreciation for why frivolous PR pitches are not welcomed but rather viewed as a waste of time.

- *Job shadow with a reporter (print and broadcast)* — Going out in the field to work on a story from start to finish is an excellent way to understand the entire life cycle and process of information gathering and distribution, also referred to as the news cycle — from being assigned a story idea to identifying sources, experts or witnesses; crafting the story; and submitting it for editorial review. A simple introduction and/or request on social media can potentially lead to a day (or more) of invaluable exposure and the chance to experience "a day in the life" of a journalist.

- *Interview a producer* — Over coffee/tea, smoothies, or lunch, consider having a conversation with a television or radio producer to inquire about their daily duties in the studio. Take the opportunity to ask why some stories get their attention and others do not. Ask about the criteria they use to select story ideas and what information they most appreciate from PR professionals who are pitching suggestions to them. If possible, use the conversation to pitch a sample idea and ask them to critique your content. Use the constructive feedback to refine and enhance professional development.

- *Collaborate in the editing bay or editing suite* — Even if a PR professional has few or limited audio or video production skills, it is well worth the effort to spend several hours in the editing bay as podcasts, interviews and productions are merged together from various files to tell a story. It is an enlightening process to begin with hours of footage, sounds, images and interviews — to see what is left behind and what is used to make a story complete. During the time spent with an editor, inquire about why certain sound bites were selected and which elements combine best to create compelling content.

- *Ask for a PR critique* — Reaching out to a local PR professor on campus or a PR professional in a local PRSA (Public Relations Society of America) chapter is a good way to get constructive feedback on content. Draft a sample media pitch and accompanying script for the story idea and ask for input on how to improve. If possible, request written comments and advice on things to add or delete to refer back to at a later date. Finally, ask the PR professional about their approach to pitching story ideas to the media and about what works best to produce the results they want.

- *Freelance during the summer or semester for a nonprofit organization or print publication* — There are countless organizations in need of editorial support from new writers seeking to enhance their skills. Consider reaching out to a local charity or a local publication to gain additional experience in copywriting and editing while simultaneously building a strong portfolio of published pieces. During the process, be sure to keep each draft of an article or profile piece to compare how similar or different the original piece is to the final, published piece. Use that information to better understand how editorial decisions are made and what information is required to create well-written content.

- *Watch the news* — So much can be gained from simply watching the news with a critical eye on the details. Pay attention to the lead stories that open the top of the newscast. Take note of how many individuals are interviewed, how many different scenes or backgrounds are part of the story, and what information the on-site reporter shares with the audience. Ask yourself if any crucial information is missing — or how you might have written the story differently to be more effective.

- *Write sample pitches and scripts* — Write mock pitches related to the same story idea for radio, television and online; examine their similarities and differences in approach to understand what works best on each respective platform. Review the process to understand where and when to use various types of content, such as sound bites (audio interviews), B-roll (general video footage), stock images (staged photographs), and live stand-up interviews with individuals who are pertinent to the story.

There are a lot of ways to gain experience and additional expertise, but nothing compares to actually getting out in the field and doing the work.

4.3 — ELEMENTS OF NEWSWORTHINESS

What makes something newsworthy is fairly predictable. Asking a few basic questions can inspire the PR practitioner to identify ways to present desirable content in a way that gets media coverage:

- What does the public have a right to know?

- What does the public need to know?

- What does the public want to know?

- What does the PR client want its stakeholders to think, know, feel and do?

Listed here are some common explanations and context to help identify newsworthy content:

- The safety and security of the public are at stake (e.g., natural disasters, active crime scenes, communicable diseases, security breaches).

- The public has a "right to know" and a "need to know" about the situation to make informed decisions for themselves and their families.

- The topic affects a large portion of the population or viewing audience.

- The issue or topic is trending or going viral on social media.

- There is "breaking news" that many other media outlets are covering, so it becomes a competitive advantage to also have a reporter on the scene.

- The story encompasses multiple newsworthy factors and components that make it mandatory to cover.

- The story is evolving, and new information is available to share.

"Newsworthy" Elements to Incorporate Into PR Writing Documents and Media Pitches

Generally speaking, news values are "criteria that influence the selection and presentation of events as published news" ("News Values," 2024). These following values help explain what makes something "newsworthy."

Local Connection or Proximity

There's a common adage in the news business that "all news is local news," meaning that if the stories being told don't have a proximity factor, or a direct, local connection to the people they're being told to, then they aren't really newsworthy. In short, people care about things that affect them and care less about things that don't.

Impact

How will this news affect the audience, and what are the consequences related to this news story? The more people affected by something, the more newsworthy the story becomes. Hearing about a small outbreak of an infectious disease in another state might get mentioned in the evening news wrap-up, but this doesn't generate much coverage. Understanding that a global pandemic is going to shut down schools and businesses and require everyone in the country to shelter in place and stay at home for weeks or months ignites wall-to-wall coverage (nonstop morning, noon and nighttime media) for weeks and months on end. The COVID-19 story impacted almost everyone in multiple ways, so the coverage was nonstop until the impact lessened.

Conflict

Anyone who has ever watched the news, a soap opera, a play, or a movie knows that conflict is a key element of compelling content creation, narration and storytelling. By nature, conflict creates tension and a sense of belonging where individuals get to side with a character or a cause that connects with them. Frequently used as a literary technique to manage challenges among protagonist and antagonist characters, conflict is popular because its resolution also provides closure for the audience and achievement of some specific goal.

Human Interest

A key component of effective storytelling involves human interest, a factor that makes news more relatable and easily understandable because the individuals featured are undergoing circumstances that people can connect with through experience or observation. One of the more popular types of stories that generally get coverage is "reunion" stories. Whether they involve military personnel returning from deployment and making a surprise visit to their child's school or long-lost relatives separated at birth and reunited through social media or DNA searches, these moving stories are inherently emotional and relatable because they pique curiosity and leverage the power of human interest.

Celebrity

Because celebrities are well known and often have national or international prominence and recognition, they attract a lot of attention, both on traditional media and social media platforms. As a result, adding a celebrity factor to a news story makes it almost immediately newsworthy — especially if the celebrity is highly visible or currently working on an intriguing project or campaign. A corner lemonade stand in a neighborhood to raise donations for a local charity is a nice idea but not that interesting to local news crews. The same lemonade stand with an A-list celebrity handing out cups of lemonade while on break from shooting a blockbuster movie is likely to open up the noon news segment, complete with the reporter purchasing lemonade, interviewing the celebrity, and telling listeners and viewers how they too can support a worthy cause and be served lemonade by one of their favorite celebrities.

Relevance

Why does the audience care about this issue or news story? The concept of relevance means that there is a connection to the audience and that the information is something they want to know more about, think about or care about. If a significant portion of the audience believes the content has value and is relevant to their lives, then a media outlet is more likely to devote resources to covering the story.

Timeliness

Is the news story occurring, developing or scheduled to happen in the immediate future? Those are questions to consider when assessing the timeliness of content. At the core of news is the word "new," which means the newsworthiness value increases in direct proportion to how new the information is and how quickly the story unfolds. Unfortunately, the rush to get a story out first often results in inaccurate or incomplete reporting, which can be damaging and confusing to readers and viewers. Even when there is an opportunity to align a quality PR pitch with breaking news, it is important that the information being provided is honest and accurate.

Magnitude

The term magnitude is often used in the context of discussing earthquakes and how severe the tremors and resulting damage will be. In the same regard, a story about a faucet leaking in the cafeteria of a local elementary school does not carry the same magnitude as a story about a broken water main line on the busiest street in the city that will stall rush-hour traffic for hours. Magnitude is about the number of people affected by a situation and how serious the consequences or impact will be.

Novelty or Uniqueness

People are naturally drawn to things that they don't see every day, which is why "novelty" or "unique" stories often get a lot of attention. A traffic jam at 5:30 p.m. is not news; however, a traffic jam on the highway caused by a flock of chickens from an overturned truck is breaking news. It is not uncommon to see wall-to-wall coverage of rare or unusual events such as a solar eclipse, an unidentified flying or aerial object captured on camera, royal ceremonies overseas, and space shuttle takeoffs and landings. Listeners and viewers often tune in because of the rarity of such occurrences and because some of them may be once-in-a-lifetime events.

4 .4 — NEWSROOMS: THEN AND NOW

When news access for most people was limited to one local daily publication, three basic network television stations, local AM and FM radio stations, and nonexistent social media, getting traction and media coverage was fairly straightforward. News departments were segmented and organized by "beats" — issues/topics designated for consistent coverage — and reporters were assigned specific duties in an organized manner that clearly distinguished writers, editors, proofers, designers/layout professionals, reporters, producers and directors. For the most part, individuals had one dominant skill and spent their time working in that one area. Today, newsrooms are a lot different and the competition is fiercer; lead times are shorter, deadlines are more frequent, and journalists are competing not only with other publications and media outlets but also with citizen journalists equipped with smartphones and self-described influencers with an online audience.

To be successful in creating newsworthy content, it helps to think the way our colleagues in the media think and understand what is important to them and to their respective audiences. Also, remember that news is a business, and sometimes news decisions are influenced by the fact that specific types of content can often increase viewership. For example, news that is interesting or fascinating but not necessarily informative might get significant airtime anyway, simply because footage showing what happened at the city council meeting, though informative, isn't always as interesting. Even though online content is endless, there is limited time and space within news broadcasts to fit in all the stories available to share. Tough editorial decisions often result in noteworthy and newsworthy content not making the broadcast because there is not enough time to showcase all of it. The PR professional's job is to understand how a newsroom works, identify which factors influence what gets aired, and find the right individual to pitch and advocate for coverage. What follows are some approaches to content creation and media pitching that might help generate positive results.

All News Is Local News

People care about things that affect them or the people they know. When seeking to tailor pitches to journalists or media personalities, it is helpful to think in local terms — "How does this story affect or impact people within a local viewing audience?" "How does this content resonate with the people listening or watching?" — even if it is a global audience. Identify the local angle or the "at-home effect" and use that perspective to make the pitch relevant to the journalists' audiences.

Think Like a Journalist

Think like an effective, successful journalist. When pitching story ideas, be sure to ask and answer the questions a journalist is going to have. Can the information being shared be fact-checked and verified? Is there someone available for an on-the-record interview? Is there another perspective to consider that also needs to be addressed? Are there competitors, detractors or opponents to the issues or topics of note? Are the basic 5Ws (who, what, when, where, why) answered sufficiently? How does the story affect the audience? What is the impact, benefit, threat or value to the audience? Is the topic something people care about? Is there a larger trend in the news that the idea can connect with or leverage for more coverage on a larger scale? By answering these questions and doing the necessary prep work in advance, a PR professional can greatly increase the likelihood of securing the coverage they want on behalf of their client.

Understand the Media Platform

Just as important as knowing the audience is understanding the platform where information will be shared. Do visuals drive the content of the story? Do clear audio interviews and sound effects make the difference? Is the online platform limited by the number of characters that can be shared or the length of time content remains visible or accessible? Does the outlet require multimedia content with photos, videos and clickable hyperlinks? Submitting content in the correct format greatly increases the chances it will get published.

Create Shareable Content

Even traditional print publications and broadcast outlets are competing for online views, clicks and shares on their digital platforms. Pitching shareable content — meaning words and images that consumers are likely to pass along to someone else within their influencer circle — increases the chances of a story getting picked up. Beyond the main publication or broadcast, editors and producers also must consider how much traction a story can gain online, and that often results from "sticky" stories that people want to tell other people about. An oldie but goodie type of shareable content that is still popular is Top 10 lists in some iteration, with an expert explaining why the audience must do something, use something or read something. Examples include Top

10 things to tell your teen before they leave for college, Top 10 things to pack for the perfect vacation, and Top 10 places to visit before they're gone forever. These types of stories and pitches often employ scarcity (limited availability) and social validation (also known as peer pressure) to attract readers and viewers.

Align Editorial Ideas With Advertising

In theory, within the executive suites of various media outlets, advertising content and editorial content are two separate conversations, and one should not influence the other. However, in the real world, advertisers often make decisions about paying for placement based upon the type of editorial content that consistently is produced. Alternately, editorial content can be influenced by the potential to attract lucrative advertising dollars. The lesson for PR practitioners is to identify alignment between story ideas and the related advertising content to make a stronger case for why a particular article, feature or profile might be relevant to audience members.

Understand the News Cycle

Having a thorough understanding of news cycles and how news stories circulate and (often) recur will assist new PR practitioners in their daily duties of finding and pitching stories that get media coverage. As mentioned earlier in the chapter, relevance is one of the common and reliable elements of newsworthiness that can help strengthen the likelihood of piquing interest from a journalist. Relevance focuses on how closely an audience is connected to a story topic and whether the content has direct application for them. A relevant story contains something the viewers or readers know about, care about or frequently think about because it affects their daily lives.

Relevant content is often recurring content, and some news stories are reliably consistent because they happen within a predictable timeframe or on a regular schedule, such as monthly city/town council meetings, quarterly reports and annual holiday celebrations. When a PR professional identifies important cyclical recurrences in the news and effectively ties aspects of a client's priorities into the news cycle, there is an increased opportunity to successfully pitch a story and secure quality media coverage that is newsworthy, relevant and timely for the target audience.

Here are three simple ways to approach, identify and categorize story ideas using the news cycle to determine and drive content creation: 1) There is an *initial story* that introduces information to the audience for the first time. 2) There is often a *follow-up story* that serves as a reminder about the initial story and provides new information or updates to the original reporting. 3) The news cycle concludes with an *anniversary story* about the same topic, which offers a wrap-up and summary about the beginning, middle and end of the news story.

4.5 — CRAFTING STRONG MEDIA PITCHES

Using a sample pitch for a florist (Beaucoup Bouquets), here is a demonstration of how the PR agency or PR representative can use research or data to leverage the cyclical nature of news in connection with a holiday and then generate multiple opportunities for positive coverage.

Client Overview and Media Approach

Beaucoup Bouquets is a local florist that specializes in colorful blooms and floral bouquets for all occasions. The company has a quality website, robust social media presence, and strong brand identity in the community as a result of making financial donations to the school system and local charities. The owners of the florist are seeking ways to expand their customer base through a strategic, PR-based awareness campaign. One recommended tactic is conducting a national survey about the most popular types of flowers purchased for Valentine's Day and publishing the survey results along with an interactive map that shows which states or cities primarily purchase different types of flowers. Next, using the information provided, an initial media pitch can be drafted to leverage the client's activities and accomplishments to secure positive media coverage.

Initial Story Pitch for Beaucoup Bouquets

In this fictitious example, the PR professional is reaching out to a journalist named Troy, who has covered similar stories or topics in the past. The sample pitch makes mention of the reporter's history of articles and incorporates that information to develop a stronger pitch.

> Dear Troy,
>
> I enjoyed reading your story on allergen-free floral options for Valentine's Day. The article was an informative and entertaining piece on how receiving flowers on Valentine's Day for some people can be an allergy-filled nightmare. Here is another story idea that your readers will appreciate. My client Beaucoup Bouquets is a local florist that publishes an annual report about which types of flowers are most frequently purchased for Valentine's Day. The national survey is conducted online and updated each year. The results from last year are available now, and the new survey for this year is open for respondents to log their answers. Below is a link to the survey results. Also, one of the company's co-owners and floral design artists is available for an interview to provide expert advice on selecting the right blossoms for Valentine's Day. There are photos available, along with a brief video that explains the basics of floral arrangements. Valentine's Day is just two weeks away, so we can schedule an interview later this week on Thursday or Friday, at your convenience. Here is my direct contact information if you'd like me to send over additional background information for your review. I look forward to working with you.

Potential Story Lead for Beaucoup Bouquets

A local florist published a survey that can help consumers select the right flowers for Valentine's Day. Every February, Beaucoup Bouquets launches a survey to find out which types of flowers are most popular as gifts on the special day. You can visit the florist's website and click on a map of the state to see how it measures up against other parts of the country. The company owner also offered tips on how to arrange the perfect bouquet and which flowers are least likely to cause a reaction for individuals with allergies.

Follow-Up Story Pitch

In the wake of a successful story, there are still more opportunities to strengthen the relationship with the journalist as part of ongoing media relations activities. A brief follow-up note or email serves several purposes, including acknowledging that the story was viewed, thanking the journalist for their effort to produce the story, and laying the groundwork for another successful pitch by providing updates and details for a future story idea.

> Dear Troy,
>
> Great article on the Valentine's Day flower survey. This is a quick note to let you know that the survey results from this year are in and available to update your readers. In addition to the interactive map, there is a chart that shows which flowers are most popular in each region of the country — along with a one-page guide that makes recommendations for the ideal month to purchase the most popular types of flowers. I can assist in scheduling a follow-up interview with the florist's co-owner again and send over any additional information you need.

Anniversary Coverage Pitch

An anniversary follow-up reminder is also a good way to keep the positive coverage going and maintain communication with the journalist or media outlet. Similar to newsrooms, PR agencies often utilize editorial calendars to track and schedule opportunities for story ideas and/or follow up on stories that already have been produced.

> Dear Troy,
>
> It's that time of year again. A year ago, you informed your readers about the most popular Valentine's Day floral options. Once again Beaucoup Bouquets is launching its annual survey to report on which flowers get the most love across the country. Since the last article, the survey report has expanded to now include data city by city or through a local zip code search. Basically, readers can now see which floral arrangements are most popular in their neighborhood. I'm available to coordinate an interview with the co-owner of the florist and send over photos, video links and a fact sheet on Beaucoup Bouquets. I will follow up by Friday — but feel free to reach out to me sooner if you have any questions.

In this example with Beaucoup Bouquets, the newsworthy elements include relevance, impact and timeliness — based on a predictable news cycle for an annual holiday that occurs on the same date every year — making the story easy to schedule, pitch and plan for in advance.

PR PLANNING CHECKLIST FOR NEWSWORTHY MEDIA PITCHES

Here is a convenient checklist to make sure you are well equipped and have prepared the basic information a journalist needs to decide whether your pitch is worthy of consideration:

- Targeted media list with complete contact information
- A primary media pitch and timeline that aligns with the journalists and their audiences; a secondary pitch or different angle to consider in case the first one doesn't connect
- News release with quotations and/or a basic media kit (news release, fact sheet, backgrounder)
- Basic B-roll (generic video footage) that coincides with the topic and helps explain the story
- One sheet or infographic with data visualizations to explain complex information
- Industry professional or subject matter expert (SME) to serve as an additional source of information
- PR client who is an authorized spokesperson and trained to conduct media interviews and speak comfortably on the record on camera
- Captioned headshots and/or industry photos

Additional Media Pitch Strategies

Here are some additional concepts to use in shaping media pitches and identifying story ideas that get picked up by the media based on news cycle coverage. The key to success is finding an angle within the trend that connects to the client and provides newsworthy information to the public.

Trends

Hitching a local story to a regional or national trend is a surefire way to increase media pickup, because the story is already getting a lot of attention from multiple outlets. Trends also tend to have a large geographical impact, making the story relevant to more individuals. Examples of common trends include topics such as college enrollment figures, hiring practices, charitable giving during the holidays, fluctuating gas and fuel prices, and economic growth.

Designations

With just a simple online search, it will become evident that almost every day is National [Something] Day and certainly every month is National [Something] Month. These designations are often manufactured and promoted by PR professionals as part of large campaign strategies, then used to enhance interest from the media. If the PR practitioner looks carefully, there is likely a designation of some type with a relevant correlation to their clients' agendas for every day on the calendar.

Annual Events and Reminders

The previous scenario with Beaucoup Bouquets was an example of using annual events or holidays and reminders within the news cycle. Also important to remember from the example was the substantive piece of research that was pitched to the journalist — not just a promotional opportunity to feature a florist on Valentine's Day. The key to successful pitches and creating newsworthy content is making sure there is real news at the core. An easy approach to "hitching and pitching" a client to a less-than-notable holiday is to create an indirect connection to establish a correlation — meaning that when a customer thinks of *x*, they also think of *y*. For example, a retail battery store might leverage National Favorite Toy Day as a reminder to check or replace the batteries in all handheld games and toys. "As you celebrate National Favorite Toy Day and practice or play games on your favorite devices, don't forget to refresh the batteries in all your gadgets to ensure the fun continues all year long. This message is brought to you by your local Battery Store." Another example is the twice-per-year messaging about changing the batteries in smoke detectors, which often accompanies reminders about setting clocks back or forward for daylight saving time.

Subject Matter Experts

Introducing a subject matter expert from your client's team to discuss a specialized industry is an effective way to pitch an idea and gain the interest of media. Providing access to an SME utilizes novelty based on scarcity, as there are probably not a lot of experts who are knowledgeable or skilled in that particular area. Widespread issues like cybersecurity or cybercrimes, which can affect anyone and often have far-reaching effects, are popular topics that consumers often want more information about to protect themselves and their data from breaches or theft. Areas that focus on a specialized training or skill set are also popular with journalists, as audiences often cannot gain access to the individuals on their own.

Research, Major Reports and Data Dumps

The U.S. Census is completed only every 10 years, but the implications and impact of the census data are broad and vast. Census information and stories about census data often have a two-year runway, as the process involves collection of the information as well as political infighting about how the information should be collected, who should be included, and what the legislative consequences will be as a result of the new data on demographics and demographic shifts across the country. Additionally, major reports and data dumps — large amounts of statistical data that are made public or widely available — are reliable sources of inspired content as part of the news cycle.

Data Visualization

In storytelling, seeing is believing and a picture is worth a thousand words, as the sayings go. At the height of the COVID-19 pandemic in 2020, shocking statistics about the spread and toll of the virus saturated the news from morning until evening. Accompanying the headlines were endless scrolls (rolling text along the bottom of a screen) and correlating graphics that indicated "COVID-19 hot spots" on a map showing where the virus was concentrated across the country. The same concept of interactive mapping is also used to identify areas of drought, airline/airport flight cancellations, Election Day voter turnout and more.

Good Vibes and Feel-Good Stories

Predictably, every year a news agency releases information about how the proliferation of negative news stories and the volume of content on social media are overwhelming people and making them feel less optimistic about the future. In essence, people are sick and tired of too much bad news. In response, the opportunity to share positive and good news is a popular way to attract more readers and viewers. Because negative news often receives more attention, good news can stand out and gain more visibility because it is less common in news feeds and more inclined to be shared as a way to uplift others. Where there is an opportunity for the PR practitioner to offer good news and benefit their client, it's a win-win.

Community Involvement

Incorporating public participation and community involvement into the news cycle is an effective way to introduce content and story ideas, because charitable organizations and local nonprofits often have applications and deadlines that generate news value while at the same time extending opportunities for everyday people to get involved in their communities. By developing story angles and pitches that include specific ways to participate, upcoming deadlines, and clear calls to action, journalists are given relevant and timely information to consider that their audiences will likely be interested in and respond to.

Policy Changes, Rules and Regulations

Any local changes or updates to public policy fit well in the news cycle planning process, because the information is considered "need to know" for those who are affected. This type of information includes local street closures, holiday hours for government offices, sidewalk repairs for safety protocols, new hours of instruction for year-round schools, voter registration sites and hours, etc. Public information is newsworthy because it is relevant to and affects a large number of people within a common geographic area.

Holidays

Holidays celebrate and commemorate national accomplishments, religious observances, military engagements and seasonal transitions. They often produce days off from school or the office and opportunities to disconnect from business as usual and reconnect with family, friends and loved ones, giving them broad and universal appeal. Not a Thanksgiving holiday goes by without seeing stories and hearing commentary from experts at turkey-manufacturing companies and local fire stations sharing details on preparing the perfect holiday meal with turkey — and not burning down the house in the process of preparing that meal.

Evergreen Content

Evergreen content is always fresh and relevant, rarely has a time limit, and is known for its long shelf life and universal impact on society. It is easy to think of evergreen content in the news cycle as "ol' reliable" content that people always care about and want to hear more about — from exercise habits to fancy time-saving appliances and devices to weight loss programs to smartphone apps to retirement savings. The list goes on and on, but savvy PR professionals keep an updated list of go-to evergreen content ideas, which they can use to align with client messages and craft effective media pitches.

The value in understanding news cycles is knowing how and where to look for content that journalists want to report and that audiences want to learn more about and share with others. News cycles help shorten the timeline for identifying substantive, newsworthy information and pitching stories of interest by utilizing past coverage to predict the need or desire for future coverage.

CHAPTER SUMMARY

Knowing what makes content newsworthy is a valuable skill to have, because it increases the likelihood that the content created by the PR professional will attract the interest of the media and result in positive media coverage for the PR client.

It is worthwhile for PR practitioners to get familiar with the list of elements that make news worth covering and then work to incorporate at least one of those elements into the content being developed. Starting with a strong, attention-grabbing headline is important, since many people look only at headlines before deciding which stories to read or explore further. Also, having a good understanding of how newsrooms work and how news cycles evolve can help predict where there will be opportunities for media coverage.

Finally, the ability to craft and pitch a great story idea that appeals to relevant readers and viewers completes the cycle for effectively creating and delivering quality content to audiences.

KEY TERMS

celebrities	news cycle
conflict	novelty
evergreen	proximity factor
headline	relevance
human interest	timeliness
magnitude	title

DISCUSSION QUESTIONS

1. Which element of newsworthiness do you think is most important or effective in pitching story ideas to the media?

2. Why is it important to understand how print and broadcast newsrooms operate?

3. Why do some important news stories not get a lot of media coverage?

WRITING EXERCISES

1. Write a compelling six- to eight-word headline announcing a new course at your college that teaches PR students how to ethically and effectively use artificial intelligence to enhance PR writing.

5 PR DOCUMENTS CREATED FOR THE MEDIA

LEARNING OBJECTIVES

5.1   Learn basic sections and understand components of writing a news release.

5.2   Learn the purpose and process of writing a media advisory.

5.3   Organize basic sections and understand the significance of writing a fact sheet.

5.4   Understand which documents make up a comprehensive media kit.

INTRODUCTION

The documents highlighted in this chapter are the most frequently utilized PR writing communication tools because of their longevity of use in the industry and effectiveness to convey information to the media and various target audiences across different platforms.

Documents created primarily for distribution to the media are usually formatted in Associated Press (AP) style to align with long-held professional standards for uniformity, consistency and accuracy. When combined, these common documents — news releases, media advisories and fact sheets — make up the basic formation of a media kit, which is discussed in more detail in Chapter 6.

A consistent theme about documents that are formatted for and distributed to the media is the element of newsworthiness. Throughout the creative development process, keep in mind the sole purpose of creating and sending news releases and/or media kits isn't just for the sake of getting publicity by publishing content; it is providing relevant, useful, valuable and interesting information to journalists and their respective audiences while also advocating for the PR client.

There are a number of factors that contribute to the news value of a story, many of which have been explained in Chapter 4. Generally speaking, news values are "criteria that influence the selection and presentation of events as published news" ("News Values," 2024). Here is a brief overview of some of the more popular and essential components that contribute to newsworthiness. Remember, the more newsworthy elements the story has, the more likely it is to get media coverage and gain traction with target audiences.

- *Local connection or proximity*— Identifying the local angle within a story or its connection to local readers and viewers increases the chances for a story to get media coverage, because people generally care more about issues that affect them and individuals who are close to them.

- *Impact*— The number of people who will be affected by the issue being covered underscores the importance of impact. The greater the number of people affected by something, the greater the newsworthiness of the story to the media's audiences.

- *Conflict*— Conflict or tension between opposing sides is almost always newsworthy. PR professionals are responsible for presenting information honestly and fairly, even while advocating for a client on a particular side of the issue.

- *Human interest*— Human interest angles in stories allow the readers or viewers to connect with something familiar, whether on an emotional, personal or professional level.

- *Celebrity*— Because celebrities are well known and often have global brand recognition, their presence or connection to a story makes it instantly newsworthy and of greater interest to a broader audience.

- *Relevance*— The concept of relevance in storytelling means that there is a connection to the audience and the topic or issue is something they want to learn more about because of its potential effect or impact on their lives.

- *Timeliness*— News is all about "new" information and informing the public about events or areas of concern that are occurring or upcoming in the near future. The timeliness factor also presents an opportunity for journalists to provide new information to their audiences.

- *Magnitude*—Magnitude is related to the number of people affected by a situation and how serious the consequences or impact will be on them or their surroundings.

- *Novelty or uniqueness*— Novel or unique stories are focused on topics that people don't necessarily see or hear every day, so they attract more interest through general curiosity.

5.1 — NEWS RELEASES

What is a news release? Also commonly called a press release, a news release is a communication tool and common PR writing document that provides basic information about a topic, issue, announcement or event on behalf of an individual, company or organization to inform and educate the media and their respective audiences and to ultimately gain positive media coverage for the organization that distributes the release. For decades, within the PR industry, news releases have been the PR workhorse documents and done a lot of the heavy lifting related to providing research, answering questions from journalists, introducing background and context around high-profile issues, and presenting story ideas for the media to consider covering.

What Is the Purpose of a News Release?

The purpose of a news release is to present a newsworthy story idea in a generally accepted format that can be utilized by journalists to develop a complete story. In most cases, the objective for developing a news release is to inform or persuade, but in some instances it is also to respond to content or commentary circulating in the media that might impact the organization. Though news releases are primarily written and formatted for journalists, the content is written with specific publics and target audiences in mind — audiences that are reached through various media outlets and journalistic networks. Audiences are broad groups that receive similar messaging, while publics are microtargeted groups within audiences that share common interests or connections to the message or brand and for which content is specifically tailored. As an example, participants attending a conference or presentation about athletics make up a broader audience that also has smaller (and sometimes overlapping) publics that focus on specific sports and games like tennis, golf, soccer, basketball, football and baseball. For a direct messaging campaign about sports, a general message may resonate with the entire audience, but information about an upcoming golf tournament or a new line of golf clubs is relevant only to the golfing-involved public, a segment of the audience.

How Are News Releases Formatted?

News releases are written in AP style, with traditional media audiences in mind. Adaptive versions of news releases might be reformatted or shortened to accommodate online sites with content limits or social media platforms that provide a brief snippet and then link to additional information on secondary web pages. Along with the standard AP style, news release construction is based on inverted-pyramid style, which places the most important information at the beginning (or top) of the release — answering the questions who, what, when, where, why and who cares — and providing less important details about the news release subject as the document progresses.

Additionally, the news release provides the story angle, idea or pitch to journalists, which serves to pique their interest and ideally persuades and encourages them to write a full article or broadcast a complete news story for their respective audiences. It is also helpful to journalists when news releases include a quotation from a high-ranking executive or the most relevant leader within the organization. Though often written or "tweaked" by the PR practitioner, the quotation needs to reflect the intent and voice of the speaker. Quotations are useful for journalists, as they are preapproved upon publication or release to the media and help the journalist save time in completing a story; thus, the quote is readily available and may decrease the need for a follow-up interview.

Background and contextual content within a news release helps underscore the news value and explains why a journalist might want to cover the story. Though PR professionals have an obligation to work as advocates on behalf of their clients, there is also a priority to understand the needs of the journalists and their respective audiences and to present story ideas and content that is useful and relevant to them.

Most news releases conclude with a boilerplate, or a summary paragraph about the organization issuing the news release that provides basic background, history, mission and contact information to the journalists. Though boilerplates are often overlooked, they provide pertinent details that help better inform the journalist and include resources about the company or organization in case more details are needed.

Though most news releases are produced and distributed in a digital or electronic format, there occasionally is the need to print news releases in hard-copy form for inclusion in a media kit or as part of a direct-mail campaign. In terms of formatting and appearance, news releases are often typed using Times New Roman in 12-point font, unless there is a specific type/font combination that is required by the corporate branding and style guidelines. Key section markers on the release include the contact block with the PR professional's name, agency name, phone number and email address. News releases are printed on letterhead that includes the company's logo and contact information. There is a document title ("News Release") that helps to identify the document correctly as part of a larger media kit, and then the remaining content is written in Associated Press style. A release date or embargo informs journalists when the news release is approved for use and distribution; an embargo provides the information in advance but requests that it not be used immediately.

At the beginning of every news release is an AP-style-formatted dateline, which is a city or city and state (depending upon AP style) of origin for the story content. The release body is double-spaced and organized by a lead paragraph (also referred to as a lede in journalism classrooms and newsrooms) in the inverted-pyramid style format, which starts with the most important information being included first. There is also a quotation from a leader within the company or organization, background information that informs the journalists about the story opportunity, and a summary boilerplate paragraph that provides a brief overview about the company issuing the news release and its contact information.

See Figure 5.1 for a news release template.

Who Receives the News Release?

Though it seems like almost everyone is on some type of distribution list that eventually will allow them to receive a news release, the document in its original formation was designed to go to media outlets and journalists, who would then consider creating a broader piece or long-form story. However, with most organizations publishing and distributing news releases on their own websites and owned platforms, the media is now just one of several other target audiences that might be on the recipient list.

How Are News Releases Distributed?

There are dozens of ways to distribute news to journalists and target audiences; however, a handful of basic and reliable distribution processes should be familiar to all PR professionals seeking media coverage for a story. What follows is a short list of distribution tools to consider when sharing news releases.

FIGURE 5.1 ■ **News Release Template**

Name

Organization

Phone

Email

NEWS RELEASE

(document title: ex. news release, media advisory, fact sheet, etc.)

FOR IMMEDIATE RELEASE – XX/XX/20XX

CENTERED HEADLINE GOES HERE, ALL UPPER CASE, NO MORE THAN TWO LINES

(Make sure headline highlights the client, summarizes the release and uses a verb)

DATELINE (city and state in AP Style) – News releases are one effective means of reaching the media and ultimately the target audience. Each news release, like a news story written by a reporter, should focus on one key point. The lead paragraph is written in inverted pyramid style and answers the basics: who, what, when, where, why, how and who cares?

Valerie Fields, instructor for Public Relations Writing, said: "The release should be clear and concise with a strong lead and always include a quotation. News reporters and editors receive hundreds of releases daily. It is important that your release is easy to read and use."

The body of the release should begin about one-third of the way down the page so as to leave enough room for the editor to write remarks. It should be double-spaced for easy reading and editing. Remember – about three typed lines equal one column inch of typeset copy.

At the bottom of the first page, it is useful to leave at least a one-inch margin and indicate either the end of the release (### or –30- or [end]) or that more information follows by inserting (-MORE-). If more information follows, try not to break paragraphs or sentences in the middle. Never break a word and complete it on the next page.

-MORE-

(Continued)

FIGURE 5.1   ■   News Release Template *(Continued)*

RELEASE PAGE SLUG/TITLE - Page 2

Include a slug line – an abbreviated headline and page number – on subsequent pages in case they get separated.

Use correct AP style for spelling, use of titles, abbreviations and the like. Aligning the content with the media outlet's format makes each release easy for editors to use. Don't forget to check spelling, punctuation and grammar. Avoid puffery and flowery adjectives and adverbs.

Close with a summary boilerplate with contact information. This last paragraph provides one or two sentences to describe the organization submitting the release and its mission, products and services. These basic details or general facts serve as a reference point and source of information for the journalist to ensure accuracy for their story.

# # #

Email Contact Databases

Email contact databases are probably the most basic and least involved process of the news release sharing and distribution options. PR professionals who have built a contact list of journalists can simply review the list and see which relevant individuals or outlets are likely to be receptive to the story idea. Once the news release is complete, edited and proofed, and approved by the client, it can simply be embedded within an email body along with an introductory media pitch or included as an attachment and sent directly to a short list of media contacts.

Electronic Media Databases and List Builders

Electronic media databases and list builders streamline and simplify the effort to find the right media contacts for news release distribution. There are numerous free online resources that can be identified through a basic online search tool, while there also are paid database and list-building services that allow purchasers to input the filtered search criteria they need and purchase contact lists that can be used for distributing news releases via email or direct-marketing tools.

Free News Release Distribution Sites

Free news release distribution sites may not secure the same level of reach as some paid services, but they are worthy of consideration when elevating awareness and expanding audience reach are crucial objectives of the PR campaign. Basic accounts for free distribution services usually require an email address and password to access the portals. The correctly formatted news release is uploaded into the site and then posted online within the site and potentially distributed to other affiliate partner sites, which provide additional exposure for the original poster of the content.

Paid News Release Distribution Sites

Paid news release distribution sites are probably the most commonly used and effective tool to gain widespread coverage for a story, as PR writing professionals can target geographic areas or media outlets and topics, which increases the likelihood of presenting the news release to the correct individual who is likely to cover the story. Prices per news release distribution can range from several hundred dollars to several thousand dollars depending upon the length of the news release and the distribution channels selected.

Media Relations Pitches and Follow-Up

These approaches require more hands-on actions, connections and conversations by the PR practitioner. Though more time-consuming, these activities are often more productive because the root of media relations is about relationships — professional relationships built over time on trust and reliability between the PR professional and the journalist. Though a journalist may have seen the story idea go across on a particular subscription or distribution service, a follow-up phone call from a PR colleague whom they know and trust and can rely on to coordinate interviews, provide photos and background information, secure quotations, or answer questions and provide access might make all the difference between covering a story and ignoring it.

News Aggregator Sites and Apps

News aggregator sites and apps scan stories and information published online and compile them within a single source site. PR practitioners can leverage the power of owned media platforms (websites, blogs, video channels) to publish their own SEO optimized content and then rely on algorithms, keywords, trending topics and aggregators to pick up the story and amplify it across other platforms.

Online Influencers

Influencers have gained more credibility with PR practitioners for news release and media pitches as individuals' trust of traditional news sites and sources have begun to decline and people have relied more heavily upon recommendations and suggestions from individuals they trust, admire or respect. Presenting a story idea and securing mentions or endorsements from a popular influencer with a large online following can be even more effective with some audiences due to the trust factor. Though media and content regulators are more closely scrutinizing online influencers and requiring more transparency and disclosures from them about their compensation or relationship with brands, they still carry a lot of influence with audiences and can be extremely effective in increasing visibility for a story idea or PR campaign.

Owned Media Platforms

Owned media platforms are a form of controlled publications or broadcasts that the client or organization issuing the news owns and also can leverage to amplify story ideas and opportunities. Examples include websites, blogs, podcasts and webinars. Owned media represents the O in the PESO Model (Paid, Earned, Shared and Owned), a model of content curation and strategic communication that is used to gain visibility, engage with audiences, and amplify messaging. The model is widely credited to U.S. consultant and author Gini Dietrich.

RSS Feeds

RSS feeds are subscriber-based aggregators that can be organized and customized for readers to prioritize topics of interest or favorite content sites. Publishing and distributing news releases through owned media platforms as well as free and paid distribution sites increases the possibility of the content also being picked up by news aggregators and distributed through select RSS feeds.

Social Media Posts

Posts within the PESO Model are considered to be "Shared" content, as the purpose of posts is online community engagement with the expectation that information will be shared with others. Using relevant social media and social networking sites to distribute news release content is one of the most cost-effective tools available, considering the massive audiences and reach that are generated online. In addition to basic content posts and hyperlinks, many social media and social networking sites have internal search and database tools or filters that allow account holders to build custom lists or databases within the site and export them into an external spreadsheet or customer relationship management (CRM) application that can be used for direct messaging or direct marketing and outreach.

Are News Releases Still Relevant?

Even in the age of direct messaging and social media, the need for news releases remains strong for several reasons. First, news releases and the way they are written provide a comprehensive overview of information needed for basic yet effective storytelling. Next, journalists are always in search of good stories for their readers, viewers or subscribers, so they rely on news releases from PR professionals to help identify quality sources and interesting story ideas that they might not otherwise discover on their own. Last, because news releases are written in AP style, they adhere to basic journalistic standards that are easy to incorporate into the style and format that most traditional publications and media outlets can easily use, which reduces the need for heavy editing or rewriting. At their core, news releases are news stories that advocate on behalf of a client or cause — but when done correctly, they are still newsworthy and have a lot of value for the journalists who receive them.

See Figure 5.2 for a sample news release.

5.2 — MEDIA ADVISORIES

Written for and distributed solely to journalists, a media advisory — sometimes called a media alert — makes up the second component in a basic media kit. As a note, the term "media alert" is more often used for breaking news versus general announcements or upcoming events. A media advisory functions like an invitation to the media to attend and cover a specific event — usually an in-person press conference.

FIGURE 5.2 ■ Sample News Release

Vortex Inc.

Mykaela Drummond, Media Contact

Vortex Inc.

608-555-6789 mobile phone

mdrumm@vortexinc.bizz

NEWS RELEASE

FOR IMMEDIATE RELEASE – 08/13/20XX

VORTEX INC. LAUNCHES NEW FITNESS APP: VORTEX VIBES

MADISON, Wis. – Vortex Inc., a leading innovator in technology solutions, will unveil its new, groundbreaking fitness application, Vortex Vibes, on Aug. 20 during the company's annual meeting at corporate headquarters in Madison. Designed to revolutionize personal fitness tracking, Vortex Vibes empowers users to seamlessly monitor their daily fitness activities with unparalleled accuracy and ease.

With the global health and wellness industry experiencing unprecedented growth, leaders at Vortex Inc. recognized the need for a comprehensive fitness tool that integrates seamlessly into users' daily routines. The Vortex Vibes app utilizes state-of-the-art technology to track various metrics including steps taken, distance traveled, calories burned, and active minutes, providing users with invaluable insights into their fitness progress.

Avery Michaels, CEO of Vortex Inc., said: "We are thrilled to introduce Vortex Vibes to the market. Maintaining a healthy lifestyle is more important than ever in today's fast-paced world. Vortex Vibes empowers individuals to take control of their fitness journey by providing them with the tools and insights needed to achieve their goals."

Key features of the Vortex Vibes app include:

- Intuitive Interface: Vortex Vibes boasts a user-friendly interface, making it easy for users to navigate and access their fitness data at a glance.

- Comprehensive Tracking: From steps taken to calories burned, Vortex Vibes tracks a wide range of fitness metrics, allowing users to gain a holistic understanding of their activity levels.

- Personalized Insights: Vortex Vibes provides users with personalized insights and recommendations based on their unique fitness goals and activity patterns, helping them stay motivated and on track.

- Integration Compatibility: Vortex Vibes seamlessly integrates with popular fitness devices and platforms, ensuring users can easily synchronize their data across multiple devices.

Vortex Vibes is now available for download on iOS and Android devices, with a variety of subscription options to suit individual needs.

About Vortex Inc.

Founded in 2018, Vortex Inc. is a leading provider of innovative technology solutions. With a commitment to excellence and a passion for innovation, Vortex Inc. strives to empower individuals and businesses with cutting-edge tools and resources to thrive in today's digital landscape. For more information about Vortex Inc., visit http://www.vortexinc.bizz

# # #

Media advisories answer the basic questions and outline in detail the information that is relevant to working reporters, such as featured speakers, event itineraries, interview opportunities, appropriate attire, parking availability, satellite uplink details, accessibility to electrical outlets or wireless internet, and more, to facilitate comprehensive coverage for a potential story idea.

See Figure 5.3 for a media advisory template.

What Is the Purpose of a Media Advisory?

The purpose of a media advisory is to pique the interest of potential journalists by providing enough information about a potential story idea that they are inclined to inquire further or attend a press conference to get more information to write a story or produce a broadcast segment about the topic or subject featured in the media advisory. In addition to answering the basic questions and providing background information for the journalist, the media advisory also invites the journalist to an event or announcement — usually a press conference — and includes an agenda or itinerary and logistical details about the event along with a list of resources available to anyone covering the story.

How Are Media Advisories Formatted?

The straightforward and basic formatting of the media advisory makes it one of the most easily identifiable documents housed within a media kit. Since media advisories are created exclusively for the media, the content is written in AP style using 12-point Times New Roman typeface, unless the corporate branding guidelines dictate otherwise. Media advisories share the same standard headings and markers as the news release, including the contact block with name, phone number and email address for media follow-up; a document title ("Media Advisory") and release date information ("FOR IMMEDIATE RELEASE"); a dateline representing the city and, if needed, the state; and page slugs to indicate "more" text on additional pages, along with the page numbers and closing hashtags (###).

Media advisories take the inverted-pyramid style and 5Ws to a different level by literally writing out the questions and providing the answers. The document is targeted to media audiences, so it is formatted to address the specific questions working journalists likely will ask as well as provide logistical details that help reporters know who or what resources are available while covering a story and which individuals might be available for photos or interviews.

Who Receives the Media Advisory?

Unlike news releases, which are often posted on the issuing company's website or sent directly to target audiences through direct-marketing channels, media advisories are written and distributed exclusively to alert the media about an upcoming announcement or event and to invite journalists and freelancers to attend a press conference where additional information will be shared by a company representative. The distribution of the media advisory is similar to the options available for distributing news releases, and the information is shared through a combination of one-on-one, free and paid distribution services.

FIGURE 5.3 ■ **Media Advisory Template**

Name

Organization

Phone

Email

MEDIA ADVISORY (template)

Release Date Info - 00/00/00

DESCRIPTIVE, ACTIVE HEADLINE GOES HERE IN ALL CAPS

DATELINE—In some cases, an introductory paragraph describing the event or topic is appropriate – similar to the lead paragraph in the news release. A media advisory functions like an invitation to the media to attend and cover a specific event (often a press conference or major announcement). Information is organized in blocks that answer What, Who, When, Where, and Details. Use the advisory to provide all pertinent details that are relevant to working media e.g., featured speakers, event itineraries, attire, parking, satellite uplink details, access or passwords for wireless internet, etc.

WHAT: Describe in no more than two sentences <u>what</u> is to occur that calls for media attention. The WHAT is flush left; indent the information to make it easier to read. Format the document in AP style.

WHO: This can address persons of prominence who are involved in the event or program. Keep this brief also.

WHEN: The day/date and time are included here. Also include a rain date, if relevant. If there is an RSVP or registration deadline, be sure to indicate that information within the media advisory. To help the reporter/photographer/videographer know when key activities occur, it is helpful to include a schedule of what will take place.

Scheduled activities:

1:05 p.m.   Welcome by company President Jo Schmo

1:15 p.m.   Keynote address by guest speaker Kym Dough

2 p.m.   Awards presented to outstanding volunteers

WHERE: This should provide information about the location; including building, room, address, directions or any other specific details that will enable reporters and visitors to easily find the location.

DETAILS: This section provides logistical information for the reporter to use. It's also helpful to include interview and photo opportunities, or any special instructions to assist the media in effectively covering the event.

# # #

How Are Media Advisories Distributed?

Like news releases, media advisories are shared with journalists using one or more of the following options:

- Email contact databases
- Electronic media databases and list builders
- Free news release or media advisory distribution sites
- Paid news release or media advisory distribution sites
- Media relations pitches and direct phone, email or social media follow-up

Are Media Advisories Still Relevant?

Though more limited in scope in that they are distributed solely to a media audience, media advisories are useful tools to assist with pitching story ideas to media and informing journalists about pertinent details needed to adequately prepare for covering a story idea. As long as media outlets are seeking to develop and publish content every day, there will be a need for media advisories from PR representatives to help identify potential story ideas and media coverage opportunities. Media advisories will continue to be relevant as long as there is a need for news.

See Figure 5.4 for a sample media advisory.

5.3 — FACT SHEETS

Fact sheets introduce background, historical and research information about the company to help the journalist write or produce an accurate story about the organization being featured in the article. Fact sheets are often included with a news release and media advisory to constitute a basic media kit.

Typically one to two pages in length, the fact sheet is mostly free of narrative or commentary from the PR agency or the brand it represents. In theory, the fact sheet is an objective document that includes only verifiable information that helps a reporter during the research phase of story development. However, as with most information, the facts that are included may direct or redirect a potential article toward a certain direction or story angle. For example, a media kit from a community farming organization may include a fact sheet that lists the numerous health and nutritional benefits of locally grown fresh produce but omit facts about pesticides, pollution or other effects on the environment. The inclusion of certain facts or the omission of other facts can influence the outcome of a story and also tip the balance in coverage, affecting how information is presented to target audiences. Though advocacy is a tenet of PR professionalism, honesty and transparency cannot take a back seat for the sake of convenience. Truth telling in public relations work must always remain a steadfast principle and priority for practitioners.

See Figure 5.5 for a fact sheet template.

FIGURE 5.4 ■ **Sample Media Advisory**

Vortex Inc.

Mykaela Drummond, Media Contact

Vortex Inc.

608-555-6789 mobile phone

mdrumm@vortexinc.bizz

MEDIA ADVISORY

FOR IMMEDIATE RELEASE – 08/13/20XX

VORTEX INC. TO HOST EXCLUSIVE UNVEILING OF 'VORTEX VIBES' FITNESS APP

MADISON, Wis. – Vortex Inc., a leading innovator in technology solutions, invites technology media representatives to attend an unveiling event for the company's new, groundbreaking fitness application, Vortex Vibes. Designed to revolutionize personal fitness tracking, Vortex Vibes empowers users to seamlessly monitor their daily fitness activities with unparalleled accuracy and ease.

What:	Vortex Inc., a pioneer in technology solutions, will unveil its revolutionary fitness application, Vortex Vibes, during a special press event at the company's annual meeting session.
Who:	Avery Michaels, CEO of Vortex Inc., will deliver remarks highlighting the features and significance of Vortex Vibes in the health and wellness industry.
When:	Tuesday, Aug. 20, 20XX

Itinerary:

11 a.m.	Welcome and Opening Remarks – Leigh Thompson, Vortex Chair
11:15 a.m.	Vortex Vibes Product Overview – Avery Michaels, Vortex CEO
11:30 a.m.	Vortex Vibes Unveiling and Product Demonstration
Noon	Lunch
1 p.m.	Closing Remarks – Avery Michaels, Vortex CEO

Where:	Vortex Inc. Headquarters I Auditorium 4560 Vortex Ave. Madison, Wisconsin
Why:	Vortex Vibes represents a groundbreaking advancement in personal fitness tracking, leveraging cutting-edge technology to empower users to achieve their fitness goals. This exclusive press event provides an opportunity for journalists to have hands-on access and gain firsthand insights into the app's capabilities and its potential impact on the health and wellness landscape.
Details:	Media registration is required. Please RSVP via email to: mdrumm@vortexinc.bizz. Free parking for media vehicles is available in the V-North parking lot at Vortex Inc.

# # #

FIGURE 5.5 ■ Fact Sheet Template

Name

Organization

Phone

Email

FACT SHEET (template)

Release Date Info Details - 00/00/00

BRIEF HEADLINE IDENTIFIES SUBJECT OF THE FACT SHEET

What is the Fact Sheet?

At the top of the fact sheet, include a brief summary statement followed by bulleted information about the organization, product or service, and the overall PR campaign, etc. The fact sheet is a research-focused document that can include facts, statistics, and data to help the journalist accurately cover a story idea. Be sure to keep the focus on what the audiences (media, journalists, reporters, consumers, customers, etc.) want and need to know.

Fact Sheet Content and Organization

● Content included in a fact sheet should answer questions the media and public will likely have about the company.

● Bulleted information may be presented as sentence fragments, phrases, or complete sentences, but it's best to be consistent within each fact sheet.

● Information contained in a fact sheet is organized by categories using headers and sub-heads to clearly and concisely share details with the reader.

Fact Sheet Spacing

● It is acceptable to single space bulleted items and double space between bullets. Just be sure to keep the writing clear and easy to comprehend.

● Indent information within a bulleted item so the information lines up clearly.

  ○ Example 1 – include [more] if the content takes up more than one page.

  ○ Example 2 – include page slugs and page numbers such as Fact Sheet, Page 2 and ### to indicate the end of the fact sheet.

# # #

What Is the Purpose of a Fact Sheet?

The purpose of a fact sheet is to provide additional objective content to the media and assist in securing accurate media coverage about an organization, product, service, industry or corporate brand. The information contained within fact sheets is objective and verifiable data, which better informs the reader by providing unbiased information. Facts sheets usually accompany other documents like news releases and media advisories as part of a broader-reaching media kit for announcements, special events and PR campaigns. Facts sheets are normally distributed to the media, but the information contained also may be repurposed for nonmedia audiences and presented in a more visually appealing format such as an infographic, which displays and explains facts and data using graphic design elements.

How Are Fact Sheets Formatted?

Fact sheets are written using AP style and 12-point Times New Roman typeface, unless the corporate branding guidelines dictate otherwise. They also share the same standard headings and markers as the news release and media advisory, including the contact block with name, phone number and email address for media follow-up; a document title ("Fact Sheet") and release date information ("FOR IMMEDIATE RELEASE"); a dateline representing the city and, if needed, the state; and page slugs to indicate "more" text on additional pages, along with the page numbers and closing hashtags (###).

Content included in a fact sheet should answer questions the media and public will likely have about the company. Information contained in a fact sheet is organized by category, using headers and subheads to clearly and concisely share details with the reader. Factual information is listed in bullet-point form underneath each corresponding header or subhead. Bulleted information may be presented as sentence fragments, phrases or complete sentences, but it is best to be consistent within each fact sheet. It is acceptable to single-space bulleted items and double-space between bullets and sections; the idea is to make the writing clear and easy to comprehend.

How Are Fact Sheets Distributed?

Fact sheets often accompany news releases and media advisories as part of a larger media kit and are shared with journalists using one or more of the following options:

- Email contact databases
- Electronic media databases and list builders
- Free news release, media advisory and fact sheet distribution sites
- Paid news release, media advisory and fact sheet distribution sites
- Media relations pitches and direct phone, email or social media follow-up

See Figure 5.6 for a sample fact sheet.

5.4 — MEDIA KITS

Though all media kits are not the same — depending upon the purpose, client, product or service being represented — they all serve the basic purpose of providing information to the media with the intent to gain positive media coverage and elevate awareness about a specific issue or topic.

FIGURE 5.6   ■   Sample Fact Sheet

Vortex Inc.

Mykaela Drummond, Media Contact

Vortex Inc.

608-555-6789 mobile phone

mdrumm@vortexinc.bizz

FACT SHEET

FOR IMMEDIATE RELEASE – 08/13/20XX

VORTEX INC. LAUNCHES NEW FITNESS APP: VORTEX VIBES

Vortex Inc., a leading innovator in technology solutions, unveiled its new, groundbreaking fitness application, Vortex Vibes, on Aug. 20. The Vortex Vibes app empowers users to seamlessly monitor their daily fitness activities with unparalleled accuracy and ease.

Key Features of Vortex Vibes:

- Comprehensive Tracking: Vortex Vibes tracks various metrics including steps taken, distance traveled, calories burned, and active minutes, providing users with valuable insights into their fitness progress.

- Personalized Insights: Vortex Vibes provides users with personalized recommendations and insights based on their unique fitness goals and activity patterns, helping them stay motivated and on track.

- Integration Compatibility: Vortex Vibes seamlessly integrates with popular fitness devices and platforms, ensuring users can easily synchronize their data across multiple devices.

- Vortex Vibes is available for download on iOS and Android devices, with a variety of subscription options to suit individual needs.

Benefits of Fitness Apps:

- Fitness apps offer a wide range of features, including activity tracking, workout planning, nutrition tracking, social sharing, and personalized coaching.

- Many apps leverage technology such as GPS, accelerometers, and heart rate monitors to provide accurate data and insights to users.

- Accessibility: Users can access fitness apps anytime, anywhere, making it convenient to track their progress and stay motivated.

- Personalization: Fitness apps offer personalized recommendations and insights based on individual goals, preferences, and performance.

Future Trends in Fitness Technology:

- AI and Machine Learning: AI-powered algorithms analyze vast amounts of data to deliver personalized recommendations, optimize workouts, and predict future trends in health and fitness.

- Virtual Reality (VR) and Augmented Reality (AR): VR and AR technologies create immersive fitness experiences, allowing users to participate in virtual workouts, explore new environments, and interact with virtual coaches and peers.

# # #

Media kit documents also may include a news release, a media advisory, a fact sheet, biographies, executive speeches, a quotation sheet, a backgrounder, an infographic, headshots, marketing collateral materials, an organizational chart, product samples, etc.

Digital media kits include an electronic version of the same documents found in a traditional media kit along with additional digital assets such as a logo file, B-roll, marketing collateral, and hyperlinks to other owned media content (e.g., blogs, websites, social media commentary, video channels).

The basic components of a media kit, which are the news release, media advisory and fact sheet, have been introduced and explained earlier in the chapter. Next is a list — along with brief explanations — of additional documents that are oftentimes included in media kits to assist journalists in writing or producing complete and accurate stories.

Backgrounders

A backgrounder is an informational document that offers some historical context about a company and provides more detailed information about its founding, leaders, history, mission, vision and goals. The organization of a backgrounder is often chronological, guiding the reader through the founding of the organization to its present-day activities. Backgrounders also may include historic photos and images that help narrate the company's story. Backgrounders are double-spaced, and document lengths can range from one to five pages, depending on how long the organization has been operating.

Biographies

A biography (bio) is a detailed description of an individual's life and includes the person's name, title and organization along with an overview of their current role and responsibilities. It may also highlight the person's career history, professional associations or affiliations, awards, honors, industry recognitions, and personal information such as family and hobbies.

Headshots

A headshot is a professional photograph of the subject that pictures them close up and shows their face and a little of the background or scenery. Headshots are accompanied by a brief photo caption that identifies the individual shown in the photo.

Infographics or One Sheets

An infographic is usually a one-page document with strong graphic design elements that presents data, statistics or complex information with visual representation to make the information easier to understand. One-sheets are usually one-page documents that feature a product or service overview and are used as part of a larger promotional campaign to educate and inform readers.

Marketing Collateral or Marketing Communications (MarCom) Materials

Often referred to as collateral materials or MarCom, these controlled publication documents tend to be more promotional in nature, with creative designs and layouts. Examples include brochures, flyers, posters, direct-mail postcards and newsletters, which offer more insight into a company and share more of the brand's voice and persona.

Organizational Chart (Org Chart)

Organizational charts visually represent the hierarchal structure within a company, organization or institution and explain the internal structure of various roles and responsibilities within it. Including an organizational chart as part of the collateral materials can assist the media in understanding the company's overall operations and identifying the appropriate contact to profile or interview for a story.

Product Samples

For companies launching or introducing new products into the marketplace, including free product samples (within a media kit) for journalists to test or review and write about is a good way to ensure the story is an accurate reflection of the actual item(s). Providing product samples can be an efficient and often lower-cost option, because samples are readily available as existing inventory. Also, interacting with tangible items is more productive than relying solely on a written description.

Quotations

Quotations (or quotes) are the exact words spoken by an individual about a particular subject or in response to an interview question. They are used to provide context, give a voice to the story, and also present a verbatim perspective from a company representative. Though PR practitioners are often called upon to edit, proof or "tweak" quotations by company executives, the words should genuinely reflect the individuals' sentiments and be approved by them in advance.

Speeches

Executive or political speeches, which are prepared statements developed to deliver to an audience, are often included in media kits to make sure journalists accurately quote the speaker and to confirm that the media has the necessary access to detailed information and/or transcripts of their comments for inclusion in a feature story or profile article.

PR TOOLKIT: COMMON PR DOCUMENT REMINDERS

The following information serves as a quick checklist of key information that should be included in each common PR document.

Press Release

- Name, client/PR agency contact name, phone, email
- Release date and release status (e.g., "FOR IMMEDIATE RELEASE," "EMBARGO UNTIL XX/XX/XXXX")

- Document title ("News Release")
- Headline
- Dateline (ALL-CAPS CITY, AP style state name)
- Lead paragraph (inverted-pyramid style; answer who, what, when, where, why, details)
- Quotation (key organizational leader or high-ranking executive)
- Boilerplate summary paragraph
- Page slugs (abbreviated headline and page number, "more," "[end]" or "###," etc.)

Media Advisory

- Name, client/PR agency contact name, phone, email
- Release date and release status
- Document title ("Media Advisory")
- Headline
- Dateline
- Summary lead paragraph
- Information blocks (what, when, where, details, e.g., media interviews, photo opportunities, cost for admittance, attire)
- Page slugs

Fact Sheet

- Name, client/PR agency contact name, phone, email
- Release date and release status
- Document title ("Fact Sheet")
- Bulleted list of accurate, relevant, factual information
- Page slugs

Photo Captions

- Name, client/PR agency contact name, phone, email
- Release date and release status
- Document title ("Photo Caption")
- Headline
- Dateline
- Photo caption (includes names and identifying information for people in the photo [left to right] and a general summary of the visual image that emphasizes the significance of the photo)
- Photo credit (e.g., "Photography by Fotos4U©")
- Page slugs

Public Service Announcement

- Name, client/PR agency contact name, phone, email
- Release date and release status (e.g., "FOR IMMEDIATE RELEASE," "EMBARGO UNTIL XX/XX/XXXX")
- Document title ("PSA")
- Headline
- Dateline (ALL-CAPS CITY, AP style state name)
- Run time ("00:15" or "00:30" or "00:60") — broadcast only

- Lead paragraph (inverted-pyramid style; answer who, what, when, where, why, details)
- Content represents a nonprofit organization or public interest story only
- Boilerplate summary paragraph
- Page slugs

Broadcast News Release (VNR/ANR)

- Format is similar to that of a public service announcement but can also represent a for-profit interest or organization
- Name, client/PR agency contact name, phone, email
- Release date and release status
- Document title
- Headline
- Dateline
- Run time ("00:30" or "00:60")
- Audio or video cues (announcer, voice-over, close-up, medium shot, fade to black, etc.)
- Typeface and spacing (Courier 14 point, double-spaced; single copy block for ANR audio only; two-column copy block for VNR video cues and video copy/script)
- Tag line and disclaimers
- Page slugs

Speech

- Name, client/PR agency contact name, phone, email
- Document title ("Speech")
- Speech length (run time, e.g., "5 minutes")
- Speech heading and speech delivery details (e.g., "Campaign Speech for Company President — PRSSA Annual Conference on [time and date] at [location] for [purpose]")
- Headline
- Speech copy (double-spaced; write for the ear)
- Page slugs (abbreviated speech headline, page numbers)

Letter to the Editor

- Block letter style (date, even left margin, address block, salutation to editor, double spacing between paragraphs)
- First-person narrative; letter represents an individual
- 200-250 words, based on publication guidelines
- Include name, address, phone number and signature of individual writing the letter

Op-Ed Piece

- Addressed to the editor of a specific publication (most recipients want exclusivity)
- Focus on a specific, timely, relevant topic that has been a focus in the publication's recent coverage
- Op-ed author should present a level of expertise or direct influence on the topic being addressed
- 750-850 words, based on publication guidelines
- Include name, address, phone number and signature of individual writing the op-ed

Direct-Mail Letter

- Block letter style (date, even left margin, address block, salutation, single-spaced copy and double spacing between paragraphs)
- Introductory paragraph
- Call to action; incentive to persuade purchase, action, decision, etc.
- Company background/overview statement
- Follow-up call to action ("Call today," "Log on today," "Return this coupon," etc.)
- Contact information (toll-free number, website, return correspondence, etc.)
- Postscript ("P.S.") message (reiterate incentive; most-read section of direct-mail letters)

Brochure

- Logo
- Layout (standard two-fold is 8½" × 11" portrait orientation with three panels on each side — often mislabeled as a "trifold"; consider blank panel for self-mailer brochures)
- Organizational contact information
- Mission or vision statement
- No time-sensitive information in copy
- Good use of white space for easy reading
- Photos with captions and details relevant to brochure content
- Consistent color scheme, typefaces, fonts and text sizes

Newsletter

- Logo
- Publication title
- Issue/edition info (e.g., "Volume I, Issue 2")
- Publication date (e.g., "Spring 2025" or "April 14, 2025")
- Slogan or tag line
- Table of contents
- Calendar of events
- Layout generally consists of two or three columns
- Oversized pull quotes and graphics can enhance layout
- Main article with jump line(s)
- Photos with captions
- Page numbers

Public Relations Plan

- Name, client/PR agency contact name, phone, email
- Date
- Document title ("Public Relations Plan")
- PR plan outline
  - Overall objective
  - Goals
  - Strategies
  - Tactics

- ○ Plan of action/timeline/task list
- ○ Measurement tools
- ○ Estimated budget
- ○ Contact information

AP Style Reminders

- Spelling: Word-processing spell-checker does NOT catch errors in ALL CAPS
- Proper noun spelling errors
- Datelines: City in ALL CAPS and state in Uppercase-lowercase AP style
- State abbreviations (U.S. Postal Service and AP style often differ)
- Month abbreviations
- Address abbreviations ("1234 Main St." vs. "1234 Main Street")
- "That" versus "which" usage
- Titles capitalized prior to names, lowercase following names
- "Its"/"it's"; "their"/"there"/"they're"; "your"/"you're"
- No comma needed before "and" in a series (also referred to as an Oxford comma)
- Comma needed after year when used with specific date (e.g., "Jan. 1, 2026, is a holiday")
- No "00" needed for top-of-the-hour times (e.g., "4 p.m.," not "4:00 p.m.")
- "Noon" or "midnight," not "12:00 a.m." or "12:00 p.m."
- Double-check use of words for numbers one through nine, numbers for 10 and above; always use numerals for ages
- Read copy aloud and/or backward to catch common errors
- Double-check facts and spelling, then check again!

SUMMARY

News releases, media advisories and fact sheets are the core documents that constitute a basic media kit. News releases provide broader, general information for pitching potential story ideas to journalists; media advisories invite working journalists to attend and cover announcements or special events; and fact sheets offer journalists and readers relevant objective background information on a particular subject. Supplementary documents often found in complete media kits include backgrounders, biographies, headshots, infographics, marketing collateral materials, organizational charts, product samples, quotation sheets and speeches.

All of the documents profiled in this chapter are created for the media and used individually or collectively as part of a media relations effort to share information, secure media coverage and communicate key messages about a product, service, cause, brand or PR campaign to target audiences.

KEY TERMS

aggregator sites

backgrounder

biography

boilerplate

collateral materials

fact sheet

headshot
influencers
infographic
MarCom
media advisory
news release
news values

one-sheets
organizational charts
PESO Model
product samples
quotations
RSS feeds
speeches

DISCUSSION QUESTIONS

1. Why are news releases still so popular with PR professionals and journalists?

2. What is the purpose of a media advisory, and what information does it contain?

3. Which documents could be included in a media kit to launch a new mobile app?

WRITING EXERCISES

1. Write an AP style lead paragraph using inverted-pyramid style that announces an upcoming event on campus.

6 PROACTIVELY PITCHING AND ATTRACTING MEDIA COVERAGE

LEARNING OBJECTIVES

6.1 Define media relations.

6.2 Formulate a plan to pitch story ideas to the media and gain coverage.

6.3 Recognize the key components of building a quality media list or media database.

6.4 Identify how to prepare for and plan to host a press conference.

6.5 Learn how to write and assemble a basic media kit.

6.6 Understand how crisis communication and feature articles can be used for media relations.

6.7 Determine how feature articles can be leveraged to gain more coverage in media relations.

INTRODUCTION

The efforts related to suggesting story ideas to the media and working to attract media coverage fall under the PR industry sector of media relations. This chapter focuses on learning which tools are needed to support media relations activities and to assist journalists in writing accurate stories based on the information provided by the PR professional. Building media databases, hosting press conferences, using basic PR documents to create media kits, and leveraging crisis situations as opportunities to enhance media relations are helpful skills for PR practitioners to have in their professional toolkit.

As discussed in previous chapters, creating newsworthy content that gets coverage is only the beginning of the process. Once quality content is drafted, approved and ready for distribution, there are a number of tools, tactics and timelines to implement to make sure the right information gets to the right individuals at the right time.

This chapter will provide an overview and examples of how to prepare to share news or pitch story ideas to journalists, and how to plan events that attract and gain media coverage.

6.1 — MEDIA RELATIONS

The media relations aspect of public relations work is often stated as a scope of work within a PR campaign, but it is frequently misunderstood in terms of what it entails and how to do it well. In many cases, soft skills and intangible interpersonal skills constitute the work of media relations, with the objective of building quality and mutually beneficial professional relationships with journalists. The idea behind media relations is to establish reliable connections with working media professionals to periodically pitch ideas and secure positive exposure on behalf of a client or cause. The PR professional's role in the media relations process is to create access and to become a reliable source for credible content that has value to journalists and their respective audiences.

Media relations is not an exact science — mainly because it requires so many immeasurable and irreplicable components, making it generally not scientific at all. Without question, there are surveys and reports that detail the best times and methods to contact journalists, offering some reliable methodologies. However, networking, friendships and established relationships — coupled with the occasional cold calls — can go a long way in the process as well. The fact that media relations work relies heavily on personalities and persuasion also makes it an artistic endeavor, one that is well suited for outgoing professionals who understand the importance of consistently providing quality service and committing to the long-term process of building professional relationships.

News is a business, and PR professionals are suppliers of information for that well-established business model. Individuals who understand the news business, the news cycle and the value of newsworthy content are those with a higher likelihood of being successful in their work. It is also important to factor in the significance of professionalism and proficiency to build credibility with journalists — meaning practitioners in the PR industry should avoid pitching empty ideas and nonsubstantive content for the sole purpose of seeking advertising or self-serving, free promotional coverage for clients. Suffice it to say, simply representing great clients for good causes is insufficient. And just being a nice person is not enough. Indeed, content is king and quality counts.

Looking back, media relations has adapted and changed a lot over the past few years. Notably, the shelter-in-place restrictions brought on by the start of the pandemic in 2020 vastly changed how corporations and organizations conducted business, and they also significantly changed how news was covered due to the extended period of time that businesses were closed, employees worked remotely from home, and media interviews were done via video conferencing instead of live, on the scene, or in person.

In response to these ubiquitous shifts in business operations and daily activities, PR professionals also changed their process of disseminating information to the media, choosing instead to use digital platforms and online gatherings in place of in-person media events, such as press conferences. Though there were countless disruptions to "business as usual" and a major shift in daily operations, the benefits of hosting virtual events quickly became evident, as PR professionals were able to extend the geographic reach of invitations to journalists for relevant news and simultaneously decrease the costs and resources needed for event planning and reserving facilities to host events. The ability to livestream on social media or set up a video conference link and simply send out invitations for guests to log on from anywhere in the world made gatherings much more cost-effective and efficient in terms of planning, travel and logistics.

6.2 — PITCHING THE MEDIA

A media pitch (letter or email) is a written message created for an individual journalist, reporter or media representative that is designed to pique their interest in covering a client, topic or story idea. Pitching story ideas to journalists is a key aspect of media relations work and generating coverage for clients.

Content in effective pitch documents should clearly explain what the story idea is, how and why it is relevant to the reporter's audience, and what resources you can make available as the PR contact in helping to coordinate coverage of the story.

It is also helpful to have background materials available to share with the journalist to help them accurately and effectively cover the story. These materials may include a basic media kit (news release, media advisory, fact sheet, executive biographies and organizational backgrounder) along with high-resolution photos and the company logo (if requested).

Research is the first step in effective media pitching; identifying the correct media outlet and journalist for the story — based on their area of focus — and then following up with tailored content in a way that aligns with their platform. That means being prepared to provide photos and to coordinate an in-person or telephone interviews for print publications or providing B-roll (general video footage related to the topic) and suggesting a location with relevant background visuals for television interviews. Finding the right person for a media pitch begins with building a quality media list or media database to enhance media relations activities. Chapter 18 also includes a list of tips for sending quality media pitches to journalists.

Sample Media Pitches

Two sample media pitches are provided here. Be sure to pay attention to the differences between the two sample pitches, noting what makes each effective or ineffective. An ineffective email pitch might look like:

> To Whom It May Concern:
>
> My name is Hannah Williamson, and I work as the PR coordinator for Raindrop Bottled Water. The client is pledging to give away a million bottles of water to communities hit by disaster. They plan to make their first donation this month to the local nonprofit ShareCare that is sending volunteers to several locations around the world. Let me know if you'd be interested in covering this event or if you have any questions. Thanks!
>
> Alternatively, an effective email pitch might look like:
>
> Dear Roger Covington,
>
> Based on your longtime coverage of local nonprofits and their disaster relief efforts, I'm certain you know how important clean drinking water is to communities in need. After a natural disaster, one of the most requested items for residents is access to safe, clean water. Our client ShareCare is pledging to give away 1 million bottles of water to communities

devastated by recent flooding. The first phase of their donation will be commemorated at a charitable event on Friday, March 4, at 2 p.m. at their main office located at 212 Pineview Lane.

I'd like to invite you to attend this event and share information about the ShareCare pledge and how your readers can contribute to saving lives. I read your recent report on how this area leads the region in charitable giving, and this is another opportunity for residents to positively impact the lives of others.

For your convenience, a media kit is available, along with photos and brief video footage of some Raindrop Bottled Water and ShareCare volunteers at a local relief event. I will follow up with you via email on Tuesday afternoon to answer any additional questions or to assist in scheduling interviews with the Raindrop Bottled Water community relations director, Torry Nielson. Thank you in advance for your consideration. I look forward to meeting you!

Hannah Williamson, PR Coordinator

(555) 583-0428 mobile

HWilliamson@prcompanysite.com

Note how the first pitch is a bit generic and lacks important information. Also, the first pitch shifts responsibility for advancing the conversation onto the journalist — increasing the likelihood that the story doesn't receive coverage. The second pitch provides background, context, specifics, relevance, resources and details for following up.

TIPS FOR BEGINNERS: THE SECRETS TO BEING A PR PRO

Public relations professionals don't necessarily tell people what to think — they tell them what to think about. When you watch the news or peruse the daily headlines, you're taking in information that has already been determined by someone else to be worthy of your time and attention. Behind the scenes, a skillful PR pro crafted a message and pitched an idea to the media to bring to your attention. If you've ever watched a program and wondered, "How did that person or business end up being featured?" then you've seen the results of a PR pro at work.

For the record, here's what public relations is: the art and science of communicating a specific message to a target audience (or audiences) to achieve a desired result with measurable outcomes utilizing various multimedia vehicles and outlets. And here's what PR is not: lying, spinning the facts or hiding the truth to protect clients from bad publicity. As in any industry, there are "good guys" and "bad guys," but the key to being a real PR pro is understanding that accurate, honest, timely communication is the secret to success.

Let's do a quick review on the evolution of PR: Traditional PR makes use of news releases, press conferences, wire services, media kits, interviews and special events to accomplish various communications objectives. Now we have the world of digital and social media, which extends that reach into websites, interactive blogs, microblogging, social networking platforms, webinars, podcasts, webisodes, video streaming and mobile marketing apps.

Finally, there is personal PR, which exceeds the reach and role of digital, social and traditional PR tools and integrates the person with the brand. Personal PR communicates who you are as an individual in addition to how you function within an organization. It speaks as much to what you do as it does to how you do it — what you care about and how and where you spend your time, money, resources and energy. The convergence of old and new public relations tools has resulted in a robust industry that allows novices or professionals to take control of the communication flow and become expert multimedia storytellers across town or around the world.

Virtual Footprints

First, the good news: Technology and digital media have made communicating instantly and frequently available to anyone with access to the internet. Now, the bad news: Technology and digital media have made communicating instantly and frequently available to anyone with access to the internet. The virtual footprints you leave behind show the online community who you are, where you've been and what you care about. When you establish a presence online, it's nearly impossible to erase those footprints — especially those that might be damaging or detrimental. Remember that potential customers or clients will not make a distinction between the "public" you and the "private" you. So, if your online image contradicts or conflicts with the business and professional image you want to project, the solution is simple: Delete it and don't repeat it.

Tell Your Own Story

PR pros must have the ability to recognize trends, anticipate reactions and reasonably predict outcomes based on past occurrences. Effective PR pros help themselves or their clients reinvent and reinforce their relevance in the marketplace so as to reach new audiences and increase inherent value to existing ones. The secret to being a PR pro is to be first at telling your own story. Sometimes this means tooting your own horn, and sometimes it means beating the competition to the punch. Half the battle of successful public relations — just like in business — is getting there first.

6.3 — BUILDING A MEDIA LIST OR MEDIA DATABASE

The need to develop quality media lists is always a priority in the PR industry, and any opportunity to acquire accurate and frequently updated lists should be considered. There are countless businesses that provide media database search and development tools as products available for purchase to help PR professionals locate the correct contacts in media relations work. The options available to build quality media lists range from manually searching news sites and entering data into a spreadsheet, to renting or leasing access from list developers, to subscribing to media database and media monitoring services that range in price from hundreds of dollars per month to tens of thousands of dollars per year, depending upon the number of users and quantity of services purchased.

A media list or media database is a document containing relevant media contacts and their contact information for the purpose of distributing updates and pitching story ideas to gain media coverage (see Figure 6.1). It is quite common and expected to have numerous lists — organized by topic, PR client needs, media types or geographic location. Though media database services provide much more than basic contact information (including details such as social media preferences, influencer rankings and media biases), a basic media list includes the necessary information to provide information to a journalist and then be able to follow up with them using the details included in the database. The most important factor for media lists is keeping them up to date, regularly confirming that the lists contain the correct names, phone numbers, email addresses, locations, and coverage topics or beats. Fortunately, most media database subscriber services provide automatic updates to media contacts as part of the licensed agreement.

Professional social networking sites such as LinkedIn can serve as a valuable tool for developing media contacts and building original media databases, which can then be used for targeted contacts and pitches to journalists. Using the search tool and filters, professionals can narrow down and identify potential contacts by geography, interests and roles/titles. This greatly decreases the timeline for identifying the right contacts at specific media outlets and publications.

One of the most common complaints journalists have about working with PR professionals is receiving pitches that are unrelated to their beats or specialized areas of coverage. Sending email blasts or posting generic messages to journalists that are not relevant to their work usually backfires by eroding the PR practitioner's credibility and deteriorating the relationship between the two professionals. It is worth the time and effort to target messages and to tailor content for specific journalists or media personalities to ensure the information they receive has value to them and their readers, listeners or viewers.

6.4 — PRESS CONFERENCES AS A MEDIA RELATIONS TOOL

When there is a major news announcement from a company or organization, a proven tool in media relations is the traditional press conference, a media-focused event that invites journalists to attend and learn more information from the entity hosting the press conference. The purpose of the press conference is to distribute additional information to journalists about the announcement and to provide answers to reporters' questions in a Q&A format. Traditionally, press conferences are in-person events, with a designated spokesperson at the podium to

FIGURE 6.1   ■   Sample Media List/Media Database

Miami Media List

Outlet	Name	Role	Email	City	LinkedIn	Phone	Notes	Conversation Starter
Bloomberg Markets	Michael Smith	Reporter / Senior Writer	<hidden>@bloomberg.net	Miami	https://www.linke din.com/in/micha	<hidden>		
Glamour Latinoamerica	Marck Gutt	Travel Writer	<hidden>@hotmail.com	Miami	http://mx.linkedin. com/pub/marck-g	<hidden>		
MotorSport.com	Joe Jennings	Contributing Writer	<hidden>@motorsportnetwo rk.com	Miami		<hidden>		
The Miami Herald	Theo Karantsalis	Contributing Writer	<hidden>@springyleaks.com	Miami	http://www.linkedi n.com/in/karants	<hidden>		
Newser	Luke Roney	Staff Writer	<hidden>@newser.com	Miami	http://www.linkedi n.com/pub/luke-r	<hidden>		
Glamour Latinoamerica	Valeria Pérez Fraga	Editorial Director	<hidden>@condenast.com.m x	Miami	https://mx.linkedi n.com/in/valeria-p	<hidden>		
Family Magazine	Janet Jupiter	Publisher	<hidden>@bellsouth.net	Miami	https://www.linke din.com/in/janet-j	<hidden>		
USA Today	Alan Gomez	National Correspondant & Reporter	<hidden>@usatoday.com	Miami	https://www.linke din.com/in/alan-g omez-21b1299	<hidden>		

moderate questions and responses. As an alternative, it is also possible to invite journalists to attend a virtual press conference, where they can join a video conference session via hyperlink and submit questions via text or voice.

Press conferences are planned and coordinated to make announcements and share information with journalists. However, having a full room can go a long way in building confidence and boosting morale among company team members who are a part of the effort. In addition to journalists, other individuals who may be selected to attend a press conference include company executives, local elected officials, community partners and relevant stakeholder group members who have a vested interest in the news being shared. Although those individuals are not there to ask questions, they can be a source of moral support and help present a strong, united front on behalf of the organization. See Figure 6.2 for a press conference checklist.

FIGURE 6.2 ■ **Press Conference Checklist**

Press Conference Checklist
By Jake R Brady
Customize, print, share & use this list at: checklist.com/press-conference-checklist

- ☐ Preliminary Actions
  - ☐ Determine location, time and date.
  - ☐ Notify media of conference's location and time.
  - ☐ Have room/area confirmed.
  - ☐ Have speakers identified and confirmed.
  - ☐ Produce media kit/other documents required.
  - ☐ Anticipate and arrange for necessary site security.
  - ☐ Arrange for video and/or audio taping.
  - ☐ Check availability of parking.
  - ☐ Make follow up calls to media.
  - ☐ Arrange reception area/sign-in for media.
  - ☐ Brief your staff on the subject, spokesperson, and schedule.
- ☐ Statements and News Releases
  - ☐ Obtain written statements for your spokesperson.
  - ☐ Make copies of news releases for media.
  - ☐ Develop anticipated questions and answers for the spokesperson.
  - ☐ Ensure that all credit union material is approved for release.
  - ☐ Assemble press kits and background information.
- ☐ Conducting the Conference
  - ☐ Prepare media kits for handout.
  - ☐ Assign staff to direct media to the briefing room.
  - ☐ Log the names of media representatives who attend.
  - ☐ Start video and audio recorders.
  - ☐ Open the conference.
  - ☐ Monitor the questions and answers closely.
  - ☐ Prepare conference notes.
- ☐ Event Follow-Up
  - ☐ Wrap-up release distributed.
  - ☐ Send thank you e-mail to VIPs.
  - ☐ Send pictures of the conference to local newspapers.
  - ☐ Monitor the media for event coverage.

If hosting a press conference is not the right solution, there are other ways that PR professionals can get the word out to their audiences:

- Business wire or newswire distribution services

- Direct email pitches to journalists

- Company website articles and blog pots

- Company social media sites (photos, videos and posts)

- Company webcasts, live streams or podcasts

These external distribution channels, internal sites and "owned" content platforms can effectively supplement external media coverage — and in some cases replace the need for a press conference. There are some questions PR professionals should ask before scheduling a press conference:

- Is this news important, relevant and impactful enough that journalists will leave their offices to attend the press conference?

- Is there a credible, trained representative who can serve as the spokesperson for the organization and effectively respond to questions from reporters?

- Are there additional representatives or subject matter experts available to attend who can assist in answering specific questions, if needed?

- Is there enough time to professionally prepare, plan and schedule a press conference so that the news is shared and published in a timely manner?

- Does the organization have access to a location that will accommodate the journalists, communications professionals, organizational leaders and related stakeholders?

When Should a PR Professional Plan a Press Conference?

A press conference may be appropriate in the following situations:

- When there is a major news announcement that affects a large number of people, creates a significant economic impact on the community, or includes a major celebrity or public figure who is of interest to the public.

- When there is more information to share than is feasible for a news release or media pitch email sent to journalists.

- When the news announcement creates more questions than answers and journalists will likely follow up with requests for more information.

- When conducting individual interviews is not practical and it becomes more efficient to address several reporters at one time.

- When misstatements about the organization hosting the press conference have been made in the media and there is a need to correct the record.

- When there is an emergency or crisis situation that requires a lot of information to get out quickly and to reach as many people as possible.

- When the organization needs to make a public statement or clarify its position about a related topic or trending news story that affects the public.

What Preparation Is Needed for a Press Conference?

The prep work leading up to the press conference is just as important as the conference itself. Part of the advanced planning includes defining key messages that need to be shared and also training the authorized spokespeople to effectively deliver those messages. That preparation may include developing internal media prep Q&A documents along with fine-tuning messaging strategies and key talking points, which are rehearsed in advance with the communications team during mock interviews and media training sessions. Once the messages have been defined, it is time to focus on logistics.

Where Should a Press Conference Take Place?

If there is a conference room or auditorium large enough to accommodate the group, press conferences are often held onsite at the company or organization's headquarters. However, if that is not an option, reserving a hotel ballroom or conference meeting space is a good alternative. The space should be reserved with needs of the media in mind, meaning there should be quality audio (microphone and speakers) in a larger room, space reserved for television cameras, good lighting, a podium or lectern that has room for microphones to record the individual speaking, accessible electrical outlets, and a branded backdrop and/or staging area for still photography or one-on-one television interviews. Be sure to confirm there is adequate parking for news vans and satellite trucks, if needed. After the location is confirmed, it will be necessary to select the date and time — being mindful to avoid any major conflicts with previously scheduled events that might also attract media coverage and take away attendance from the press conference.

When Should a Press Conference Take Place?

Many press conferences occur on Tuesday, Wednesday or Thursday — primarily to avoid Monday morning overloads and Friday "working for the weekend" disinterest. Keep in mind that when the news is important enough, professional journalists will show up to do their jobs. Selection of the date and time for the press conference also has a lot to do with the timing of local newscasts and publication deadlines for daily and weekly print media outlets. Many press conferences are held in the morning to give broadcast teams time to get out of production meetings and print journalists time to write their articles and file them for publication by their midafternoon deadlines.

Once the location, date and time are confirmed, that information — along with an agenda or media advisory — can be shared with invited journalists and other stakeholders to provide logistical details and a list of speakers who are available for photos and/or interviews. Notifications can be sent by direct email, social media posts, media wire distributions, word-of-mouth conversations or mailed invitations if there are items to be shipped in advance.

6.5 — WRITING AND ASSEMBLING MEDIA KITS

Another important factor to consider in planning a press conference is what types of materials will be needed to distribute to attendees. Packets containing media kits, product samples or other promotional content require a longer lead time for printing and production. If there are no items that need to be handed out in person, developing an electronic press kit (EPK) or digital media kit that is available via email, link or website download is an easy and cost-effective option to get pertinent information to the journalists in advance.

Finally, once the press conference logistics have been confirmed and guests have been invited, it is good practice to make follow-up phone calls or send emails to journalists one to two days in advance to confirm their attendance and to inquire about any additional information needed to assist them with covering the story.

Here is a short checklist of written materials or documents that PR professionals are responsible for creating in preparation for hosting a press conference. The news release, media advisory and fact sheet are shared in advance as part of the media kit. The additional materials help clarify or support the story angle and help prepare the client and spokespeople to deliver accurate and quality remarks at the press conference — and in the follow-up period after the press conference concludes.

- News release

- Media advisory

- Fact sheet

- Email pitches

- Media prep Q&A document

- Copy and content for promotional materials (flyers, brochures, infographics, etc.)

- Messaging strategy and talking points for speakers

- Introductory and closing remarks for company officials

- Follow-up thank-you letters, notes or emails to journalists and stakeholder attendees

PR TOOLKIT: FUTURE TRENDS IN MEDIA RELATIONS

In 1980 the CNN network launched and introduced news in homes around the clock. From that day until this day, the demand has only grown. To meet that demand, PR pros will likely embrace new technologies and platforms such as artificial intelligence to support content development, audience engagement and media monitoring activities. Professionals in the

PR industry will continue to accelerate content creation models and meet the increased demand for 24/7 visual content.

Emerging technologies will be explored to push the envelope for clients — to position pioneers on the edge of innovation and to increase clients' return on investment. Innovations like virtual reality training and simulations for crisis communicators will increase; meta-verse product placement will add to the integrated marketing mix; online 3D avatar influencers will become the new spokespeople for meta-based media; and in-home micro targeted press briefings (or flash briefings, as they're called) will be delivering custom content to in-home users.

So, what does that look like? Let's say a luxury vehicle brand suffers a manufacturing or product malfunction and needs to issue a recall. Fifty years ago, the automaker communications team would call industry journalists, then mail out a hard-copy report about the recall, which car owners also would hear about in a recall letter from the company and on the 6 p.m. evening news and maybe read about it the next morning in an article in the daily newspaper.

Now, the luxury brand communications team will issue a worldwide news release on a paid newswire service, post a notice on the company's website, share the recall notice on its social media platforms, include a video message from its research and development executive team, send push notifications to subscribers across all digital platforms, and then monitor cable and network news coverage to evaluate media pickup and distribution along with social media commentary, which is measured by quantitative sentiment analysis to determine the level of consumer response to reputation management.

Where we're heading next is hyperfocused targeting with real-time adjustments. So for that same luxury brand, yes, there will still be a news release for those traditional media outlets about the product recall, but there also will be a social media release that is interactive with photos, hyperlinks, quotations from company executives, video footage showing the vehicle and the recalled parts, and an interactive QR code form that allows customers to schedule maintenance appointments. Those individuals who are engaged with that brand in the alternate metaverse — who own, for example, NFTs (i.e., nonfungible tokens) of the vehicle — will receive a notification on their smart devices, and all vehicle owners will receive a targeted communication via their personal virtual assistant, Alexa or Siri or Bixby, keeping them up to date and informed in real time of all that happens without relying solely on journalists or a specific media outlet but instead strategically combining them for maximum reach and coverage. This results in customized communication and engagement platforms that combine PR tools of the past and embrace innovative tools for the future. Essentially where the PR industry is going is not either traditional media or social and digital media; it's all of the above and more.

6.6 — INTRODUCING CRISIS COMMUNICATION AND HOW TO LEVERAGE IT

Though it sounds counterintuitive to the work of public relations, there are times when clients want less media attention and to get out of the spotlight. More often than not, it is during times of crisis — a period of operational disruption, when bad things are happening and negative attention is growing — that corporate executives or business owners want to focus solely on undoing the damage that has been done and getting back to "business as usual."

By nature of their definition, crises attract attention — especially media attention — because they usually have a large-scale impact, which attracts the public's interest. Crisis communication involves the process of developing and distributing messages to relevant stakeholder audiences. A common saying in the crisis communication field is that "every crisis is an opportunity." Depending upon how the crisis situation is handled, it may represent an opportunity to leverage the media attention and advance a positive narrative, or it may become a PR disaster that becomes a case study on what not to do during a crisis.

Specifically when business conditions are not ideal, the media relations role in crisis communication is a crucial part of the job. As a PR professional, making the commitment to being open, honest and transparent with the media and stakeholder groups can make navigating a difficult situation less challenging. Regardless of the situation (an exciting new product launch or a crisis communication press conference announcing negative news), the job of the PR professional remains the same, which is to serve as a credible and reliable source of accurate and timely information.

To get started and become familiar with the crisis-related aspect of media relations, here are some basic definitions and terminologies related to the field of crisis communication, a specialized area within public relations:

- Crisis — a potentially hazardous, threatening or damaging natural or human-created situation that poses a threat to life, safety, property, reputation or standard operations. Take note: A crisis is unpredictable but not unexpected. Rule #1 in crisis communication: People first.

- Crisis management — the orchestrated response to a crisis with the objective of restoring normalcy.

- Crisis communication — the managed process and flow of communication and messaging strategies to all affected audiences. Effective crisis communication reflects a strategic and coordinated process of articulating specific messages to key stakeholder audiences to inform, educate and reassure them during all phases of crisis management and recovery.

- Dark site — a prepopulated, remotely activated website dedicated solely to crisis communication activities and messaging.

- Emergency preparedness — the advance planning process for training and preparing for appropriate crisis responses.

- Emergency operations center (EOC) — the official location for coordination of crisis management and response.

- First responders — the initial personnel on-site to deescalate and/or resolve a crisis situation.

Generally speaking, the risk factors for crisis assessment are measured by (Impact) × (Likelihood) = [Crisis Preparation + Crisis Response]. This basic formula can help PR

FIGURE 6.3 ■ Crisis Risk Map

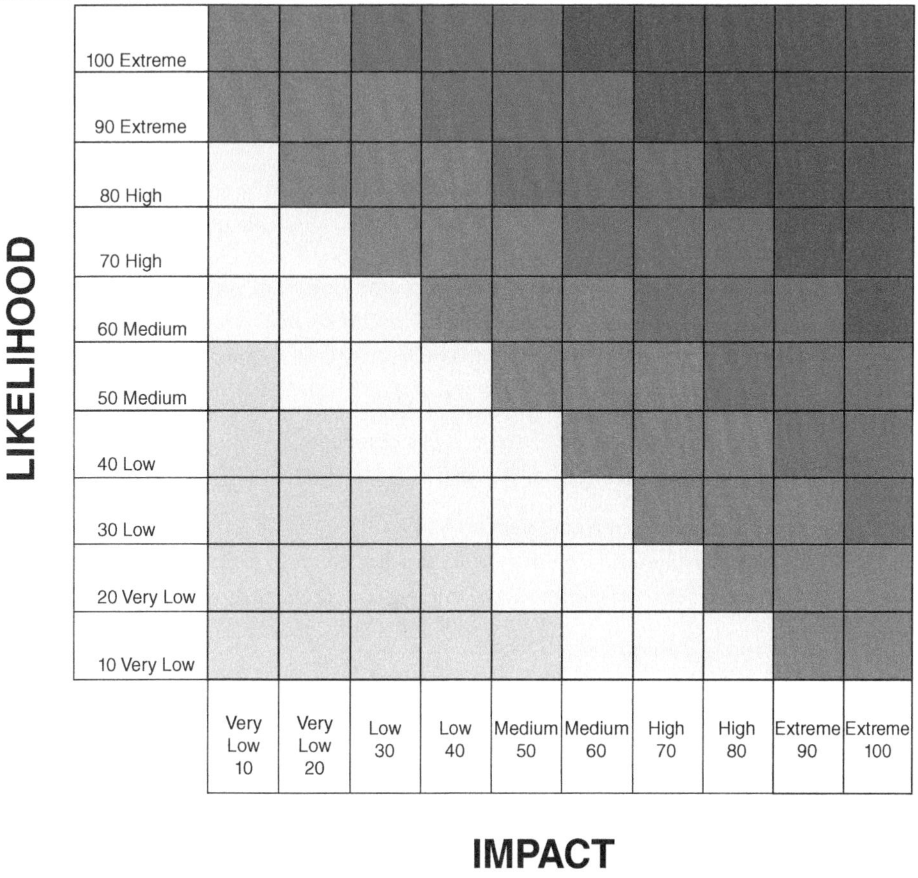

professionals understand and prepare their responses for potential crisis scenarios. See Figure 6.3 for a crisis risk map example.

Here are some factors to consider in assessing crisis potential:

- Nature of the business and potential risk factors
- Experience of the current leadership and management team
- History of past crisis events and crisis communication track record
- Current reputation and perceptions with stakeholders
- Prominence of the company/organization
- Organizational culture and social climate
- Communication reporting structure

- Status of current public relations and crisis communication team
- Presence of a crisis management plan and crisis communication plan
- Frequency of crisis communication drills and media training sessions

Sample Outline for a Crisis Communication Plan

Consider this sample outline containing different components of a crisis communication plan:

- Plan overview:
  - Identifies how and when to use the crisis communication plan
  - Explains how the organization defines a crisis and when to activate the plan
  - Offers instructions on how often to update the plan and practice crisis drills
- Crisis definitions:
  - Identify likely organizational crises and assessments
  - Rank impact and likelihood of crisis scenarios relevant to the organization
- Current crisis overview/situation analysis:
  - Provides background information about what led to the crisis situation
  - Gives additional context about the existing environment surrounding the crisis
- Crisis communication stakeholders:
  - Define audiences affected by the crisis situation
  - Define audiences that can affect the organization experiencing the crisis
- Communication flow chart and/or grid
- Crisis response guidelines and checklist
- Crisis communication team members:
  - Provide contact information to the crisis communication team members
  - Provide instructions for who to contact at each step throughout the crisis
- Crisis management team members:
  - Provide contact information for the crisis management team members
  - Provide an overview of roles and responsibilities for team members
- Key media contacts and media outlets with complete contact information
- Company/organization fact sheet
- Messaging strategy:
  - Key messages
  - Key audiences
  - Authorized spokespeople
  - Communication platforms (preferred and priority)
- Potential media questions

- Media do's and don'ts guidelines

- Social media plan

- Evaluation and recovery questions and forms

- Templates for potential crisis situations:
  - News release
  - Media advisory
  - Holding statements
  - Social media posts

- Sample media kit documents:
  - News release
  - Media advisory
  - Fact sheet
  - Backgrounder
  - Executive bios and photos
  - Official media statements

- Forms:
  - Incident report
  - Media inquiry log
  - Press conference/media sign-in sheet
  - Evaluation form

Crisis Analysis, Action and Communication

To begin formulation of an initial crisis communication response, it is helpful to observe, ask and answer some basic questions to help shape strategic messaging.

Questions to ask with regards to crisis analysis include:

- What do we know?

- What don't we know?

- What situation do we have right now?

- What does it mean now and in the immediate future?

Questions to consider for crisis action include:

- What do we want? (goal setting)

- How do we get what we want? (strategic planning)

- What do we do? (tactical actions)

Common crisis communication questions include:

- What do we need stakeholders to know, think, feel and do?

- What do we say? (messaging content)

- How do we say it? (form and strategy)

- Where do we say it? Which platforms are appropriate?

Consider the additional points and priorities in the "Tips for Beginners: When Crisis Strikes" box in this chapter when performing media relations duties and providing guidance to clients about how to navigate and leverage media attention during a time of crisis.

TIPS FOR BEGINNERS: WHEN CRISIS STRIKES

When it comes to handling a crisis, it's not a question of "if," it's a matter of when and how. No company is crisis-proof, because a crisis can occur at any time for any number of reasons. A company can be the victim of a crisis, the unintended victim of a crisis or the manufacturer of a crisis. Regardless of the problem's source, the results are often just as devastating and damaging if a crisis is handled poorly.

A crisis is any natural or human-caused threat that can potentially harm a company. The range of crises that can affect an organization is vast and wide, from severe weather, computer hacks and terrorism to product malfunctions, ill-advised social media posts, poor customer service, financial mismanagement and inappropriate relationships. No company is too large or too small to face a crisis, and no matter the size of an organization, having a crisis response and crisis communication plan in place is mandatory.

The recent parade of crises poorly handled by large multinational corporations has been astonishing, most of them the result of self-inflicted wounds and a refusal to follow some basic crisis communication rules that should be obvious.

Rule #1: People First

Policies and procedures do not take priority over people and their safety. No matter what has happened and how badly things have gone or how much money has been lost, any and all remarks to the public must begin with an acknowledgment of the people who have been hurt, harmed, injured, targeted or negatively impacted.

Rule #2: Tell the Truth . . . Fast

During a crisis, when people don't have information, they create it. Good, bad or ugly, any information and communication voids will be filled with rumors and speculation, which are difficult to control and impossible to contain. If the organization at the core of the crisis doesn't tell its own story, someone else will — to the company's detriment.

Rule #3: Take Responsibility and Don't Blame Others

The reason many companies fail the crisis test is because their leadership is afraid to take responsibility for what has gone wrong, lest it be seen as an admission of guilt that can later be used against them in a court of law. The problem is that lawsuits often take years, but the court of public opinion — fueled by traditional media and social media — requires an immediate reaction and an immediate response. Blaming the victim or saying nothing at all are guaranteed to fail.

For professionals who handle crises for companies, an unspoken rule is that you cannot communicate your way out of something you behaved your way into. In other words, they understand that clients, customers, media and the public don't just want empty words — they want a change in behavior, procedures and operations to avoid a repeat of the crisis in the future. It's not enough for a company to publish a canned statement or talking points and then hide behind vague explanations and platitudes in hopes that people will forget the incident and move on to the next thing.

Crisis assessment/planning, crisis management and crisis communication all require a plan — a written plan — that can easily be understood and implemented at a moment's notice. Any small business that doesn't have a crisis management plan or crisis communication plan in place can follow these basic steps to get started:

Crisis Risk Assessment/Planning — Create a list of all potential threats to the business. Include broad categories of threats and then list potential specific threats by answering the following questions: What can possibly go wrong in this company? If something goes wrong, who will be affected? Of all the bad things that could happen, which of them are most likely to happen, and which are least likely to happen? (Is the company more likely to get robbed or sued? Are there products that can hurt people or merely inconvenience them if there is a malfunction? Is there a lot of customer traffic where people can be targeted, or are most customer interactions taking place remotely or online?)

Crisis Management — Develop an action plan for the most likely crisis situations and make a list of all individuals, entities and organizations that need to be contacted when a crisis occurs. This should include first responders (police, EMS, fire department, etc.), executives and management, investors and stockholders, legal representatives, media contacts, and the spokespeople authorized to speak on behalf of the company. Crisis managers are on duty until the crisis is resolved and the organization begins to recover.

Crisis Communication — Identify and limit the number of people who can talk to the media and provide official comments, and make sure that they are all saying the same thing. Prepare templates or written documents in advance that can be filled in with specific details when a crisis occurs. Make sure that the affected organization tells its own story and controls the flow of communication about the crisis. Encourage the spokespeople to answer questions truthfully and outline when and how additional information will be provided as it becomes available. Finally, provide details that will assure the media and public that the crisis is being properly addressed and that corrective action is being taken.

During a crisis, it is important to communicate a cohesive and consistent message with stakeholders through all relevant media platforms where you know your message will be heard. Currently, social media moves the fastest and with the greatest sense of urgency, so it's important to have a social media plan in place to immediately communicate with people. Make sure all user IDs and passwords are easily accessible to individuals authorized to comment on social media sites. Confirm that each social media post is accurate and approved by the crisis communication team to avoid making a bad situation worse.

The objectives of any crisis plan are to restore operations to normalcy, to rebuild trust with stakeholders and to reestablish the organization's positive reputation. Regardless of the crisis, it can be successfully handled with planning, training and proper plans in place.

6.7 — FEATURE WRITING AS A MEDIA RELATIONS TOOL

In rare instances, the PR professional can conduct research and interviews, write and edit a feature article, and propose getting it published or posted as written in its entirety. A well-written, fair and balanced profile piece on a person or subject of interest is yet another way to gain media coverage for a client. Smaller budgets and limited resources at many smaller publications are creating voids in their ability to adequately and consistently cover all the news topics that may interest their readers.

Similar to pitching the story idea, a PR professional can pitch producing the entire feature article and offer the publication rights to a desired media outlet, a win-win scenario that gets quality content into the marketplace and helps complete content requirements for the newspaper or magazine outlet.

Feature stories have a little more creativity and personality than most straight news stories. The articles tend to "feature" an individual, product or issue and provide additional details and narrative about the featured subject from beginning to end.

The construction of feature articles is very simple: introduction, body and conclusion. The feature story still incorporates many of the same elements as a news release but offers more flexibility in narration and storytelling. The feature style is less objective and provides more insight and commentary to bring the subject to life throughout the piece. Common types of features include personality profiles, product launches and organizational profiles.

Here is a list of possible ways to open a feature lead paragraph:

- Lead with a metaphor (says that one thing is another)

- Lead with a simile (says that one thing is like another)

- Lead with an analogy (simplify complex ideas)

- Lead with a quotation (powerful, memorable and shareable)

- Lead with an anecdote (relatable storytelling; emotional connection)

- Lead with a joke (just don't do it!)

CHAPTER SUMMARY

There are many tools at the disposal of PR professionals to assist in their media relations work, using content and events to attract and secure positive media coverage. Learning how to perfect pitching techniques is worthwhile to increase the likelihood of matching the right story idea with the right journalist. At the core of successful pitching and media relations are well-written documents that accurately convey the messages of the client. PR professionals will find media database software to be a valuable tool and worthwhile investment. Using media lists, media kits, custom feature articles and press conferences expands opportunities to meet and connect with new journalists and to secure quality media coverage on behalf of clients.

KEY TERMS

crisis

crisis communication

crisis management

dark site

emergency operations center (EOC)

emergency preparedness

feature stories

first responders

media database

media list

media pitch (letter or email)

media relations

press conference

DISCUSSION QUESTIONS

1. What does media relations work entail for PR professionals?

2. What are some of the considerations in deciding to host a press conference?

3. Name some of the information included in a quality media list or media database.

WRITING EXERCISES

1. Write a three-sentence statement to provide to journalists during a campus data breach crisis situation where you do not have any answers or confirmed information to share about the crisis. This media holding statement should acknowledge the crisis, avoid speculation, and provide details about next steps to be taken by the crisis communications team.

7 WEBSITES, ONLINE AND SOCIAL MEDIA CONTENT, AND AI

LEARNING OBJECTIVES

7.1 Learn how to write for the web.

7.2 Understand the importance of online newsrooms in media relations.

7.3 Use key words and phrases to enhance search engine optimization for online content.

7.4 Plan, outline and publish a blog.

7.5 Utilize artificial intelligence (AI) apps and software as supplemental writing tools.

INTRODUCTION

Content creation for websites, online commentary and social media platforms is constantly adapting to how readers consume information — in many cases while they're distracted or on the move. Though there is a large audience of readers and viewers using laptops or desktops at home and work, there is also a continual, surging population of individuals who are reading and scrolling through unlimited volumes of information from the palm of their hands.

Mobile devices, including smartphones, e-readers, tablets and digital notebooks, are just some of the technological options that allow people to access information from the internet. Content creators should be keenly aware of how their target audiences engage with online content using these devices and develop material with those priorities in mind.

7.1 — WRITING FOR THE WEB

Brevity, clarity and shareability are the common traits of online content, whether the outlet is a webpage on a website, a blog or a social media site. Brevity is important for keeping readers' attention — especially when screens are smaller, attention spans are shorter, online reading speeds are slower, and more online competitors are vying for viewers' attention.

Clarity is always important, but it is particularly so with online content, because its non-linear structure allows readers to click, scroll and jump around within content. Clarity ensures that no matter where the reader navigates within the verbiage, the message is clear and easy to understand. Shareability is the trademark of online content for a number of reasons. First, a lot of online content is user generated, so it seamlessly reflects the voice of those who are participating in online conversations. Second, web-enabled widgets and plug-ins, which are tools that enable additional functions on a webpage or social media site, encourage site visitors to forward, share, republish and print information found online.

Three additional things to keep in mind when developing online content are the importance of creating conversational copy that is easy to read and understand; writing engaging content that encourages readers to respond, react and share it with others; and incorporating key search terms for search engine optimization (SEO) that make it easier to find the information being published and to gain maximum exposure and reach.

Websites

A website is an internet-based collection of material about a particular subject, organization, institution or company that is organized by individual webpages that readers navigate using tabs or links to access information online. Viewers of website content are looking at the information on a computer monitor or mobile screen, and they are using mouse clicks or finger scrolling to read or view multimedia elements. Generally speaking, websites serve as a digital home base or "hub" for a company, institution or nonprofit organization to centralize information and to provide easy and instant access for viewing, printing, downloading or sharing content. Many other online resources, such as blogs and social media platforms, may redirect readers to the main website, which likely contains more detailed background information about the company. Websites can range in length, style and function, offering anything from a single landing page with basic text and images to numerous tabs and pages with elaborate designs, prolific imagery and countless ways to interact with the content.

Writing and designing content for a webpage means creating it with large and small screens in mind and with a clear understanding of how readers navigate through a page. Generally speaking, the human eye is naturally attracted to larger content first, hence headlines. From childhood and elementary school, students are taught to read words and then sentences from left to right, moving vertically down a page, so that is the natural reading pattern to follow with online content as well. Also, the eye is drawn to vibrant colors and motion first, so placement of website copy can be designed using those basic elements of layout and design and reader comprehension to attract attention and increase engagement.

Like every other outlet, material written for the web should be clear and easy to understand and presented to align with how online audiences access and navigate content. That means copy or content for webpages and websites should be written based on the three principles listed earlier in the chapter: brevity, clarity and shareability.

This chapter is noticeably absent of references to marketing research studies and recommended social networking or social media sites because of the rapidly changing landscape and frequent introduction of new platforms into the online marketplace. Basically, by the time a study is published or a new social media brand is launched, the next one in the queue is already on the way, ready to replace or displace the competitors. With more and more content being repurposed for online placement, the best approach for teaching about writing online content is to focus on the core principles and foundational skills that relate and apply to all content creation, with specific emphasis on how to tailor that information for online consumers.

No matter how or why they started, almost every website or online platform subsequently has introduced the ability for users to upload, download and share multimedia content, which has made video production more popular and in demand than ever. Visit any website, and it is likely to be overflowing with big, bold photos that incorporate motion or animation; hyperlinks and anchor links to increase search rankings; SEO-enhanced content; and incentives and premiums, including promotions, discounts and giveaways, to entice readers to spend more time on the page and to take some specific action. All of these options are ways to increase engagement, which is another way of saying two-way communication and interaction between the publisher of the content and the target audience.

Headers and Hyperlinks

Headlines and subheads are useful in organizing online content and helping readers more easily navigate through a lot of text. Larger headlines naturally get noticed first, and subheads (smaller, categorized headlines) can be used to narrow the focus of a topic and to consolidate information into smaller segments to improve reader comprehension.

A hyperlink actively engages the reader by connecting text or images to additional text, images or external content relevant to the topic. A user can simply click the hyperlink to move from their current online reading location to another part of the webpage, a different webpage, another website, or a different document or multimedia file altogether. Anchor links function in a similar way but solely within the same website and often on the same web page, basically moving the reader from one point on a webpage to another point to decrease the amount of scrolling or skimming of content needed.

Quick Tips to Enhance Website Navigation

The ease — or lack thereof — with which website visitors can effortlessly move around and find the information they are seeking could be the difference between whether they frequent the pages and engage with the content or exit the site and never return.

- Focus on brevity, clarity and shareability for content creation.

- Write the way consumers read and search; write for quick scrolling and skimming.

- Use widgets and plug-ins that allow site visitors to share content and enable more features beyond basic viewing of information.

- Employ fewer words and include more captioned photos and multimedia video content.

- Always incorporate a "call to action," asking the reader to do something or take a specific action, to help measure engagement and also to increase buy-in from site visitors.

- Write to an individual in front of a global audience to make content more relatable.

- Offer discounts, premiums, freebies and promotional opportunities to attract site visitors.

See Figure 7.1 for a sample webpage layout.

7.2 — ONLINE NEWSROOMS

Online newsrooms can do a lot of the media relations work for a PR practitioner seeking to distribute information about their client or cause. Often placed on a company's website under a specific tab for "News" or "Newsroom," these webpages serve as a repository for multimedia content available for journalists and non-media site visitors. Electronic newsrooms or e-newsrooms may contain clips or footage from past media coverage, news releases, sound bites from company officials, executive biographies, infographics or white papers, headshots, media kits and more. Here are some brief introductions to information that might be found within the online newsroom for an organization, along with explanations of how and why that information is useful.

FIGURE 7.1 ■ Sample Webpage Layout With Section Markers

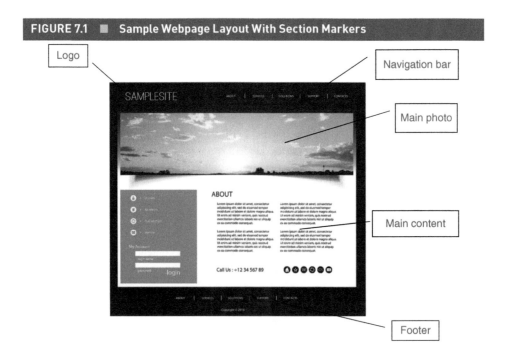

Press Releases or News Releases

These standard media relations documents are used to pitch story ideas or provide general information to the media about a topic or upcoming event. Publishing news releases in the online newsroom makes it easier for journalists to find research and background information to assist in story development and also streamlines the distribution process of getting information out to various media outlets.

Video Profiles and Video Content

Video content within an online newsroom can include one-on-one interviews with key executives or generic B-roll footage that provides additional content and context for a broadcast production. The footage is presented in a format that is easy to incorporate into a broadcast package and may accompany a news release or media kit to help tell an accurate story.

Executive Bios

Though many websites include executive profiles within similarly named "About Us" or "Meet Our Team" navigational tabs, including complete executive biographies along with professional headshots of the individuals is a good way to make sure journalists have access to the information needed to correctly identify key leaders within an organization and to ensure that details about the management team are accurate and up to date.

Headshots and Action Shots

Including a photo gallery or online photo album in the newsroom decreases the need to schedule additional photo shoots to secure images that accompany a news story and also presents an opportunity to advance the brand narrative of the organization by using key photos of individuals, products or projects under development to control the storytelling and present the company in a positive light. Including high-resolution photos that are easy to download from the online newsroom is an effective way to distribute visual content to the media.

Position Papers and White Papers

Position papers are public-facing documents that clearly articulate the stance a company or corporation takes on a particular issue, topic or subject that is relevant to the organization and its stakeholders, customers or investors. Position papers often address high-profile subjects or regulatory issues that may affect the company and its operations or stock price. White papers are well-researched publications that are considered "owned" content that the company creates to inform the public or make the case for a specific argument related to its industry. The topics can range from a food-processing plant presenting data and statistics on why genetically modified food is or is not safe for consumption to an electric vehicle manufacturer discussing pollution, emissions and environmental regulatory policies for the industry. Making these types of documents available to the media and the general public for download helps elevate awareness about the organization and increases the likelihood that their story is told effectively across various types of media outlets.

Media Kits

Posting media kits that are available for download by the media and others is an effective and cost-efficient option for amplifying a story and expanding its potential reach to target audiences across unlimited geographic and demographic markets, since anyone can access the materials with just the click of a button or hyperlink. Media kits are a combination of media relations documents used to inform journalists about a topic, client or event and also to provide background details or historical information to help produce an accurate news story. At a minimum, a media kit might contain a news release, media advisory, fact sheet, executive biographies and company backgrounder. More detailed multimedia kits also can include photos, videos, speech transcripts, infographics and white papers.

How-To Videos

During the height of do-it-yourself (DIY) television series, posting "how-to" videos online surged due to consumer popularity. They also became a great tool for PR professionals in elevating clients' brands. These relatively inexpensive productions require a subject matter expert, good lighting and a quality camera to capture a real-time demonstration or edited series of instructions teaching viewers how to build something, make something, cook something or accomplish a specific task. Oftentimes, the comments section for responses to the videos is left open to showcase how relevant or well received the information was by its target audience viewers, at the same time increasing publicity for the organization that posted the how-to video.

Media Coverage From Other Outlets

Highlighting previous articles or in-depth media coverage from various other outlets may serve to encourage a journalist to follow up and develop another story because there is proof that the company or client is newsworthy to audiences. Some companies post an "In the News" reel in the online newsroom to highlight print and broadcast stories that have featured them in the past and to showcase the level of publicity the product, service or cause has secured among its target audiences.

When it is possible to build online newsrooms as part of a company's overall website, PR practitioners should lobby for their inclusion to augment media relations efforts, to streamline the content distribution process and to increase awareness about a client or brand by making relevant content easily available online. In cases where sensitive or copyright-protected information needs to be shared, online newsrooms can be safeguarded using passwords or dual verification notices to ensure that only authorized individuals gain access to the materials posted online. The ease and frequency with which online newsrooms can be updated make them a great and efficient tool for communication professionals.

7.3 — WEB SEARCH ENGINE OPTIMIZATION (SEO)

Content creators should endeavor to write online material that will easily be discovered by search engines, resulting in Page 1 search results, Top 10 search result listings and ultimately, more website visitors.

Whether it is a webpage, blog, or e-release (electronic news release), the expectation is always that the PR writing professional has developed the content with search engine optimization (SEO) in mind. This means that in a document, the headline, subhead and lead paragraph all contain key words, terms or phrases that align with how online users seek out information — and how search engine algorithms scan and catalog content and search results for online users. Before writing a headline or boilerplate paragraph that solely emphasizes the PR client or focuses on their products and services, it is worth considering which questions people who are seeking more information are likely to ask. Once a list of questions is complete, consider using some of the key words or phrases and incorporating them into the copy being developed to increase the likelihood of higher search engine results and secure greater visibility.

Though both Google and YouTube attract millions and billions of online visitors and views and offer countless other functions, both of these popular sites top the list for their ability to provide top-notch search results. Even though various Google apps allow users to create and share files, manage multimedia content, and send and receive emails, Google is probably best known for its expansive search engine. And though YouTube has dominated the video-sharing stage for almost two decades, it too is considered a top search engine for online users. Search engines use algorithms based on a combination of page visits, reciprocal page links, updated content, keywords and search terms, webpage header tags or title tags, and other metrics to direct visitors to specific and relevant websites based upon the initial search request.

Simple SEO Reminders

Writing online content with SEO in mind is a quick and easy way to improve search results and rankings for a client, hence boosting their overall visibility in the marketplace.

- Create content based on commonsense, user-focused "search intent" questions, terms and phrases to develop relevant headers, page titles and copy for higher-ranking search engine results.

- Update content frequently to reflect online search habits, and accompany photos and video content with keywords and relevant phrases to enhance search results.

- Don't focus solely on promoting the client or the campaign, but rather develop questions based on what clients or customers would ask to find more information. Be consistent with SEO copy enhancements by regularly inserting keywords and relevant phrases into headlines, titles, subheads, and main-body copy or content to increase the likelihood of being found online during a web search or automated search engine retrieval.

- To supplement traditional news releases or media kits, also publish and distribute SEO e-releases (electronic or digitally formatted news releases) that are posted online and written to achieve higher search placements and rankings based on search engine algorithms.

- Incorporate widgets (small programs or apps that can be added or plugged in) in webpages along with embedded links that allow site visitors to perform important tasks such as archiving, bookmarking, printing and sharing content with others.

7.4 — BLOGS

Blogs are online journals or issue-centric webpages that are populated with conversational or informational content and frequently updated to provide fresh commentary for readers, subscribers and viewers. Originally launched as "web logs" and then truncated to "blogs," these online sites are ubiquitous from individual, nonprofit and corporate publishers seeking to connect with readers through online discussions and engagement.

In 2023, there were more than 600 million blogs out of approximately 2 billion websites worldwide, with over 31 million active bloggers in the United States publishing at least one blog post per month. Needless to say, that is a lot of content competing for readers' attention.

A basic search on blog topics will reveal an unlimited number of blogs focused on every conceivable topic. The purpose of a blog can be multifaceted, based on the publisher, the topic and the audience. Some blogs reflect the solo voice of an individual sharing their thoughts, ideas and interests with like-minded individuals, while other blogs provide research, data and statistics to inform audiences about topics that may affect their everyday lives. Blogs can be fun, serious, informative, entertaining or simply reflective, based on the vision of the author. What most blogs have in common, though, is an engaging approach and a conversational tone that resonates with the people who follow it.

In its infancy, the concept of blogging was introduced as an opportunity to publish an online periodical that built and maintained an audience by publishing frequent and reliable posts about a particular topic or issue on a consistent schedule. Whether the posts were daily, weekly, biweekly or monthly, readers generally knew what to expect and when to expect it. As the blogging universe — or blogosphere — expanded with more and more novice writers, the expectation for routine content simultaneously decreased, giving way to more informal, relaxed and conversational content published randomly or intermittently, at the whim of the author.

Planning a Blog

Blogs can be an effective public relations campaign tactic as part of a larger strategic approach to communicating with target audiences. Before launching a blog, the PR professional needs to clearly define the purpose of the blog and the target audience and the specific publics within the audience. Next, there needs to be a unique angle that will set the blog content apart from the volumes of information already available, whether it be a niche topic or area of expertise; special access to celebrities, public figures or privileged information; or a unique storytelling angle that differentiates the blog and sets it apart from the competition.

Once the topic has been decided, the blog will need a name, which will be used in promotions and search engine optimization to attract more readers and ultimately drive more traffic to the brand's main hub site or website. There is no definitive number of blog posts required within a week, month or year, so the frequency with which any specific blog is published or updated may vary greatly. However, there is an expectation from the blog's audience that the author(s) will post frequently enough to engage those who are interested in the topic and in accordance with whatever was promised or promoted.

Once the frequency is determined, the author of the blog can utilize attention-grabbing headlines and bold graphics along with video interviews, music and other multimedia content to capture and keep the attention of readers and subscribers. It is worthwhile to periodically review industry research, white papers or infographics to get new ideas about how to improve search rankings and to keep readers coming back for more. Some common ideas for blog topics include Top 10 lists, best/worst comparisons, common mistakes people make, lists of proven tips, how-to articles or videos, and rankings or reviews of popular products, software or services.

Similar to websites, the design and layout of blogs can differ greatly depending upon the topic and audience. From a single page to a multipage layout with a branded theme, blogs cover the spectrum in terms of how they appear to readers and subscribers. There are numerous blog host sites and servers that provide visual themes and standardized templates that make creating and publishing a blog very simple, essentially aligning the creative process with the most basic word-processing software content management systems (CMS) to facilitate easy plug-and-play methods for generating the content needed to populate the blog page(s).

Attracting blog subscribers and securing repeat blog site visitors are direct functions of posting interesting topics and consistently publishing quality content that is informative, insightful and easy to understand. Care should be given to crafting meaningful and effective blog titles, blog post headlines, subheadings, introductory paragraphs, quotations and calls to action. Well-written blogs can build brand awareness, extend audience reach, attract new clients or customers, and establish credibility in the marketplace. Quality content that is enhanced with SEO tools also can drive more traffic to a client's website and generate supplemental traditional media coverage.

The next section provides guidance for outlining and organizing blog posts from WordPress, one of the most popular sites for hosting, building and publishing blogs.

What Is a Blog Post Outline?

A blog post outline is a simple document that describes the angle and structure of your article. It makes it easier to write clearly and efficiently while staying focused on your topic. A good outline should include the following items:

- Your topic: What are you writing about?

- Your angle: What's your perspective on that topic?

- Your structure: What specific points will you make to support your angle?

You can also include working titles, though some writers prefer to write headlines after their post is finished. This helps make sure your selected headline actually fits the finished article. Here is a sample of a blog post outline:

- *Introduction (what's the angle of this post?)*
- *Main point 1*
  - *Subpoint 1*
  - *Subpoint 2*
  - *Subpoint 3*
- *Main point 2*
  - *Subpoint 1*

- ○ *Subpoint 2*
- ○ *Subpoint 3*

- ● *Main point 3*

  - ○ *Subpoint 1*
  - ○ *Subpoint 2*
  - ○ *Subpoint 3*

- ● *Conclusion*

- ● *Optional call to action (CTA)*

Source: Sailer, B. (2022, September 20). How to quickly create a blog post outline (template). https://wordpress.com/go/content-blogging/blog-post-outline-template/Simple Blog Post Reminders

Blogs are ubiquitous channels that cover almost every conceivable topic. Along with the following tips, focus and frequency are two key factors that can make blog posts successful.

- ● Begin with answering "What's in it for me?" from the audience's perspective.

- ● Use active words and visual storytelling to engage readers.

- ● Write clearly and concisely using present tense.

- ● Focus on one topic per post and incorporate keywords and relevant phrases based on how audiences seek out information.

- ● Back up blog content with facts and data to underscore specific points.

- ● Incorporate photos, videos and other multimedia content to engage the reader.

- ● Edit and proof for accuracy in spelling and grammar to build credibility with the audience.

- ● Include inspiring quotes or trivia to keep content fresh.

- ● Reference current events to demonstrate relevancy for the audience.

- ● Link back to a main hub website or social media platform to extend audience reach.

- ● Include tags and hashtags to make blog topics or conversations easy to follow online. Tags are public-facing keywords that describe or explain a post, and hashtags are words or phrases preceded by a hash sign or octothorpe (#) that are used to group online conversations and simplify searching for or following trending topics online.

Social Media Writing

Since its inception, social media has enabled people all over the world to create and share information, converse, and exchange ideas within online communities around the globe through the development of communications-based applications and virtual networks.

What all social media sites have in common is user-generated content that is designed to educate, inform, influence, enrage, entertain, persuade and engage others who participate within shared online spaces. Depending upon the social media platform, individuals posting comments generally adhere to a basic set of guidelines established by the host site that provide instruction and parameters regarding format, length and acceptable content.

Developing content for social media and using social media as part of a larger public relations campaign is now standard procedure for most public relations practitioners. Career site Indeed.com (Indeed Editorial Team, 2024) listed 14 of the top job titles with significant social media duties or responsibilities:

- Brand manager
- Blogger
- Content curator
- Content strategist
- Creative director
- Data analyst
- Digital project manager
- Digital strategist
- Marketing associate
- Social media community manager
- Social media coordinator
- Social media intern
- Social media specialist
- Social media manager

Regardless of which platform is being used, writing for social media, social networking, and online communities must always be relatable and conversational while still adhering to basic writing guidelines and standards of spelling, grammar and style. Though social media is known for its excessive use of abbreviations, emoticons and emojis (representations of facial expressions formed using combinations of keyboard characters as well as digital icons used to express emotions), overuse of these items within a professional setting can diminish the writer's credibility and make audiences less inclined to take the writer seriously.

Keep in mind that the names and brands of social media and social networking sites may change, evolve or expand, but the priority should always be on developing and posting relevant, interesting, engaging and useful content to keep audience members captive and connected. See Figure 7.2 for some popular social media site icons.

FIGURE 7.2 ■ Popular Social Media Site Icons

Source: iStock.com/Kenneth Cheung

Consider these rules of engagement when developing online content for social media sites:

- Write for the reader. Be sure to approach content with the "What's in it for me?" question from the reader's perspective.

- Speak "social" and use platform-appropriate language based on the selected social media site, giving consideration to imagery, abbreviations, and use of abbreviations and emojis as well as following online community guidelines.

- Write in a conversational tone that encourages two-way communication and invites user engagement with the post, whether it be to comment, elaborate or share with others.

- Employ the use of first and second person in posts, making use of contractions and "I" and "you" and "we," as opposed to the standard third-person objective voice often used in journalistic writing and professional PR writing documents.

- With the exception of acceptable abbreviations, adhere to basic rules of spelling and grammar to enhance credibility, build trust and avoid confusion with online audiences.

- Focus on tags, headlines and hashtags to expand online audience reach and amplify social media posts. Tags are short text descriptors of who or what is shown or shared, headlines and subheads introduce social media posts and themes, and hashtags are words or short phrases preceded by a hash mark or octothorpe (#) that help organize online conversations and make them easier to search and follow across platforms.

- Craft headlines based on the way online audiences search, think, speak and seek out information.

- Use multimedia content when appropriate, including photos with hyperlinks and captions, scrolling text, video content, music, alt text embeds for individuals with hearing and/or visual impairments, and more.

- Use interactive content with surveys, polls and short quizzes to increase engagement, to attract more views and to increase the chances that someone will share the content with their online followers.

- Be sure to incorporate SEO into headlines and use keywords in content along with search tools and content amplifiers like social media handles (@) and hashtags (#) to help organize and extend the reach of online conversations.

- Include some type of call to action (CTA) that asks the reader or viewer to take some type of action and further engage with a social media post.

See Figure 7.3 for a sample social media post and consider how it follows these rules of engagement.

FIGURE 7.3 ■ Sample Social Media Post

Joe's Coffee House
29 September 2025

Celebrate #GlobalCoffeeDay with us today!

👍 Like   💬 Comment

PR TOOLKIT: ONLINE TOOLS

In addition to well-written content that is relevant and useful to audiences, PR professionals can leverage other online tools to reach new audiences and elevate awareness about a client or brand.

Wikis are online sites built mainly through user-generated content that are then updated and maintained through collaborative contributions. By reviewing researched and approved content and adding it to a wiki site, communication professionals representing individual brands can secure even more visibility than they would using owned media content online.

Linktree is another online tool for customization and promotion that collects and combines all relevant links to other online resources in a single location. Because some social media sites do not allow links to competing sites, a Linktree page can be useful by functioning as a repository for cataloging and displaying all important web-based resources and webpages for a client.

QR codes or quick-response codes are matrix bar codes that are hyperlinked to website URLs, email addresses, PDF files or other promotional content that can be accessed online. When there are length restrictions or limitations on how much copy can be shared, a QR code graphic is a good alternative that provides direct access to additional information that is useful for audiences. QR codes also can be customized with a logo and brand colors to align with the overall visual identity of an organization or company.

Content and Copyrights

Just as with any traditional PR campaign, there is a need to consider online integrity and copyright protections for clients, brands and consumer audiences when it comes to social media content creation. Part of the responsibility of ethical PR practices is ensuring that content is honest and transparent and also making sure that there are no content copyright violations or trademark infringements.

Infractions of this kind are managed by the Federal Trade Commission (FTC), which asserts, "Our mission is protecting consumers and competition by preventing anticompetitive, deceptive, and unfair business practices through law enforcement, advocacy, and education without unduly burdening legitimate business activity." As discussed in Chapter 16, trademark protections are for intellectual property consisting of a recognizable icon, sign, design or creative expression that identifies and distinguishes a certain product or service from competitors. Copyright protections belong to the creator of original works of content, such as song lyrics, poetry, computer software, art or literary works. Exceptions to copyright protections for original creations occur in the context of employees working for companies or organizations and freelancers operating under negotiated "work-for-hire" contracts that transfer the rights of ownership to the company.

The volume of information and imagery online offers easy access for authors to "borrow" ideas or creative content without purchasing, licensing usage, or appropriately attributing credit. It is important to know that copyright violations can create legal liability for PR professionals or PR agencies, which both have a responsibility to adhere to standards of professional practice. As a result, there is a growing number of lawsuits against PR agencies that publish or distribute false or misleading information or produce creative content that violates fair use or copyright protections for original work. A good rule of thumb is to not post anything that is not an original creation or is not cited, purchased or licensed for use.

The Lanham Act

According to the online free legal dictionary, the Lanham Act of 1946, also known as the Trademark Act (15 U.S.C.A. § 1051 et seq., ch. 540, 60 Stat. 427 [1988 & Supp. V 1993]), is a federal statute that regulates the use of trademarks in commercial activity. Trademarks are distinctive pictures, words and other symbols or devices used by businesses to identify their goods and services. The Lanham Act gives trademark users exclusive rights to their marks, thereby protecting the time and money invested in those marks. The act also serves to reduce consumer confusion in the identification of goods and services.

Can PR professionals remain committed to the tenets of honesty, transparency and fairness in online communities and on sites where the content cannot always be verified and the sources cannot necessarily be confirmed? The answer is yes. Notwithstanding the avalanches of easily accessible online material, PR professionals are better served by using more comprehensive PR strategies and approaches than relying solely on social media and web-based communication channels.

Online Privacy Considerations

In addition to trademark and copyright violations online, infringements of individual privacy rights are rampant due to the level of anonymity the internet offers. Whether it is using someone's work or ideas without permission, posting harassing content as a form of revenge or retaliation, or misrepresenting the voice or opinions of others, online privacy issues are ubiquitous on social media sites.

In addition, products, services, campaigns, apps and online games that are geared toward children must take extra steps to protect young audiences. PR professionals working on content that is designed for younger markets need to be aware of the safeguards needed and the policies in place to protect children and their right to privacy.

As defined by the Federal Trade Commission, the Children's Online Privacy Protection Act (COPPA) protects children's privacy by giving parents tools to control what information is collected from their children online. According to the COPPA website, "the Act requires the Commission to promulgate regulations requiring operators of commercial websites and online services directed to children under 13 or knowingly collecting personal information from children under 13 to: (a) notify parents of their information practices; (b) obtain verifiable parental consent for the collection, use, or disclosure of children's personal information; (c) let parents prevent further maintenance or use or future collection of their child's personal information; (d) provide parents access to their child's personal information; (e) not require a child to provide more personal information than is reasonably necessary to participate in an activity; and (f) maintain reasonable procedures to protect the confidentiality, security, and integrity of the personal information. In order to encourage active industry self-regulation, the Act also includes a "safe harbor" provision allowing industry groups and others to request Commission approval of self-regulatory guidelines to govern participating websites' compliance with the Rule."

Libel and Defamation Online

The Associated Press (AP) stylebook specifically addresses three principals of legal risks related to libel and defamation for published news reports: 1) the report contains incorrect information that harms someone's reputation; 2) the report contains correct information that invades someone's privacy; or 3) the report contains material that is subject to someone else's copyright.

By definition, defamation is injury to reputation; when written or published in print or online or broadcast via radio or television, it is called libel, and when spoken, it is called slander. General standards to prove defamation include:

- The statement was published and made accessible to other people through print, broadcast or online platforms;

- The subject is identified or identifiable within the published reports;

- There is some type of harm or injury, which could take the form of financial loss, emotional suffering, mental anguish, reputational damage, etc.; and

- The issuer or publisher of the content was negligent and showed malicious intent.

PR practitioners are wise to understand the laws related to defamation; to follow the guidance issued by the AP in developing and publishing content to protect the integrity of the industry and safeguard audiences from reputational harm; and to protect practitioners, clients and agencies from legal jeopardy. That being said, when leveraged effectively, writing for the web presents an enormous PR opportunity with countless avenues to create strong messages that reach and resonate with local, regional, national or global audiences.

7.5 — ARTIFICIAL INTELLIGENCE AS A WRITING TOOL

PR practitioners and communication professionals everywhere are discussing the ramifications of rapidly advancing artificial intelligence tools and what the ethical, efficiency and employment effects will be on respective industries.

Much like the internet, smartphones and word-processing software, AI is a tool that can be used to improve skill sets and extend an individual's professional ability. The inclusion of AI in this chapter is not to introduce a replacement for skilled writing ability but rather to introduce instruments that can be used to enhance and expedite the research and brainstorming processes that kickstart creative content development.

Generally speaking, predictive and generative AI models "learn" from patterns, themes and structures that are inputted into the systems and then generate new data that shares or reflects similar characteristics. The following (unedited) narrative demonstrates the current capabilities of AI to generate content in response to a specific and concise prompt. Similar to the traditional writing process, results can be refined and regenerated to produce a better final product.

This excerpt was generated based on this prompt: "Write an introductory overview about Artificial Intelligence and ChatGPT and their uses and implications for communication professionals and Public Relations Writing. Include a bulleted list of highlights, benefits, and shortcomings."

ChatGPT

Introduction: Artificial Intelligence (AI) has emerged as a transformative technology that is revolutionizing various industries, including communication and public relations. One of the remarkable applications of AI is ChatGPT, an advanced language model developed by OpenAI. ChatGPT can generate human-like text and engage in natural language conversations, making it a valuable tool for communication professionals and public relations writers.

Overview of Artificial Intelligence and ChatGPT: Artificial Intelligence refers to the development of computer systems that can perform tasks that typically require human intelligence. AI systems, such as ChatGPT, utilize deep learning algorithms and large datasets to understand and generate human-like text, making them capable of carrying out conversational interactions. ChatGPT has been trained on a vast corpus of text from the internet, enabling it to generate coherent and contextually relevant responses.

Uses and Implications for Communication Professionals and Public Relations Writing:

Content Generation: ChatGPT can assist communication professionals and public relations writers in generating high-quality content, such as press releases, blog posts, and social media updates. It can provide inspiration, suggest ideas, and help refine drafts, saving time and effort.

Language Enhancement: AI tools like ChatGPT can help communication professionals enhance their writing skills. They can receive real-time feedback, suggestions for improvements, and learn from the model's ability to produce fluent and persuasive text.

Customer Engagement: ChatGPT can be employed to create chatbots or virtual assistants that interact with customers, addressing queries, providing information, and even resolving complaints. This enhances customer experience and streamlines communication processes.

Social Media Monitoring: AI-powered systems can monitor and analyze social media conversations, enabling communication professionals to gain insights into public sentiment, identify emerging trends, and engage with the audience in a more targeted and effective manner.

Highlights of Using AI and ChatGPT in Communication and Public Relations Writing:

- Enhanced content creation and ideation processes

- Improved writing skills through real-time feedback and suggestions

- Efficient customer engagement and support

- Deep analysis of social media conversations for informed decision-making

- Time-saving and increased productivity for communication professionals

Benefits:

- Increased efficiency: AI tools like ChatGPT can assist communication professionals in producing content faster and more efficiently.

- Enhanced creativity: ChatGPT can provide novel ideas and perspectives, inspiring innovative communication strategies.

- Improved accuracy: AI-powered tools can help identify errors, inconsistencies, and potential biases in writing, ensuring more accurate and reliable content.

Shortcomings:

- Lack of contextual understanding: While ChatGPT can generate coherent responses, it may occasionally lack deep understanding of context, leading to potentially inaccurate or inappropriate outputs.

- Ethical concerns: AI-generated content may raise ethical issues, such as the dissemination of misinformation or the potential for manipulation.

- Dependence on training data: ChatGPT's responses are based on the data it was trained on, which can inadvertently perpetuate biases present in the training dataset.

- Loss of human touch: Relying solely on AI for communication may lead to a loss of personalization and the human connection that is essential in public relations.

Conclusion: Artificial Intelligence and ChatGPT offer significant potential for communication professionals and public relations writers. These technologies can streamline content creation, improve writing skills, enhance customer engagement, and provide valuable insights. However, it is essential to recognize their limitations and carefully consider the ethical implications associated with their use to ensure responsible and effective communication practices.

Source: OpenAI. (2023). ChatGPT (Mar 14 version) [Large language model]. https://chat.openai.com/chat.

Consider another excerpt, generated with this prompt: "Write a bulleted list of 10 professional, ethical, and legal challenges posed by the use of artificial intelligence in PR Writing for public relations and communication professionals."

ChatGPT

Privacy Concerns:

- AI can gather and analyze vast amounts of personal data, raising ethical issues related to privacy, consent, and data protection regulations.

Bias and Discrimination:

- AI algorithms may inadvertently perpetuate bias and discrimination, leading to negative public perceptions or even legal challenges.

Transparency and Accountability:

- The opacity of AI decision-making can make it difficult to attribute responsibility for content or decisions, raising concerns about accountability.

Intellectual Property:

- PR professionals must navigate legal issues related to the use of AI-generated content, including copyright and plagiarism concerns.

Authenticity and Trustworthiness:

- Maintaining the integrity of information and ensuring AI-generated content is truthful and credible is a challenge for PR professionals.

Automation vs. Job Displacement:

- The use of AI for writing can lead to concerns about job displacement, requiring ethical considerations regarding workforce implications.

Manipulation and Misinformation:

- Unethical use of AI in creating deepfakes or spreading disinformation challenges PR professionals to address trust and credibility issues.

Regulatory Compliance:

- Compliance with evolving regulations and guidelines for AI usage in public relations, such as disclosure requirements, is essential.

Accountability for Errors:

- When AI-generated content contains errors or misinformation, PR professionals may need to address the consequences and rectify them swiftly.

Ethical AI Development:

- Ensuring AI systems are developed and used in an ethical manner, with a focus on social responsibility and sustainability, is an ongoing challenge for PR professionals.

Please note that these challenges may evolve over time, and public relations professionals should stay informed about the latest developments and ethical guidelines in the field of AI and communication.

Source: OpenAI. (2023). ChatGPT (Mar 14 version) [Large language model]. https://chat.openai.com/chat.

CONCLUSION

Writing for the web requires a commitment to writing consistently and with brevity, clarity and the intent for shareability so as to create interesting, relevant, useful and engaging content for online audiences. Whether the content is being developed for a website, blog or social media platform, it is important to write clearly and concisely using a conversational tone and appropriate "social" language that aligns with online community guidelines and standards. Infusing content with key words and phrases based on how audiences think, speak and seek out information will increase search engine optimization (SEO), which is useful in making content easier to find in search results.

Content creators must be aware of trademark and copyright protections and avoid misusing or misrepresenting material that belongs to someone else. Creating content also requires due diligence to ensure that children are protected and to avoid potential reputational harm to others through online publications or posts.

Enhancing well-written copy with music, photos and videos is an effective way to attract and expand online audiences and to increase engagement with readers and viewers. Online platforms make it possible to have conversations and build virtual communities around the world, blurring geographic boundaries. Simply following basic rules of style, spelling and grammar — and applying common sense and common decency in creating content and communicating with others — opens a world of possibilities for launching successful messaging strategies and PR campaigns.

Finally, content creators should consider how AI can enhance and expedite — but not replace — their writing. The following excerpt was generated based on the prompt: "Write a 4-sentence closing summary paragraph on a PR Writing textbook section titled Artificial Intelligence as a Writing Tool."

> In conclusion, the section on "Artificial Intelligence as a Writing Tool" in this PR Writing textbook illuminates the transformative role that AI is playing in the field of public relations and communication. It highlights the potential of AI-powered tools to enhance efficiency, accuracy, and creativity in crafting compelling PR content. By harnessing the capabilities of AI, PR professionals

can streamline their writing processes, access valuable insights, and stay ahead in an ever-evolving industry. This chapter serves as a valuable resource for understanding the dynamic synergy between AI and public relations, providing essential knowledge for future PR practitioners.

Source: OpenAI. (2023). ChatGPT (Mar 14 version) [Large language model]. https://chat.openai.com/chat.

KEY TERMS

blogs

hyperlink

online newsrooms

position papers

website

white papers

DISCUSSION QUESTIONS

1.   With information overload and so many online sources of competition for readers and viewers, what are some effective content creation strategies for attracting more readers?

2.   What is COPPA, and why is it important in regulating online content for young audiences?

3.   Why are tags, handles and hashtags useful in developing online content?

4.   What is the significance of search engine optimization (SEO) and its relevance for PR writing professionals?

5.   What impact will artificial intelligence have on PR writing and the public relations industry?

WRITING EXERCISES

1.   Create a prompt for an artificial intelligence language app to help generate ideas for improving written online content and enhancing SEO.

8 WRITING SOCIALLY CONSCIOUS CONTENT

INTRODUCTION

This chapter on socially conscious content is an introduction for public relations practitioners (whose professional duties often include creating content about social issues, environmental topics and newsworthy events), emphasizing the importance of respectful and responsible language in messaging that is shared with people across the nation and around the world. Social consciousness also includes being mindful of big-picture messaging and its long-term effects as opposed to prioritizing immediacy and short-term PR campaign results for the sake of increased publicity or awareness. Whether the content relates to the environment, social responsibility, inclusion or awareness, social consciousness is a crucial component of creating meaningful and effective dialogue within campaigns and respectfully connecting with diverse audiences everywhere.

8.1 — HOW TO APPROACH SOCIAL ISSUES

Public relations professionals, content creators and communication experts are often placed in the unique position of crafting messages and distributing statements that influence public discourse and potentially elevate some conversations above others. The ability to heighten awareness and shape public perception on important topics should not be taken lightly. This is an important responsibility, and it should be treated as such.

There have been countless social justice, freedom, equality and environmental sustainability movements — among others — throughout the years that have captured the interest of individuals and corporate brands alike. PR agencies and brand ambassadors are cautioned against co-opting, hijacking, or aligning with popular movements solely for the sake of gaining exposure or increasing market share. In socially conscious writing, authenticity is the common denominator for effective campaigns, ensuring that a company or organizational brand and its mission, vision and values statements align with the cause being promoted or embraced.

In this instant-communication era, it takes only minutes or seconds for the public to see through a phony campaign that is conducting "performance activism" just to advance the appearance of sensitivity or fairness without actually putting in the work to support or advance those initiatives or priorities.

In diverse societies with multiple races, ethnicities, cultures, religions and political ideologies, it can be challenging to say anything without the risk of offending one, two or 20 different groups all at once. Also, evolving value systems and social norms make what used to be acceptable or tolerable no longer the case. Keeping up with accurate terminology and nomenclature within communication professions requires dedication and a commitment to pursuing accuracy and understanding how to respectfully engage with various groups.

The expectation for PR practitioners is not to know every term, label, acronym, historical reference or advocacy group that represents every segment of the population. Rather, the responsibility is to acknowledge the differences that exist and to do the necessary research to accurately, fairly and respectfully identify them when relevant to the campaign or messaging strategy. For example, there may be instances where communicating with seniors (individuals over the age of 65 years) is not relevant at all because the product, service or topic is not targeted to this group. However, if the product launch is designed for mass consumption and age is not a factor, it is appropriate to include messaging, language, topics and images that are inclusive of this particular demographic group and also to communicate that intentional thought and consideration is being given to their unique needs and concerns, which may vary from those of other targeted age groups. To some extent, inclusion overlaps with mindfulness — of being aware of who and what is relevant.

Being inclusive in content and imagery isn't as simple as switching out pictures and inserting a representative from every age group, every ethnicity, and all different cultures. Developing inclusive content is a matter of practice and a way of doing business, not an isolated episode or campaign. It begins with the research, the planning, the creative process, design and development, production, and delivery of a PR campaign.

Corporate Social Responsibility (CSR)

Business News Daily defines corporate social responsibility (CSR) as a type of business self-regulation with the aim of social accountability and making a positive impact on society. Some ways that a company can embrace CSR include being environmentally friendly and eco-conscious; promoting equality, diversity and inclusion in the workplace; treating employees with respect; giving back to the community; and ensuring that business decisions are ethical.

Environmental, Social and Governance (ESG) Scores

According to U.S. News & World Report, an ESG score is a rating that evaluates how sustainably a company is conducting business. A favorable ESG score could compel investors to invest in a company, either because investors see the company's values as aligned with their own or because investors view the company as sufficiently shielded from future risks associated with issues such as

FIGURE 8.1   ■   Sample ESG Graphic

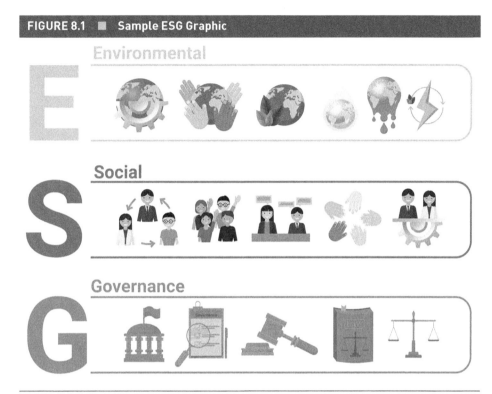

pollution or poor corporate governance. The environmental component of an ESG score considers a company's carbon emissions, energy consumption and whether it is working to address climate change. The social component takes into account the diversity within the company and employee satisfaction. Last, the governance part evaluates the company's board diversity, executive pay, corporate culture and business ethics, among other things. See Figure 8.1 for a sample ESG graphic.

Triple Bottom Line for Sustainability in Corporate America

According to business.com (Fernandes, 2024), the triple bottom line is a sustainability-based accounting method that focuses on people, profit and planet. The triple bottom line differs from traditional reporting frameworks because it includes ecological and social aspects that are often difficult to measure. The idea is that by improving in any one sector, the company overall will improve in performance.

8.2 — THE ROLE OF INCLUSION

Regardless of which PR campaign model is being used — ROPE (Research, Objectives, Programming, Evaluation), RACE (Research, Action, Communication, Evaluation), PACE (Planning, Action, Communication, Evaluation), GRACE (Goal-setting, Research, Assessment, Communication, Evaluation), or ROSIE (Research, Objectives, Strategies, Implementation,

Evaluation) — inclusion at every level is the key that delivers effective results and diminishes the likelihood of a glaring error that could have been addressed at the outset with a diverse set of perspectives throughout the development process. The following sections focus on developing a comprehensive PR campaign and also highlight potential pitfalls that can occur when socially conscious concerns are omitted in planning and implementation.

Research

Regardless of the industry at the core of a PR campaign, research is the first step in ascertaining what is known and what information is needed to contribute to the planning and goal-setting phase of the campaign. Research findings answer the "Why" question that shapes the "How" response in planning and implementation. Research results are only as good as the pool from which they are drawn. If 1,000 people are surveyed or polled, but of those 1,000, more than 90% are statistically homogenous, it is nearly impossible to extrapolate information and apply insights from the research to the total populace, because the research is not an accurate reflection of the campaign's general target audience.

Similar scenarios are frequently encountered with pharmaceutical- and health care-related PR or marketing campaigns, where limited research on small population samples creates unintended consequences because the research pools lack diversity. During the COVID-19 vaccine clinical trials launched in 2020, numerous marketing and PR campaigns conducted outreach to recruit more women and individuals from diverse populations and minority groups in the United States to ensure that the efficacy, side effects, risks and rewards were consistent across patient groups and to use the inclusive clinical trial process to enhance the element of trust, which was required to encourage and boost vaccine rates.

Planning

The planning phase of a PR campaign maps out the objective, goals, strategies and tactics along with specific actions to be taken and deadlines to meet. Inclusive planning can prevent a lot of headaches on the back end, because it invites more opinions and diverse perspectives into the conversation, which can help identify pitfalls or potentially offensive or tone-deaf content during the initial stages.

In 2018, clothier H&M faced immediate pushback and backlash from around the globe for a hoodie sweatshirt modeled by a 5-year-old Black male model that featured the statement "coolest monkey in the jungle" in bold, capital white lettering (West, 2018). Historically and sadly, according to multiple historians, the terms "monkey" and "ape" have been used as racial slurs against people of African descent in Europe and America from as early as the 16th century. Ironically, the company's inclusion and diversity statement at the time stated, "In an inclusive and diverse environment, everyone can contribute to optimizing decision-making and team performance by reflecting and relating to our employees, customers and communities." In response to the outcry, H&M initially issued a partial apology for causing offense but continued running the ad in select markets. Additional pressure forced the company to stop selling the sweatshirt altogether and to publish the following statement on its website:

We agree with all the criticism that this has generated — we have got this wrong and we agree that, even if unintentional, passive or casual racism needs to be eradicated wherever it exists. We appreciate the support of those who have seen that our product and promotion were not intended to cause offence but, as a global brand, we have a responsibility to be aware of and attuned to all racial and cultural sensitivities — and we have not lived up to this responsibility this time. (H&M, 2018)

In addition to the apology and suspended sale of the garment, H&M also hired a new leader for diversity and inclusiveness who ushered in a new set of procedures to avoid repeating the same mistake. Some of the diversity, equity and inclusion (DEI) initiatives were:

- Increasing the number of quality checks on products from one to five

- Creating an internal system to flag potentially offensive clothing or content

- Launching a system where at least a dozen individuals review any photos to be uploaded online

- Hiring a Nigerian American as the North America head of inclusion and diversity

- Pledging $500,000 in June 2020 to the NAACP Legal Defense and Education Fund, Color of Change, and the American Civil Liberties Union

Creative

The creative development process of PR campaigns is probably the aspect most familiar to people outside the industry. Without question, the creative components of campaigns are not limited to pictures and videos. Creativity encompasses and blends elements of imagination, vision, purpose and messaging with the objective of motivating people to take specific actions. Creative content harnesses the power and energy of possibility and potential, encouraging practitioners to challenge the status quo and expand the boundaries of how to connect and engage with target audiences.

Inclusion in the creative phase offers the benefits of unique experiences, backgrounds, observations and understandings of how people consume and interact with messages. Senior team members working alongside younger team members can share insights and analysis on previous campaigns and their effectiveness while also collaborating about the potential for success using new platforms or emerging technologies.

The creative meeting of the minds doesn't just result in cool graphics or viral videos; it lays the groundwork for unlimited ideation and brainstorming that brings new and unexpected ideas to the table. Generally speaking, people from different generations don't think about things the same way because their lived experiences can differ greatly because of changing times, information, technology and societal standards. People from different cultures don't necessarily interpret information the same way because words and phrases have different contexts, meanings and significance.

It is impossible for anyone to know everything about everyone else. Part of the remedy is to make sure there is diverse representation at every level of the creative process and to examine and inspect content for accuracy, relevancy, appropriateness and respect. For certain, humor varies across racial, cultural, sex and gender, and age groups and across every other demographic category, which makes incorporating jokes, sarcasm or satire into campaigns particularly risky and subject to error. But if a comedic campaign is the big idea, it will behoove the creative team to consider the nuance, phrasing and semantics of every single word or phrase to ensure the message has the intended effect.

Several years ago, in response to an increase in violence against Asians — exacerbated by online trolling and discriminatory comments made against Asians during the pandemic — creative agency Anchor Worldwide launched an integrated creative marketing campaign to combat the spread of Asian American Pacific Islander (AAPI) hate crimes in New York (Anchor, n.d.). The campaign focused on an apparent new pharmaceutical product that claimed to end racism. The packaging had a powerful and impactful accompanying statement that underscored the campaign's key message: "The only cure for racism is 'love, compassion, introspection, empathy, courage, and conscience.'" The directions on the package read: "If you are experiencing irrational anger or biased thoughts against AAPI individuals, introspect thoroughly and seek help from https://stopaapihate.org. Have authentic conversations about racism with your friends, family, and inner network. Learn about the history of AAPI, immigration, discrimination, resistance and unity. If you witness a racist episode please don't hesitate to report it to local authorities." A corresponding QR code was printed on the packaging that directed customers to the website for more information.

The creative design was noticeably absent of eye-catching imagery. The final product featured a box with vibrant yellow graphics and black text; there were no diverse faces of young people or menageries of cultural icons — just a simple and clear message that kept the focus where the campaign creators wanted it to be. Contributing factors that enhanced creativity included product placement, industry acknowledgments and awards, online influencers, and an authentic message that aligned with stated core values.

Diverse voices and perspectives are important to include during the creative process.
Source: iStock.com/Bobboz

Action and Implementation

Sometimes quality research and inclusive planning are not enough to prevent disaster when the actions taken are inappropriate or the implementation is tone-deaf in execution. Here are five unrelated examples of organizations that received media attention for their campaigns, ranging from nonprofits to major consumer brands to an athletic apparel powerhouse to a Broadway production.

First, a statewide, invitation-only, women-oriented political and economic advocacy group launched a campaign that included development of a new website for its members and potential supporters. The organization was known for its successful and accomplished membership roster, which featured members with decades of experience in law, corporate America and entrepreneurship. The average age of the membership was 60 years old; however, when the first draft of the website went live, every woman pictured appeared to be under the age of 40, which caused quite a stir within the membership — many who loudly proclaimed that the website was not reflective of a single member. In the process of creating a vibrant and compelling site with a lot of attractive and diverse representatives, the web developers failed to accurately represent the target audience. As a result, the entire site was taken down and all the images were replaced to reflect the existing members.

Next are Pepsi and Dove. With their considerable resources, experience and long track records in the creative space, it is challenging to understand how creative-campaigns-gone-wrong made it from the ideation table to the public without any intervention or second-guessing on the appropriateness of launching the campaigns from a sensitivity perspective. In 2017, beverage maker Pepsi aired a short film commercial using footage reminiscent of the Black Lives Matter protests against police brutality. The video featured television celebrity and entrepreneur Kendall Jenner, who spontaneously joins the protest activities and hands a can of Pepsi to one of the officers, which results in the crowd cheering and infers that peace and unity resulted from this act. Within minutes, the harsh online reaction became a trending topic, commenting on the lack of sensitivity by the company and the actor by minimizing the real sacrifices that individuals make for social justice. Within one day, the ad was pulled and the company released the following statement:

> Pepsi was trying to project a global message of unity, peace and understanding. Clearly we missed the mark, and we apologize. We did not intend to make light of any serious issue. We are removing the content and halting any further rollout. We also apologize for putting Kendall Jenner in this position.

In spring 2017, the Dove body-wash brand aired a 46-second ad with the tag line "Beauty comes in all shapes and sizes." The camera then shows various body-wash bottles of different shapes and sizes, representative of traditional female body type labels (pear shaped, short and round, tall and slender, curvy, etc.) It didn't take long for the overwhelmingly harsh response and sarcastic replies on social media to roll in — essentially reminding Dove that its messaging (traditionally known for not body shaming) was completely off base for a company with decades of content around body positivity branding and acceptance.

Wait, there's more. In fall 2017, Dove soap aired a social media ad that featured images of a Black woman wearing a brown shirt who lifts her shirt in subsequent frames to reveal a white woman wearing a white shirt underneath the original woman (perceived as Dove soap washes away brown to reveal white). Cue the outrage and criticism from all different groups of people who thought the ad was ignorant and insensitive at best and outright racist at worst. Even defenders of Dove found it difficult to explain and interpret in any other way, though further research and review of the entire set of footage reveals additional images that were less stereotypical, demeaning and offensive in nature. But the damage was already done. Dove issued a statement on Twitter on Oct. 7, 2017: "An image we recently posted on Facebook missed the mark in representing women of color thoughtfully. We deeply regret the offense it caused" (Dove, 2017).

Sometimes small campaigns can go global and go wrong — even if that is not the intention. The internet and social media now dictate that there are no small mistakes, so it is worth the effort to take the time to review materials for any potential offense they might cause. In 2012, a simple print ad published at a local gym in Germany, created by athletic shoe giant Reebok, stated in big, bold text: "Cheat on your girlfriend, not on your workout." The global response was swift, and the ad was pulled within hours. The company also issued the following statement: "We regret that some offensive Reebok materials were recently printed. The signs were removed as soon as we were made aware of them. I can assure you that Reebok does not condone this message or cheating in any way. We apologize for the offensive nature of these materials, and are disappointed that they appeared at all" (CBS Boston, 2012).

Another consideration for campaign implementation is accessibility — making sure those with vision, hearing or physical impairments can conveniently access campaign content. In October 2022, a theatergoer with hearing loss was singled out during a Broadway show by a lead actress from the *Hadestown* production for using a captioning device that allowed her to follow along with the show (Evans, 2022; Serna, 2022). The actress mistook the device for a recording instrument, which is not allowed to be used in the theater. The victim shared in an Instagram post that the actress "reprimanded" her "not once but twice, at least" and called the experience "super embarrassing." She went on to say, "My hearing is such that I need captioning devices for when I see a show. And to kind of be ostracized and publicly ridiculed really hurts." Immediately following the incident, the producers of the show and the theater owner connected with the audience member and offered an apology and an opportunity to return and see the show again. In addition, they thanked her for bringing the issue of accessibility to their attention. In a joint statement, the organizations said, "The incident yesterday is a reminder that this is an ongoing process needing constant revisiting and renewal" regarding their commitment to accessibility in all forms. Though the initial harm was already done, there was swift acknowledgment from the venues along with an apology and corrective action to prevent future recurrences, as well as an offer to the audience member to make amends to help repair the harm caused to the individual and the extended damage done to the hearing-impaired community.

Evaluation

The process of evaluation allows campaign creators to reflect on what worked and what didn't work quite as well, and also to review and compare current results with previous results to establish patterns and/or improve from past mistakes and lessons learned. A marketing research survey of advertising and marketing executives indicated that a lot of creative agencies are not more proactive in diverse and inclusive campaigns for fear of getting it wrong and suffering the consequences as in the previous five scenarios. Knowing that simply reinforces the need to incorporate inclusion into business models, increasing shared responsibility and accountability for creative content.

Though focus groups often occur at the beginning stages of a campaign during the research phase, there is great value in hosting focus groups throughout the entire creative development process and conducting beta tests to get an idea of how the public will respond to a campaign and whether any of the components are lacking in inclusivity or may be potentially offensive to any groups.

There's a common adage in the creative space that states, "You cannot manage what you cannot measure." Building in metrics for diversity, equity, inclusion and accessibility can help inform and improve the creative process and make it more beneficial and rewarding for everyone involved. Metrics allow practitioners to measure progress or stagnation and report back to teammates, clients, colleagues and stakeholders for accountability. The metrics also can be useful when a brand is questioned or challenged about their inclusion efforts and their commitment to social issues and topics. Brand alignment with social causes should represent a natural cohesion with the mission and stated principles and values.

The Associated Press stylebook is a good resource for PR writing professionals to keep in their library, not only for writing according to widely accepted journalistic standards but also as a reference on correct usage and terminology when reporting on, referring to or crafting messages to different groups of people around the world. It is also recommended that practitioners keep handy an updated list of advocacy groups that represent diverse communities and populations as a tool for quickly reaching out to resources and contacts who can assist in clarifying correct usage.

8.3 — HOW TO BUILD CREDIBILITY WITH DIVERSE AUDIENCES

Mutual respect is built and earned by establishing and maintaining trust. For the purposes of PR writing, that means taking the initiative and necessary time to learn more about communities outside the one(s) with which PR professionals identify.

The only way to create accurate and inclusive content is to understand the diverse communities impacted by or connected to the messaging. Inclusive writing as a practice is a lifelong endeavor and requires a commitment to learning, adapting, and encountering narratives and sentiments that may be new, different or challenging. However, inclusion is a good first step. That means, when reviewing content, it should be edited and proofed through the lens of different perspectives and its potential impact on those communities. As an example, does the language or tone elevate one group over another? Do the images leave out important demographic groups that are part of the target audience? Is the language appropriate and respectful of all human beings, regardless of status, education, income or affiliations?

Toastmasters International is a nonprofit educational organization that teaches public speaking and leadership skills through a worldwide network of clubs. In a brief overview titled "Speaking to Diverse Audiences," the organization offers six tips for giving a speech or presentation to an audience of people who speak various languages or have differing cultural backgrounds:

- **Enunciate clearly.** If possible, try to speak with a neutral accent to better include all audience members.

- **Don't speak too fast.** Remember that the normal pace of speech in one language might become incomprehensible for people relatively new to that language.

- **Be careful with metaphors.** Some metaphors that are appropriate in one culture can be offensive to another; even slight changes in pronunciation can completely alter the meaning.

- **Know the meanings of words outside your native language.** Unless you are absolutely sure of the meaning and pronunciation of a word you are using in a given language, do not use it.

- **Avoid slang, jargon and idiomatic expressions.** Diverse audiences may not understand slang from a given country.

- **Be mindful of body language, eye contact and personal space.** Posture, mannerisms and eye contact speak volumes, and what is taken for granted in one culture might be considered offensive in another.

Socially conscious content is the incorporation and integration of social responsibility and awareness into public relations messaging to diverse audiences. The development of this content also considers the societal effects and impact of words and images that are introduced into the public discourse. To put it more concisely, words matter.

To be sure, sometimes content creation is just as much about knowing what not to say as it is about knowing the right thing to say and the appropriate way to say it. Avoiding divisive descriptors is usually a good starting point, and reaching out to various groups or reviewing guidance from various resources decreases the likelihood of writing or publishing something offensive or inappropriate.

Diversity and inclusion should be integrated into all creative materials and content.

Source: iStock.com/gmast3r

What Is Diversity, Equity and Inclusion (DEI)?

The field of diversity, equity and inclusion is ever expanding as it works to enlarge the tent of inclusion in the workplace and society at large, endeavoring to bring traditionally underrepresented or overlooked voices and perspectives to the forefront as full participants in collective decision-making at every level.

The University of North Carolina at Chapel Hill's School of Journalism and Media defines diversity as:

> Any point of difference among individuals, variety; especially among different types of people. It includes a recognition and appreciation of differences and finds value in these differences because they are necessary for promoting growth and learning for all community members. Diversity can be measured across many variables — age, race, ethnicity, sex, gender identity, sexual orientation, socio-economic group, geography, religion, thought, philosophy, perspective, disability and veteran status.

As defined by Built In (Heinz & Urwin, 2024), an online community for startup and tech companies, DEI is any policy or practice designed to make people of various backgrounds feel welcome and ensure they have support to perform to the fullest of their abilities in the workplace. Diversity refers to the presence of differences within a given setting; in the workplace, that may mean differences in race, ethnicity, gender, gender identity, sexual orientation, age and socioeconomic background. Equity is the act of ensuring that processes and programs are impartial and fair and provide equal possible outcomes for every individual. Inclusion is the practice of making people feel a sense of belonging at work.

- **Diversity** is the reality and presence of differences that may include age, race, gender identity, religious beliefs or practices, sexual orientation, ethnicity, socioeconomic status, language, (dis)ability, political ideologies, perspective, etc.

- **Equity**, which differs from equality, works to promote fairness, justice and impartiality in laws, policies, procedures, processes and the distribution of resources within systems and institutions. Whereas equality emphasizes equal access to resources, equity acknowledges historical and systemic challenges that may affect the ability to take advantage of resources and opportunities and instead focuses on the effective allocation of resources needed to reach an equal outcome.

- **Inclusion** is about openness and accessibility that welcome diverse groups and individuals within an organization to fully participate and engage equally. Inclusion efforts are often put forward as a solution to expanding participation levels and incorporating more voices and perspectives that traditionally have been left out of advancement and development opportunities and decision-making processes.

What Is Inclusive Language?

Creating content that features inclusive language is about more than inserting a few buzzwords and randomly including the names of different marginalized groups or traditionally underrepresented populations. Inclusive language takes into consideration the fact that topics in the news and media discourse often overlap a variety of target audiences, and it is important to make sure that diverse perspectives are represented and diverse voices are heard throughout the conversation.

More importantly, it is presumptuous to think that any homogenous group of individuals can adequately or accurately speak for or fully represent the interests of others without their input. Inclusive language consistently expands audiences that can and will engage with PR campaigns while also enhancing social capital among diverse groups on behalf of the PR client.

Avoid Slurs and Slang

Even for the most creative and edgy PR campaigns, slurs and slang should be avoided, because they likely will offend people and create negative backlash for the PR agency that publishes the content. Slurs are offensive language used to stigmatize people, and slang is informal and relaxed verbiage that is often used in a euphemistic format in place of a more respectful term.

Include Accessibility

Accessibility is also related to inclusion, ensuring that everyone within an audience has equitable access to information. As an example, a helpful tool to facilitate inclusion is "alt text" on the web. This embedded text accompanies photos, images and other multimedia content to give an explanation of and context for what is shown. Users can read the text or enable an audio reader to vocalize the textual descriptions.

Here is an excerpt from the "disabilities" entry in the AP stylebook to help guide language use and informing writers about how to accurately and respectfully develop content for those within this group:

> Disabilities. The terms disabilities and disabled include a broad range of physical, psychological, developmental and intellectual conditions both visible and invisible.
>
> Perceptions of disabilities vary widely. Language about disabilities is both wide-ranging and evolving. Disabled people are not monolithic. They use diverse terms to describe themselves. Many, for example, use the term *people with disabilities*. Both *people with disabilities* and *disabled people* are acceptable terms, but try to determine the preference of a person or group.
>
> Use care and precision, considering the impact of specific words and the terms used by the people you are writing about.
>
> When possible, ask people how they want to be described. Be mindful that the question of identity-first vs. person-first language is vital for many. The terms disabilities and disabled are generally embraced by disabled people and are acceptable when relevant. (Associated Press, 2022, p. 207)

Recognize Bias in Language

When developing content, it is useful to keep in mind that everyone brings their own sets of biases and past experiences into the equation. Biases are generally thought of as learned or inherent prejudices against or in favor of certain individuals and groups.

Referencing the concepts of "otherism" and framing can help PR writing professionals identify bias in their daily work activities. Otherism is a divisive phenomenon involving exclusion of individuals and groups based on perceived difference and then using language to reinforce the distance and create separation. Framing is all about how information is presented and which attributes within the content are highlighted or downplayed in terms of relevance or importance.

For example, in a news story about students celebrating their university's athletic victory over a top rival, using a word like "riotous" instead of "celebratory" can send a strong message and alter the nature of the story. As another example, in social justice protests, publishing the term "mob" versus "protesters" significantly changes the tone and how the information will be perceived. In those examples, the language and terminology choices are determined at the development phase with writers and then shared with the public. It is the responsibility of all professional communicators to be accountable for the language used to represent others. The following terms explain how certain mental and psychological processes affect communication.

- *Implicit bias* is defined as the attitudes or stereotypes that unconsciously affect our understanding, actions and decisions, influencing actions, judgments or behaviors toward specific groups solely based on traits or characteristics such as their appearance, demographic profile or associations.

- *Confirmation bias* is the tendency of people's minds to seek out information that supports the views they already hold and interpreting information through an established lens that reaffirms existing beliefs.

Knowing and understanding that unchecked bias and ignoring stereotypes, assumptions and generalizations can be hurtful to others and harmful to the communication process is a good reminder to always review terminology, usage and content and to give thoughtful consideration to language and its potential effects and impact on people's lives.

Words Matter

One way to help students envision the significance and impact of inclusive visual imagery is through an example using college recruiting materials. This also highlights the importance of knowing and understanding the target audience and acknowledging how words and images may resonate with respective groups.

Imagine a traditional brochure for higher education that is targeted to high school students, their parents, and high school guidance counselors. Instead of being available online in a digital format or accessible via hyperlink or QR code scan, there are only hard-copy versions available in the front office of high schools and at various local libraries. Content in the brochure focuses on a very rigid and inflexible curriculum with only in-person class attendance as an option. Finally, the photos in the brochure feature students who all appear to be at least 25 years old. The question to high school students is, "Do you see yourself represented in this brochure?" In this example, the language doesn't speak to the students. The images don't reflect the students or their friends and affiliate groups. The curriculum format is disconnected from how many students desire to learn. If the authors and developers of the brochure don't make the effort to understand the audience, it is highly unlikely that their recruiting activities will be successful. When audiences are not included or represented respectfully and equitably in messaging, they are less likely to engage with or pursue the opportunities shared.

Using Gender-Neutral Language

The AP stylebook entry on "gender-neutral language" is quite extensive, providing guidance on appropriate language and descriptions for common professions, jobs and roles that might appear in writing. The entry reads: "In general, use terms for jobs and roles that can apply to any gender. Such language aims to treat people equally and is inclusive of people whose gender identity is not strictly male or female." The instruction goes on to suggest balancing the guidelines with simple common sense, respect and adaptability as language and nuance within language evolves. "Treatment of the sexes should be evenhanded and free of assumptions and stereotypes" (Associated Press, 2020, p. 125). Demonstrating these ideas, Table 8.1 provides examples of AP style gender-neutral language for jobs or roles.

Cancel Culture

To be sure, no movement is without its detractors. With the amplification of more voices, perspectives and opinions on social media and cable television, the opposition to diverse commentary is just as prominent and vocal.

The terms "canceled" and "cancel culture" emerged in the 2000s as a way to reject or protest against objectionable content or actions by individuals, organizations and corporations that the public deemed offensive, inappropriate or unacceptable. Depending upon one's perspective, cancel culture can be framed as a proactive response to police bad behavior or a defensive overreach to silence certain voices and opinions that may be seen as divisive.

TABLE 8.1 ■ AP Style Gender-Neutral Language for Jobs or Roles	
Previous Usage	**Preferred Usage**
businessman or businesswoman	business owner or businessperson
chairman or chairman of the board	chair, board chair, or chairperson
fireman or firemen	firefighter
mailman	mail carrier or letter carrier
mankind	humanity, humankind, humans
manmade	artificial or synthetic
policeman or policewoman	police officer
stewardess	flight attendant
waiter or waitress	server

Online encyclopedia Wikipedia defines cancel culture this way:

Cancel culture is a phrase contemporary to the late 2010s and early 2020s used to refer to a cultural phenomenon in which an individual deemed to have acted or spoken in an unacceptable manner is ostracized, boycotted, shunned, fired or assaulted, often aided by social media. This shunning may extend to social or professional circles — whether on social media or in person — with most high-profile incidents involving celebrities. Those subject to this ostracism are said to have been "canceled."

The term "cancel culture" came into circulation in the late 2010s and early 2020s and has mostly negative connotations. The term "call-out culture" is used by some as more positive verbiage for the same concept.

Some critics argue that cancel culture has a chilling effect on public discourse, is unproductive, does not bring real social change, causes intolerance, and amounts to cyberbullying. Others argue that the term is used to attack efforts to promote accountability, to give disenfranchised people a voice, and attacks language that is itself free speech. Still others question whether cancel culture is an actual phenomenon, arguing that similar forms of boycotting have existed long before the origin of the term "cancel culture." ("Cancel Culture," 2024)

Merriam-Webster dictionary defines it as "the practice or tendency of engaging in mass canceling as a way of expressing disapproval and exerting social pressure" (Merriam-Webster, n.d.). More recently, in pop culture and politics, cancel culture is routinely applied to deny access to exalted media platforms, *to remove celebrity status or esteem, and to reduce popularity or visibility for an individual or group based on perceived inappropriate or offensive comments, speech, or behavior.*

In a diverse society, it goes without saying that all professional communication-oriented organizations must embrace and express their commitment to establishing inclusive standards for membership and practice within the industry. The next sections in this chapter also will share several official DEI statements from various sectors. Take notice of the length and specificity of the statements and how they each reflect the mission and vision of the organization that published them.

PR TOOLKIT: BEING YOU | PRSSA NATIONAL DEIB STATEMENT

PRSSA members are creative alone, but together we are visionaries. This means PRSSA members must be their authentic selves, practice inclusivity and be responsible for each other — all with respect and understanding infused within our communication. For PRSSA and the public relations industry to grow and evolve, being creative is not enough. We need visionaries to ensure we will be a more empathetic, dynamic and innovative organization and workforce.

Inclusion is not just about having "a seat at the table." It's about ensuring everyone's voice is heard and fully considered. PRSSA recognizes the importance of listening to all voices and experiences to forge a viable Society that aids the profession and future professionals in serving diverse and increasingly multicultural publics.

The most obvious contexts of diversity include race, ethnicity, religion, age, ability, sexual orientation, political belief, gender, gender identity, country of origin, culture and diversity of thought. However, in a rapidly changing society, diversity continues to evolve and can include class, socioeconomic status, life experiences, learning and working styles, personality types and intellectual traditions and perspectives. These defining attributes impact how we approach our work, connect with others and move through the world.

PRSSA encourages its members to always respect, embrace, celebrate and validate each other's differences. These diverse and inclusive practices, when done proactively, contribute to the growth of our Chapters, the public relations industry, the communities in which we live and work, and ourselves.

PRSSA members are the future of the industry. It is our responsibility as bright, young leaders to be the change we envision.

Source: PRSSA. (n.d.). Being you | PRSSA national DEIB statement. In *PRSSA diversity toolkit 2023–2024* (p. 6). https://www.prsa.org/docs/default-source/prssa-docs/about/prssa-diversity-toolkit.pdf?sfvrsn=ce661 73c_10

Examples of Official Statements

As this chapter concludes, a number of official statements on diversity, inclusion and DEI are displayed to offer further insight into how different companies and organizations prioritize inclusion in their business models. Consider, compare and contrast the following statements.

PRSSA

PRSSA's diversity statement is as follows:

PRSSA embraces all individuals regardless of background, culture, education, major, age, disability, gender and sexual orientation. PRSSA recognizes the importance of different experiences, perspectives and voices in making a viable Society that aids the profession. (PRSSA, n.d.)

Table 8.2 provides language guidelines from PRSSA on race, ethnicity and origin.

Amazon

The following is Amazon's diversity and inclusion mission statement:

Diversity, equity, and inclusion are good for business — and more fundamentally, they're simply right. Customers represent a wide array of genders, races, ethnicities, abilities, ages, religions, sexual orientations, military status, backgrounds, and political views. It's critical that Amazon employees are also diverse and that we foster a culture where inclusion is the norm. Amazon prioritizes equal pay, and since we've been measuring and publishing the ratio over the past several years, women have earned between

Identity	Explanation	Example(s)
African American/Black	"Black" and "African American" are not always interchangeable. Some individuals prefer the term "Black" because they do not identify as African and/or American. Individuals may identify as "African," "Afro Caribbean," "Afro Latino" or other.	Refer to groups as Black students, Black faculty members, etc., not "Blacks." Consider the necessity of using race within your text. Ask yourself: "Would I mention 'white student' or 'white faculty member' when discussing others?"
Asian, Asian American, Pacific Islander	"Asian" refers to people who are citizens of countries in the Far East, Southeast Asia or the Indian subcontinent or to people of Asian descent. Asian Americans trace their origins to these regions. "Pacific Islander" includes Native Hawaiian, Samoan, Guamanian, Fijian and other peoples of the Pacific Island nations. Use "Asian"/"Pacific Islander" when referring to the relevant population in its entirety. Otherwise, use the preferred term of the individual or group.	Refer to groups as Asian students, Asian faculty members, etc., not "Asians." Consider the necessity of using race within your text. Ask yourself: "Would I mention 'white student' or 'white faculty member' when discussing others?"
Hispanic, Latin(o/a) and Latinx	"Hispanic" refers to people from Spanish-speaking countries. "Latino," "Latina" or "Latinx" is a person of Latin American descent who can be of any background or language. If the individual or group does not identify as either "Latino" or "Latina," the gender-neutral term "Latinx" can be used. When referring to a group, generally use "Latinx" as it is gender inclusive.	People from Mexico, Cuba and Guatemala who speak Spanish are both Hispanic and Latin(o/a)/Latinx. Brazilians who speak Portuguese are Latin(o/a)/Latinx but not Hispanic. Spanish-speaking people in Spain and outside Latin America are Hispanic but not Latin(o/a)/Latinx.
Native American	"Native American" is preferred unless the individual or group specifies otherwise. Occasionally, some prefer "American Indian"; however, this is not universal.	The term "Indian" is used only when referring to people from India, not for Native Americans.
People of Color	Sometimes we don't use the term "people of color," because not all people have the same experience. Instead, refer to groups by their name.	Do not use the term "colored people"; use "African American," "Asian," and "Hispanic" vs. "people of color"

(Continued)

TABLE 8.2 ■ PRSSA Race, Ethnicity and Origin Language Table *(Continued)*		
Identity	**Explanation**	**Example(s)**
Underserved/ Underrepresented	Do not use the term "minority" to describe students from diverse backgrounds. When referring to multiple groups of students from diverse backgrounds, use "underserved/ underrepresented students"; however, use the specific group title when possible.	"LGBTQ+ students," "Black students," "undocumented students," etc.
Immigration Status	Do not use the words "illegal immigrant" or "illegal alien" to refer to individuals who are not U.S. citizens/permanent residents and do not hold visas to reside in the U.S. or have not applied for official residency.	"Undocumented students," "undocumented individuals," etc.

Source: PRSSA. Appendix: Race, ethnicity and national origin. In *PRSSA diversity toolkit 2023–2024* (p. 20). https://www.prsa.org/docs/default-source/prssa-docs/about/prssa-diversity-toolkit.pdf?sfvrsn=ce66173c_10

99.8 and 100.0 cents for every dollar that men have earned in the same jobs. We also believe it's critical that we increase opportunity for underrepresented groups to enter the technology workforce. We created Amazon Future Engineer, a childhood-to-career computer science education program designed to inspire and educate millions of students globally from underserved communities to pursue careers in computer science. It's not only that diversity, equity, and inclusion are good for business—it's more fundamental than that. It's simply right. (Amazon.com, n.d.)

Dell Technologies

Dell Technologies' diversity and inclusion statement is found below:

At Dell Technologies, we believe that diversity is power. Our goal is to build a future workforce that champions racial equity, values different backgrounds and celebrates unique perspectives. Our ongoing commitment to diversity and inclusion is how we address societal challenges and unlock innovation. It's how we win as a company — and win the right way. (Dell Technologies, n.d.)

United Way

United Way's diversity statement is as follows:

United Way fights for the health, education, and financial stability of every person in every community.

We take the broadest possible view of diversity.

We value the visible and invisible qualities that make you who you are.

We welcome that every person brings a unique perspective and experience to advance our mission and progress our fight for the health, education, and financial stability of every person in every community.

We believe that each United Way community member, donor, volunteer, advocate, and employee must have equal access to solving community problems.

We strive to include diversity, equity, and inclusion practices at the center of our daily work.

We commit to using these practices for our business and our communities.

Join us in embracing diversity, equity and inclusion for every person in every community. (United Way, n.d.)

The Walt Disney Company

The Walt Disney Company's diversity and inclusion statement is as follows:

From our media networks to our movie studios, from our theme parks to our products, very few companies touch the hearts and minds of generations of people around the world the way Disney does. With this rich opportunity comes a deep sense of responsibility for creating the most authentic stories and experiences. Today, audiences are rapidly diversifying, new generations are shaping the nature of work, and changes in society increasingly impact employees everywhere.

Our focus and intent encourage people from every nation, race/ethnicity, belief, gender, sexual identity, disability, and culture to feel respected and valued for their unique contributions to our businesses. It informs our guiding principles and defines our relationship with guests and consumers, who trust and believe in the Disney brand in ways that are meaningful to them. Simply put, diversity and inclusion remind us all — from Disney fans to employees — that we belong. (Walt Disney Company, n.d.)

The White House

The following is a description of the Executive Order on Diversity, Equity, Inclusion, and Accessibility in the Federal Workforce:

This Executive Order reaffirms that the United States is at its strongest when our Nation's public servants reflect the full diversity of the American people.

Even with decades of progress building a Federal workforce that looks like America, the enduring legacies of employment discrimination, systemic racism, and gender inequality are still felt today. Too many underserved communities remain under-represented in the Federal workforce, especially in positions of leadership. This Executive Order establishes an ambitious, whole-of-government initiative that will take a systematic approach to embedding DEIA in Federal hiring and employment practices.

When public servants reflect the communities they serve, the government is more effective and successful. (White House 2021)

CONCLUSION

PR practitioners are called upon to create socially relevant content that reaches the masses, and incorporating steps toward developing inclusive language can help them achieve success. Whether addressing corporate and environmental issues, social justice and activism, or topics related to diversity, equity and inclusion, the ability to respectfully communicate with diverse audiences is a professional requirement.

There are countless ways to incorporate socially conscious content into PR messaging and campaign materials. The importance of approaching content development with a focus on diversity and inclusion cannot be overstated, as it has the ability to bridge societal gaps and expand opportunities for unified approaches to building a stronger society.

KEY TERMS

biases

corporate social responsibility (CSR)

diversity

equity

framing

GRACE

inclusion

PACE

RACE

ROPE

ROSIE

DISCUSSION QUESTIONS

1. Why is it important for the messaging in public relations campaigns to model inclusive language?

2. What are some common mistakes in PR writing related to diversity, equity and inclusion? Can you think of any national PR campaigns that missed the mark on DEI issues?

3. What are the potential pitfalls of PR campaigns that use exclusionary language or messages that are not socially conscious and relevant?

4. What are some available resources for PR practitioners in becoming more adept at writing inclusive content for diverse audiences?

WRITING EXERCISES

1. Write eight to 10 key words or phrases you think should be included within an effective diversity, equity and inclusion statement for an international corporation that sells retail apparel for adults and children.

9 THE STORY BEHIND THE IMAGE

LEARNING OBJECTIVES

9.1 Identify key elements that make up a complete photo caption.

9.2 Understand how the process of photo selection and photo captioning works.

9.3 Learn how to write clear, concise, compelling photo caption content.

9.4 Recognize the concepts of accessibility, fair use and copyright as they apply to photos and captions.

INTRODUCTION

As more and more PR content relies on visual components, the ability and need to craft quality, well-written photo captions will continue to increase. The majority of content that is created by public relations professionals as part of ongoing media relations outreach efforts will include photos, videos and multimedia content. Specifically, still photos or images capture a single moment in time, and it is the responsibility of the PR practitioner to provide an accurate account of what is shown in the description of the photo along with relevant background information and supplementary context that adequately informs the reader. It is important to remember that not all photographs are accompanied by a complete story or write-up in media publications, so it is imperative that the photo and its caption effectively communicate the intended message.

9.1 — WHAT ARE PHOTO CAPTIONS?

A **photo caption** is text that accompanies a published photograph and explains the significance of the photo, describing who/what is pictured and what is occurring in the image. For PR purposes of distributing captioned photos to the media, caption content should utilize the inverted-pyramid format, concisely answering the questions who, what, when, where and why using one or two sentences. It is important for photo captions to be specific with dates and locations, because captions are sent to various media outlets with different publication and production schedules. As a result, there is an increased likelihood that the same photo will be printed or published at different times, depending upon the media outlets' daily, weekly or monthly production deadlines. Providing detailed information ensures that the photo and the accompanying caption are accurately represented in reproduction.

What Are the Essential Elements That Constitute a Quality Photo Caption?

The following is a brief checklist of crucial elements to include in photo captions that are distributed to journalists:

- **Contact block** — This block of contact information includes the PR representative's name, contact phone number and email address as a reference point in case the journalist has questions or needs clarifications about the photograph or its subjects.

- **Document title or content title** — "PHOTO CAPTION" is the name of the embedded or attached document in an email message or the title line that precedes the actual caption content. The purpose of the title is to make it clear that the content that follows accompanies the photo and also ensures that the caption is not misused, omitted or mistaken for a pull quote or some other editorial feature.

- **Release date and release status** — "FOR IMMEDIATE RELEASE" accompanied by the date provides confirmation to the journalist receiving the photos and captions that they are approved for use in the publication or production. The release date notification also acknowledges whether a photo has been published before and when (e.g., "PHOTO ORIGINALLY PUBLISHED 00/00/0000").

- **Caption headline** — The header for a photo caption is short and to the point, labeling the context of the photo and the essence of what is occurring. Caption headlines are usually no more than four to six words.

- **Dateline** — Similar to news release datelines, the dateline city in a photo caption is written in ALL CAPS and formatted in AP style to identify the location of the photo or the place where the action in the photograph is occurring.

- **Caption content** — In one or two sentences, a photo caption identifies who or what is in the photograph along with why it is relevant. The caption should succinctly answer the basic who, what, when, where and why questions and offer a general summary of what the reader sees in the photo. For photos with multiple people, individuals should be named or identified from left to right.

- **Photo credit** — A photo credit is a copyright acknowledgment of the rightful owner of the image and expressed permission to publish or broadcast the image. Professional photographers often provide the preferred verbiage to attribute for appropriate credit (e.g., "Photo used courtesy of XYZ Photography" or "Photo Credit: The PicsRUs Studio").

- **Page slugs** — In many instances, the PR professional prepares several photos and captions that will be sent to different many outlets. In the case where a document or email message contains multiple photos and captions, page slugs contribute to a clear understanding of how many pages of captions there are and where the reader is within the document.

There are countless cliches created to convey the importance and significance of a single image to the human eye and mind. It is not uncommon to hear sayings such as "A picture is worth a thousand words" or "A photo captures the essence of a single moment in time." Photo captions augment photographs and images and enhance readers' understanding and comprehension of the relevance and significance of the story through imagery and text.

A quality photo caption should be accurate and complete, providing a clear description of what is in the photo and the appropriate context to explain the significance of the photo and why it was taken and shared. Since not all captioned photos are accompanied by a complete news article or story, it is important that the caption be thorough and written well enough to stand alone without any additional long-form content.

9.2 — HOW DOES THE PHOTO CAPTIONING PROCESS WORK FOR PR PROFESSIONALS?

Sometimes, there is one primary photo that accompanies a news release or media kit that needs to be captioned before it can be shared with the media. In that scenario, it is fairly easy to write a single caption and then distribute it along with other media-oriented content. On other occasions and for special events, writing captions is a marathon process that requires numerous captions tailored for different types of media outlets operating on varying publication deadlines.

As an example, if a PR client hosts a formal gala with celebrity attendees and a charitable theme and targets several audiences, photos from the event are relevant to a lot of different media outlets that publish related content. At the conclusion of the gala, the event photographer may send over hundreds of photos for the PR professionals to review, select, caption and distribute to secure the maximum amount of media coverage. Out of the hundreds of photos, there may be a total of 15 quality photos that align with the potential media outlets. Each photo needs to be captioned, and each caption should be written in a way that connects with the target audiences.

If a particular photo focuses on the celebrity who attended the event, the media advisory, photo and photo caption will be sent to celebrity and lifestyle publications and online celebrity news outlets. A different photo of the celebrity pictured with the executive director of the charity might be captioned and sent to local daily and weekly newspapers in the hometown and also to publications that feature celebrity lifestyles. If the celebrity or executive is a high-profile individual who also identifies with a specific demographic, then the write-up, photo and caption also can be distributed to those media outlets. Some of the publications will need the information within hours, others within days, and some need the information for production but will not actually publish the content for another month. The PR professional's job is to know and understand where the story opportunities are and to understand the journalists' respective deadlines — and to meet them.

Not all images are the same, so it is beneficial to adhere to basic guidelines about photo captions to clearly communicate with readers and viewers.

Captions for Social Media Content

Online captions should be written with the user experience (UX) in mind, meaning professional communicators should acknowledge that attention spans are short, screens are small, and compliance with accessibility standards is important. Online captions are often geared toward engagement, compelling readers to respond or react to posted content. Along with the standard information that explains the image and what is happening in the picture, social media photo captions often include a question for the reader to answer or issue a call to action, motivating them to "like" or share a post. Consider this example: "Remember this celebrity? You won't believe what they look like now! Click here to see them now." Online captions tend to be more conversational and informal in tone, as the target audience is mostly consumers and end users versus professional journalists.

Captions for Images With Nonhuman Subjects

It goes without saying that people love their pets. In many cases, animal lovers or animal welfare organizations that work to protect and support "furry friends" have names for the animals. When featured in a photo, animals with names should be identified by their name and their species or breed, as seen here: "Cobalt (r) is a French Bulldog available for adoption and currently residing at the Altamonte Animal Shelter."

Captions for Photos With Large Groups or Unnamed Individuals

When it is not feasible or productive to name everyone pictured in a photo, another option is to identify the group or event that connects the people in the picture. See the following example: "Runners gather at the starting line for the Friends & Family CureRun marathon charity event on Sept. 8 in Dallas, Texas."

Captions for Photos With Inanimate Objects

Captions for photos of things should clearly describe what is seen in the picture and explain why the image is important. This practice is demonstrated here: "A massive sinkhole swallowed two vehicles on Saturday, Oct. 31, at the 2 Dollar Warehouse on Main Street in Rileyton, Delaware. Contrary to online rumors, the sinkhole was not a Halloween prank to attract more customers but rather a ground collapse that posed a threat to pedestrians."

Captions for Pictures That Include a Public Figure or Celebrity Subject

At special events when a celebrity or public figure is in attendance, there are often a lot of photos of individuals gathered because of the celebrity presence. Identifying the celebrity in the photo first is acceptable, because the story often revolves around their attendance. See, for example,

"Actor John Doe (center) signs autographs with fans on April 23 during a lunch break outside the set of the new movie 'Title Here' in production in Solar Springs, New Mexico."

Captions for Archived or Previously Published Photos

Photos are not always new or "for immediate release" because they have been published before. This is often the case with standard headshots of elected officials or high-profile corporate executives. Sometimes, photos of iconic or historic images are archived or filed with news outlets and used repeatedly as part of standard media coverage. "In this file photo, President Jane Doe greets visitors at the Military Heroes Memorial in Washington, D.C., on Jan. 1 to commemorate the anniversary of their sacrifice and to thank them for their service."

TIPS FOR BEGINNERS: CHECKLIST FOR WRITING EFFECTIVE CAPTIONS

- Check all facts, including name spellings, titles, dates and locations, for photo caption content to ensure accuracy.
- Write in the present tense, using active voice, when possible.
- Identify all main subjects and major actions captured by the image.
- Identify photo subjects from left to right, seated to standing, or from primary named subject to secondary subjects.
- Don't just state the obvious in a caption (e.g., "John Smith stands beside Jane Smith"); provide additional context for why the individuals are standing together in the photo.
- Write captions that can stand alone without being accompanied by an article or long-form editorial content.
- Include specific dates (days and months) and locations in photo captions.
- Write captions using the inverted-pyramid format, answering the questions who, what, when, where and why.
- Avoid subjective language or judgmental statements in a caption that are a matter of opinion and perspective (e.g., "unruly fans," "angry protesters," "boisterous students").
- For archived or previously published photos (found within an existing library of previously captured and published images), be sure to indicate that status detail in the caption release date information and within the context of the caption (e.g., "In this university yearbook photo taken in May 2024, Professor A.B. Caldwell accompanies graduating seniors to Shepherd Auditorium to receive their degrees during the spring commencement ceremony for Talmont College in City, State.")
- Use descriptions to identify a main subject in a photo that has multiple people (e.g., "Widget Inc. CEO Michal Freulen (holding the trophy) celebrates with the sales team on Dec. 30 in the company's regional Topeka, Kansas, office to conclude another successful year.")
- Use punctuation for clarity in specifying directions and locations of subjects in a photo (e.g., "Nate Torres, far right, presents Employee Achievement Awards to seven Big Company team members on Jul. 14 during the annual meeting in Chicago, Illinois.")

AP Style Caption Tips

Ethics is an important concern when using photos and captions for distribution to the media. Within the news values section of the AP stylebook, the content written about photos provides guidance on general standards of practice to follow to maintain the integrity of the photos used and to appropriately describe the images within the caption text.

Per the AP stylebook, in general, photos should not be digitally altered from their original image, with the following exceptions: a) minor adjustments such as cropping and color correction and b) removal of irrelevant background images or details that do not alter the facts or significance of the photo. To the extent possible, all photo subjects should be clearly identified in the caption body, accompanied by the date, location and a description of the activities taking place.

9.3 — WRITING GREAT CAPTIONS

The photo caption template in Figure 9.1 offers tips and suggestions for explaining the content, context and relevance of what is occurring in a photo and how to concisely convey that information to readers.

Photo Caption Example

Figure 9.2 features two women overlooking the New York City skyline with their backs to the camera. A sample caption, created using the photo caption template in Figure 9.1, demonstrates how to incorporate all the details needed to adequately inform the reader about what they are seeing in the photo.

FIGURE 9.1 ■ **Photo Caption Template**

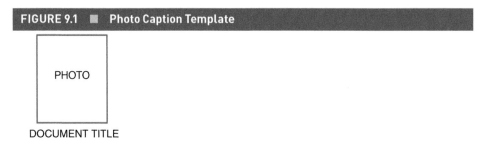

PHOTO

DOCUMENT TITLE

                                        RELEASE DATE INFORMATION FOR MEDIA

CAPTION HEADLINE

DATELINE – Photo caption body identifying the Who, What, When, Where and Why of the photo.
[Photo Credit: Source of Photo]

###

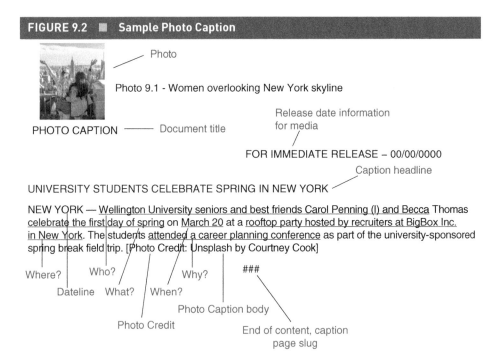

FIGURE 9.2 ■ Sample Photo Caption

Incomplete Versus Complete Photo Captions

In this brief exercise, let's take the opportunity to compare a quality, complete caption with an incomplete caption for the photo in Figure 9.3 to examine how they are different and why complete caption content is more helpful to the reader.

Consider this first caption: "Lightning struck several structures yesterday during a powerful storm system that left thousands without power." From a public relations and media relations outreach perspective, Caption 1 only confirms what is clearly obvious in the photo, which is that lightning is striking. The photo caption does not clearly state where the storm is or why the photo is relevant to readers. Now, consider this caption: "Lightning bolts illuminate the sky and strike a landmark abandoned building on Aug. 9 during an evening electrical storm in Wautega, North Dakota, leaving more than 1,000 homes without power. Customer service representatives from the Home Supply Store offered free demonstrations to customers the next day at the same location, providing training on how to safely operate home generators and restore electricity in the wake of the storm."

As a PR representative for the Home Supply Store, this image and the caption will underscore the importance of the products and services offered by the client, which include using a generator to restore power in homes during electrical outages. The caption content not only explains what is occurring in the photo but also includes the date and location of the storm. Additionally, the caption offers context that clarifies why the photo and information in the caption are relevant to the reader.

Caption Writing Exercises

Now, try out these five caption-writing exercises:

FIGURE 9.3   ■   Lightning Striking During an Evening Storm

Source: Photo by Michael D on Unsplash

Writing Exercise 1

Write and punctuate an AP style caption for Figure 9.4 that clearly identifies the individuals in the photo and the relevance of the photo to technology-oriented media outlets.

- Details: Group is called Women of Color in Technology

- Activity: IT team group photo during "Code Women" conference lunch break

- Date and Location: Friday, Nov. 14, at Waterfall Conference Center in Sacramento, California

- Team member names (13) from left: Ariana Jeffreys, Maria Rolando, Michelle Kendrickson, Ana Pollard, Mikka Shepard, Aleah Pope, Sandra Dillard, Joanna Beard, Kia Johnson, Anna Stewart, Lola Whellon, Natasha Little, Kiera Smith.

Writing Exercise 2

Write an AP style caption for Figure 9.5 that explains the activity and relevance of the photo without using subjective or judgmental language and opinions.

FIGURE 9.4 ■ Women of Color in Technology Group Photo

Source: Photo by Christina @ wocintechchat.com on Unsplash

FIGURE 9.5 ■ Police and Demonstrators in Paris, France

Source: Photo by Koshu Kunii on Unsplash

- Details: Two unnamed women stand in front of a police barricade on the streets of Paris.

- Activity: Social justice rally and march in France to end discrimination around the world.

- Date and Location: December 28, 2020, in Paris, France.

Writing Exercise 3

Write an AP style caption for Figure 9.6 that clearly identifies the individuals in the photo and the relevance of the photo to business-related media contacts.

- Presenter: Mark Williamston, sales manager at StartUps Innovation Space

- Details: Making a sales pitch to potential business partners for a joint-venture opportunity

- Activity: Local entrepreneurs attend a presentation regarding business joint ventures

- Date and Location: Tuesday, June 8, at Ridgemont Business Complex in Redfalls, Washington

FIGURE 9.6 ■ Man Presenting to Group in Warehouse Setting

Source: Photo by Austin Distel on Unsplash

Writing Exercise 4

Write an AP style caption for Figure 9.7 that clearly identifies the subjects in the photo and the relevance of the photo to nature-oriented and outdoors-featuring publications.

- Details: Elephant family, from left: Tazo, Sophie, and matriarch Bella go out for a stroll at the Masai Mara National Reserve in Kenya.

- Activity: Protected wildlife on a reserve are shown in the picture to encourage conservation efforts.

- Date and Location: Sunday, Sept. 14, in Kenya (eastern Africa)

Writing Exercise 5

Write and punctuate an AP style caption for Figure 9.8 that clearly identifies the individuals in the photo and the relevance of the photo to arts and entertainment media outlets.

- Details: Dance troupe is called Rainbows & Raindrops.

- Activity: Four women practice their dance routine before an on-campus dance competition.

- Date and Location: Saturday, March 12, in Sigman Theatre on the campus of Maylord University in Greenberg, Missouri.

FIGURE 9.7   ■   Elephant Family in Kenya, Africa

Source: Photo by David Heiling on Unsplash

FIGURE 9.8   ■   Four Female Performers at Dance Rehearsal

Source: Photo by Ketan Rajput on Unsplash

9.4 — ACCESSIBILITY CONSIDERATIONS

Every social media platform that incorporates visual content also provides a way for content creators to include captioning for those with visual or hearing impairments. PR writing professionals should make clear captions a part of the deliverables for online content, affixing clear and concise descriptions of photos and video content to align with accessibility standards and formats for all audiences.

Captioning or Closed Captioning

Captioning for multimedia content refers to displaying interpretive text on a monitor or screen to convey audio or visual content for individuals with visual or hearing impairments — or individuals who simply appreciate additional explanations regarding onscreen activities. Captions that transcribe spoken words make it easier for audience members to follow along, and captions that describe visual content can be used to explain subtle or hard-to-see video elements and background actions that might otherwise be overlooked. Effective captions should accurately communicate onscreen actions so that viewers can following along with or without high-quality audio and video footage.

Clickbait Captions

As defined by Wikipedia ("Clickbait," n.d.), clickbait is a text or a thumbnail link that is designed to attract attention and to entice users to follow that link and read, view, or listen to the linked piece of online content, being typically deceptive, sensationalized, or otherwise misleading. For PR writing professionals, clickbait captions can be tempting to create because they are likely to attract more attention to online content. However, using misinformation or disinformation for the purposes of securing more hits or impressions is unethical. The responsibility required for professional content creators aligns with the ethical standards and guidelines highlighted in Chapter 2 that reiterate the roles of honesty and integrity in professional practice.

Photo Copyrights and Permissions

It is important to verify that any photos being used as part of a PR campaign or storytelling initiative by a PR professional or on behalf of a client are used within the acceptable boundaries that protect copyrighted content. Copyrights are part of federal law and protect original works, including photographs and content. Professionals should use or post only photos and images that have been officially secured for the stated purposes and distribution or purchased for usage within the parameters of the license. There are numerous stock photo sites that provide expansive catalogs of images, scenes and staged pictures (often with models or actors) and can be purchased for editorial usage or commercial productions.

Even with purchased or licensed usage, it is imperative that images not be used in an offensive or disparaging manner that could unfairly link the individuals or locations pictured with inappropriate content or activities. The AP stylebook guidelines for journalists state: "AP images must always be accurate . . . We avoid the use of generic photos or video that could be mistaken for imagery photographed for the specific story at hand, or that could unfairly link people in the images to illicit activity" (Associated Press, 2022, pp. 1095–1096).

PR TOOLKIT: CONSTITUTIONAL FAIR USE AND COPYRIGHTS

The following excerpt is published by the U.S. Congress to offer guidelines on the First Amendment, copyright laws, and constitutional fair use.

Article I, Section 8, Clause 8:

[The Congress shall have Power . . .] To promote the Progress of Science and useful Arts, by securing for limited Times to Authors and Inventors the exclusive Right to their respective Writings and Discoveries.

Copyright, by its nature, may restrict speech — it operates to prevent others from, among other things, reproducing and distributing creative expression without the copyright holder's permission. The Supreme Court has thus recognized that some restriction on expression is the inherent and intended effect of every grant of copyright. Even so, the restrictions on speech effected by copyright are not ordinarily subject to heightened scrutiny. . . .

Copyright law's other First Amendment accommodation is the fair use doctrine. Fair use is a privilege that permits certain uses of a copyrighted work, for purposes such as criticism, comment, news reporting, teaching, scholarship, or research, without the copyright holder's permission. Courts assess whether a particular use is fair using a multifactor balancing test that looks to, among other considerations, the purpose and character of the use; the nature of the copyrighted work; the amount and substantiality of the portion used; and the economic impact of the use on the market for the original work. Fair use also considers whether a use is transformative — that is, whether it adds something new, with a further purpose or different character, altering the first with new expression, meaning, or message. Fair use serves First Amendment purposes because it allows the public to use not only facts and ideas contained in a copyrighted work, but also expression itself in certain circumstances. (Constitution Annotated, n.d.)

Social Media Captions

Newer social media sites, which represent the rapidly growing group of channels and platforms, require captioning as part of the storytelling process — taking into consideration that many users are watching short-form narration with low or no audio and relying mostly on captions within each frame to relay the content. For that reason, it is helpful for content creators to write accurate and descriptive captions to provide additional context for videos, along with verbatim transcripts to mirror words that are being shared by onscreen subjects. Captions and subtitles on many social media sites are a standard part of the narrative that viewers expect.

Tags and Hashtags

In addition to photo captions, textual content accompanying online photos often includes tags and hashtags. Tagging labels or assigns words to images to make them easier to find in online searches, which also plays a role in improving search engine optimization (SEO). A hashtag (also known as the pound key, tic-tac-toe sign, or octothorpe, depending on the age of the person identifying it) is a symbol that proceeds short words and phrases to enhance online searches and to connect online topics and conversations as part of a trend or theme. Here are some examples: #PRWriting #PhotoCaptions #NationalDayOfGiving #StayStrong #HappyNewYear.

Hashtags are frequently used to galvanize online movements and to unify people with common causes or concerns and connect them across online platforms. The hash symbol itself is a useful search tool that serves as the common denominator for identifying specific content within online discourse, news content and social media posts.

CONCLUSION

Photo captions are a routine aspect of PR writing that help explain content, context and nuance within visual images. Photo captions accompany pictures that are published in print or posted online, and closed captioning is used with multimedia content to provide interpretive information about what is occurring on camera or onscreen. Well-written, clear, concise captions enhance storytelling in traditional and digital media formats. Effective photo captions assist readers and viewers with reading and comprehension whether or not there is an accompanying full news story or feature article.

KEY TERMS

hashtag	tags
photo caption	user experience (UX)

DISCUSSION QUESTIONS

1.   What is the purpose of photo captions in media relations work?

2.   What information other than the basic 5Ws should photo captions contain?

3.   What are some media distribution opportunities for photos and captions to increase the potential for media coverage?

WRITING EXERCISES

1.   Write a brief social media photo caption for an image that features two identical red hearts beside each other to be published on Feb. 14 for Valentine's Day.

INTERNAL COMMUNICATION TOOLS

LEARNING OBJECTIVES

10.1 Identify effective internal communication tools available for research in PR writing.

10.2 Understand why and how to launch and implement a SWOT analysis.

10.3 Evaluate an existing communications plan by conducting a communication audit.

10.4 Learn how to write a PR plan and incorporate metrics to measure success.

10.5 Develop a comprehensive checklist for effective media engagement.

INTRODUCTION

Making internal audiences a priority is always a smart move, and many times the answers being sought already exist inside the company. For sure, public relations is widely known for its promotional external communications — media-focused or public-facing content that is crafted for journalists or targeted directly to end users and consumer groups. However, it's important to keep in mind that category of content is the end result of an initial internal communication process that is used to survey the landscape and understand what the problems and possible resolutions of those problems might be. Additionally, many of the tools used to connect with internal audiences also function in dual roles and can be adapted for internal or external usage.

Finding the right answers for a client's public relations and strategic communication campaign begins with asking the right questions. Using a few proven techniques to analyze and understand internal audiences is a good way to develop a strong foundation for eventually building creative and effective external communication campaigns.

Generally, the first steps to launching a new creative campaign include research and planning. PR practitioners cannot begin to develop the strategic "how" until they know the basic answers to who, what, when, where and why. Thorough research provides insights and analysis into the current situation, target audiences, and previous communications efforts or activities and their respective successes or failures. The planning aspect develops a broad overview of the challenges and potential opportunities, overlaying them with available resources, timelines and a budget to fund the campaign.

Internal audiences refer to groups that are within or "inside" a particular organization as opposed to audiences that are outside — or external — observers and not involved in day-to-day leadership or operational activities. Platforms and tools that are used for internal communications include email, intranet, memoranda, conference calls, staff meetings, team-building exercises, newsletters or e-newsletters (electronic newsletters), voicemail, SMS text messages and group chats, desktop news feeds, and team project management software.

10.1 — PR RESEARCH AND PR PLANNING

Let's do a basic review of how the need for a PR campaign might materialize. A company may be experiencing declining sales or increasing competition and may want to elevate their brand's awareness through a PR campaign. A company also could be receiving a lot of negative media coverage or negative comments on social media that influence the decision to be more proactive with external communications. A company might also be new or in the startup phase and seeking ways to establish a stronger position in the marketplace. Through the process of advertising in industry trade publications, in social media posts, via word of mouth, or by submitting an official request for proposal (RFP) for an agency, solicitation for a creative firm is carried out with the expectation that companies specializing in creative content will respond and propose ideas on how to solve the communication problems that have been identified.

To get the right answers, PR professionals must begin with asking the right questions. In many instances, those questions arise from the results of a thorough analysis that paints an accurate picture of how the company is doing and how the company is viewed through the eyes of its stakeholders — groups and individuals who can affect or are affected by the company's activities. Here are some sample basic, introductory questions to jump-start the process:

- What does the company do well enough for it to be highlighted in external communications?

- Where are the opportunities for improvement to make the company more successful?

- What has social listening revealed about the relationship between the company and its stakeholders?

- What trends in society and media are working to the advantage of the company?

- What trends in society and media are working toward the detriment of the company?

- Which words come to mind and reflect top-of-mind awareness when the company's brand name is mentioned?

- What are some of the ways the company can strengthen or increase loyalty from its existing customer base?

- Does the company have a clear and compelling mission and shared values that allow stakeholder groups to become brand ambassadors?

- Is diversity, inclusion and Equity (DEI) a foundational part of the company's mission, purpose and values, and is it clearly communicated to diverse audiences?

- Does the company have a crisis communication plan in place to quickly respond to challenges and communicate with stakeholders during a crisis situation?

10.2 — CONDUCTING A SWOT ANALYSIS

A common management and analysis tool used in strategic planning for business development and creative communication plans is a SWOT analysis, an acronym that refers to the assessment of an organization's Strengths, Weaknesses, Opportunities and Threats.

As it relates to public relations planning, the results of the SWOT analysis provide insights into the status of internal and external communications activities and the organization's standing with its various audiences. Conducting a thorough SWOT analysis allows the PR practitioner or communications team to be introspective in its review process by studying internal factors, including the organization's strengths and weaknesses.

Strengths are operational pillars that support the company or institution and help build its reputation for success by fulfilling objectives, achieving established goals, and delivering on the mission and stated values. Internal strengths can be revised or reinforced at any point, because control of these factors resides within the organization and its ability to adapt to external factors as needed. As an example, excellent customer service may be a strength and part of the brand's reputation. That strength can be built upon and reinforced through ongoing training and implementation of new ways to surpass the expectations of customers and deliver excellent service.

Weaknesses are considered vulnerabilities that potentially expose the organization to risk or harm — internal factors that can be altered or changed by leadership or management as needed to protect the company's interests. Once identified, internal weaknesses can be addressed and resolved to eliminate the possibility of harm in a particular area. For example, if the information technology (IT) team identifies a software vulnerability in the e-commerce shopping cart on the business website, a patch or fix can be applied to reduce the likelihood of a cyberattack on the company. An internal decision to address a problem can immediately resolve the issue and eliminate the weakness.

Opportunities represent external environmental factors (economic, societal, political, etc.) outside the organization's control that, if taken advantage of, may benefit the company and contribute to its reputational or overall success. For example, a company cannot control economic policies put in place by the federal government; however, if those policies are favorable to the organization, they can be leveraged to its advantage and utilized to propel the company toward greater success.

Threats are external factors that can threaten or harm a company or exploit the company's weaknesses to produce further harm. Though an organization may not be able to directly control the source of the threat, its leaders may be able to mitigate harm or sidestep a direct hit through planning and a timely communication response. Just as positive economic policies can be leveraged, negative economic forces, such as an economic recession, can threaten the viability of a company. Advanced strategic planning may help better position a business to avoid some of the negative effects of threatening factors beyond the company's control.

The following figures display different SWOT analyses. See Figure 10.1 for a SWOT quadrant layout, Figure 10.2 for a SWOT column layout, and Figure 10.3 for a SWOT infographic.

The benefits of conducting an effective and thorough SWOT analysis are numerous. For starters, the SWOT results provide a clear assessment of the true nature of the organization for which a communications plan and messaging strategy will be developed. It's not enough in PR writing to create random goals and strategies and to employ creative tactics. Any quality campaign must reflect the true values of the company and its mission — and then accurately communicate those priorities to specific audiences in a memorable and compelling way.

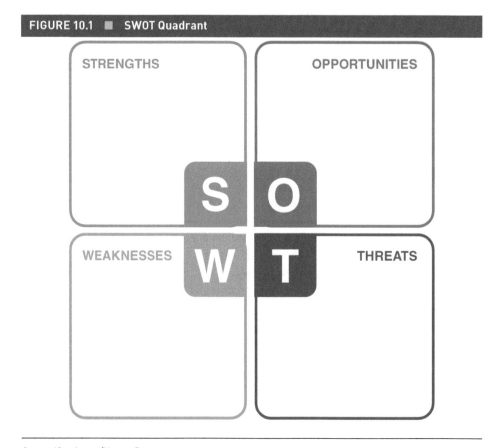

FIGURE 10.1 ■ SWOT Quadrant

STRENGTHS

OPPORTUNITIES

WEAKNESSES

THREATS

Source: iStock.com/Nastya Bevz

FIGURE 10.2 ■ SWOT 4-Column Table

SWOT ANALYSIS

Lorem ipsum dolor sit amet, consectetur adipiscing elit, sed do eiusmod tempor incididunt ut labore et dolore magna aliqua Duis aute irure dolor in reprehenderit in voluptate velit esse sed do

Strengths

Lorem ipsum dolor sit amet, consectetur adipiscing elit, sed do eiusmod temp or incididunt ut labore et olore magna aliqua. Ut en im ad maim veniam

Weaknesses

Lorem ipsum dolor sit amet, consectetur adipiscing elit, sed do eiusmod temp or incididunt ut labore et olore magna aliqua. Ut en im ad maim veniam

Opportunities

Lorem ipsum dolor sit amet, consectetur adipiscing elit, sed do eiusmod temp or incididunt ut labore et olore magna aliqua. Ut en im ad maim veniam

Threats

Lorem ipsum dolor sit amet, consectetur adipiscing elit, sed do eiusmod temp or incididunt ut labore et olore magna aliqua. Ut en im ad maim veniam

Source: iStock.com/ribkhan

FIGURE 10.3 ■ SWOT Infographic

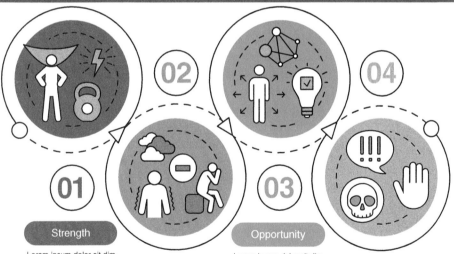

Source: iStock.com/bsd studio

10.3 — COMMUNICATION AUDITS

A communication audit is generally a long and comprehensive report that details all of the internal and external communication activities of a company, organization or institution. The audit examines what tools are in place and how effective they are at meeting the stated mission and communication goals of the company. Additionally, the communication audit identifies internal stakeholders and external stakeholder groups and how effectively the brand communicates with those groups.

A quality communication audit provides invaluable information to the PR professional to gain a better understanding of how to develop an effective communications campaign for the client. Because the audit reviews and assesses all existing communications currently in place, the results, conclusions and recommendations section may identify areas for improvement and opportunities to implement new or more effective communication strategies.

Communication audits are internal documents and therefore are not required to be written in Associated Press (AP) style, which is reserved for content developed for the media. Individuals receiving a copy typically include the client's leadership and management team, the client's communications and/or marketing team, and the PR practitioners who will be working on the upcoming PR campaign.

A three-step process is used to create the framework for a thorough communication audit: 1) research, 2) analysis, and 3) evaluation. The research section of the audit incorporates historical background content, including the founding, mission, vision and values. It also includes quantitative and qualitative data that sheds light on the quality of communications inside and outside the operations of the organization. If there have been any particularly successful or unsuccessful communication campaigns, that information is included in the audit as a point of reference that provides guidance for future campaigns.

The analysis section does the heavy lifting of the report by reviewing, measuring and assessing internal and external communications, including but not limited to print, broadcast, online, social media, marketing, promotional, crisis and corporate communications and related messaging platforms. Analysis of social media and web-based blogs and sites might review when the content was posted; how often it is updated; how relevant the content is to readers and subscribers; how well content is written for search engine optimization (SEO); how many subscribers, followers or fans engage with the site; how many style or grammatical errors there are; how many reciprocal links are included in the copy; and many more details that paint of picture of how well the communications content achieves its purpose.

Finally, the evaluation section often includes a SWOT analysis and a list of conclusions and recommendations for how better to move forward with enhanced or improved communications activities. As a reminder, SWOT stands for Strengths, Weaknesses, Opportunities, and Threats. Strengths and weaknesses are internal and within the control of the company or organization, while opportunities and threats are external and outside the control of the company or organization.

Most agencies and textbooks share a similar outline for the sections that need to be included in the communication audit. The format is similar to a research paper or formal presentation in that the text is double-spaced and organized by sections and content. Page numbers and generous 1-inch margins are common, leaving some space for comments and notes about the audit findings or recommendations. What follows are the standard sections commonly found in a communication audit.

Title Page

At a minimum, the communication audit title page should include the name of the client, the title ("Communication Audit"), the name(s) of the author or authors, and the date of the report.

Table of Contents

The table of contents (TOC) should include a list of each section or subsection found in the report along with the page numbers corresponding to the first page of each section.

Executive Summary

This section is a detailed, high-level overview of what is included in the report. It is often joked that this may be the only section the client reads, so make sure it includes all the pertinent information in a snapshot so that the most important discoveries, concerns, findings and recommendations are shared.

Introduction

The communication audit introduction not only introduces the report, it also introduces the company or organization and provides information about its founding and history. The introductory section clearly lists the mission, vision and values statements along with basic information about the company's structure and products or services.

Audit Goals

This brief section articulates why the communication audit is being conducted. Understanding the "why" when undertaking such a large project helps the PR professional "begin with the end in mind." Audit goals may relate to understanding stakeholder perceptions about the organization or soliciting input and feedback about whether to rebrand the entire organization.

Methodology

Research is an essential part of the communication audit, as are the tools used to conduct the research. The methodology section lists and describes the research tools that were used to acquire information to develop the report. Some of the tools often used are surveys, questionnaires, interviews and polls.

Audit Diary

An audit diary is a reconciliation and accounting of research and methodologies to confirm the work that was done to complete the research. The audit diary simply lists the date, time and location of activities that occurred to compile information during the research phase.

Results of the Audit Process

Once the research and an assessment of all internal and external communications is complete, the results portion of the document reports out on what was found and what the information represents. Not only does this section provide analytics, but it also offers insight and guidance on what next steps should be taken based on the findings.

Conclusions and Recommendations

After the executive summary, this section is the most likely to be read by the client to get a better understanding of what needs to be done to improve the organization's communications. Also included in this section is the SWOT analysis and a list of recommended action items for improving future communications strategies, documents, and messaging for internal and external audiences and publics.

Appendix

Tables, graphs, charts, interview transcripts, raw research data, etc., can be found in the Appendix section of a communication audit. This section includes any additional information or content that was used in the process of data collection to inform the contents of the audit.

10.4 — PR PLANS AND INCORPORATING METRICS

A comprehensive public relations plan is one of the more common, useful and helpful documents that a new PR practitioner will create and use for most client campaigns. The internal PR plan developed for the client's knowledge and the PR practitioner's guidance are essentially an outline and a road map demonstrating how to implement and execute a PR campaign from start to finish.

At the beginning and as an introduction for the client, the PR plan provides a snapshot assessment of the environmental landscape, current situation, and associated rationale for why the plan is needed. This opening situation analysis explains any background information and influencing factors that may affect the client and what prompted the need or desire to launch a new campaign. The PR plan may be needed to address a growing problem, take advantage of a current opportunity, maintain a pattern of existing growth, jump-start stalled progress, or counter negative media coverage. Regardless of the motivation, the PR plan document lays out a step-by-by approach for what needs to happen, when it needs to happen, and who needs to make it happen.

The situation analysis (also referred to as a "situational analysis") provides context around the unique opportunity to be leveraged or the problem that the PR plan is designed to solve. Used as the opening paragraph at the top of the PR plan, the situation analysis shares insights on internal and external factors and provides a brief assessment of the company's strengths, weaknesses, opportunities and threats, which will be used to guide development of the plan's overall campaign objectives, goals, strategies, tactics, actions and timeline.

Following the situation analysis is a clear statement of the PR plan goal and objectives. Though the terms "goals" and "objectives" are sometimes used interchangeably in different sectors — journalism/media, business and professional schools — the purpose of stating them is to identify a clear result and focal point for accomplishment and the related steps needed to solve the problem or maximize the opportunity. This statement generally begins with an infinitive — an active, present-tense statement in the form of "to do" that indicates action (e.g., "to increase awareness of [New-Product Name] among targeted primary existing customers by launching a 6-month social media campaign that features celebrity influencers using and endorsing the product). For clarity purposes, notice that the PR campaign statement of intent also includes a specific methodology and timeline, both with inherent metrics that can be measured during the evaluation period.

TIPS FOR BEGINNERS: FORMULA FOR WRITING AN EFFECTIVE PR CAMPAIGN GOAL OR OBJECTIVE

The goal of the campaign is the overarching purpose for why you're launching the campaign. Everything listed in the PR plan beneath the goal should work toward fulfilling the specific campaign objectives, meaning that the actions, tactics and strategies should lead to fulfillment of the overall objectives and goal.

S.M.A.R.T. Goal/Objective Formula

Formula: [Infinitive and action verb] + [campaign objective of client's product/service] with [targeted audience] by launching [time period] [communications channel(s) featuring tactical solutions].

Example: To increase awareness of [New-Product Name] among targeted primary existing customers by launching a 6-month social media campaign that features celebrity influencers using and endorsing the product.

Targeted Audiences

In a communications plan, targeted audiences are the individuals and groups of people with whom you most want to engage in a dialogue about the brand through various communications channels. Those channels are determined based on the demographic and psychographic profiles of the audiences and coincide with the media platforms through which messages are sent and received to accomplish a specific outcome.

For purposes of the PR plan, the top three targeted audiences are identified as primary, secondary and tertiary: the first and most important priority group; the second and next group that might benefit from a crossover opportunity or ancillary promotions; and the third group, which isn't necessarily a focal point or budgetary priority but offers additional opportunities for exposure and increased awareness for the company.

A small, regional mobile smart device company on the West Coast introducing a new, upgraded version of an existing device might be interested in getting its current customer base to purchase the newest version. As this target audience is already familiar with the brand and already using the current model of the product, they represent an easy and obvious choice as a primary targeted audience to engage with the upgrade. Customers currently using a competitor's mobile smart device might be a potential secondary audience who could be appealed to with messages that focus on new features and benefits of the upgraded device that their current device does not have. Finally, individuals who are new to the mobile smart device market (first-time users or purchasers, such as newly employed college graduates) are an ideal tertiary audience. As new consumers in the purchasing space, they may need more information, education and awareness about the products and options available; however, they can be introduced to the brand and become potential lifelong customers.

Maintaining that order, the PR plan section for target audiences would include a brief description and audience profile:

1. Primary — Existing customers of brand [old device] who want to upgrade; employed professionals ages 25-55 years old on the West Coast

2. Secondary — Brand competitor customers desiring an upgrade; employed professionals ages 25-55 years old on the West Coast

3. Tertiary — West Coast-based, newly employed college graduates seeking to enter the mobile smart device market; first-time users or purchasers

S.M.A.R.T. PR Plan Objectives

PR campaign objectives are prioritized lists that help organize and realize the ultimate purpose for the plan. They outline and specify the steps needed to implement a strategy and accomplish the ultimate goal. The S.M.A.R.T. acronym is used to assist PR practitioners in creating complete and comprehensive goals and objectives that encompass details that can be easily explained, implemented and measured. The meaning of S.M.A.R.T. in PR campaign implementation will be described next.

S — Specific

Does the written or stated objective reflect enough detail that it's clear what needs to be accomplished, who's responsible for the activities, and when the tasks will be completed?

M — Measurable

Can you quantify the results of actions taken during implementation of the PR campaign? Is there a baseline by which the campaign achievements can be measured?

A — Attainable/Achievable or Actionable

Is this objective possible and within reach based on the personnel and resources available? Are the outlined goals and objectives practical, and can they be quickly acted upon?

R — Realistic or Relevant

Does this objective align with the mission, vision and purpose of the company, and does it work toward fulfilling the stated purpose of the campaign?

T — Timely or Time Sensitive

Is there a clearly defined starting point and ending point for the campaign and the intermediate steps in the process of implementing the campaign? Are there deadlines or benchmarks built into the campaign calendar that reinforce accountability and keep the process moving forward in an expedient manner?

Examples of S.M.A.R.T. in Practice

The S.M.A.R.T. approach is merely a guideline for writing clear and understandable goals and objectives. Here are three examples of what is typically a list of three to five campaign objectives included in a PR plan:

- Write and distribute three press releases in February and March about the new mobile smart device using a paid distribution service that targets technology writers and producers on the West Coast; conduct journalist/media follow-up with email pitches and interview opportunities.

S.M.A.R.T. analysis: There is enough detail and specificity for a client to understand exactly what is going to get done. The metric represented by three press releases can be quantified. If only two press releases are completed, the objective was not accomplished. Even for a small team, writing three press releases over the course of two months is an attainable, relevant and reasonable means of increasing awareness about a new product launch to journalists who cover technology. The time element is included by listing February and March as the months to complete the tasks.

- During Q1 (first quarter of the year), pitch 25 print, broadcast and freelance journalists and bloggers who cover technology on the West Coast to interview and cover the new mobile smart device as a featured segment.

S.M.A.R.T. analysis: Though the names and contact information aren't included, there is enough information for the client to understand that a targeted list of 25 journalists and media outlets will be used to pitch story ideas. The incorporated metric is 25 contacts, which is quite achievable given the numerous channels, outlets and platforms available for connecting with journalists and bloggers. As the pitches are targeted toward individuals who cover technology, the approach is relevant and realistic, with a time-focused element of first-quarter activity.

- During Q2 (second quarter of the year), secure one celebrity social media influencer with 1 million+ followers to use and endorse the mobile smart device as part of their lifestyle for 30 days, engaging their followers with 3× weekly posts on Instagram and TikTok.

S.M.A.R.T. analysis: Securing a celebrity influencer is clear and measurable, based on the description that defines the desired online audience following. Since celebrity endorsements are often paid gigs, it's a fairly straightforward process to include payments in the budget to cover relevant fees. The associated product aligns with audiences who are familiar with technology and likely have a social media presence, so the content is relevant and realistic for what needs to be accomplished. The time element is highlighted for the second quarter of the year.

General S.M.A.R.T. Advice

Ask these basic questions to ensure the S.M.A.R.T. guidelines are in place:

- If anyone not associated with the client or the campaign reads this goal or objective, will they know and understand what is supposed to happen?

- Can I quantify the results of this goal or objective by measuring a starting point and an ending point that identifies success or failure?

- Can this be done with what's in place, and does it make sense and fulfill the overall purpose of the campaign?

- Is this practical and beneficial and in alignment with the brand message?

- Is it clear when this element of the campaign begins and/or ends?

PR Strategy

A strategy answers the question "How are we going to accomplish these goals and objectives?" Strategy represents an informed approach that relates to and aligns with a specific audience or key public. Strategies tend to be broader in scope and reach and can be broken down into smaller segments, and they often are correlated with audience-specific communication channels and media platforms.

Using categorical strategic approaches can be helpful in developing effective strategy statements, especially when needing to differentiate strategies from tactics in a PR plan. As an example, a strategic approach for increasing awareness could be Celebrity Association, which answers the strategic "how" for increasing awareness about the featured product or service. One might consider using Celebrity Association to enhance brand loyalty and increase awareness about a new product by recruiting five TikTok celebrity influencers to demonstrate that current users upgrading to the new mobile smart device will enhance daily living and improve social status with peers, for example.

Pay attention to how the strategy addresses the desired outcome of enhancing brand loyalty and increasing awareness with a specific primary audience of current device users. It also specifies which platform to utilize and how to leverage that channel, which is by recruiting celebrities to endorse the product with their followers on social media.

Strategy planning is also where message design is formalized and finalized. Usually, messages are audience specific and developed in two parts: primary messages and secondary messages. The primary part of the message focuses on the purpose of the campaign and reinforces the "what" you want the audience or public to know, along with the appeal that answers "why" the public should respond or react to the message. The secondary process of messaging focuses on the rationale and acts as validation for the primary message. It may include data, facts, statistics, testimonials or background information that supports the overall messaging strategy.

In a PR plan, the tactical section is where we often see the creative ideas emerge. Since it's easy to confuse strategies with tactics, think of tactics as tools — the tools that will be employed to accomplish the strategic approach and implement the "how." Generally speaking, tactics cannot be broken down into smaller parts or approaches and often include specific media channels or brand-name outlets. For example, this might look like posting one endorsement from a satisfied client about the new product on X (formerly Twitter) each day for three weeks, including a captioned customer photo with a link to the website and two relevant hashtags, and tagging the customer and a celebrity endorser in the post.

Most PR plans also include a section for actions, often organized as a to-do list, and the budget. Actions outline specific duties along with the person or group that is responsible for performing the tasks and the associated deadline for completion. The budget is an all-inclusive breakdown of costs and expenses associated with implementing the campaign. Often a spreadsheet is used to organize campaign elements by the types of work, products or services needed to fulfill the campaign. Budget line items might include hourly rates for all campaign personnel (including employees and subcontractors), paid news release distribution wire services, paid social media ad campaigns, fees for celebrity influencers, photography fees, videography and editing services, campaign team overhead expenses, travel, profit margin, etc.

PR Plan Metrics

Metrics are quantifiable tools that allow a PR professional to monitor and measure the impact and reach of a communications campaign. Clear metrics tools and platforms that are communicated at the beginning and during the development of a PR campaign also can help manage and support reasonable client expectations. It's not unusual in the course of creating content for clients to hear them say something along the lines of "I want our video to go viral," even if the product or service that is being promoted or publicized isn't that interesting or captivating to online audiences. It's also not unusual for clients to have unrealistic expectations about what the results of a PR campaign should be; after all, their interests and focus are on their company — not the competition, popularity, budget or other background factors that may influence the success of other online content. An initial conversation about the approach, metrics and anticipated reach, engagement, interactions and results can help manage expectations at the beginning and help define what success for the brand looks like for the client's campaign.

Background and Research

A thorough review of background information that focuses on the environmental landscape and societal factors influencing the client and the client's communication plan helps guide the process and assist the PR practitioner in making good decisions toward developing a comprehensive PR plan. A quality background study also identifies previous issues or repeating patterns that may affect a new campaign launch. Quantitative and qualitative research provide important details and context and establish the basis for developing the campaign, based on empirical data that reflects the sentiments of the target audiences and key publics.

Situation Analysis

The situation analysis basically informs users of the PR plan about how they arrived at the point of needing a PR plan. It describes events leading up to the current situation, along with a description and explanation of the problem to be solved or the opportunity to be leveraged.

Core Problem or Opportunity

The core problem or opportunity is a succinct statement that articulates the main issue that needs to be resolved by the campaign or the external opportunity that can be seized and utilized to advance the goals and objectives of the campaign if properly leveraged. The statement encapsulates the motivating factor for why the campaign is being developed for implementation.

S.M.A.R.T. Goals and S.M.A.R.T. Objectives

The S.M.A.R.T. acronym can be used for objectives or goals to ensure their consistency with the outlined components: Specific, Measurable, Attainable/Achievable, Realistic/Relevant, Timely or Time Sensitive. The PR campaign goal highlights the big-picture result that is desired by taking specific steps toward fulfillment, and the individual objectives are usually listed as three to five bulleted items that when accomplished help achieve the No. 1 ultimate result for the campaign.

Core Audiences and Publics

Targeted audiences are key groups of people for whom campaign messaging is developed. Publics are smaller groups within audiences that share demographic or psychographic commonalities that shape and narrow the strategic messages. As an example, a company that provides educational and tutoring materials may determine that parents are one of their target audiences and educators represent another. Within those audiences are smaller, more segmented key publics, which might include parents of elementary school children or high school teachers.

Key Messaging and Platforms

Oftentimes, there is a broad and singular primary message that communicators want to share on behalf of a client, and it appeals to all audiences and publics. Then there are segmented secondary messages that specifically appeal to particular publics that may have varying or differing opinions and viewpoints or unique motivations and self-interests that influence their decision-making and behavior.

Strategies and Tactics

Strategies and tactics address the "how" and targeted approach to fulfilling campaign requirements, along with outlining the tools that will be used to do so. Strategies, tactics and messaging are usually coordinated to fine-tune messaging for key publics.

Actions and Timelines

Actions are a to-do list of tasks and the groups or individuals responsible for completing them, complete with dates and deadlines to confirm progress reports and when projects are finished.

Checklists and Accountability

As part of the actions and timeline section in a PR plan, checklists and assignment lists are used as a form of accountability to make sure someone answers for work that needs to be done to keep the campaign implementation on schedule.

Budget

Budget worksheets can be designed on a single-page spreadsheet that categorizes and lists potential campaign expenses by the type of work, services or products needed to implement and execute the campaign. The budget includes all elements of the campaign, from personnel, research, content creation and production to travel and accommodations.

Evaluation and Metrics

The criteria for evaluation should reflect the stated S.M.A.R.T. PR campaign goal and objectives listed in the plan. Ideally, each strategy and tactic also includes an inherent metric so that the evaluation section of any results report can be clearly listed for review and discussion. Evaluations are important for charting future courses and documenting what worked and what didn't work during the campaign. That information also helps establish "best practices" for the client and adds to the cache of reliable approaches and tools for the PR practitioner.

Summary Reports

A thorough summary report that includes an executive summary and overview of the campaign highlights is a useful tool in helping client executives understand what took place and why, what was accomplished, what performed well or not so well, and how much it cost to achieve the measured results. The report also summarizes the overall return on investment (ROI), or what the client got in return for the money and resources that were invested.

10.5 — MEDIA ENGAGEMENT CHECKLIST

Much like the initial research that prepares and shapes the framework for a successful PR campaign, the written media prep Q&A document prepares and shapes the framework for a successful media interview.

A media prep document is an internal communication that is used to prepare the client to respond to potential questions and statements made about their organization. The document also lists the interviewer, date, time, location, media outlet background and logistical details to ensure a smooth interview process. The private — often confidential — document is used to anticipate and prepare the interview subject for any and all questions while also outlining in bullet points the proposed messaging strategy and approved talk tracks. The idea behind this document is to prepare the client well enough that there are no surprises and that no questions from the reporter or journalist will catch the interviewee off guard. Your role as the PR practitioner and media-training coach is to ensure the comfort level and delivery of answers to all anticipated questions: the good, the bad and the ugly.

The opening section of a media prep Q&A document provides background information about the media outlet requesting the interview; interview, publication or show details, such as format and political affiliations and ideologies; and any additional information to make sure the interviewee knows in advance what to expect. Essential information also includes the name(s) of the interviewer, the name and type of media outlet, the format of the interview (e.g., live or pre-recorded), the length of the segment, and when the show or segment will air if it's being taped to air at a later date. Figure 10.4 displays a graphic depicting the structure for strategic messaging.

The common denominators for strategic communication and strategic messaging are planned and intentional content. Everything is anticipated, planned, prepared and scripted — down to the amount of eye contact, rate of speech and word choice.

The countless disastrous interviews available to view while watching the news during any crisis situation make it appear that there is no preparation, planning or strategy at all. However, when done correctly and consistently, any interview (even during a challenge or crisis) can be

FIGURE 10.4 ■ Umbrella Strategic Messaging

Overarching theme of Messaging

Strategic Communication

- **Strategic messaging (umbrella)**

- **Talk tracks (handle)**
  Various topics of planned communication.

- **Talking points (grip)**
  Anecdotal content and supporting details.

Plan. Process. Purpose.

viewed as an opportunity to elevate the brand, control the flow of communication, and advance the narrative of the company as it aligns with the larger corporate mission, vision and brand.

The Q&A section of the document basically lists all of the potential questions that will be asked during an interview and includes the appropriate, approved (by the communications and legal teams, if needed) responses in bullet-point format.

Consider the following sample media question and response for a Q&A prep regarding a scenario in which communicators are asked who is responsible for the defective manufacturing of a new mobile smart device.

- [Company Name] is committed to manufacturing quality products and ensuring excellent service that exceeds our customers' expectations.

- There is an ongoing internal investigation to determine the origination of any mobile smart device that did not meet our high production standards.

- Once that investigation is complete, we will issue a report to our customers and to the public, along with our plan to implement any necessary steps to continue our track record of producing quality devices and delivering excellent service.

Pay close attention to the intentional and carefully selected wording that does not embrace or repeat the negative or inflammatory language used in the question while also promoting core statements that reinforce the brand identity. In terms of formatting, it is acceptable to include complete sentences if they are short and easy to repeat; however, bulleted lists of sentence fragments are acceptable for quick reminders of the talking points. To that end, large blocks of text are difficult to memorize and deliver under pressure and also come across as scripted, forced or unnatural. The bulleted format with sentence fragments can simply include key words, phrases and terminology that prompt a more robust response to the question.

TIPS FOR BEGINNERS: HOW TO DEVELOP A STRATEGIC MESSAGING PLAN

Consider the following concepts when putting together a strategic messaging plan:

- **Strategic Response**— crafts the theme of how questions will be answered. (Ex. Transparency.)
- **Talk Track**— identifies potential topics or issues for inquiry and formulates a response based on the strategic theme. (Ex. Transparency in hiring. Transparency in finances. Transparency throughout the investigation and reporting.)
- **Talking Points**— provide supporting data, statistics and anecdotal narrative that reiterate or validate the larger messaging strategy and talk tracks. (Ex. [Company Name] has a 98% customer service rating, so we look forward to continuing that tradition of excellence and transparency in how we operate. Ex. Once the investigation is complete, in the spirit of transparency, we will share the findings with our customers and the media.)

- Successful media interviews are the result of frequent and consistent practice, practice and more practice. Answering tough questions on a deadline and often under the bright, hot lights of television cameras is not comfortable or natural. Preparation is the key to success, and that preparation is built upon repetition and practice — until the responses are comfortable and the delivery is effortless. To conclude, let's quickly review media do's and don'ts to help make your interview-prepping process go more smoothly:
  - Do answer the question, directly and briefly
  - Don't answer questions that aren't asked; stay on message
  - Do speak confidently and with authority
  - Do use clear, concise language
  - Do use active/visual words
  - Do use specific words and phrases that are accurate and relevant
  - Do present one idea at a time
  - Do stop talking when you've answered the question; rambling is dangerous and reckless in communications
  - Do get to the point quickly
  - Don't exaggerate and don't minimize the significance of an event
  - Don't guess or speculate if you don't know the answer; refer the reporter to the appropriate source who can answer correctly
  - Don't repeat loaded language within the question; those words will become your words in a direct quote
  - Don't say "No comment" — it's often perceived as deceptive or an admission of guilt
  - Do use the "sandwich technique" to wrap sensitive or difficult news
  - Do ask questions for clarification if you don't understand the question
  - Do your research and know your subject matter
  - Do relax — reporters sense fear

See Figure 10.5 for a sample media prep Q&A document that helps prepare clients for media interviews.

Run of Show

Event planners and PR practitioners cannot fully appreciate the value of a run of show document until attending an event that doesn't have one. The run of show is a detailed, logistical production schedule and outline of a special event that includes every speaker, transition, pause, performance or activity that occurs from hours before the program starts until the last dessert is served and the event host says goodnight and wishes everyone farewell. Many detailed run of show documents also include the verbatim scripts of each speaker and how long they should last, especially if the production is televised and must stay on schedule.

If possible, all presenters, speakers and participants should attend an abbreviated practice session or run-through of a special event to become familiar with the room, stage, lighting, teleprompter, etc. If that isn't feasible, the run of show document should be shared in advance with all program participants with the goal of ensuring everyone is familiar with their role and the overall flow of the show.

See Figure 10.6 for a sample run of show document.

FIGURE 10.5 ■ Sample Media Prep Q&A Document

Vortex Inc.

MEDIA PREP / MEDIA Q&A

Vortex Inc. Television Interview   July 30, 20XX

"On the Hot Seat" Talk Show (8/24/XX)

WHOT News | www.whot.news.com

TV Show:	On the Hot Seat
Show Host:	Jenn Peeples
Show Guest(s):	Avery Michaels, Vortex Inc. CEO
Show Topic:	Technology Trends
Interview Date/Time:	Saturday, Aug. 24, 20XX
	9:30 a.m.
Interview Location:	WHOT News Station
	4000 News Blvd.
	Madison, WI
Interview Format:	In-Person; Live, In-Studio Pre-Recorded
Show Airs:	Sunday, Aug. 25, 20XX
Show Details:	Avery Michaels will arrive at the WHOT studio at 8:30 a.m. for a prep session.
	Station Contact: (608) 555-1234 front desk
Show Overview:	"On the Hot Seat" is a community television talk show that features business, political, and civic leaders to discuss relevant issues for viewers.

Media Q&A:

Q1: What sets Vortex Vibes apart from other fitness apps on the market?

- Vortex Vibes stands out due to its comprehensive tracking capabilities, intuitive interface, and personalized insights.

- Unlike many fitness apps, Vortex Vibes seamlessly integrates with popular fitness devices and platforms, ensuring users can easily sync their data across multiple devices.

- Our app's personalized recommendations and insights based on individual goals and activity patterns help users stay motivated and on track.

[more]

FIGURE 10.6 ■ Sample Run of Show

5:00 p.m. – 6:00 p.m.	Room setup and arrival of VIPs to green room
5:30 p.m. – 5:55 p.m.	Jazz band begins playing in reception area for guests
5:55 p.m.	Doors open for guests to begin seating
6:15 p.m. – 6:17 p.m.	Emcee approaches the podium to make welcome comments

Emcee Samuel Brickson:

Good evening, everyone – and welcome! We're so glad to welcome you to tonight's celebration. It's wonderful to gather together in person again. We have an amazing lineup of speakers and performers here tonight, so please sit back and relax …

Now it's time to kick off our program. It's my pleasure to invite to the stage the CEO of our platinum corporate sponsor. Please help me welcome, Mr. Gerald Pearson!

6:18 p.m. - 6:23 p.m.	Gerald Pearson remarks:

Good evening, everyone – and thank you so much for coming out. We have a fantastic program planned, but first I want to introduce a video produced by our corporate communications team about our company's 100-year commitment to renewable energy …

6:24 p.m. – 6:30 p.m.	Cue video. "Renewable for Life" video plays on all monitors
6:31 p.m. – 9:27 p.m.	Details of each activity or sequence of events – and the respective timeframe it lasts
9:28 p.m. – 9:30 p.m.	Emcee Samuel Brickson:

Congratulations again to all our award winners and thank you to our corporate partners who helped make this night possible … We appreciate your support and hope you enjoyed the evening. Please be safe and have a wonderful evening. Goodnight.

# # #

CHAPTER SUMMARY

Internal communication tools are helpful for the PR writing practitioner and the client for whom the tools are created. A SWOT analysis allows those working on a campaign to get an inside glimpse of the structure of a company and its overall communications planning efforts.

The communication audit — a comprehensive report detailing all internal and external communications activities — offers a thorough assessment of what's currently in place and how those communications are performing with the key publics.

A PR plan is one of the common tools used to direct a PR campaign. Based on the findings and recommendations from the SWOT analysis and the communication audit, a PR plan can be developed to guide the messaging strategy for target audiences associated with the campaign. Once the PR campaign is underway and the media begins to respond, a media prep Q&A document helps prepare the client for conducting successful interviews with the media.

KEY TERMS

communication audit

media prep Q&A

metrics

run of show

situation analysis

SWOT analysis

DISCUSSION QUESTIONS

1. What purpose does conducting a SWOT analysis serve in developing a communications plan or PR campaign?

2. How does a public relations plan help guide the communications process for a PR practitioner and their client?

3. What information does a quality communication audit provide for the organization and the communications team?

WRITING EXERCISES

1. Write a one-page public relations plan to launch a new downloadable app called myBaby Tunes, targeted to new parents, which records their infant's cries and mixes them into a song.

2. Write five anticipated questions and their respective bulleted responses for a media prep Q&A document for an automobile manufacturing client facing a major vehicle recall of 1 million vehicles due to a faulty braking system that causes the brakes to wear out prematurely.

3. Develop a messaging strategy and write the talk track and talking points for your client — the executive director of a small, local nonprofit that rescues neglected animals — to support a response to the question "What makes your animal rescue center a worthy cause for the community to support with their donations?"

11 EXTERNAL COMMUNICATION TOOLS

INTRODUCTION

Beyond AP style media-focused documents and public-facing PR campaigns and creative content, organizations often need to communicate en masse with external audiences — people and groups positioned outside the company or institution and its daily operations — to inform or educate them about new activities or information that is relevant to them. Many of the tools used to connect with external audiences also function in dual roles and can be adapted for internal or external usage. This chapter will highlight those documents and give a brief explanation of how they are used to effectively communicate.

As part of a company's broader communication strategy, it's important to adjust external messaging content to fit with the audience's knowledge level and comfort level. Most importantly, external audiences want to hear what's important to them and what's in it for them from corporate messengers. When writing for an external audience, the PR writing professional needs to consider the viewpoint of the recipient and answer the question they likely will have: Why are you sending this information to me? Then, ask yourself: What is it the company wants the recipient to know? And what is it the company wants the recipient to do? Answering those two questions will fulfill the basic requirements of primary and secondary messaging by appealing to the goals of informing, updating or educating and also addressing the motivations or self-interests of the person on the receiving end of the communication.

11.1 — INTERNAL AND EXTERNAL COMMUNICATION DOCUMENTS

A short list of common PR publications or documents that can be used for internal or external corporate mass communication purposes include:

- Memoranda (also called memos)
- Newsletters or electronic newsletters (e-newsletters)
- Direct-mail letters

Memos

In short, a memo or memorandum is a brief (usually one-page) written correspondence that conveys a specific point of information in a concise format. The top header section of the memo includes the document title "MEMO" or "MEMORANDUM" at the top; a "To" line that lists the name of the recipient(s) for whom the memo is being written; a "From" line that includes the name, department or source author of the memo; the date when the memo is being distributed; and a subject line that briefly describes the purpose of the enclosed content. The correspondence beneath the header section provides details about the information being shared and what actions or steps — if any — the reader needs to take to follow up or comply with the information contained. Standard memo content formatting is single-spaced text, with double-spacing between paragraphs. In practice, external memos are also used to formalize an agreement or understanding between parties, hence the specialized document titled "MEMORANDUM OF UNDERSTANDING."

See Figure 11.1 for a sample memo header.

FIGURE 11.1 ■ Sample Memo Header

MEMORANDUM

TO:	Our Customers
FROM:	Office of the President & CEO
DATE:	January 1
RE:	Happy New Year!

Memo content begins here. The purpose of a memo is to concisely convey information to the recipient in a written document.

The format is single-spaced text that is double-spaced between paragraphs. An official corporate memo is printed on hardcopy or electronic letterhead.

No valediction (closing greeting such as "Sincerely,"), contact information or signature line is needed at the bottom of the memorandum. Often the writer or the originator of the document will include their initials beside their name in the top header section as an indication that the content is verified from their desk or office.

Newsletters or E-newsletters

A newsletter is a controlled publication that can be printed in hard copy or delivered electronically to a targeted group of individuals who have an interest in the content included in the document. Used internally, newsletters can speak directly to employees of an organization to discuss human resources matters or leadership directives that will affect people who work for the company. For external purposes, a newsletter can be designed in a more creative format to increase engagement and can be sent outside the company to share news or updates or to solicit input or feedback about products and services. Subscriber newsletters, association or membership newsletters, and community newsletters are examples of public-facing or external newsletters that are created to connect a company directly with external publics.

Figure 11.2 displays a sample electronic (digital) newsletter, or e-newsletter, using Latin filler text.

Direct-Mail Letters

Direct-mail letters are often associated with marketing campaigns that appeal to customers or potential customers in an effort to persuade them to purchase a product. But wait . . . there's more. Yes, direct-mail campaigns frequently lead with a sales and marketing priority, which is then used as a tool to build a database and relationship with the recipient. However, there are other uses for direct mail to mass audiences, including product updates, recall notices, public health notifications, local governance, and updates about public policy that might affect readers' activities or livelihood.

Figure 11.3 displays a sample direct-mail letter layout.

11.2 — USE FEATURE ARTICLES TO SUPPORT PR CAMPAIGNS

Feature articles are creative and insightful tools to use to support a larger PR campaign while also educating the target audience and bringing increased awareness or positive media attention to the client. Instead of developing a "straight news" press release for distribution to the media, the PR professional can conduct research and interview the client for the purpose of writing an in-depth feature article that introduces or provides more information about an individual, a new product or service, or innovative ideas and advancements within the company.

As the name indicates, a feature does just what is says — it features a subject throughout an article from the beginning to the end. A feature article is distinct from straight news because it does not follow the inverted-pyramid style, which quickly gets to the main points in the first (or lead) paragraph and then adds less pertinent details further down in the story. Feature articles also tend to be less objective and more subjective, focused on positive aspects of the subject in the article that the campaign is designed is highlight.

FIGURE 11.2 ■ Sample E-Newsletter Layout With Latin Filler Text

Source: iStock.com/JDawnInk

By nature, feature articles tend to be written in a more creative style, using a delayed lead, descriptive modifiers, and more creativity in a less structured format. The answers to the 5Ws (who, what, when, where, why) are still answered, but in a more relaxed and engaging way.

FIGURE 11.3 ■ Sample Direct-Mail Letter Template Layout

4Life Nautilus Incorporated　　　**[Letterhead or Sender Address]**
123 Exercise Way
Vancouver, Washington 98765

March 6, 2026　　　**[Date]**

Mr. John Smith　　　**[Recipient Name and Mailing Address]**
456 Fitness Avenue
Los Angeles, CA 90001

Dear Mr.Smith,　　　**[Salutation]**
As a valued member of the Nautilus family, we are committed to ensuring your safety and satisfaction with our products. That's why we're reaching out to inform you about an important update regarding your recent purchase, the 4Life Nautilus ProForm Power 995i Treadmill.

In partnership with the Consumer Product Safety Commission, we have identified a potential safety concern with a specific component of the ProForm Power 995i Treadmill. While no incidents have been reported, we believe it is essential to take proactive measures to address any potential risks to our customers.

We are initiating a voluntary recall of a limited number of ProForm Power 995i Treadmills due to a potential issue with the power cord. In rare cases, the power cord may become damaged, posing a small risk of electrical shock. Your safety is our top priority, and we want to ensure that you can continue to enjoy your workouts without any concerns.

As part of this recall, we are providing you with a complimentary replacement power cord for your ProForm Power 995i Treadmill. The replacement cord is designed to meet our rigorous safety standards and will ensure the continued safe operation of your treadmill.

Your replacement power cord will be shipped to you within the next 4-6 weeks. In the meantime, we advise you to refrain from using your treadmill until the replacement cord has been installed. We understand the inconvenience this may cause and appreciate your cooperation in prioritizing safety.

If you have any questions or require assistance with the replacement process, please don't hesitate to contact our customer service team at 800-555-1234, Monday through Friday, between 9 a.m. and 5 p.m. PT. You can also visit our website at www.4lifenautilus.ux/recall for additional information and updates on the recall process.

Thank you for your understanding and cooperation in this matter. We remain committed to providing you with high-quality products and exceptional service.

Sincerely,　　　**[Valediction]**

Alice Fitness　　　**[Signature]**

Alice Fitness
Customer Care Manager
4Life Nautilus Incorporated

P.S. If you have not received your replacement power cord by April 10, 2026, please contact us immediately at 800-555-1234. Your safety is our priority, and we want to ensure you can resume your workouts as soon as possible.

[Postscript]

Common types of features include personality profiles, product profiles, service overviews and organizational profiles.

The construct of a feature article is basic, beginning with an attention-grabbing introduction, a main body that profiles the featured subject, and a clear ending with a memorable conclusion. Accompanied by a captioned professional headshot, product photo or project site image, the feature package can be published on a company's owned media platforms (e.g., website, blog and social networking sites) or pitched as syndicated content to smaller trade association or community publications that are in need of extra content. Here are some possible feature leads that can be used to capture the readers' attention in the opening paragraph:

- Lead with an analogy (makes hard-to-understand ideas easier to comprehend)

- Lead with an anecdote (shares a memorable story or situation involving the featured subject)

- Lead with a joke (just don't do it; funny to one group may be offensive to another)

- Lead with a metaphor (says that one thing is another)

- Lead with painting a picture or setting the scene (speak in pictures that "show and tell")

- Lead with a simile (says that one thing is like another)

- Lead with a statistic (impressive percentages or uncommon factoids are memorable)

- Lead with a quote (quote the featured subject or a well-known public figure for effect)

Here are some of the most common ways to end a feature article:

- Close with a call to action (assign a task or follow-up activity for the audience)

- Close with an emotional appeal (get the audience to think and feel)

- Close with a quote (quote the featured subject or a well-known figure for effect)

- Close with a reference to the opening (remind the audience where you started)

- Close with a summary (remind the audience of the key points and highlights)

11.3 — FOR-PROFIT VERSUS NONPROFIT ANNUAL REPORTS

The role of PR writing professionals is more prominent than often realized when it comes to drafting content for annual reports. Much like its name states, an annual report is a once-a-year document that corporations and nonprofit organizations publish to update investors, shareholders and contributors with a year-in-review accounting of financial operations and activities, along with a summary of operations and accomplishments. With the exception of financial documents and financial statements from a certified public accountant's office, much of the content included in the annual report is written by the public relations or communications team. Examples of content include letters from the board chair or president, an introduction to the annual report, a year-in-review narrative, customer or client success stories, photo captions, next-year projections and an annual report cover letter.

All public companies are required to file annual reports with the federal Securities and Exchange Commission (SEC). The SEC is an independent government oversight agency that is responsible for regulating the securities market (financial assets such as stocks, bonds or options) and protecting investors. Though nonprofits do not have the same legal requirement to file annually, many larger nonprofits produce and publish an annual report (hard copy or digital) to share financial details and community-focused achievements with their donors to make the case for continued support and additional contributions toward their endeavors.

Much like any other publication, it's important to *know your audience* when writing for an annual report. Keep in mind that the primary audience for corporate annual reports is individuals who have invested money into the growth and development of the company and therefore have an ownership stake and a keen interest in the survival and success of the business. Though nonprofit contributors may not technically own a portion of the organization, many still donate money, volunteer time, provide resources and want an official report on how their investments have benefited the community or other stakeholder groups.

Even though annual reports have a reputation as financial reporting documents, in many instances they also are used as promotional and marketing pieces as a result of more creative design, unique layouts and presentation, vibrant photos, and compelling content, in addition to the mandatory balance sheets, income statements, and cash flow reports. A lot of different publics rely on annual reports for the important financial information they contain.

List of potential stakeholders for for-profit annual reports:

- Shareholders

- Potential investors

- Employees

- Business partners

- Customers

- Suppliers

- Vendors

- Financial planners and investors

- Hedge fund managers

- Media

11.4 — ANNUAL REPORTS

Annual reports are documents created to engage with external and internal stakeholder groups. These are millions of investors that reply upon these documents, so there are required sections that must be included to fulfill federal SEC filing requirements, discussed in the next sections.

Annual Report Sections

Although there are no mandated formats for an annual report, a review of most corporate annual reports will reveal a number of sections that are consistent for all for-profit annual report documents. What follows are descriptions of those common sections.

Letter From an Executive

Whether it's the board chair, president, CEO, executive director or a joint letter from top executives, most annual reports open with a first-person correspondence from a leader of the company or organization that addresses events and operations from the past year. Usually one to two pages in length, the letter offers an optimistic narrative about what the company has done and how the organization has performed — and what projections are in place for the upcoming year. The letter is often accompanied by a headshot and the author's signature. The PR professional assigned to write the letter can review previous letters or correspondence and conduct a brief interview with the executive to draft a letter that accurately reflects the voice of the author(s).

Description of the Organization, Products and Services

The nuts and bolts of the finances for an annual report can be found in the financial statements and the financial audit and letter from a certified public accountant. However, near the beginning of the annual report, readers commonly find a section that describes what the company produces and sells and how it makes money. There may be product line descriptions and an overview of services, along with a revenue snapshot reflected by percentages of earnings for each line of business showing how much they each bring into the company. This section also may highlight any additional brands or subsidiaries of the company and discuss or explain any differentiation in accounting practices or any changes or additions to the stated line of business.

Financial Summary

The primary target audience for an annual report is shareholders — individuals who have invested money into the company in expectation of a financial return — so their interest is how the company is performing from a financial standpoint. This section of the report demonstrates financial trends for the company over a 10-year period, or lifetime annual revenue if the company is younger than 10 years old. The financial summary in graph or chart form also displays visual trends to easily explain to any reader whether the company is making money, losing money or holding steady from year to year. Accompanying the financial summary, an official letter of audit from a certified public accountant (CPA) is generally required, providing analysts and investors with external validation that the company is operating in good faith and that its accounting practices meet the generally accepted accounting principles.

Notice of Form 10-K Availability

Form 10-K is an official document provided by the Securities and Exchange Commission (SEC) that corporations are required to complete as an annual report submission. If the company is required to complete the form, the company also is required to inform its investors of the availability of the form. Annual Form 10-K filings are required for the company to be in compliance with federal regulations. In general, public or private companies with more than $10 million in assets and more than 2,000 investors — or with tradable shares valued at more than $700 million — are required to file Form 10-K.

Chief Financial Officer (CFO) Analysis and Management Letter

A letter from the chief financial officer is an important section of the annual report because it discusses the company's most recent financial performance, typically over the past two years. Investors and analysts look to this letter, which represents the top financial executive within the company, to provide additional insights and analysis into the financial health of the company and the leaders' ability to direct the company toward profitability and produce high-yield returns for its investors.

Financial Statements

Financial statements are drafted directly from the reports generated by the bookkeeping or accounting software system and provided by the chief financial officer (CFO), so they are not written by the PR practitioner. The financial reports most often included in this section are the income statement (also known as the profit & loss statement or P&L statement), balance sheet, and cash flow statement. Historically, these reports made up the heart and soul of an annual report, as they reflect the financial health of the company and help investors make high-dollar decisions as to whether or not to continue investing or recommending investments into the company.

Stock Price

The stock price represents the value of a single ownership share in the company. An annual report will include the closing year's end stock price and a chart or graph reflecting the performance of the stock prices throughout the year, along with an explanation for any extenuating circumstances that may have positively or adversely affected the stock price in an exceptional way.

List of Board Members, Directors and Officers

Accountability and conflict of interest are important factors for consideration when investing in a company. Every annual report will include a list of its leadership and management team, including board members, directors and officers (executives on the board). In most cases, officers are elected or appointed by the board of directors.

Nonprofit Annual Reports

A nonprofit organization is a legal entity organized and operated for a community-focused or social benefit. Though many larger, national nonprofits may earn a lot of money, the funds are redirected back into the organization to continue providing goods and services for the public good as opposed to generating a profit and dividends for its investors or contributors.

Because nonprofit organizations are generally not publicly traded businesses on the stock market and have no shareholders, there is no SEC or federal requirement to file an annual report. However, because most nonprofits are highly dependent and reliant upon the generosity of external donors, publishing an annual report is a good way to showcase the accomplishments of the previous year, highlight employees and volunteers and their positive impacts in the community, and make appeals for donors to continue supporting the organization. Common sections that can be found in nonprofit annual reports include:

- letter from the board chair

- description of services provided

- geographic locations, philanthropic reach and community impact

- list of executives, board members, directors and officers

- standard financial statements and certified public accountant audit letter

- footnotes explaining any necessary and relevant information that affects financial performance

Generally speaking, nonprofit annual reports tend to be shorter, easier to read and understand, and more aesthetically pleasing than a lot of for-profit annual reports. The reports are shorter because there are no mandatory financial filings or federal requirements to be met. They tend to be written in plain language and easier to read because the audience is not a financial investing group seeking analysis and documentation but rather individuals and organizations that support the work and services the nonprofit provides. Finally, the document is designed for storytelling and narration about the past year's accomplishments and positive impact for those in need instead of focusing mostly on how much money was made and what the return on investment will be. Usually, a few standard sections of content are found in nonprofit annual reports that require the writing skills and storytelling expertise of a public relations professional.

Letter From the Board Chair

Diverse boards that reflect a cross-section of community leaders are often a hallmark for non-profit organizations. As the leader of that group, the board chair, along with the other officers and board members, is elected or appointed to offer guidance, governance and fiduciary (financial) support for the growth and expansion of the nonprofit organization and its network. In the letter from the board chair, the message is designed for all stakeholders to highlight the accomplishments of the past year and appeal to donors for their continued support. Generally one page in length, the letter is a direct appeal from the board chair to the community.

Description of Services

Nonprofit organizations have a reputation for doing a lot of good work throughout the area where they are located. As a matter of practice, when bad things happen, many people look to nonprofits to step up and assist through disaster aid and relief, employment assistance and job training, feeding the homeless, supporting those with physical and developmental disabilities, and much more. Highlighting the good work done in the name of service to others is where non-profits can shine with their storytelling and narration. The PR practitioner may need to conduct research and site visits, interview service recipients and volunteers, or accompany nonprofit service providers on calls in the community to adequately capture the essence and share through storytelling how the organization positively impacts the community.

Geographic Reach and Community Impact

Nonprofits across the country span the full spectrum when it comes to size, scope of services, and reach. Some have service areas limited to one local neighborhood, while others may have a national presence and international reach based on their vision, mission and scale. As a result, making the case for financial support from large foundations and major donors is often connected with the nonprofit's ability to expediently respond to and positively impact large service areas and support thousands of people during challenging times. The PR professional can educate readers and shed light on the reach and impact of an organization by showcasing content and visuals that reflect diverse regions, populations and circumstances in which significant funding is required to adequately respond and provide assistance to those in need.

Success Stories

Nonprofit work makes a difference, and success stories are an excellent way to quantify and document that good work. Through interviews, imagery and narration, profiling individuals whose lives have been changed for the better because of the nonprofit's work is an effective way to ensure that readers of the annual report know their contributions have gone to good use. This section of the report also supports the recommended expenditures for programming activities in the community and provides additional context and narrative to substantiate the financial reports and appeals for support. Though the focus of nonprofit annual reports goes well beyond basic financial information, many key publics rely on the narrative and yearly highlights contained within the document.

Here is a list of potential stakeholders for nonprofit annual reports:

- Major donors and potential donors

- Organization members

- Employees and volunteers

- Fundraisers and foundations

- Community partners

- Board member and advisers

- Media

11.5 — UTILIZING POSITION STATEMENTS

More information about position statements or position papers is included in Chapter 17 of this textbook. In this chapter, the focus is on how a position paper can be used to further engage with external audiences.

A position paper is an official document published by an organization to clearly articulate its stance on an issue. Though the statement may contain research and data, it falls short of being classified as a research document because it does not focus on objectivity. The paper represents a specific viewpoint and often is used to advance an agenda.

The purpose of a position paper or position statement is to clearly and unequivocally inform readers and viewers where an individual or organization stands on a specific issue or topic so that customers, supporters and investors can make informed decisions about their alignment with the company or person based on its support of or opposition to a particular subject. The document may attempt to present both sides of an issue or argument but likely refutes the claims of the opposing side within the statement to further the viewpoint of the organization.

The process for writing a clear and concise position paper or position statement begins with articulating a specific point of view. The premise of the paper is followed by anecdotes, statistics, supporting evidence and content to support or further explain the author's position. Several options for concluding a position document include a call to action, a content summation or a statement that creates a lasting and memorable impression. Here is a sample template that explains how to structure and format a position statement.

TIPS FOR BEGINNERS: HOW TO FORMAT A POSITION PAPER OR POSITION STATEMENT

Figure 11.4 displays a sample position paper, also known as a position statement.

FIGURE 11.4 ■ Sample Position Paper

POSITION STATEMENT

11/30/2024

Position Statement Title Goes Here

This is my introduction. Here is where I'm going to clearly state the position that represents the interests of the client. The voice of a position statement is generally third person, objective – using the pathos (emotional), logos (reason), and ethos (credibility) appeals to connect with audiences. The formatting and appearance on the page are similar to the news release layout. The document is double-spaced, with paragraph indents and page slugs that indicate where a reader is within the document.

In-text citations in MLA or APA style are acceptable to prevent instances of plagiarism or copyright infringements.

This paragraph begins the "body" of the document and makes the case through data, statistics, research, or anecdotes to inform the reader and persuade their thinking. The reason for third person narrative in persuasion is because there is often a "hostile" audience that will not align with the views or assertions in the document.

[more]

(Continued)

FIGURE 11.4 ■ **Sample Position Paper** *(Continued)*

POSITION STATEMENT – Page 2

Using phrases such as "our priorities" or "things that unite us" will in fact isolate some individuals and create further distance between the author and the reader. Using the second person narrative and telling the reader what they need to do or expressing how they might feel may cause the individual to react in a defensive manner. Consider this: "We know that keeping our children safe is something that is important to you and one of your top priorities." Maybe. Maybe not. For a hostile or defensive reader, the reaction can be that "my children are not your children." Or for a neutral reader, "I don't even have children – you don't know anything about me."

Also, the document is the voice of the company or institution, and all individuals may not fully align with the positions the company takes. Using "we, our, your" language gives the impression that everyone at the company feels the same way, which is not necessarily accurate. Providing a distinct line between individual employees/representatives and the corporate collective also offers some professional protection from legal liability related to controversial issues.

Finally, the conclusion of the position statement reasserts the opening statement and summarizes the primary points; issuing a direct or indirect call to action, if needed. At the end of the last paragraph, the hashtags or pound keys indicate the end of related content.

#   #   #

11.6 — WRITING SPEECHES

A speech is a monologue prepared for delivery to an audience to inform, entertain or persuade. Whether they are printed on paper or spoken and delivered with no visual aids, most speeches are designed to be presented by one speaker to a group.

Speeches

PR professionals are frequently called upon to write initial drafts of speeches for executives or politicians to assist in crafting the right words that will connect with, motivate or inspire an audience to take action or embrace an idea. One of the most important and significant aspects of speechwriting is to know the audience. Another one of the most important and significant aspects of speechwriting is to know the speaker. The writer needs to embody the voice, tone, tenor and style of the speaker so that the words seem authentic and believable when the speaker delivers them. The writer also needs to know as much as possible about who's going to hear the speech when it's delivered so they can write on a level that is commensurate with the audience and their ability to relate or comprehend what is being said.

A growing industry for writers to consider is ghostwriting, where professional writers are hired to write, edit and proof literary works, books or speeches that are credited to another person as the author. Ghostwriters are secured by authors on a "work for hire" basis, meaning that they generally create content and release the ownership rights to it for a fee. Professional speechwriters focus most of their time and energy on creating speech copy and assisting the speaker(s) in confidently and comfortably delivering the content to the respective audiences.

There are four basic modes of speech delivery: scripted, memorized, impromptu and extemporaneous. Whether a speaker is using a mobile device, giving a presentation on a monitor, or informally speaking off the cuff, the point of the speech is still likely to inform, entertain or persuade the listeners.

Scripted

A scripted speech is written verbatim and often printed on paper, loaded into a teleprompter, or made visible to the speaker so it can be delivered word for word. Script speeches are usually prepared for a formal event or presentation, where the accuracy and order of the words is very important.

Scripted speeches are well researched and may include references and citations to confirm the accuracy of the content and acknowledge credit for references to other people's work or information. They are prepared in advanced and often practiced numerous times by the speaker to perfect the delivery. The PR professional writing the speech has the responsibility of confirming the accuracy of the speech content, writing the copy, editing and proofing the final version, and possibly rehearsing and coaching the individual giving the speech on proper delivery style and presentation.

Don't look for a lot of spontaneity or candid remarks with a scripted speech. It is delivered in a formal and straightforward manner with the purpose of conveying information in an exact manner. Even humorous speeches that are written for special occasions and meant to entertain may give the appearance of being spontaneous, but they actually are written in a very concise manner with every word planned and spoken with intention.

Memorized

A memorized speech is just that — speech verbiage researched, prepared and written out in advance and then committed to memory by the speaker. The speech may be printed out in hard copy during practice sessions but is generally delivered without notes or aids during its formal presentation. The upside of a memorized speech is that there is no concern about technology glitches from a malfunctioning TV monitor or teleprompter. The downside is that the speaker may be nervous or simply forget parts of the speech.

Similar to a scripted speech, a memorized speech is often researched and written in advance so there is ample time for preparation. The writer may organize the content using mnemonic tools to help the speaker more easily commit the content to memory. As an example, if there are three main points in the body of the speech that need to be shared, the writer may begin the correlating paragraphs with a fact or transition listed in alphabetical order.

For instance, a political speech may be designed to motivate people to support the candidate. To ensure all the important points are covered, the first paragraph of the body is about Altruism, the second is about Believing in a cause greater than yourself, and the third is about Community. As the speaker delivers the content, the A-B-C mnemonic device applied to each paragraph helps keep the speech in order.

Memorized speeches are delivered without notes and with few props or visual aids. The focus is on the content and the credibility of the speaker. Without practice, there is a risk of memorized speeches sounding stiff and rehearsed, so it's important for the speechwriter to give the speaker plenty of time to prepare and rehearse the speech to increase the comfort level before presenting in front of an audience.

Impromptu

The word "impromptu" means done without planning, organization or practice. Considering how important speeches are and how likely a speech is to be recorded and shared around the world online and across various social media platforms, delivering content without any planning, organization, or practice seems like a risky proposition. At any rate, impromptu speeches are presented quite often, and as the name states, the speeches are generally deemed "off the cuff" or "on the fly" remarks. There is no significant writing role for the PR practitioner as it relates to an impromptu speech, other than continual guidance and coaching for clients to make sure there are reputational guardrails in place in advance to prevent them from saying something they'll regret or saying something that undermines the mission and values of their brand.

An impromptu speech has no formal preparation and is delivered at a moment's notice by the speaker. Impromptu speech opportunities may arise when an unexpected guest is in the audience and is asked to give remarks, or if an invited guest is running late or unable to attend an event and an alternate speaker is asked to fill in last minute. Because there is no preparation, impromptu speeches have no research, no written notes, and no visual aids in place to deliver the message. The speechwriter may provide some tips or guidance on how to approach spontaneous requests for remarks, such as using the inverted-pyramid style that features the 5W questions. Using that style as a guide, impromptu remarks mentally can be organized by addressing who, what, when, where, and why.

Depending upon the quality of the speechmaker, an impromptu speech delivery can range from moving and sincere to rambling and cringeworthy, based on the content. The speech is delivered spontaneously, with no notes or formal remarks — and very little (if any) advance preparation. If the speaker is completely caught off guard, they may be nervous or hesitant. These scenarios may occur in a classroom setting when a student is called upon unexpectedly, in a professional setting when an employee team member is asked to provide a project update, or in a social setting when a VIP guest is asked to greet the audience. If the speaker is accustomed to being called upon without prior notice, they may simply rely upon past speeches and occasions to cobble together remarks that fit the event and resonate with the audience.

Extemporaneous

An extemporaneous speech is a hybrid that blends elements of a scripted speech, based on the amount of research and preparation required, and a memorized speech, based on the lack of formal documents or notes provided to assist in its delivery. Though an extemporaneous speech is defined as one given without advance planning, that doesn't mean the speaker is unprepared. An extemporaneous speech is likely delivered by an expert who is well versed in the topic or subject matter and who previously has shared their remarks on numerous occasions. A commonplace setting for extemporaneous speaking is in a college or university classroom, where the professor is presenting a topic they have researched, studied, and presented countless times.

Preparation for an extemporaneous speech is based upon previous research, study, and accumulation of knowledge about a subject. The speechwriter may assist the speaker with additional research or fact-checking; however, most of the knowledge already has been acquired. Since the speaker is likely an expert, the PR practitioner can assist in preparing for a smooth presentation by creating notes, updating the presentation format, or developing visual aids to reinforce the message with the audience.

An extemporaneous speech is not scripted and read from a piece of paper or a mobile device, and it is not memorized and spoken verbatim; rather, the speech is shared in an organized manner based on the wealth of knowledge the speaker has obtained over the years. For support, the speaker may rely on brief notes or bullet points to make sure all key points are covered or presentation slides that help the audience follow the presentation.

Speech Delivery

Delivering a quality speech is more than just speaking the right words for the prescribed amount of time. The speechwriter's job is to help the speaker understand the audience and connect with them through the words that are selected and the actions or gestures that accompany those words. As PR practitioners, it's important to know the audience and write a speech that is on par with the audience members' education and/or familiarity with the topic. It's also imperative to coach the speaker on how to interact with the audience and use their nonverbal skills (eye contact, body language, tone, etc.) to communicate and connect with the audience in a way that puts both the messenger and the recipients at ease. An essential part of incorporating movement and gestures into a speech is done through speech cues, which are directions written into the speech body to prompt specific actions.

Speech cues are stage directions provided to the speaker within the body of the speech to prompt a specific action or movement or to prompt a particular response from the audience. Here's an example of how a speech cue to get the audience to interact with the speaker might appear:

"Good morning, everyone! ***[Raise right arm]**** Raise your hand if you're excited to hear the speakers featured on today's program."

Notice that the speech cue is formatted in boldface and italics to make it stand out (and to prevent the speaker from reading or repeating those directions) and positioned prior to the comments to get the audience to respond, so that the speech cue action corresponds with the words and flows seamlessly with the speech remarks.

Speech Formats

On paper, speech documents should include a contact block in the upper left corner with the PR practitioner's or speechwriter's contact information for easy access in case there are any questions or in case any clarification about the content is needed. The speech itself should have a title and header that includes the speech delivery information, so the speaker knows which speech they have, and reminders for where, when and why it's being presented. Prolific speakers may have a number of speeches to present for different types of audiences, and the speech delivery information helps keep them organized. Also, providing a speech with clear speech delivery details offers clarity and reduces the likelihood of confusion or presenting the wrong speech to an audience. The speech delivery header should include the name of the person delivering the speech, the date and time the speech will be given, the location for the speech, and the audience for whom the speech is written. It's also helpful to include draft versions and updates in the page footer to confirm that the proofreaders and speaker have the correct, edited and final version of the speech that is to be given. Speech text is double-spaced on the page using a serif font that is at least 12-point type, large enough to easily read at a glance. Include page numbers and page slugs so that if the speech is dropped or assembled out of order, it can be easily reordered so the speaker can continue with minimal interruption.

The contextual construction of a speech is fairly straightforward. There is an introduction, a main body and a conclusion. The introduction is used to capture the audience's attention and inform them about the purpose of the speech and what they can expect to hear. The main body of the speech is the "meat" of the content. This section includes the main points that the speaker wants to make and any supporting research, data or statistics to support those claims, if the intent is to educate or inform. For a speech designed to honor someone or entertain at a special occasion, this main-body section might include three to five memories or anecdotal snippets that highlight an individual's life or accomplishments. Finally, the conclusion is where the speech wraps up and reminds listeners of what they have just heard and leaves them with a call to action (next steps to take), an inspirational thought, or a memorable line.

Speech Presentation Materials

Visuals aids to support a speech can include handouts, flip charts, props, demonstrations, or presentation slides that are projected for the audience to see. Any presentation materials that are part of a speech should be easily accessible to the speaker and seamlessly incorporated into the presentation so as not to detract from or become a distraction for the speaker. Since technology glitches abound, the speaker should be prepared to deliver an effective speech with or without any additional presentation materials.

In addition to writing the speech content, the PR practitioner also may need to write and design the presentation materials or presentation slides. Here are some tips for creating quality presentation slides that enhance the speech and support the speaker.

TIPS FOR BEGINNERS: PREPARING PRESENTATION SLIDES

When preparing presentation slides, consider the following advice:

- Select a professional template design and layout that is branded in conjunction with the organization the speaker represents.
- Adhere to the company or organizational brand standards in selecting typefaces, fonts, colors and graphics. If no branding or style guide is available, select a common easy-to-access and easy-to-read type for text on the slides.
- If using a design template with a dark background, use light-colored lettering for the text; if using a template with a light background, use dark-colored lettering for the text to create contrast and make the presentation materials easier to view and comprehend when projected for the audience.
- Don't overcrowd slides with too much text and too many graphics. If possible, include no more than 30 words or three bulleted paragraphs per slide.
- Focus on one main idea or concept on each slide.
- Use charts and graphs to simplify and visualize complex data and financial information.
- Use photos or graphics in a consistent manner (as a border, as a design element, as a point of emphasis, etc.)
- Embed graphics and videos into the presentation (if file size allows) so they are accessible with or without a stable wireless internet connection (Wi-Fi).
- Include page numbers (slide numbers) on each presentation slide.
- Include a contact information slide at the end so that the audience can follow up if they have additional questions. Include the speaker's name, preferred contact phone number and email address, and social media handles as well as a website URL.
- Edit and proof the presentation slides for spelling and grammatical errors; ensure that all names are spelled correctly and that the contact information is accurate.
- Coach the speaker to rely on the quality of their presentation, not on the presentation materials. The focus should be on the speaker and the speech, not the audiovisuals.

TIPS FOR BEGINNERS: SAMPLE SPEECH TEMPLATE

Figure 11.5 provides a template to guide the speechwriting process.

FIGURE 11.5 ■ Sample Speech Template

Contact Name

Email

Phone

SPEECH

Date - 00/00/0000

"The Catchy Title of my Speech Goes Here"

[Speech delivery information; speech delivered by Speaker Name at Event/Location Name on Location Date to Audience Group]

Speech content starts here. A speech is a monologue prepared for delivery to an audience to inform, entertain, or persuade. Whether they are printed on paper or spoken and delivered with no visual aids, most speeches are designed to be presented by one speaker to a group.

There are four basic modes of speech delivery: scripted, memorized, impromptu, and extemporaneous. The PR professional may need to assist the speaker with research, writing, editing, proofreading, and rehearsing delivery of the speech to an audience.

When drafting a speech on paper, be sure to double space the lines of copy and make the text large enough to read at a glance. This example is printed in Times New Roman, 14 points.

Speeches have a defined introduction, body with three main points, and a conclusion. Speeches should be practiced in advance to make sure they fit within the time limit given by the event organizer. To prevent confusion, use page numbers and page slugs to make sure the reader of the speech does not get lost or confused. ***[Speech cues should be set off in brackets and/or bold italics to make them stand out so the speaker does not read the words.]*** After the speech cue is listed, the speech copy can continue with regular type.

Speeches are a powerful way to connect with external audiences and make a lasting impression.

# # #

Once the content is complete, there is additional logistical information to include in the document to make sure the speaker has all the information they need to adequately prepare to deliver the speech. Here is a short checklist of elements to include in a speech and details to confirm with the speaker:

- PR rep contact name, agency name, phone, email

- Draft version and date

- Document title ("Speech")

- Speech length

- Speech header with delivery date, location and occasion (e.g., Campaign Speech for Company President, PRSSA Annual Conference in Chicago, Ill., on June 12 at 11:30 a.m. CST)

- Speech title

- Speech copy (double-spaced; written in the voice of the speaker)

- Page slugs (abbreviated speech headline, page numbers)

CHAPTER SUMMARY

Communicating with external audiences beyond planned promotional campaigns is a significant part of the job for a public relations professional. External audiences are made up of key publics and stakeholder groups that operate outside the daily activities and operations of the company and are vital to the success of any communications strategy. Though external audiences have varying interests, it's important for the practitioner to tailor messaging specifically to those groups and measure the level of effectiveness.

There are many tools in the communications toolbox for a PR professional to use, and some of those tools can serve a dual purpose in targeting internal and external audiences. Documents or publications like newsletters, direct-mail letters, memos and feature articles can speak directly to individuals and groups to convey a message. Annual reports can be utilized in a number of ways, including meeting federal guidelines for keeping investors and the media informed about the performance of a company, promoting the good work of the company, and publicizing the company's positive attributes in a controlled publication. Speeches are ubiquitous in these days of 24/7 media and online streaming content. Using quality content that connects with the target audience, speeches are a powerful way to communicate and make a lasting impression.

KEY TERMS

annual report

direct-mail letters

extemporaneous speech

feature articles

ghostwriting

impromptu speech

memo

newsletter

position statement

speech cues

DISCUSSION QUESTIONS

1. Discuss some of the different types of newsletters or e-newsletters and how they may differ for an external audience versus an internal audience.

2. What are some of the key differences between a for-profit versus a nonprofit annual report publication?

3. How can a PR professional or speechwriter prepare to effectively emulate the voice of the speaker in a speech document?

WRITING EXERCISES

1. Write a speech to persuade a local community audience to support paying higher taxes to build better schools using the following three topics or concepts as the main points of the speech: common grievance(s), common goal(s), common good.

2. Select a popular auto-manufacturing company and write a position statement clearly articulating the company's position on electric vehicles. State the position and provide three to five relevant points in the main body to support the position.

3. Write a feature opening paragraph and follow-up supporting paragraph(s) introducing Posh, a golden retriever, as this year's winner of the National Dog Show. Be sure to use a creative feature lead, but still answer the 5 Ws in a more relaxed approach.

12 WRITING TO SECURE PR OPPORTUNITIES

LEARNING OBJECTIVES

12.1 Review and analyze different types of business solicitation document.

12.2 Learn the standard sections of an RFP response.

12.3 Follow the process of RFPs from distribution to response to understand how it works.

12.4 Review key considerations for a successful RFP response.

12.5 Understand the role of PR Writing as part of business development.

INTRODUCTION

The idea of this chapter, Writing to Secure PR Opportunities, is not just about earned media interviews or product placements with online influencers. The conversation is much bigger and goes much deeper than those types of activities. This chapter delves into the origin of campaigns and client acquisition, answering the questions, "How does it all begin?" and "Where does it all begin?"

New professionals on the entry rungs of the PR ladder often are assigned new clients based on their need to gain real-world experience and their flexibility to add new projects to their schedules. Often the expectation is for new team members to quickly review client files, research the company, get familiar with the PR plan, and hit the ground running without missing a beat. What isn't always apparent is how the client came to exist on the agency's roster or project grid and the circumstances that fueled the client's need to hire an outside agency for assistance.

Business solicitation documents come in several different shapes, sizes, and formats. Most common to PR agencies is the Request for Proposal (RFP) document, which requires a formal written response to indicate interest in pursuing the project opportunity. This is where the skills of a talented PR writing professional come in. RFP responses can be long and tedious in their construction, especially for someone new to the process. This chapter discusses various business solicitation documents, questions to ask before and during the RFP response process, and key considerations for successful RFP pitch presentations.

12.1 — BUSINESS SOLICITATION DOCUMENTS

There are a lot of abbreviations and acronyms in the PR industry, so practitioners might as well get familiar with all of them to knowledgeably talk shop with clients, colleagues, and co-workers. This next set of documents that PR professionals often write in response to bid requests are known mostly by their acronyms.

The documents below represent different types of solicitations that announce a new opportunity or upcoming project in the works and invite eligible vendors to respond as potential suppliers of goods and services needed.

Request for Proposal (RFP)

A Request for Proposal (RFP) is probably the most common type of bid or solicitation document that PR professionals respond to in pursuit of new business opportunities. An RFP is an official solicitation submitted by a business, nonprofit or government agency announcing a new project for which they are seeking qualified contractors to respond and complete the work. The RFP document describes and defines the project or scope of work — and guidelines on how and when to respond — to attract viable contractors and agencies to respond. Sometimes a budget range is included, but in many cases, it is not, leaving the market wide open for the most creative, competitive, and cost-effective responses to compete for the contract award.

The length of RFPs can range from a one-page description of a project and the deadline for responses, to a 150-page document (usually issued by a government agency) filled with project details, contractual legalese, insurance requirements, security clearances, employee verifications, non-conflict of interest statements, and budgetary qualifications. With some basic online searches, it is easy to see how much variety there is in the types of RFPs currently open for bid. Generally speaking, marketing-driven, private companies seeking creative agencies invite more creativity and flourish in RFP responses, as opposed to governments and municipalities, which often take a minimalist approach such as specifically requesting uninspired responses using plain recycled paper and staples or paper clips only for binding instead of a professional portfolio with professionally designed, printed, and bound presentation materials.

As it relates to RFPs for creative agencies — and depending upon the type of company, agency, or organization making the request — the types of products and services requested can run the gamut from conducting research and writing white papers, to redesigning an identity package and website for a total brand rebuild, to launching an international, multimedia public relations campaign that seeks to persuade residents to support a particular cause. Common creative RFPs include the following:

- Public Relations Services

- Marketing and Public Relations

- Website Development and SEO

- Social Media Management

- Video Production & Editing

- Advertising & Direct Marketing

- Media Relations & Crisis Communications

- Branding & Graphic Design

RFPs are not the only documents in play that seek to attract and recruit responses from agencies. After reviewing some of the lesser-known solicitations, this chapter will offer further guidance on how to craft a quality RFP response.

Request for Quote (RFQ)

Targeted toward suppliers of goods and services, a Request for Quote (RFQ) typically is a correspondence sent to companies that provide tangible widgets, gadgets, or devices that have a specific unit price or are available for wholesale purchase (bulk quantities at a reduced cost). Within the RFQ, the issuing agency provides a list and description of what is needed, along with the desired quantity and the date the items are needed. The responding agency submits an RFQ response on company letterhead that includes the agency's trade name, a contact person's name, the federal Employer Identification Number (EIN) or Tax Identification Number, company physical address, company mailing/billing address, telephone number, website URL, primary contact email address; and a detailed quote of the items available for sale that correspond to the request, along with the quantity available, the date they can be shipped or delivered, and the per unit price or bulk rate, if applicable.

Request for Information (RFI)

This solicitation is distributed to a list of suppliers or vendors requesting information about the type of products and services — or scope of services — the recipient can provide. Once submitted, the information gathered is often used to create a database of potential vendors and suppliers that can be called upon to respond for future contracting or proposal opportunities.

An RFI response is an informal, but still professionally written document that includes the responding agency's trade name, a contact person's name, the federal Employer Identification Number (EIN) or Tax Identification Number, business or industry classification NAICS codes (North American Industry Classification System), company physical address, company mailing/billing address, telephone number, website URL, primary contact email address, number of years in business, geographic service area, and a detailed overview of the company's capabilities and ability to work on the proposed project.

Request for Tender (RFT)

Used mainly in the public sector or issued by a government agency, a Request for Tender (RFT) is an invitation for suppliers to bid on supplying a product or service. The document is a formal, structured invitation to suppliers to submit a bid to supply products or services. In the public sector, it is required by law that this RFT process be open to the public and managed fairly and free from favoritism. Request for Tenders often are issued when the project of note is greater than $25,000. An RFT process is used to procure the most cost-effective solution based upon evaluation criteria outlined in the RFT.

Invitation for Bid (IFB) or Invitation to Bid (ITB)

Similar to a Request for Proposal, this document, often issued by government agencies to solicit contractors, focuses more on cost than creativity. An IFB describes the planned project in detail, including scope of work and timelines, and details submission requirements, minimum qualifications, mandatory service standards, and any required warranties. The process is often more straightforward and streamlined because the determining factor for selection is based primarily on the budget.

Letter of Interest (LOI)

As part of the duties of Purchasing and Supply Chain Management (acquisition of goods and services to augment the development, manufacturing, and production process), purchasing officers sometimes issue a request for a Letter of Interest (LOI) from prescreened contractors and creative agencies that are qualified and have been approved to do work for the department or division unit. Specifically, if the complete scope of work and final Request for Quote (RFQ) or Request for Proposal (RFP) are not yet finalized and approved, the agent may distribute a general description of the anticipated project and ask creative agencies to submit a Letter of Interest indicating their qualifications and plans to bid on the work once it opens for responses.

A Letter of Interest will include the responding agency's trade name, a contact person's name, the federal Employer Identification Number (EIN) or Tax Identification Number, company physical address, company mailing/billing address, telephone number, website URL, primary contact email address, number of years in business, geographic service area, and a detailed overview of the company's capabilities and ability to work on the proposed project. The LOI also may request a list of project references where similar work was completed in the past and their contact information to verify the company's ability to successfully perform on the contract.

TIPS FOR BEGINNERS — ABOUT NAICS CODES

A NAICS Code is a self-assigned business or industry category within the North American Industry Classification System and represents a company's primary business activity. The NAICS system was developed for use by federal statistical agencies for the purpose of collecting and analyzing commerce-oriented, statistical data related to the U.S. economy. Upon review, thousands of business sectors and fields are represented in the system to measure the manufacturing, production, and sale of goods and services by corporations and small businesses across the country.

The use of these codes is mostly relevant for filling out forms and documenting the type of work being represented in the RFP process, and ultimately estimating sales and revenue figures for the PR industry on an annual basis.

The NAICS Code for Public Relations is 541820. As described by the coding system, "This industry comprises establishments primarily engaged in designing and implementing public relations campaigns. Campaigns are designed to promote the interest and image of their clients. Establishments providing lobbying, political consulting, or public relations consulting are included in this industry," — according to the www.naics.com website. Entries for the 541820 NAICS Code include the following: Public Relations Agencies, Public Relations Consulting Services, Public Relations Services, Political Consulting Services, Lobbying Services, Lobbyists' Offices.

Other related industry NAICS Codes include

- 541820 — Public Relations Agencies
- 541800 — Advertising, Public Relations and Related Services
- 541810 — Advertising Agencies
- 541840 — Media Representatives
- 541613 — Marketing Consulting Services

12.2 — RFP RESPONSES

Among the list of solicitations, most common in the creative and agency landscape is the issuance of RFPs, so the focus of this section is how to expertly craft an RFP response to secure new or additional PR opportunities. It's no secret that RFP responses can be tricky, particularly when there is a direct appeal for creative "big ideas," but no guidance on the budget. The PR professionals writing the RFP response often walk a tight rope on giving enough information to entice the company to want more, but not giving up too much so that it feels like creating a campaign for free — only to have someone else take the ideas and run with them or meld them into another agency's communication plan. Common sections of an RFP Response will be explained next.

RFP Cover Letter

Beyond submitting the response on time and in the requested format, the RFP cover letter is the next best opportunity to make a good impression. The cover letter is a one-page correspondence, signed and dated by an executive or officer, printed on company letterhead that introduces the agency and expresses interest in winning the contract, offering solutions, leveraging opportunities, and successfully implementing the campaign.

Use the cover letter as a tool to explain the agency's strengths and track record for working on similar projects. Keep the brief content customer-focused and solution-oriented. Be upbeat, optimistic, and offer hints about the exciting proposal that follows.

Executive Summary

The executive summary highlights the most relevant and important aspects of the enclosed proposal. No more than one or two pages in length, this summary clearly identifies the solutions and proposed process designed to meet the client's needs. If creativity is allowed, the use of a photo or a well-designed graphic can demonstrate some of the agency's strengths and presentation skills. The executive summary is no place for subtly or gradually getting to the point. This is the portion of the proposal that an executive or decision maker is most likely to read, so it needs to accomplish a lot in a short amount of time and space. Get to the point quickly about how the recommended approach addresses the current needs, surpasses the competition, aligns with the client's mission, goals, and values, and provides a substantial return on investment (ROI).

About the Agency

This section introduces the public relations agency and describes its qualifications to successfully complete the project. The information shared includes company background details, interesting facts about the agency's founding, and discusses the agency's core values. This presents an opportunity to share a brief overview of the capabilities of the organization and the primary focus area of business. Explain what the company does well and why the agency is the best choice for this particular project. Finally, include the physical address of the agency and describe the geographic footprint of the work the agency does, referencing local, regional, national, or international clientele.

Meet the Team/Agency Bios

Clients want to know who they will be working with if an agency is hired to do the job. Including photos and bios of high-ranking or well-known executives may seem impressive, but it can be risky if those individuals do not plan to be involved in the campaign in a meaningful way. Be sure to include the names and photos of individuals who will actually be working on the account, so as not to misrepresent the account team. In this section, it is better to include all relevant team member names and photos so that the potential client can see who will be working on the account and how large the assigned team is to make sure there are enough personnel to sufficiently support the work. Unless requested, it is not necessary to include complete resumes or curriculum vitae, but rather a brief paragraph for each team member will suffice, listing their relevant skills, experience, and expertise respective to work on the account.

RFP Strategic Response

A detailed strategic response is the heart and soul of the RFP response; and the portion of the document that is likely going to win or lose confidence in the agency's ability to do the work. To begin this section, include a situation analysis and then detail the client's core problem or opportunity. Align content in this section with the campaign goal and objectives that the enclosed proposal accomplishes. Without giving away the entire campaign, also suggest a creative approach and possible strategies and tactics to support the idea. Be sure to note in the proposal that the final campaign will be created based on actual research findings that are conducted as part of the planning phase of the campaign.

Provide context to the situation analysis by shedding some light on occurrences that led to this moment of needing to issue an RFP and desiring to launch a new campaign. Clearly list the campaign goal and the individual objectives proposed to fulfill that goal. Paint a picture of the strategic approach as an example of what is possible if the agency is selected. State the strategies in a proactive formula that demonstrates how the organization will benefit from the plan: Company XYZ will experience [specific objective] by employing [specific tactic], which aligns with current [Company XYZ mission or values].

Case Studies and References

This section demonstrates the agency's previous work and capabilities to perform the proposed work based on its scope of work and qualifications. Previous case studies included identify the name of the project, the scope of services requested, the budget and timeline for implementation, and the outcome or metrics of the campaign to demonstrate successful completion. If permitted, include a contact name as a reference, along with the contact's phone number and email address, so the potential client can follow up to inquire more and ask details about the agency's performance on the job.

Sample Portfolio of Related Work

Including additional samples of related work from the agency's portfolio presents another opportunity to demonstrate and showcase the team's creative ability and familiarity with the proposed scope of work included in the RFP. Demonstrating proficiency and successful outcomes on similar projects builds confidence with the client, underscoring that there is not a steep learning curve for the agency and that the selected team can quickly develop and launch a new campaign. The PR agency should select a few pieces or campaigns to highlight, to avoid overwhelming the RFP selection team with massive amounts of content. This is a situation where less is more, and the professional work should speak for itself.

Calendar, Schedule and Timeline

The calendar, schedule and timeline sections outline the process of how the proposed campaign will be researched, planned, implemented, and evaluated. It's often helpful to include a calendar of events or a Gantt organizational chart that lists sample activities during a specified time period and how they will be assigned and accomplished based on the client's requested schedule for completion. Figure 12.1 displays a sample Gantt chart, which is often used for planning and scheduling in PR campaigns.

Budget

The final budget section can easily be described as the most important section of an RFP response, because if the client cannot afford to pay the amount budgeted or if the proposed budget exceeds the RFP's recommended budget range — the agency will not win the contract. If a target budget is included in the RFP, the agency response and campaign budget should fall within that range. If no budget recommendations are given, the PR agency team should develop

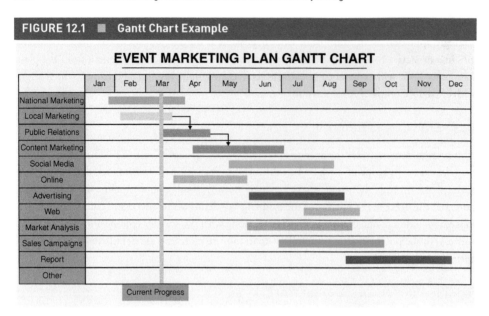

FIGURE 12.1 ■ Gantt Chart Example

EVENT MARKETING PLAN GANTT CHART

a solid campaign with a competitive budget that delivers a lot of bang for the buck; meeting or exceeding the client's expectations while still making a profit for the agency.

Before beginning the RFP response and contemplating budgets, the PR team needs to review the RFP and the issuer of the RFP to ascertain what role the budget will play in the final selection. Generally speaking, for-profit private companies or businesses seeking large-scale, creative campaign approaches are not necessarily motivated or constrained by a lowest bidder environment (as is commonplace with government RFPs that are funded by taxpayer dollars). On the other hand, if the solicitation is a bid document (versus an RFP) and clearly states that budget is the determining factor, then the PR team should take that under advisement and adapt the strategic response and budget as needed.

For clarity and convenience, the budget section can be formatted in a table or spreadsheet that lists hourly rates, fees, and basic line-item expenses for personnel, creative content, production expenses, and overhead expenses, with a bottom line total or budget range, based on the client's request. Figure 12.2 depicts an RFP budget worksheet.

An important reminder: for government RFP or Bid responses, be sure to include the exact sections and formatting requested, within the length and total page count specifications given. Complete the RFP response on any mandatory forms provided for submission, and stay within all stated timelines and budgets, as directed. Following their directions is the key to success. Review the verbiage below to gain an understanding of how little flexibility there is for some RFPs.

Listed here are the first five notices (from a government agency) in a numbered list of more than 20 separate instructions to vendors planning to respond to an RFP for Public Relations, Marketing, and Advertising services:

FIGURE 12.2 ■ RFP Budget Worksheet

PUBLIC RELATIONS BUDGET (MONTHLY)

20XX Projected Expenses

PUBLIC RELATIONS	Jan	Feb	Mar	Apr	May	Jun	Jul	Aug	Sep	Oct	Nov	Dec	20XX Total
SUBSCRIPTIONS													
Press release service (e.g. PRWeb)	$100	$100	$100										$300
Research/contact service (eg. Cision)	$100	$100	$100										$300
Reputation monitoring software (eg. Vendasta)	$100	$100	$100										$300
CONTENT													
Press releases	$100	$100	$100										$300
Newsletters	$100	$100	$100										$300
Reports	$100	$100	$100										$300
Guest posts	$100	$100	$100										$300
EVENTS/TRADESHOWS													
Admission	$100	$100	$100										$300
Transportation	$100	$100	$100										$300
Accommodations	$100	$100	$100										$300
Meals	$100	$100	$100										$300
MEDIA RELATIONS/AWARDS													
Dinners	$100	$100	$100										$300
Gifts	$100	$100	$100										$300
Award entry fees	$100	$100	$100										$300
AGENCY													
Retainer fees	$100	$100	$100										$300
Expenses	$100	$100	$100										$300
Other	$100	$100	$100										$300
TOTAL	$1,700	$1,700	$1,700	$0	$0	$0	$0	$0	$0	$0	$0	$0	**$5,100**

20XX Actual Expenses

PUBLIC RELATIONS	Jan	Feb	Mar	Apr	May	Jun	Jul	Aug	Sep	Oct	Nov	Dec	20XX Total
SUBSCRIPTIONS													
Press release service (e.g. PRWeb)	$100	$100	$100										$300
Research/contact service (eg. Cision)	$100	$100	$100										$300
Reputation monitoring software (eg. Vendasta)	$100	$100	$100										$300
CONTENT													
Press releases	$100	$100	$100										$300
Newsletters	$100	$100	$100										$300
Reports	$100	$100	$100										$300
Guest posts	$100	$100	$100										$300
EVENTS/TRADESHOWS													
Admission	$100	$100	$100										$300
Transportation	$100	$100	$100										$300
Accommodations	$100	$100	$100										$300
Meals	$100	$100	$100										$300
MEDIA RELATIONS/AWARDS													
Dinners	$100	$100	$100										$300
Gifts	$100	$100	$100										$300
Award entry fees	$100	$100	$100										$300
AGENCY													
Retainer fees	$100	$100	$100										$300
Expenses	$100	$100	$100										$300
Other	$100	$100	$100										$300
TOTAL	$1,700	$1,700	$1,700	$0	$0	$0	$0	$0	$0	$0	$0	$0	**$5,100**

1. **READ, REVIEW AND COMPLY:** It shall be the Vendor's responsibility to read this entire document, review all enclosures and attachments, and any addenda thereto, and comply with all requirements specified herein, regardless of whether appearing in these Instructions to Vendors or elsewhere in this RFP document.

2. **LATE PROPOSALS:** Late proposals, regardless of cause, will not be opened or considered, and will automatically be disqualified from further consideration. It shall be the Vendor's sole responsibility to ensure delivery at the designated office by the designated time.

3. **ACCEPTANCE AND REJECTION:** The State reserves the right to reject any and all proposals, to waive any informality in proposals and, unless otherwise specified by the Vendor, to accept any item in the proposal. If either a unit price or an extended price is obviously in error and the other is obviously correct, the incorrect price will be disregarded.

4. **BASIS FOR REJECTION:** Pursuant to 01 NCAC 05B .0501, the State reserves the right to reject any and all offers, in whole or in part, by deeming the offer unsatisfactory

as to quality or quantity, delivery, price or service offered, non-compliance with the requirements or intent of this solicitation, lack of competitiveness, error(s) in specifications or indications that revision would be advantageous to the State, cancellation or other changes in the intended project or any other determination that the proposed requirement is no longer needed, limitation or lack of available funds, circumstances that prevent determination of the best offer, or any other determination that rejection would be in the best interest of the State.

5. **EXECUTION:** Failure to sign EXECUTION PAGE in the indicated space will render proposal non-responsive, and it shall be rejected.

Take a look at the copy below, which is an excerpt from the General Provisions standard verbiage and boilerplate text used by a statewide government agency on its RFPs:

Governing Law

The contract is governed by federal law and will be construed accordingly. To the extent State law may apply, in the case where there is no applicable federal law, the State law that applies is the law of the State in which the federal government office executing the contract is located and it serves as the governing law.

Independent Contractors

The federal government retains independent contractors for the sole purpose of performing the services or providing the goods described in a contract. If subcontracting is permitted, then the term "Contractor" refers to both the contractor and all subcontractors at all levels. You must ensure that all subcontractors adhere to all of the terms and conditions of the contracts that have flow-down requirements.

Subcontracting Reporting

If subcontracting is approved under an award, you must submit a Subcontracting Report, on a semiannual basis, addressing the following for each subcontractor:

- Subcontractor's name, address, and DUNS number.

- Subcontractor's type of business concern: Minority- or Women-Owned Business (MWOB), Small Disadvantaged Business (SDB) (including ethnicity), or Veteran-Owned Business.

- North American Industry Classification System (NAICS) Code and corresponding geographic location of the subcontractor's place of performance.

- Period covered by report.

- Description of work performed by subcontractor during the report period.

- Total compensation paid to subcontractor cumulative to date.

- Percentage completion toward Subcontracting Plan goals.

Audit of Records

The federal government, through its Contracting Officer or designated representative(s), has the right to audit and examine your records and inspect your facilities in the following ways:

- Examination of Costs: The federal government agency can audit and examine your books and records, and your accounting procedures and practices, regardless of their form (e.g., machine readable media) or type (e.g., databases, applications software, database management software,).

- Facilities Used For the Contract: The federal government agency can inspect, at reasonable times, the facilities you use during performance of the contract.

Make no mistake: RFPs are serious business, and the issuing agencies don't take themselves lightly. The obligation as a PR professional responding to an RFP is to understand how the process works, know what the expectations are from the potential client, and appreciate the value of what RFP responses and the resulting contracts mean to the PR agency.

Metrics for Evaluation

Including a section in the RFP response that details the metrics built in to measure progress and accomplishments of the goal helps the potential client envision a successful campaign, because they know in advance what type of results to expect. It also demonstrates that the PR team has given thought to the entire process from beginning to end — and is planning for a successful outcome.

KPIs, also known as Key Performance Indicators, are targets that help measure progress and performance against stated goals and objectives. They are crucial benchmarks that allow the agency and client to monitor campaign results and adapt or adjust as needed. Listed here are some common metrics that agencies use as part of the campaign evaluation process:

- Earned Media Value with print, broadcast and online media coverage

- Promotional video views, downloads and viewer impressions

- Website unique visitors, web page views, site traffic and link click-thrus

- Social media engagement and content shares (e.g., retweets, posts, likes, fans, followers)

- Document downloads

- Special event and virtual event registration and attendance

- Percentage increase in phone calls or emails

- Media or industry brand mentions

Updated Guidance on PR Metrics for Evaluation

AMEC is the International Association for Measurement and Evaluation of Communication – an organization that authored a set of guidance for PR guidelines titled the Barcelona Principles. The original Barcelona Principles were launched in 2010; with two subsequent revisions. In 2015, the 2.0 update and in 2020, the revised 3.0 version of the Barcelona Principles was unveiled for the organization's 25th anniversary. Figure 12.3 displays the content shared when these updates were unveiled. A more comprehensive presentation outlining how to apply these principles is available on the www.amecorg.com website.

AMEC is the world's largest media intelligence and insights professional body, representing organisations and practitioners who provide media evaluation and communication research. AMEC grew from seven members to nearly 200 in its 25th anniversary year, representing organisations based in 86+ countries worldwide, and more than 1,000 professionals dedicated to measurement and evaluation best practice across the globe.

Here is an overview of the Barcelona Principles 3.0:

1. **Setting goals is an absolute prerequisite to communications planning, measurement, and evaluation.**

   The founding principle of SMART (specific, measurable, actionable, relevant, and time-bound) goals as a foundation for communications planning has been promoted to an *essential prerequisite*. It pushes measurement and evaluation as a core component of the planning process, articulating target outcomes and how progress towards these will be assessed.

2. **Measurement and evaluation should identify outputs, outcomes, and potential impact.**

   Previously, the Principles recommended measuring outcomes, rather than simply counting outputs. The updated principles extend this to consider longer term impact of communications strategy. According to AMEC Board Director Ben Levine, this means thinking about "the channels we are impacting, and change we would like to see through campaigns, events and activations."

3. **Outcomes and impact should be identified for stakeholders, society, and the organization.**

   From the original focus on business metrics, such as sales and revenue, the 2020 update embraces a more holistic view of performance. It allows the model to be more inclusive of a broader range of organisations and communications roles that are not necessarily profit-driven.

4. **Communication measurement and evaluation should include both qualitative and quantitative analysis.**

   "To understand the full impact of your work, it is crucial that you use the full suite of methods to measure those outcomes," summarised Levine in describing the evolution of this principle to not just quantify but also understand how messages are being received, believed and interpreted.

FIGURE 12.3   ■   Barcelona Principles Infographic

5. **AVEs are not the value of communication.**

The message remains consistent and clear; "we continue to believe that AVEs [Advertising Value Equivalency] do not demonstrate the value of our work." It is important that communications measurement and evaluation employs a richer, more nuanced, and multi-faceted approach to understand the impact of communications.

6. **Holistic communication measurement and evaluation includes all relevant online and offline channels.**

   Our founding principle that social media can and should be measured is so obvious today. The 2020 iteration reflects the game-changing shift in social communications' capabilities, opportunities, and influence, such that all relevant online and offline channels should be measured and evaluated equally. The AMEC measurement framework promotes clarity across earned, owned, shared, and paid channels to ensure consistency in approach towards a common goal.

7. **Communication measurement and evaluation are rooted in integrity and transparency to drive learning and insights**.

   Sound, consistent, and sustained measurement calls for integrity and transparency in recognition of today's attention to data privacy and stewardship as organisations comply with new regulations, such as GDPR (General Data Protection Regulation). This is also a statement that measurement isn't simply about data collection and tracking, but about learning from evaluation and applying insight back into communications planning. It recognises the need to be transparent about the context in which programmes are run and being aware of any bias that may exist in the tools, methodologies and interpretations applied.

Source: https://amecorg.com/barcelona-principles-3-0-translations/.

Barcelona Principles 3.0 is the result of a true team effort across the world. They have evolved to be applicable to the world in which the communications industry and all who work within it now operate and will continue to develop for years to come.

12.3 RFP PROCESS

Many creative agencies subscribe to paid services that routinely send new RFP opportunities to subscribers based on their industry eligibility or NAICS codes that match the services being sought. In other instances, agency leaders may receive a notice or heads-up that a company is about to issue a new RFP and request a copy so that the company can respond. There are also free websites where open RFPs are listed for anyone to see. In the case of federal, local government, or municipal RFPs, the document may reach the PR agency through direct database contact or through a registration portal that coordinates alerts and notifications based on NAICS codes and other industry-related coding systems.

After the RFP Is Issued: The Cost of Getting and Doing Business

The amount of time, energy, and resources required to sufficiently respond to an RFP can be substantial — oftentimes diverting personnel and billable hours away from current projects and overextending the current team members. Before pursuing new RFP opportunities that require a lot of writing by the proposal authors, it is important to assess whether the project or contract is really worth the effort. Here are some questions to ask before making the commitment to bid:

Can the PR Agency Afford to Pursue This Bid Opportunity and Create a Quality RFP Response?

Is it worth investing 50 hours and $2,500 in production costs and travel expenses for an in-person pitch to pursue a $15,000 contract that has 20 competitors vying for it when the agency has no previous relationship with the RFP issuer and no inside connection? Attracting new business routinely requires conducting a cost-benefit analysis to make sure the new business is actually smart business and good business for the agency.

Can the PR Agency Afford to Manage the Contract if Successful in the RFP Process?

It sounds like a silly question, but more often than realized, an aggressive, low bid to beat out the competition results in an "underbid" where the agency cannot afford to perform the job because the contract is not profitable. In this scenario, the agency is essentially paying to do business because it's losing money just to compete.

Is There Enough Time to Produce a Quality RFP Response?

In most cases, making the commitment to respond to an RFP requires a significant investment of time by the PR agency team members. Sometimes there is not a long lead time to prepare because the issuing agency is in a rush, or the RFP wasn't discovered until the last minute, or the RFP wasn't initially viewed as a good fit due to other commitments, but suddenly it becomes a priority to bring in new business. Those are all realistic situations and occurrences, but the question still remains whether there is enough time to do a good job; because a project that is half-done is essentially undone.

Is There an Existing Relationship Between the Agency and Client?

Leveraging existing relationships is part of the professional networking game, and it's no different when it comes to RFP opportunities. There's a saying that people do business with people they know, people they like, and people they trust. If an agency is pursuing a shot in the dark by responding to an RFP at a company where there is no established working relationship or prior interactions, it may be an exercise in futility. Yes, the RFP process is supposed to be open and fair, but that's often not the case — even with heavily regulated government contracts. That's not to say the opportunity isn't worth going after; but rather, understanding that 'who you know' is an important factor in determining whether an RFP is a worthwhile pursuit.

Are There Any Potential Conflicts of Interest Working on this Project?

A conflict of interest can occur when the PR agency's interests collide with external factors that can potentially affect the judgments, actions, and decisions of the agency personnel. Examples of agency conflict might be investment with or financial obligations to the issuing agency, or undisclosed personal relationships that could unfairly influence the selection process, or previous working relationships with employees that violate a nondisclosure agreement (NDA) that protects intellectual property, contract details, or trade secrets.

Has the PR Agency Successfully Performed Similar Work in the Past?

Is the scope of work for the PR agency familiar territory or is it a shot in the dark with hopes for a successful hit? Knowing how competitive the RFP process can be, it's crucial for the PR team to be honest about their capabilities and strengths, and to wisely invest their time and energy going after projects that (1) they can perform well on; and (2) don't set the team up for failure.

Is the Contract a Profitable Venture to Pursue?

A common saying in business is, "If it doesn't make dollars, it doesn't make sense (cents)." This is true for RFP responses as well. Agency leaders and teams must ask the questions in advance about whether they can afford to go after a contract — and if they can afford to win and perform well on the contract. Winning a contract isn't always a win if the cost of implementing the campaign is equal to or more than the contract amount. Team leaders should know in advance where the financial loss, break-even, and profit margin points are in the budget and then decide if the contract is worth pursuing.

Is There Potential to Grow the Contract in Additional Projects?

Sometimes a smaller (still profitable) contract is worth pursuing if the possibility of more work is on the horizon. Perhaps the issuing agency is entering the RFP process for the first time to try it out and gauge the results. Oftentimes, a client doesn't know what they need until they hire professionals to tell them and to provide additional guidance. This presents the ideal situation for a PR agency to perform well on the existing contract and then propose an expanded scope of work to keep the job going beyond the original commitment.

Will Working on the Project Enhance the Agency's Credibility and Professional Reputation?

The ideal scenario is to secure opportunities that align with the PR agency's values, maximize the team's core strengths and skill sets, and allow people to feel good about the work they're doing. Understandably, that is not always the case, but it is certainly something to aspire to as part of the decision-making process. Like any other industry, the PR sphere is tight-knit and filled with conversations about new projects and new clients. It's opportune for the agency's reputation and bottom line to work on projects that enhance their credibility and professional reputation.

Do the Client's Values Align With the Agency's Values?

Depending upon the values and morals of the leaders at the PR agency, sometimes there just isn't enough money to work with an organization that doesn't share the same values — or worse — opposes or conflicts with the agency's stated values. Requiring employees to represent or defend the reputation of a client with whom they disagree, or privately disavow, can be demoralizing to a team and detrimental to the agency. Shared values are an important consideration when determining which projects to pursue.

12.4 — SUCCESSFUL RFP RESPONSES

Keep in mind, government RFPs almost always provide a Question & Answer period where they invite questions about the RFP or RFQ via email and then issue the responses to everyone on the bidders' list, ensuring that all companies receive the same response and the same information at the same time. If given a chance to ask the issuer of the RFP questions, here are some things to consider inquiring about further.

- Is there an existing PR agency in place and is that company planning to bid on this new RFP?

- Who are the decision-makers for this RFP; what is the PR agency selection process and timeline?

- Why did the company or department decide to issue this RFP now — what is the perceived problem, challenge, or opportunity?

- What does a successful campaign look and sound like at the end of the agency engagement; how does the company or department issuing the RFP measure success?

- Is there a creative communications process from the past that worked well? And are there any creative communication processes that didn't work well?

- Are previous successful RFP responses available for review?

- What is the budget and how much of a role does budget play in the final decision? Is this a "lowest bidder" scenario where the most competitive, qualified bid wins (common with government agency RFPs)?

- How many other agencies are bidding or competing for this contract?

- What criteria or agency characteristics are most important to the selection team?

- Is there any additional information that is pertinent to the campaign that should be considered or factored into the RFP response?

Responding to RFPs can be an extremely stressful, time-consuming, and competitive process. For high-dollar contracts, it's not unusual for more than 25 agencies to be pursuing the same opportunity. In most cases, only one — or maybe two or three agencies with complementary services — will win. That means more than 20 other agencies also put in a substantial amount of time and effort to prepare and pitch their proposals, to no avail.

As a respondent to an RFP, there are some things basic things to do to make sure the time and energy spent writing the response don't result in a waste of time.

Most importantly, is to SUBMIT THE RFP ON TIME! If the due date is May 4 at 2:30 p.m. Eastern Time, that means not a minute later. Countless quality and complete RFP responses have been disqualified or discarded because they were submitted late. In this competitive arena, excuses are not welcome. Regardless of the reasons . . . congested traffic, faulty

GPS directions, incorrect address, slow Wi-Fi; it does not matter in most cases. If the RFP response is late, it is automatically disqualified. This is almost always the case with government contracts where procedural audits are common, and the rules are less flexible. In fact, the complex structure and extensive requirements of the RFP document, along with the large volume of responses, often make it necessary for RFP managers to find ways to filter out agencies. Late submissions or submissions with spelling errors, grammatical errors, and typos are easy targets to help narrow the field of potential vendors.

Another simple (maybe, not easy) step to take is to follow the RFP guidelines exactly to the letter of the written specifications. If the RFP submission details state to submit one original signed copy in blue ink; five double-sided copies on 30% post-consumer recycled paper; one electronic copy on a USB flash drive; and sign pages 3, 9, and 32 with a green marker, then that's precisely what needs to be done. Somewhere there's a person with a checklist making sure there is an original signed copy, recycled paper, a flash drive, and green ink as the basic submission standard to accept the proposal for review.

The next tip is to do some research on previous RFP processes and successful awards with the organization. If it's a private company, check out their website, social media sites, annual report, news releases (for a PR agency contact name), and any other collateral materials to pick up clues regarding the type of work they're accustomed to producing — or who might be behind their creative content. If it's a public organization that is funded with taxpayer money, the information is required to remain accessible and open to the public — with the exception of confidential trade secrets or proprietary information or intellectual property. However, the documents available as part of the public record can provide a lot of details regarding previous contractors, budget ranges, and the longevity of previous projects.

Though the RFP process in theory is to present a level playing field for all qualified agencies or contractors to respond, that is not always the case. Another tip is to read the entire RFP document to see if it seems narrowly tailored toward a particular agency. Excess specificity related to what a respondent's unique capabilities are might provide a clue that the RFP process is just a formality, and the selection has already been made, based upon how the document is written.

For example, say an innovative app developer is seeking a creative firm with national media relationships and team members who are fluent in German. The qualified agency should also manage an onsite soundstage and video editing suite, and possess a proven track record of producing award-winning content (i.e., Emmy awards), and have at least five regional branch offices located in Dallas, New York, San Francisco, Los Angeles, and Chicago. That's a pretty clear hint that they already have a company in mind — and an indication to keep looking for other opportunities.

Last, nurture new relationships and ask questions if provided the opportunity to do so. If the RFP document lists a contact name and email address or phone number, reach out to the individual to introduce yourself and your agency, and inform them of your intent to respond to the RFP. Ask some of the questions mentioned previously to gain insight about the process and the desired results. Even if the response bid is not successful, use that as an opportunity to ask for a review of the proposal and what could have made it stronger. Use every opportunity to learn and grow — and be better prepared and positioned for the next time.

12.5 — BUSINESS DEVELOPMENT RESPONSIBILITIES

As a new member of the company's team, it's important to understand how the business makes money and what a new employee's role in business development will be. Transitioning from completing assignments for a grade to tracking hours and submitting them to a bookkeeper or accountant as part of growing the company's resources is a big responsibility. Fortunately, the expectation for young PR professionals is not to be financial experts, but to have a working knowledge of how money comes in and how it goes out so that everyone within the company works together in stewardship of the agency's resources. Here are some helpful terms to know:

- billable hours —The time spent working on a project or a client's campaign that will be charged to the client; compensation for an employee's time for work to complete an assignment

- flat rate —A fixed, flat fee charged to a client for a project deliverable or specific work being done on their behalf

- hourly rate —The amount of money that is charged to a client per hour for work being done on their behalf

- retainer —An amount of money consistently paid (usually monthly) to reserve a specified amount of time dedicated toward a project or campaign

Here are some last-minute tips to keep in mind if given the opportunity to pitch the account in person:

- Rehearse the presentation several times in advance and make sure it doesn't go over the assigned time limit, which can be a cause for disqualification. Practice makes perfect, and with a room full of competitors seeking any advantage, everything matters.

- Matching outfits are not necessary, but dressing professionally — even if not on the pitch team — is a requirement as a representative of the team.

- Design clear and easy-to-read presentation materials to avoid any confusion; also plan to leave behind copies for further review by the selection team.

- Make sure all team members are familiar with the RFP response, familiar with the potential client, and prepared to answer questions at the end of the pitch presentation.

- Ask for the business. Don't assume the client knows that this account is important or valuable to the agency — and not just seen as another RFP pitch song and dance. Express interest in the client and a desire to do the work; ask for the business.

CHAPTER SUMMARY

As it relates to creative agencies, RFPs are the most common of the business solicitation documents, but there are other types of invitations and bids that also lead to new PR opportunities. The first steps toward success are entering the RFP response process with confidence that the RFP is worthy of pursuit and assurance that the agency has a reasonable chance to win the contract. There are a lot of important questions to ask in advance and several key considerations, based on whether the RFP is from a private company or government agency — and whether the agency's skill sets align with the proposed scope of work for the project.

Responding with well-written, standard sections related to the RFP document is a basic expectation. The executive summary provides a high-level overview; the strategic response outlines the campaign approach, schedule, and metrics; and the budget details how much it costs to implement the campaign and what the client can expect in return for their investment.

Finally, if an agency makes it to the final round or on to the short list of finalists, an in-person pitch is often what seals the deal. The PR team should write out scripts for the final presentation and draft crisp, clear, and engaging presentation materials to support the pitch presentation. Writing RFP responses can be time-consuming, but the process is a crucial component of business development and key to an agency's continued growth and development.

KEY TERMS

billable hours	retainer
flat rate	Request for Proposal (RFP)
hourly rate	Request for Quote (RFQ)
Letter of Interest (LOI)	Request for Tender (RFT)

DISCUSSION QUESTIONS

1. What are some of the subtle differences between business solicitation documents such as RFPs, RFQs, and RFIs?

2. What are some good reasons that a PR Agency team might decide not to pursue an RFP opportunity?

3. Discuss some KPIs to incorporate as metrics to evaluate a successful public relations campaign.

WRITING EXERCISES

1. Select a short RFP for a potential project that interests you and write the Strategic Response section that correlates to the requested scope of work by the client.

13 | PROMOTIONAL WRITING

INTRODUCTION

The two chapters in this section that explain broadcasting highlight the writing-focused elements of integrated marketing, strategic communications and traditional public relations across multiple publications and platforms including print, online, audio and video.

This chapter on promotional writing will introduce and present opportunities to fine-tune writing skills that focus primarily on promotion and publicity on behalf of a brand.

13.1 — PROMOTIONAL WRITING

Promotional writing is created with the intent to motivate consumers of the content into some desired action, whether it be to attend a concert, vote for a political candidate, purchase a product, renew a subscription, or take countless other possible actions. To those outside the profession, publicity and promotions are the sectors mostly closely identified with public relations, based on media representations and general stereotypes about what PR professionals do. Whether the promotional activity is developing content, supporting special events, or coordinating an awe-inspiring, stunning PR spectacle, at the end of the campaign the final metric is results. Did the receivers of the messaging do what was desired and take the appropriate action that helped move the PR needle one notch closer to success?

Effective promotional content often entails sensory appeal, finding ways to elicit more than just a cerebral response where the audience simply thinks about and processes what is being shared and then makes a determination on whether or not to take action. Studies in both advertising and public relations indicate that the more senses stimulated in communications, the more likely an audience is to respond.

Amusement parks have mastered the art of drawing in their customers through sensory appeal. Once inside the gates of an attraction, individuals are almost overwhelmed by the myriad sights, smells, sounds, and endless imaginings of how much fun they can have. There is loud, energetic music playing. There are flashing lights and gigantic, glowing graphics everywhere. The smell of fresh-baked goodies and treats waft in the air, teasing the nostrils and tantalizing the taste buds. Park visitors are surrounded and immersed in a 3-dimensional experience. They can feel the rhythm of the music pulsating all around them, magnetically drawing them into a sensational environment, a nonstop cascading atmosphere of fun, laughter, and enjoyment all around.

Every element of sensory appeal in promotions is intentional and designed to compel people to react or respond. Though most PR writing does not need to compete with the experience of going to an amusement park, there are some important lessons and takeaways that can be used from their model.

Writing for the Eyes

Writing for the eyes means thinking about everything in terms of visual elements. What will the viewer see that compels them to do something? This is a skill that PR practitioners use a lot because they are often writing pitches targeted toward television and broadcast journalists, who work in a visual medium. When thinking about the right words to select for visually appealing content, it is helpful to follow the advice "Show, don't tell." Consider and compare the language used in the following examples to determine which one is more engaging and effective.

Example (plain):

Fireworks Candy Cane Cupcakes are sweet, tart, and tasty all at the same time. If you like a little variety and spice in your sweet treats, try Fireworks Candy Cane Cupcakes!

Example (enhanced):

One bite of Fireworks Candy Cane Cupcakes is like the Fourth of July, whitewater rapids, and a volcanic eruption of sweetness on your tastebuds all at once. They're explosively delicious!

Though both examples introduce the cupcakes, the plain example describes them, while the enhanced example encourages the reader to imagine and experience them, using visualization and sensory-compelling language.

Writing for the Ears

Writing for the ears means thinking about content in terms of what the consumer will hear. A helpful technique in this regard is to write and listen to the content with eyes closed, so there is solely reliance on what is heard. Compare and contrast the language used in the following examples to determine which one is more engaging and effective.

Example (plain):

Symphonix wireless earbuds allow you to hear every note and every lyric with crystal clear precision.

Example (enhanced):

Symphonix wireless earbuds are so clear, you can hear your favorite artist's heartbeat with every note they sing. Throw out the wires, unplug with Symphonix and immerse yourself in pristine tunes with 3-D surround-sound music.

Both examples explain the benefits of the earbuds. The plain example simply describes them, while the enhanced example illustrates the experience and immerses the reader into the experience of wearing the featured earbuds.

Writing for the Sense of Smell

It is amazing how one particular scent can evoke a specific response or memory of a nostalgic scene from the past. It might be the smell of perfume or cologne, the scent of a favorite flower blooming in the spring, or the worst thing someone has ever smelled. Regardless of the source, memories are often connected to smells, and people connect feelings to those memories. Hence, if a PR writer can revive a favorite memory by writing about the sense of smell, it is possible to recreate a specific emotion and use that process to inspire action. Compare the language used in the following examples to determine which one is more interesting.

Example (plain):

Come down to dinner at Grandma's Kitchen for our grand opening. Enjoy homemade cooking just like Grandma makes.

Example (enhanced):

Come on in, we're open for business! The table is set, and dinner is ready and waiting for you. Grandma's Kitchen smells like Thanksgiving dinner (without the drama) every single day. At Grandma's Kitchen, it's always dinner time!

In the plain example, the reader is informed that a new restaurant is hosting a grand opening event. In the enhanced example, the reader is extended an invitation to participate and provided with a relatable comparison to a comforting memory and a specific call to action.

Writing for the Sense of Taste

Early on, the fast-food industry discovered that certain words and colors triggered a hunger response. As a result, countless shades of red, which reportedly make people feel hungry, began cropping up on restaurant signs, menus, marquees, and promotional materials. Writing for the fast-food industry was not solely about the words on the page, but also about the design and presentation of those words and their ability to elicit specific feelings, emotions, and memories related to food. Compare and contrast the language used in the following two examples.

Example (plain):

Sumptuous Sauces offers a full line of sweet and savory sauces for any dish.

Example (enhanced):

Sumptuous Sauces. We see you licking your lips in mouth-watering anticipation of our sweet and savory sauces for every dish. Some like it hot, and some like it hotter. Let's get saucy!

The plain example introduces the sauces. The enhanced example introduces a range of possibilities with the sauces and also engages the reader's imagination.

Writing for the Sense of Touch

How do you describe how something feels? This is where modifiers and compound modifiers really get a moment to shine. Writers of mysteries and thrillers are excellent at creating content that gives readers goosebumps or makes the hairs on the back of their necks stand up. In a horror or sci-fi film, it is never just dark outside; it's an eerie, hollow darkness that envelops your body, sends chills up your spine, and makes you gasp to catch your breath. Consider and compare the language used in the following examples to understand the ability of words to bring products and services to life.

Example (plain):

The sheets in our hotel rooms are the softest in the industry.

Example (enhanced):

At Hotel Haven, our guest retreats offer unparalleled rest and relaxation, with the softest sheets available to wrap you in a blanket of bliss.

The first example explains the hotel has sheets that are soft to the touch. The second, enhanced example helps the reader to envision and imagine the feeling and experience provided by the soft sheets.

Writing for Emotions or Feelings

It goes without saying, that words have the ability to build up and to tear down — just visit any social media channel or read the comments under a controversial post to understand the power of words to elicit strong feelings, emotions, and reactions. It is amazing that words alone can bring people to tears or to the brink of tears with sadness, joy, laughter, or heartfelt nostalgia. Consider and compare the language used in the following examples to determine which one is more engaging and effective.

Example (plain):

Our new fragrance Serene is light, airy, and lasts all day.

Example (enhanced):

Our new fragrance Serene embodies peace, joy, and tranquility in a bottle. Experience a sensational new scent that smells like a bouquet of your happiest memories.

The plain example discusses and describes a fragrance. The second, enhanced example not only introduces the fragrance, but packages the fragrance with words that are precious and significant for the reader; memories they hold dear and now relate to the fragrance.

Writing for Multisensory Content: Bringing Words to Life on Screens

Increasingly ubiquitous video content and Virtual Reality (VR) immersions or experiences are consistently incorporating multisensory content for audiences, subsequently pushing the creative envelope and increasing demand for interactive and captivating content.

At the heart of most compelling creative content is clear and compelling writing that demonstrates a clear understanding of the audience, the campaign goals and the media channels available for distribution. Quality PR writing can be the heart and soul of effective campaigns and serve as a bridge between brands and audiences. With so many options and demands for viewers' attention, the first order of business is to get their attention.

Teasers are a prominent feature in promotional writing and especially content for social media videos. By nature of the platforms and shortened attention spans, effective videos are short and quickly get to the point. Promotional videos or social videos posted on platforms such as Instagram, YouTube, or TikTok often use short teaser prompts or captions to attract more viewers. Instead of stating the obvious such as "Teen Falls Off Bike," which a potential viewer might ignore, the caption or header might read, "You Won't Believe What Happens Next." The possibility of something funny or fascinating happening is what compels the reader to click and watch to see what actually happens next. By the time the reader figures out it's just a teen falling off their bike, the next video is already queued up and ready to play.

The danger with that approach is potentially losing the trust of viewers by offering "click bait" where audiences are lured into watching content by misleading headlines for the sake of additional clicks that are usually connected to some type of advertising revenue for a seller. Even if the allure of more clicks or views is enticing, PR professionals are bound by a Code of Ethics, which requires integrity and honesty in their actions. Though the need and drive to attract viewers and engagement can be strong, the PR professional's interactions with key publics must be built on the bond of mutual trust and reliance that the practitioner and their respective brand are acting in good faith and in the best interest of their audience.

PR PLANNING CHECKLIST: QUICK SOCIAL MEDIA VIDEO REMINDERS

Consider these social media video tips:

- If using a smartphone, shoot the footage horizontally, not vertically.
- Shoot video in a well-lit room, where the subject is centered in the screen or slightly off-center if there are background elements that should be visible.

- Make sure the video subject looks into the camera, (not at their image) on the screen, monitor, or viewfinder.
- Make sure the audio is up high enough so that the recording comes through loud and clear.
- Do a test run and review to make sure there are no unnecessary items or people in the shot with the subject.
- Do not shoot video in front of a window or with a light source behind the video subject.
- Do not shoot video outside with the sun shining behind your subject's head.
- Do not shoot video outside if it is noisy and distracting because it is difficult to edit ore remove background noise embedded into the original audio.
- Use both hands or use a tripod to make sure the camera shot is steady.
- The following video files are generally acceptable: MP4, MOV, WMV.

Two common and basic writing tools used for development of virtual, broadcast, and online video content to motivate audiences are the Audio News Release (ANR) and Video News Release (VNR). To assist with the planning and production needs of a VNR, a storyboard — or visual outline (also explained and demonstrated in Chapter 14 of this textbook) is often used to map out the content and visuals needed for effective storytelling.

Storyboard

A storyboard is a graphics-based outline used to organize and present details about a video production. The storyboard is a useful guide for the client to envision a project and also for the video production team to understand key elements of the video that need to be incorporated. Depending upon the artistic skills of the practitioner, a storyboard can be hand-drawn with illustrations or designed using still photos and graphics. Key elements of the storyboard include time codes, major visuals, signature audio, and other significant on-camera elements. See a sample storyboard in Figure 13.1.

13.2 — BROADCAST NEWS RELEASES (AUDIO AND VIDEO)

The basic construction of a traditional print news release creates the outline for drafting audio and video news releases. In deference to the inverted pyramid style, the key elements of broadcast releases still need to answer the 5 Ws of "Who?" "What?" "When?" "Where?" and "Why?" Instead of just a printed quotation, there may be a couple of key interviews where the interview subject is speaking or visible on camera responding with sound bites that can be used to enhance the overall story. There are also additional background details and information that help the listener or viewer get a better understanding of the story. Finally, summary information and contact information as seen in the boilerplate section of a traditional print news release are included for the convenience of the audience.

Audio News Release

An Audio News Release (ANR) is an uncontrolled production in audio format that is produced (or the production is managed) by the PR or promotional team and distributed to radio stations

FIGURE 13.1 ■ Storyboard Examples

STORYBOARD Project Name: Date: **2023-01-01**
Production: Page: **1 of 1**

00:01–00:05

V/O: Did you know everyone can do their part to help protect the planet?

00:06–00:08

Music: Upbeat music "Song Title" plays

00:09–00:11

SFX: Pencil writing on paper
V/O: There are countless ways to help.

00:12–00:17

V/O: Do you have any bright ideas to help protect the planet?
SFX: windchimes tingling

00:18–00:23

V/O: The whole family can join in and work together to make good things happen.

00:24–00:30

V/O: Visit Do-Your-Part-dot-nonprofit today to learn more.

or audio broadcast platforms to share information about a newsworthy announcement, event, or client-related activity for the purpose of garnering additional media exposure and coverage. In its original format, the audio news release was the audio equivalent to radio stations of what the print news release was to newspapers and other print publications.

ANRs are considered uncontrolled, because the PR professional does not have final say or control of the finished product that airs on the radio station. However, the effort made on the front end to produce quality content with a strong news value is likely to pay off with an accurate story that strongly reflects the brand's desired narrative.

The reason ANRs are included in this chapter for promotional writing is because of the extra effort and financial investment that goes into producing them. Though the media still can take raw audio footage and add or delete to the original content, there is a greater likelihood of the final deliverable being close to what the PR professional desires because of the quality of production and editing that goes into creating the materials contained in an ANR. Essentially, media outlets are less likely to drastically edit or alter produced and well-packaged content that is relevant and broadcast ready.

How are audio news releases produced? ANRs are usually produced to match the format of the radio stations where they will be distributed; meaning if the radio station plays country music, then the accents, references, background music, or ambient sounds will reflect that genre. Ideally, the narration is voiced by a professional actor or voice talent in a soundproof studio to eliminate background noise. Appropriate sound effects and music can be added during the studio production time. The production files are generated by the PR and production teams and submitted to radio stations or podcast distributors at no charge, along with an email pitch and follow-up phone call to suggest how and why different components of the audio news release are relevant to the listening audience. General content contained within the audio news release includes the campaign title or slug, date, total running time of the segment, and contact information.

Helpful resources included with or within the ANR might be a script, recommended narration or lead-in to the ANR, and contact information in case the radio station producer has questions or needs additional information.

How does the final product look before it is distributed to the media? ANRs are typically 60 seconds long, a standard time period for radio content — and enough time to introduce a story, provide some pertinent background information, hear some quotes and sound bites from a subject matter expert (called an actuality), and present a specific call to action. The final product is a polished complete, broadcast-ready story told only in an audio format. Though the piece can be aired as is, it is not unusual for a radio station producer to edit the content to suit the station's needs or the audience's preferences for content. With so many tools available to transfer large files and content, ANRs — depending upon their length and file size — can be shared or distributed via email attachment, link to an online folder, or digital download from a website.

It is the PR professional's job to identify appropriate media outlets and to create a quality media distribution list or database to submit the ANR to for airing. Sample distribution lists might include local radio stations, regional talk radio shows, targeted industry programming, and relevant podcast producers.

Metrics for evaluating the success of an ANR include the following:

- Station demographics and daypart audience totals

- Number of times broadcast on the air or podcast site

- Media monitoring and tracking reports

- Responses to the Call to Action (e.g., sales orders, website visits, phone calls, downloads, social media shares)

Video News Release

A Video News Release (VNR) is an uncontrolled production in video format that is produced by the PR or promotional team and distributed to television stations or broadcast media outlets to share information about a newsworthy announcement, event, or client-related activity for the purpose of garnering additional media exposure and coverage. In its original format, the video news release was the video equivalent to TV stations of what the traditional print news release was to newspapers and other print publications.

VNRs are considered uncontrolled, because the PR professional does not have final say or control of the finished product that airs on television. However, the effort made on the front end to produce quality content with a strong news value is likely to pay off with an accurate story that strongly reflects the desired brand narrative.

The reason VNRs are included in this chapter for promotional writing is because of the extra effort and financial investment that goes into producing them. Though the media still can take raw video footage and add or delete to the original content, there is a greater likelihood of the final deliverable being close to what the PR professional desires because of the quality of production and editing that goes into creating the materials contained in a VNR. Essentially, media outlets are less likely to drastically edit or alter produced and well-packaged content that is relevant and broadcast ready.

How are video news releases produced? VNRs provide crucial components for storytelling to media outlets at no cost. The production costs are incurred by the PR agency and its client to develop quality content that supports a messaging campaign. The content should reflect high quality resolutions that match the level of production on a typical television station. The submitted piece should be crisp and clean, and free from excessive graphics or special effects, which might appear to be advertising versus storytelling.

Helpful elements included within the VNR are time codes, which are similar to a digital table of contents, telling the viewer where in the video content to find specific footage. Sound bites (10 to 15 seconds) and interviews with key individuals are included, as they are likely to highlight a representative of the organization or topic being featured. B-roll, a staple component of VNRs, is generic, relevant video content that supplements the primary footage and helps add variety to the piece. Finally, it is helpful to include a contact slate with a name, email address, phone number, or social media handle in case the station's producer has additional questions or needs additional information.

How does the final product look before it is distributed to the media? With so many tools to deliver files, access to a VNR might simply be a link to an online repository of content. Within the digital folder are clearly labeled files that contain: B-roll video files, sound bites and interview video files, original product still photos or images, video slates with time codes and a Table of Contents, a pitch letter or précis that summarizes the content and newsworthy angle for the media outlet, contact information, and permissions verbiage that states something along the lines of "The enclosed video footage and multimedia content are from Company Name, and the content is provided with full permission for free, unrestricted use at Station XYZ."

It is part of the PR professional's job to create a quality media distribution list or database to identify the right media outlets to share the VNR with and to follow up with a relevant pitch explaining how and why the footage can or should be used. Sample distribution lists might include local network television stations, regional cable television stations, targeted industry programming, and relevant YouTube channels.

Metrics for evaluating the success of a VNR include the following:

- Viewer impressions

- Number of times broadcast on the air

- Media monitoring and tracking reports

- Responses to the Call to Action (e.g., sales orders, website visits, phone calls, downloads, social media shares)

13.3 — AUDIO AND VIDEO PRODUCTION TERMS

In broadcast writing, audio and video cues play pivotal roles in conveying information, emotions, and narratives. These cues serve as essential building blocks for effective A/V writing and script development, adding depth and nuance to the overall communication process. The short list below is by no means a complete representation of audio/video cues; however, the definitions provide basic, foundational concepts for A/V writing and script development.

Basic Audio and Video Terminology for PR Writing

Consider these terms for audio and video in PR writing:

- A-roll — A-Roll is the main footage that drives storytelling, and it contains both audio and video components that inform, persuade, educate, or entertain the viewer.

- B-roll — B-Roll is secondary, supplemental video footage that provides additional context, background, and visual interest during storytelling.

- shot list — A detailed list of every camera shot that needs to be captured in order to produce a final video product.

Basic Elements of Video Production

This list describes basic elements of video production to keep in mind:

- Camera movements — indicate how the entire camera body and lens move to change the view or perspective of what is seen by the viewer.

- Camera/shot transitions — demonstrate how the story changes or moves from one scene to the next as part of storytelling.

- Audio/video cues — These cues prompt audio elements and video directions that dictate what is seen or heard in the final cut of a production.

Camera Shots

The following list defines different camera shots. Figure 13.2 demonstrates what these shots look like in practice.

FIGURE 13.2 ■ Sample Camera Shots

Extreme close-up (ECU)

Close-up (CU)

Medium shot (MS)

Long shot (LS)

Extreme long shot (ELS)

- Extreme close-up (ECU) — subject is very close to camera and viewer; minor details on subject are clear and noticeable, but background is not.

- Close-up (CU) — subject is close to camera and viewer; minor details are less noticeable.

- Medium shot (MS) — subject takes up approximately one-third of the screen; surrounding background environment is visible.

- Long shot (LS) — entire subject is visible on screen, and viewer is given a longer depth of vision to see surroundings and background.

- Extreme long shot (ELS) — entire subject is visible, but not with any clarity or detail; viewer has a wide range of vision that includes surrounding background environment.

Camera Movements

The following list defines different camera movements:

- Dolly in/out — Entire camera body moves in a straight line toward or away from subject.

- Truck right/left — Entire camera body moves in a straight line to the left or right, parallel to subject.

- Pan right/left — Camera body remains in a fixed position, while camera head/lens rotates right or left, as in a panoramic view. A camera pan is a horizontal movement in which the camera body remains fixed while the camera head/lens pivots horizontally.

- Tilt up/down — Camera body remains in a fixed position, while camera head/lens (nods) moves up or down, as in a floor to ceiling shot. A camera tilt is a vertical movement in which the camera body remains in a fixed location while the camera head/lens pivots vertically.

Video Transitions

The following are terms and definitions used when referring to camera transitions:

- Cut — Instantaneous switch from one shot to another; similar to the blink of an eye with a change of scenery between each blink

- Dissolve — Gradual replacement of one image with another

- Wipe — One image "wipes" the previous image away and replaces it

- Fade — Gradual change usually to or from black; "fade to black" — often used to indicate the end of a scene

Other Audio/Video (A/V) Cues

The following list includes different A/V cues:

- Sound effects (SFX) — artificial audio enhancements. Examples of sound effects can include car horns honking, leaves rustling, children laughing, dogs barking, footsteps on a creaky floor, water dripping, etc.

- NatSound — Natural sounds that accompany video footage (e.g., phones ringing in a busy office shot or traffic on the street in a congested city shot)

- Music bed — Music or instrumentals that play in the background and can be directed to be more or less prominent during the spot. Audio cues for music can include music up (louder), music under (lower), music up and out (flourish and ending).

- Voiceover (V/O) — Indicates a speaker who is not shown on camera

- On Camera (O/C) — Indicates a speaker, text or subject that is shown on camera

---

TIPS FOR BEGINNERS: QUICK TIPS TO WRITE FOR RADIO

When writing for radio, consider the following:
- Use sound effects or other audio enhancements to capture listeners' attention before diving directly into the content.
- Open with a soft lead when writing for audio productions. For both audio and video productions, indirect leads are most effective, as they engage the audience and bring them into the story. Since audiences are often distracted while consuming audio or video content, they might miss essential information if the narrator jumps directly into the story or begins with crucial content.
  - Example: "Owners of all-terrain vehicles might want to check their warranties before the end of the year. A top seller of ATVs is issuing a recall because of defective parts, but all repairs may not be covered by the manufacturer or dealer." Notice how the first sentence is a teaser — it alerts the listener that something important will follow.
- For text that will be read by an announcer, make sure the copy or script is speaker friendly and conversational:
  - Use short, simple, declarative sentences. The majority of broadcast sentences are no more than 10 words long.
  - It is acceptable to use sentence fragments. Clauses and phrases sound more like day-to-day, casual conversations — and are more relatable.
  - Avoid long strings of words or modifiers. Break them up into separate sentences or clauses — or simply delete them.
  - Avoid complicated, technical jargon. Use common words that most people readily know and understand.

- Write in the present tense, using an active voice.
- Feel free to use contractions, which are common in everyday speech. Keep the content conversational and relaxed.
- Use phonetic spelling with words that might be difficult to pronounce. Ex. Company CEO Terry Shieffer (SHEE-fur) will make remarks during the press conference.
- If you're using an acronym, write out how it is pronounced:
  - Y-M-C-A (notice the hyphens between each letter)
  - C-E-O (this is a common acronym, so it's not written out, but shown as it's pronounced)
  - NASA (no hyphens are included because NASA is how the word is pronounced)
  - N-double-A-C-P (this is the preferred use and pronunciation of this organization's name)
  - U-S Senate (notice that there is a hyphen between U and S to ensure it's pronounced "U-S" and not "us")
  - p-m, a-m
  - N-C-double-A tournament (write it out the way it should be pronounced)
- Internet addresses also should be written as they would be pronounced. So, a URL for website.com would appear in broadcast copy as [website-dot-com].
- Keep numbers as simple to say and hear as possible. Focus on the key statistics, and write out numbers as they would be pronounced:
  - If there is a large or long number, round it off. Instead of saying $1,103,809; write and say, "More than one point one million dollars."
  - $1 million (print) = one million dollars (audio).
  - 4.9 percent (print) = almost 5 percent (audio).
  - Phone numbers can be written as they appear in print: "Call area code 555-202-8972." Be sure to repeat the phone number since people are often doing other tasks while listening.

13.4 — REPURPOSING CONTENT

Traditionally, people thought of promotion and publicity as the two sides of the public relations coin; professionals hired for the sole purpose of getting positive media coverage, eliminating negative media coverage, and telling anyone who will listen how great Company A is and what great things the business is doing to make the world a better place.

Now, there is a better understanding of how effective public relations and other strategic communications processes can be used to build and strengthen relationships between brands and their audiences. The demand for promotional writing and creative content is nonstop. Fortunately, a large part of PR writing consists of redundancy, refining and repurposing original content for different audiences across different platforms.

Here are several instances of how the same original owned media content ("O" from the PESO — Paid, Earned, Shared, and Owned media — Model introduced in Chapter 5) can be repurposed (or upcycled) for promotional purposes across various media channels.

Let's use the example of fictional company FanFair Foods, which makes and sells sugar-free and zero fat amusement park snacks and treats (Yum!). The regional company targets health-conscious Generation Z consumers in the Southwest, but is now seeking to expand nationally and to reach broader demographic audiences.

Facebook

The global presence and easy access to audiences around the world make Facebook one of the most recognizable and effective social media apps for reaching a large number of people at once. Between building a dedicated network of customers and managing a paid social media campaign that allows target marketing based on geographic location and similar hobbies and interests, a Facebook campaign can be an excellent way to promote a company and expand a brand's reach.

On Facebook, a basic FanFair Foods post will include a post headline, branded image or video, and relevant call to action. The bottom of the post also can incorporate a hyperlinked button to shop or learn more.

X (Formerly and Commonly Called Twitter)

X (formerly Twitter) is considered to be a microblog, which chronicles content with the most recent tweets (messages consisting of 280 or fewer characters) posted at the top of the feed. X users engage followers and also follow other accounts of interest. A FanFair Foods tweet will consist of brief content, relevant searchable hashtags, and an on-brand photo or video of the product or a celebrity influencer enjoying FanFair Foods snacks. Options on X to expand the reach of the message include incorporating @names, or handles, and tagging key individuals in the post with online large followings.

Instagram

Instagram is a popular video sharing site that is driven by visual content. Filtered photos and videos are uploaded and combined to create online stories that are shared within a users' network. On Instagram, FanFair Foods' celebrity influencer is a well-known fitness and lifestyle coach with more than 2 million followers. Each month, the influencer posts two photos and two videos that include FanFair Foods snack products in the daily health and fitness regimen.

TikTok

Based on algorithms and viewing habits, this ubiquitous video sharing, social media site is a useful tool to build awareness with minimal investment needed for production. Fancy equipment and expensive film crews are not recommended, as most content in the 15-second to 3-minute videos is shot from the selfie vantage point, with the focus being on the subject in the video, rather than the production quality. As a note, in late spring/early summer of 2021, TikTok overtook YouTube in the United States as the platform with consumers dedicating the most time to watching video content. Here is an example of how embedded captions or content on TikTok for fictional company FanFair Foods might read: TikTok copy — [Captions] All the fun. None of the fat. #FanFairFoods

LinkedIn

LinkedIn is a powerful social networking site for business professionals. One human resources survey indicated that more than 80% of hiring managers visit a potential employee's LinkedIn page before making a final hiring decision. LinkedIn posts tend to focus less on sales and frivolous content and more on informative or educational posts and ways to broaden or strengthen a professional network. A brief presentation for FanFair Foods on LinkedIn will include a brief overview of a recent event hosted or sponsored by the company and a few slides about how to increase employee moral or enhance company culture by incorporating healthy snacks into the workday. The content also will highlight health benefits of FanFair Foods and include a key contact for more information.

Pinterest

Pinterest got its start as an online scrapbooking platform, that has grown into much more for building brand awareness. A Pinterest collection for FanFair Foods will include recipe ideas that include FanFair Foods snacks and photos of the products accompanying healthy meals and other snack-worthy activities.

Email (Direct Marketing)

Direct messages sent to key publics using email content sent to their inboxes is still one of the most efficient and effective ways to reach target audiences. An email subject line for FanFair Foods might read: Let's have some fun with FanFair Foods! The email will include an embedded photo and design/layout that is on brand with the company's colors, typography, voice and personality. The email body copy will highlight the benefits of FanFair Foods, include a list of available products for purchase, and also appeal to the needs and wants of its customers. At the bottom of the email message, there will be a specific call to action accompanied by contact information and buttons that hyperlink to the company's various social media platforms. Email messages can be created and scheduled in advance and distributed with regular frequency to maintain communication and also to establish a level of expectations for outreach to the customers. The interactive nature of the email content means that recipients can share or forward the information, engage with the brand, and contact the company with questions or to request additional information.

E-Newsletter

Newsletters in general target broad audiences with common interests. An e-newsletter for FanFair Foods will provide ample opportunity to highlight product photos, profile interesting customers or brand ambassadors who eat FanFair Foods, showcase creative recipe ideas, and list upcoming special events. E-newsletters can also include video messages from company executives and hyperlink to additional resources on healthy eating habits.

Company Blog

The key to successful blogging is consistency. Company blogs are a good way to connect with audiences and to build a following. The FanFair Foods blog is an Owned media outlet that allows readers to get to know more about the brand and to hear its authentic brand voice. Blog posts allow for more creativity and insights into FanFair Foods and also create a space for two-way dialogue and engagement with customers.

PowerPoint

Beyond the familiar static slide presentations often seen in board rooms, PowerPoint presentations with photos, videos, transitions, and animations can be designed to play like commercials or mini promotional videos to highlight important information about a company. A FanFair Foods PowerPoint presentation will be designed with the brand colors and imagery, an upbeat voice narration of a popular influencer, include important health benefits about the snack food, and conclude with a call to action to purchase the product or learn more.

Webinar

This combination of web-based presentations and seminars became extremely popular during the pandemic, which forced in-person events to be cancelled. Webinars facilitate meetings or presentations to small or large groups and can be broadcast live or recorded and shared on demand. A FanFair Foods webinar is an opportunity for company executives to speak on a panel, hear presentations on the benefit of healthy snacks from a nutritionist, and present a Question-and-Answer session for online guests to learn more directly from the presenters.

Infomercial

Informative, entertaining commercials are a mainstay in promotional writing. These scripted narrations feature products or services and focus on selling wants and needs to consumers. A FanFair Foods infomercial might appear on several different television stations and a dedicated YouTube channel. The infomercial content will feature actors searching for healthy snacking options (the problem) and identifying FanFair Foods as the obvious choice (the solution). The voiceover or narrator will include a list of FanFair Foods health benefits, feature attractive packaging, offer a comparative cost savings versus other snacks, and provide an incentive for making an immediate purchase. *But wait, there's more!* If the customer takes a specific action by a specific date, they also will be rewarded in some additional way that further engages them with FanFair Foods.

Promotional Video

With attention spans at record low levels, an effective promotional video will take less than 3 minutes to view — preferably 60 seconds or less to get its message across. A FanFair Foods promo video might feature high-energy music, attractive actors or subjects wearing trendy fashions, and highlight all the different places to enjoy FanFair Foods — at work, at home, at sporting events, at the park, in the car, on vacation.

Push Notifications

These short messages are delivered directly to an end-user or key public and appear on their mobile device home screen. The notification is automatically triggered by the app and can be delivered to the device regardless of whether an individual is actively using their smartphone. A push notification for FanFair Foods might read: Reminder! It's time for a healthy snack. You deserve it. Enjoy #FanFairFoods

According to an IBM Cloud Education article on push notifications, there are several types of notifications that use artificial intelligence (AI) to distribute AI or human-authored content: There are many ways of applying push notifications, but these are irrespective of marketing strategies, and are conventional to the channel in general. These include

1. Reminders such as in-cart actions, sign-ons and next-step actions

2. Updates, including news-related or relevant brand information

3. Deals like calls-to-action (CTAs) for sales, specials or subscription opt-ins

4. Authentications like security-based, one-time passcodes

5. PSA notifications such as civic information and weather alerts

---

Source: IBM. (2022). *What is a push notification?* https://www.ibm.com/topics/push-notifications.

Direct Mail (U.S. Postal Service)

Every Door Direct is a U.S. post office service offered that allows businesses to target neighbors by identifying zip codes for direct mail campaigns. A direct mail campaign for FanFair Foods will include a full color, double-sided postcard that is mailed directly to a household. The copy will be brief and concise and include bright, eye-catching graphics. There will be a basic product overview, list of benefits, call to action, purchasing details, and contact information.

For all the different media and social media platforms listed, the core message will be consistent across platforms: FanFair Foods is a delicious, healthy snack — and a fun way to enjoy favorite treats without the calories or the guilt of eating junk food.

CONCLUSION

Promotional writing using an integrated communications approach can create a powerful and far-reaching impact on audiences around the globe. The combination of well-researched and well-written content, along with compelling graphics, informative infographics, influencer campaigns, social media and multimedia amplification can create game-changing results.

KEY TERMS

A-roll	pan right/left
Audio News Release (ANR)	shot list
B-roll	sound effects (SFX)
cut	storyboard
dissolve	tilt up/down
dolly in/out	truck right/left
fade	video news release (VNR)
music bed	voiceover (V/O)
NatSound	wipe
On Camera (O/C)	

DISCUSSION QUESTIONS

1. What is the benefit of repurposing or upcycling content across different platforms?

2. How can an audio news release or video news release help build brand awareness?

3. What are some things PR professionals and content creators can do to capture audiences on small screens and keep their attention?

WRITING EXERCISES

1. Write a 15-second soundbite for your university's president or chancellor as part of an Audio News Release (ANR) package reminding students to stay safe during spring break.

2. Write a short push notification from client Bankify to customers reminding them to change their online banking password within the next 30 days for security purposes.

14 AUDIO/VIDEO: WRITING FOR ACTION AND CHANGE

INTRODUCTION

Evolving technology, social media channels, and ubiquitous digital platforms, along with their constant need for updates and content, require that content creators and writing professionals develop and publish informative and entertaining material that not only resonates with the audience through an authentic brand voice, but also compels people to take action. Essentially, it's no longer enough to inform, persuade, or entertain, but now the expectation is to include a call to action that aligns with readers', listeners' or subscribers' self-interests, motivations and socially conscious causes.

This chapter on Audio/Video: Writing for Action or Change discusses how to build strong messaging strategies, harness the power of storytelling, and develop compelling content that connects with audiences; persuades and motivates them to change their minds, alter their behavior, or get involved with causes in a meaningful way.

14.1 — MOTIVATING AUDIENCES

The beginning of the 21st century welcomed new technologies that introduced powerful publishing platforms and storytelling to the masses, enabling everyday people around the world to produce and broadcast content that inspired, encouraged, or enraged people to take action. No longer was the public positioned solely as recipients of information that was pushed out to them with little to no engagement. Now, the conversation had the potential to become a dynamic dialogue between companies, institutions or brands and their respective stakeholder groups. With technology advancements and increased access, the public no longer needed to rely on traditional journalists, reporters, media personalities or communication professionals to select and share information. Furthermore, everyone with a mobile phone, smart device and access to the internet had the capacity to reach countless individuals through social media and social networking platforms. Anyone with a story to tell or a grief to air could tell it to the world unfiltered.

This same time period ushered in the phrase "going viral." Much like the undesirable COVID-19 virus that plagued the world beginning in 2020, the term "viral" shares its genesis in that it refers to "contagious or highly transmissible" content that spreads quickly and widely across the internet and through online social platforms. For too many companies and practitioners, the pressure on professional communicators was to create content that would go viral — amassing millions of views in a few days or weeks. Unfortunately, that is a tall order and unlikely outcome for most content. Though no one can predict what will or will not catch on and go viral, there are some predictable and identifiable patterns in content that goes viral.

A study from college researchers who reviewed and analyzed viral videos reported that three emotions were most likely to make content go viral: anger, awe and humor. Generally speaking, viral content is memorable and shareable because viewers within connected communities usually have the same questions and reactions: Did you see that? Can you believe that? How could/did they do that? I've got to see that again!

In tandem with viral content is the notion of "sticky" content: words and images that resonate with readers and viewers and lend themselves to being memorable and shareable. The content sticks with audiences, connects with them and makes them more inclined to want to tell others about it.

Even before "viral content" was a thing, one of the first videos that embodied the concept of going viral was the "keyboard cat," which featured a feline demonstrating its musical talent by playing a tune on a keyboard. The unusual video was silly, showing something people didn't expect or see every day, and it incorporated the newsworthiness components of novelty and humor. The original author reintroduced the video on YouTube in 2007, and ultimately garnered more than 50 million views.

The famous sibling video "Charlie Bit My Finger" that featured two young brothers Harry, 3 and infant Charlie, one astonished that his brother bit him on camera, eventually logged more than 900 million views on YouTube. The video resonated with audiences, especially families with small children, because it was humorous and relatable to what goes on in households around the globe, creating a shared sense of connection for everyone who watched it. As a follow-up to the viral video's massive popularity and success, there is a direct correlation to its monetary value in exchange for reaching so many viewers. It was reported by The New York Times in 2021 that 'Charlie Bit My Finger' Is Leaving YouTube After $760,999 NFT Sale (NFT = non-fungible token).

Common characteristics of viral content include

- Universal emotional appeal
- Simple and easy to understand

- Unique or unexpected

- Awe-inspiring or mesmerizing

- Just plain funny (e.g., think children or animals on live television)

14.2 — HARNESSING THE POWER OF STORYTELLING

The internet is filled with memes, short video clips, animations, or images that embody a shared sentiment and spread quickly as a result of online sharing and amplification. The word "meme" derives from the concept of memetics (i.e., how ideas replicate, mutate, and evolve). In the context of PR writing, amplify means to expand and extend the reach of a message using influencers and social media platforms.

Traditionally, the term amplification meant to expand a narration as a form of exaggeration. It was a rhetorical device used by writers to embellish their storytelling. More recently, in PR Writing, amplify or amplification is connected to our ability as professionals to use social media tools to increase the significance of a story and to enlarge the target audience that engages with the content.

Whether it's lightning striking a centuries-old monument, a curious shark getting too close to divers, a baby tasting lemons for the first time and reacting as expected or a brown bear chasing skiers down the slope of a mountain, viral videos featuring animals, children and Mother Nature at work tend to catch on and spread quickly because they are viewed as authentic and unscripted — simply snapshots of life happening in real time. There also are other unscripted events recorded on video that suspend reality and capture the attention of the world.

In the summer of 2020, the world watched in shock and horror for more than 9 minutes as video footage from the cellphone of a teenage witness captured and broadcast the arrest and detainment of George Floyd by Minneapolis, Minnesota, police officer Derek Chauvin, an encounter that ultimately led to Mr. Floyd's death. This viral video sparked anger and outrage around the world and mobilized tens of millions of people into marches, protests, and global social movements to support the cause of racial justice. In June 2021, Chauvin was sentenced to 270 months (22 ½ years) in prison for the murder of George Floyd. Many pundits and TV analysts speculated that without the viral video footage, Mr. Chauvin would have gone unpunished, and Mr. Floyd's life and death would have gone unacknowledged. This viral video and associated content are credited with sparking one of the largest global social movements in history.

In the weeks and months following the death of George Floyd, communicators and change agents representing civil rights organizations and causes created messaging strategies, provided talking points, and published commentary about racism, discrimination and racial equity to a captive audience that was ready for action and ready for change. The difference between that moment in time compared to previous similar incidents was the convergence of credible content, education, outrage, focused attention and prolonged engagement — fueled by shared content and viral online exchanges.

In March 2022, during the early weeks of the Russian invasion of Ukraine, another enduring image and video clip captured the attention of the world. In direct contrast to Russian political and media narrative about striking military targets in the name of national defense, cameras captured numerous missile strikes and explosions demolishing residential complexes and a maternity hospital. The image shown around the world was a pregnant woman cradling her bruised and bloodied belly, one of the thousands of innocent Ukrainian civilians who became victims of the invasion. The photo and its associated video counterpart show the woman being rolled closer to the front lines on a gurney by medical and military first responders. It was reported that when told that she was going to lose the baby, she uttered the words, "Kill me now." Both mother and baby died shortly thereafter.

The still picture and complementary video footage sparked outrage for the inexcusable actions being taken and violence being directed toward defenseless individuals and vulnerable populations in Ukraine. In response to the photo and video, there was an uptick in fundraising and relief support from individuals, organizations, corporations and entire nations to help shelter and protect Ukrainian citizens.

Some of the iconic hashtags that became prominent as a result of viral content or social movements energized and fueled by social media engagement include: #MeToo (advocating against sexual harassment, sexual violence, and sexual assault); #BlackLivesMatter (advocating against systemic racism and discriminatory behavior toward African Americans); #IceBucketChallenge (also known as the ALS Ice Bucket Challenge; helping promote awareness of the disease amyotrophic lateral sclerosis [ALS] and raise donations for research), and many more.

The well-read and savvy PR practitioner will constantly monitor current events and world news to identify opportunities for genuine support and authentic engagement on behalf of a brand or brand persona. Developing respectful and relevant content, incorporating appropriate hashtags to amplify a message, and embedding useful images, links and videos are all a part of the PR writing process for inspiring action and change from target audiences in cohesion with the organizations represented.

When content connects with one or more basic motivating factors, audiences are compelled to move from being unmotivated observers to active participants.

Motivating factors within messaging that can inspire action or change include

- Passion, purpose and deeper meaning

- Incentives, benefits and rewards

- Altruism and philanthropy

- Protection from pain and access to pleasure

- Power, ego and self-mastery

- Recognition and approval from others

14.3 — AMPLIFYING MESSAGES

This section covers some common issues, topics, challenges, and opportunities to study and follow, where clients may need to develop campaigns encouraging audiences to take meaningful action.

Common Causes

In 2021, more than 115 million U.S. petitioners visited the website change.org to learn about open petitions and additionally to sign petitions they supported and to encourage others to mobilize for changes in society. By the end of that calendar year, there were more than 791,896 petitions with more than 463,883,172 signatures in total.

According to change.org, the website represents the world's largest nonprofit-owned tech platform for people-powered, social change. Over 450 million people located across more than 196 countries used the technology driven petition and associated campaign tools to speak up on issues they were passionate about and wanted to create change for the better. As the platform continues to expand in use and reach, approximately 70,000 petitions are created and supported on the platform every month, with more than 1.7 million new people joining the platform's global network of users every week.

Animal Rights and Wildlife Protection

Clients in support of animal rights advocacy might be in search of audiences who are willing to take action to protect animals from chemical and product testing. Other animal rights or protections may involve spaying or neutering pets to control animal populations, while also encouraging people to avoid illegal breeding mills and to support no-kill shelters to increase rescue pet adoptions from animal shelters.

Criminal Justice/Sentencing Reform

In connection to racial and social justice issues, these campaigns frequently require support from external audiences because individuals who are incarcerated or being detained by the criminal justice system often do not have the access or necessary resources to advocate for themselves. There are numerous nonprofit organizations and agencies that dedicate their work to reviewing legal cases, hearings and sentencing disparities and guidelines to improve and ensure equal treatment under the law.

Domestic Violence

Law enforcement officials regularly report on the dangers and uncertainty involved with domestic violence and intimate partner calls, due to the volatile nature of the situations. In addition to the personal threats and lack of safety and security for the victims, there is also an economic impact. Domestic violence has a significant negative effect on workforce productivity, accounting for hundreds of thousands of missed days at work and loss revenue due to dangerous conflicts or confrontations that jeopardize the employees' health, safety and ability to safely function on the job.

Environmental Sustainability/Renewable Energy

Corporate social responsibility (CSR) is frequently at the heart of conversations related to companies' accountability to the public regarding environmental issues and corporations' responsibility to the global community to protect the earth by limiting the amount of damage done through waste disposal and wastewater run-off or questionable manufacturing processes.

Related issues surrounding the environment inspire campaigns and messaging about renewable energy sources and ways individuals can contribute to a cleaner environment and less substantial carbon footprint.

Financial (Student Loan) Debt Cancellation

As students and new professionals entering the job market, the topic of student loans and eradicating student loan debt is a top priority. Over the years, numerous consumer debt advocacy groups and nonprofit organizations have secured the assistance of lobbying firms and public relations agency to clarify political positions about student loan debt and to push for policy changes around regulations for the student loan and financial services industry.

Gun Violence and Gun Laws

There may not be a more hotly contested debate in the country than the 2nd Amendment and related conversations about ownership of firearms, background checks and gun violence. Countless millions of dollars have poured into groups and campaigns to reaffirm the legal right to bear arms, at the same time energizing groups who oppose the status quo in response to increasing crimes committed with firearms and devastating mass shootings fueled by easy access to high-powered weapons.

Human Rights Violations

On a national and international scale, the topic of human rights violations touches everyone, highlighting issues like human trafficking to labor abuses. Many campaigns related to human rights violations center around increasing awareness of the issues and informing audiences about ways they can protect innocent victims or identify the problem and alert the appropriate authorities.

Marginalized and/or Underrepresented Groups

There are many more communities with a long list of grievances shared by historically underrepresented populations and groups who have been abused, overlooked or disenfranchised throughout the formation, foundation and development of the country. PR professionals are often called upon to assist with crafting messaging, defining priorities, articulating solutions and helping develop the official voice on behalf of people who have been marginalized in society.

Mental Health Awareness

Throughout the early part of the 21st century, the focus on mental health and well-being increased dramatically due to high-profile individuals, celebrities, politicians and public figures speaking boldly about their own personal challenges with mental health issues, helping to remove the stigma around mental health conversations by elevating and normalizing the topics.

Racial Discrimination

The ongoing struggle within diverse societies is inextricably linked to discrimination, a result of systemic and institutional racism underscored by centuries of oppression chronicled throughout

American history. Nonprofit groups, lobbyists and PR agencies are often called upon to elevate awareness about subtle, persistent and egregious acts that reinforce discriminatory practices and to shine a spotlight on efforts to diminish racism in society.

Quadruple Bottom Line

For decades there was a corporate conversation about the triple bottom line, representing people, planet, and profit. However, in the conversation or discussion about writing for change, it is necessary to add an additional area of focus — purpose. Audiences now expect and demand that corporations and the brands that they support also focus on purpose-driven messaging. The following list expounds upon the quadruple bottom line in messaging to key publics.

- Purpose-oriented messaging — Purpose in messaging indicates a commitment to issues or topics that extend beyond product sales and corporate profits and operations. As part of the brand messaging, organizations need to clearly express their positions and demonstrate their support of societal issues through statements, contributions, donations and advocacy. Purpose-driven messaging not only addresses the questions of "Who?" "What?" "When?" and "Where?"; the messaging also answers the questions "Why?" and "What?" to do next in terms of actionable steps.

- People-oriented messaging — Putting people first means that brands and their public-facing messaging prioritize the well-being and best interests of those who are connected with the brand as customers or brand ambassadors.

- Planet-oriented messaging — Focusing on the planet as a priority strengthens the corporate social responsibility component as part of a company's values statement and commitment to keeping the planet healthy and livable for generations to come.

- Profit-oriented messaging — The expectation is still for corporations to earn a profit and reward shareholders and investors with a return on investment (ROI) in exchange. Though profits are a major priority, in the quadruple bottom line paradigm, profits are not the sole driving factor, but a spoke in the wheel of priorities that reevaluates and reassigns the importance and relevance of purpose, people, planet and profit.

TIPS FOR BEGINNERS: ONLINE TIPS FOR WRITING SOCIALLY CONSCIOUS CONTENT THAT SPREADS

- Do your research to make sure the cause is credible and the players or representatives at the forefront of the movement or issue align with the respective brand values.
- Use an authentic brand voice that resonates with the mission, vision and values of the company to address the topic.

- State how the social cause affects or impacts the brand and identify areas of work or support where the brand has an authentic presence.
- Collaborate with celebrity influencers who have a genuine connection to the cause and leverage their platform as an amplifier for important social issues.
- Create or use relevant hashtags that support a cause and align with the brand voice.
- Write messages that are simple, clear and conducive to sharing and amplification.

Don'ts of Writing for Socially Conscious Causes, Action and Change

Here is a brief list of activities not to engage in (at least not as a singular action) when writing about socially conscious causes and when writing for action or change:

- Bandwagon activism is demonstrated when individuals (often celebrities or public figures) or businesses participate in a social movement because it is popular, or they feel pressured to participate by their respective stakeholder groups.

- Celebrity activism is often scrutinized when celebrity individuals or corporate brands employ celebrity figures as endorsers or spokespersons for a worthy cause. The high-profile status of celebrities as influencers also creates a significant amount of skepticism when motives are challenged or questioned. Pushing a celebrity personality to the forefront of a societal cause in which they have no real knowledge or expertise is risky and can be costly in terms of reputational damage.

- Contentious collaborations occur when a brand attempts to neutralize an external threat by developing and grooming relationships with individuals or organizations that might otherwise challenge the company's operations and harm the brand's reputation. The process is frequently discussed in terms of companies co-opting a specific issue or cause and making concessions to decrease the likelihood of negative media coverage that otherwise might be generated in response to societal demands.

- Hashtag activism is when companies or individuals demonstrate support for an issue or cause by reposting, liking, or sharing a specific hashtag and accompanying word or phrase. Companies that only post hashtags but don't demonstrate any real action toward the cause may open the door for swift online criticism from detractors or trolls who accuse the brands of talking the talk, but not walking the walk; engaging only in talk, with no measurable action.

- Performance activism is supporting or championing a cause publicly for the sake of increasing or enhancing visibility for the company or brand. This is generally viewed as exploitative and disrespectful toward the marginalized groups or communities at the core of the issue.

Kickstart the Creative Writing Process

After the initial client meetings or internal agency planning sessions, one of the first steps toward developing a campaign with production or creative development components is drafting a creative brief. A creative brief is a short document (generally 1 or 2 pages) that outlines the campaign and its final deliverables.

New hires at an agency are often tasked with writing and presenting a creative brief to the team to align all the players and get everyone on the same page in terms of project goals, objectives, messaging, timelines, deliverables and budget. To kick off the process, here are some questions to pose during the brainstorming and ideation (creative development) process:

- What is the name of the new campaign being launched and why is it the right approach?

- What do we want to accomplish?

- Who are we talking to?

- What do we want them to do after encountering the campaign messaging?

- What's in it for the customer or end user; how are their self-interests served?

- How does the brand benefit (e.g., awareness, sales, customer loyalty, reputation management)?

- What do our target audiences think, feel or believe now?

- Is the audience supportive, hostile or neutral to our brand and the core problem or opportunity?

- Do we have adequate resources available (people, financial, technology, time) to develop and maintain this campaign?

- How do we define success at the end of this campaign?

Let's review the different sections included in a creative brief and their significance to the overall campaign (see sample campaign deliverables presented in a creative brief in Table 14.1):

- *Campaign Name* — The crucial campaign name is the public facing moniker by which the campaign will be known to customers or consumers.

- *Situation Analysis* — The situation analysis offers a brief overview of the current situation and lays the groundwork for what is prompting the new campaign. The situation analysis essentially answers the question: How did we get here?

- *Core Problem or Opportunity* — This is a one-sentence statement of the primary challenge or situation to leverage.

TABLE 14.1 ■ Sample Campaign Deliverables in a Creative Brief		
Type of Media	**Quantity**	**Distribution**
30-second audio PSAs	Four (4)	Regional radio stations
60-second video PSA	One (1)	Local network and cable TV stations
Promotional graphics for blog and social platforms	Eight (8)	E-newsletter, blog, social media accounts
3-minute promotional video	One (1)	Website, YouTube channel

- *Campaign Timeline: Start/Finish* — These dates represent the beginning point and end point of the campaign launch and serve as benchmarks during the evaluation process.

- *Project/Campaign Overview* — The overview section details the strategic approach toward solving a problem or maximizing an opportunity; it also reinforces the connection between the campaign and the greater mission or values of the organization developing the campaign.

- *Target Audiences* — Often divided into primary, secondary and tertiary key publics (by level of importance or relevance), target audiences are defined by demographic and psychographic descriptors and identify who the campaign is designed to reach. Each of the key publics (smaller groups within an audience that share a common connection) may have a unique primary or secondary message that aligns with them.

- *Key Messages* — As part of the overall messaging strategies, key messages are the essential elements of a campaign that communicators want to convey to the target audience.
  - Primary Messages — relevant to all publics and audiences; in alignment with campaign goals.
  - Secondary Messages — provide additional context to primary messages with an ethos, pathos or logos persuasive appeal to various publics.

- *Audience Call-to-Action* — A request or encouragement to the audience to act or engage with the campaign in a specific way. A call to action is the behavior you want recipients of the content to model after hearing the message. In other words, what do you want them to do? (Example: Vote for this policy; Click this link; Sign this petition, Subscribe to this news feed)

- *Scope of Work* — The scope of work clearly outlines the expectations and work needed to develop, launch and implement the entire campaign.

- *Campaign Deliverables* — This section is a list of the actual items (audio, video, online content) that needs to be designed, drafted or produced as part of the campaign.

- *Campaign Evaluation and Metrics* — This section includes a brief list of the tools and metrics that will be used to determine whether the campaign fulfilled its purpose, met the objectives and goals, and succeeded based on the original plan.

Throughout the campaign, team members can review the creative brief to make sure they remain on track with the scope of work and timeline. The document is also useful for keeping everyone focused on the priorities of the campaign. See a sample creative brief template in Figure 14.1.

AUDIO AND VIDEO STORYTELLING

To get acclimated to the job, it's important to share some basic audio and video terminology that will help PR practitioners write quality scripts and provide clear direction for the videographers, directors, and producers who may be using their words to guide the creative production process.

How to Write for the Ear

Writing for the ear is a unique skill that requires the PR professional to produce content that engages sensory responses solely through what is heard. One of the key challenges in writing for audio is that listeners are often engaged in other activities or listening while distracted. It is not unusual for audience members who are listening to content also to be driving, reading, scrolling online, cleaning, napping or multitasking.

Visual storytelling or a visual narrative in public relations writing is a story told primarily through visual media with the goal of connecting with the audience in a way that solicits a desired response. The story may be told using graphics, still photography, illustrations, animation, video footage; enhanced by music, sound effects, voice narration and other audio features.

As a PR writing professional, it is not necessary to be a skilled audio producer or video editor; however, it is important to know and understand the language and be able to write quality scripts for the industry professionals who will use the scripts to produce the final deliverable.

Public service announcements (PSAs) are general audience messages created by and distributed by nonprofit organizations. PSAs can be powerful tools to inform audiences and persuade them to take a specific action, whether it is conserving energy, avoiding destructive behavior or spreading kindness and goodwill among neighbors. They typically promote positive or informative messaging that lends itself toward the greater good. Key messaging topics in PSAs might highlight subjects or opportunities related to free community events, free educational activities, or access to free healthcare resources, for example. PSAs also are frequently used to promote action or change by motivating the listeners to support a cause or get involved in a particular effort that makes a difference or has a positive impact on society. These produced broadcast messages are called spots. Whether the final product is a 30-second audio recording or a 15-second video, the spot is designed to motivate people to take action.

Three common and basic writing tools for development of broadcast and online video content to motivate audiences are a storyboard, audio PSA script and video PSA script.

- Storyboard — A storyboard is a graphics-based outline used to organize and present details about a video production. The storyboard is a useful guide for the client to envision a project and also for the video production team to understand key elements of the video that need to be incorporated. Depending upon the artistic skills of the practitioner, a storyboard can be hand-drawn with illustrations or designed using still photos and graphics. Key elements of the storyboard include time codes, major visuals,

FIGURE 14.1 ■ Sample Creative Brief Template

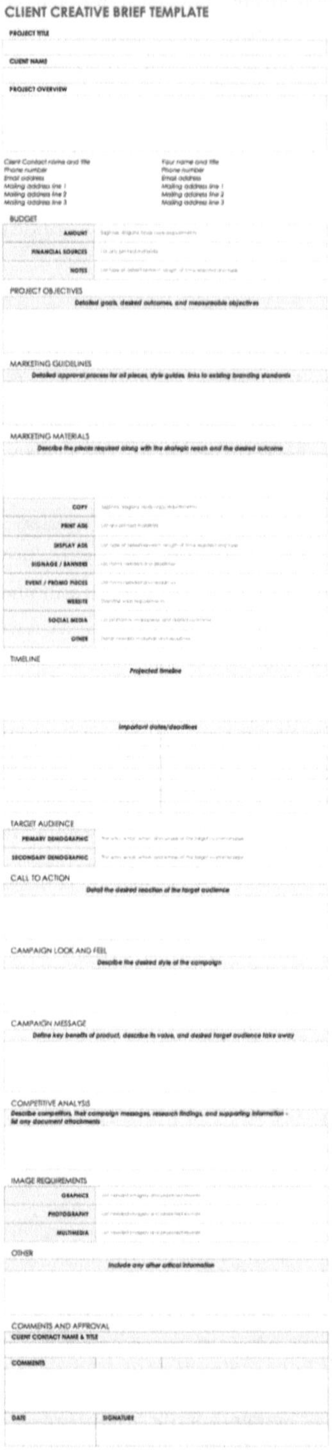

CLIENT CREATIVE BRIEF TEMPLATE

PROJECT TITLE

CLIENT NAME

PROJECT OVERVIEW

Client Contact name and title	*Your name and title*
Phone number	*Phone number*
Email address	*Email address*
Mailing address line 1	*Mailing address line 1*
Mailing address line 2	*Mailing address line 2*
Mailing address line 3	*Mailing address line 3*

BUDGET

AMOUNT	
FINANCIAL SOURCES	
NOTES	

PROJECT OBJECTIVES

Detailed goals, desired outcomes, and measurable objectives

MARKETING GUIDELINES

Detailed approval process for all pieces, style guides, links to existing branding standards

MARKETING MATERIALS

Describe the pieces required along with the strategic reach and the desired outcome

COPY	
PRINT ADS	
DISPLAY ADS	
SIGNAGE / BANNERS	
EVENT / PROMO PIECES	
WEBSITE	
SOCIAL MEDIA	
OTHER	

TIMELINE

Projected timeline

Important dates/deadlines

TARGET AUDIENCE

PRIMARY DEMOGRAPHIC	
SECONDARY DEMOGRAPHIC	

CALL TO ACTION

Detail the desired reaction of the target audience

CAMPAIGN LOOK AND FEEL

Describe the desired style of the campaign

CAMPAIGN MESSAGE

Define key benefits of product, describe its value, and desired target audience take away

COMPETITIVE ANALYSIS

Describe competitors, their campaign messages, research findings, and supporting information - list any document attachments

IMAGE REQUIREMENTS

GRAPHICS	
PHOTOGRAPHY	
MULTIMEDIA	

OTHER

Include any other critical information

COMMENTS AND APPROVAL

CLIENT CONTACT NAME & TITLE	
COMMENTS	
DATE	**SIGNATURE**

signature audio, and other significant on-camera elements. See Figure 14.2 for a sample storyboard.

- Audio PSA — An audio public service announcement is created for and distributed by a nonprofit organization and presented to radio stations or podcast producers to audiences who will only hear the content. PSAs generally are created to have broad appeal for the public good. See Table 14.2 for a sample audio PSA script. Note: The easiest way to create an audio script using a word processing document is to insert a table with two columns, which allows the script writer to easily navigate and align text independently within the two columns. As a general rule of thumb to calculate how many words need to go in the script, it is helpful to use the rate of speaking as 2.5 words per second. Example: A (60-second spot) x 2.5 words is approximately 150 words. Remember the best way to confirm the exact timing is to read the script aloud with a timer to ensure that it means the allotted time specifications given.

- Video PSA — A video public service announcement is visual messaging created for and distributed by a nonprofit organization to audiences that will see and hear content. Video PSAs are generally created to have a broad appeal and provide information for the public good. See Figure 14.3 for a sample shot list to determine necessary video content.

FIGURE 14.2 ■ Storyboard Example

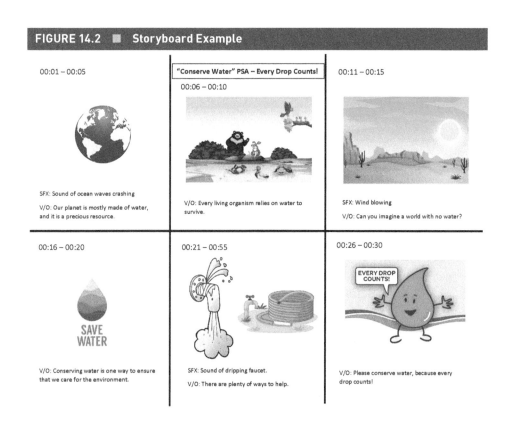

00:01 – 00:05

SFX: Sound of ocean waves crashing

V/O: Our planet is mostly made of water, and it is a precious resource.

"Conserve Water" PSA – Every Drop Counts!

00:06 – 00:10

V/O: Every living organism relies on water to survive.

00:11 – 00:15

SFX: Wind blowing

V/O: Can you imagine a world with no water?

00:16 – 00:20

SAVE WATER

V/O: Conserving water is one way to ensure that we care for the environment.

00:21 – 00:55

SFX: Sound of dripping faucet.

V/O: There are plenty of ways to help.

00:26 – 00:30

EVERY DROP COUNTS!

V/O: Please conserve water, because every drop counts!

Here are some other broadcast productions that PR writing professionals might need to prepare:

- Podcast—Simply put, a podcast is an on-demand, internet-based radio show that features streaming and downloadable audio content. Podcasts cover any and all topics, and they generally are produced in single episodes as part of a series geared toward a target audience, and then made available on demand for listening or download through a website, streaming app, smart device podcast player or app. The PR practitioner's role may include researching topics for the host, writing interview questions, drafting a media prep Q&A document and writing the intro and outro segments for the podcast announcer.

TABLE 14.2 ■ Sample Audio PSA Script	
Audio Cues, Sound Effects (SFX), and Music	**Narration or Script for Actor(s)**
SFX: Fingers typing on keyboard (notice that this audio cue is separate from the narrator script and can be positioned appropriately).	NARRATOR: Nonprofit groups use public service announcements to get publicity from radio and television stations.
	The P-S-A uses short sentences, just like a broadcast release.
SFX: Cymbal crashing!	
	P-S-A copy can be 15, 30, or 60 seconds long. The P-S-A content and music should fit with the station's regular programming.

# # #

FIGURE 14.3 ■ Sample Shot List for 'Conserve Water' Video PSA

"Conserve Water" PSA–Shot List:

1. World map highlighting oceans

2. Forest scene of animals drinking water

3. Barren desert scene

4. Graphic of waterdrop with "Save Water" text

5. Leaking and/or running faucet

6. Leaking garden hose

7. Animated water drop

- Webinar — A webinar is the combination of a web-based seminar; hence the name webinar. A seminar is defined as a presentation or meeting to provide information. Transitioning seminar content onto web-based platforms allows meeting hosts to present information from one or several speakers to groups ranging from two to hundreds of thousands in a live, prerecorded or on-demand format. The PR practitioner's role in developing webinar content may include drafting a run of show, writing and editing presenter biographers and introductions and scripting content for prerecorded videos that play during the session.

How to Write for the Eyes

Writing for the eye means envisioning what the viewer will see and hear, then putting those ideas on paper by telling a compelling story through visuals. Keep in mind, in writing for action or change, the metric for success is engagement. What did the writer or sender of the content get the recipient to do? Possible answers might include attend a meeting, join a club, sign the petition, click the link, take the survey, complete the quiz, download the article or share the post.

Here are some tips for visual scripting:

- Think and write in pictures.

- Write with imagery that excludes any audio — make the visuals tell the story.

- Write with an active voice in the present tense.

- Incorporate elements in the script that appeal to multiple senses.

- Use short, declarative statements in the script.

- When given the option; show, don't tell.

See Table 14.3 for a sample video PSA script. Note: The easiest way to create a video script using a word processing document is to insert a table with two columns, which allows the script writer to easily navigate and align text independently within the two columns. Time codes support video content, which drives the audio accompaniment.

Show, Don't Just Tell

In the spirit of efficiency and effectiveness, it is vitally important that written content also be supported by multimedia visuals that may include photographs (or pics), graphics or infographics, audio links, embedded video files and hyperlinks to other multimedia content that can be easily discovered, shared and commented about online. The following box provides several tips for the PR writing professional to incorporate into content creation for visual storytelling and writing for action or change.

TABLE 14.3 ■ Sample Video PSA Script	
VIDEO CUES ON THIS SIDE (What You See) Key Elements: Time Codes, Camera Shots, Camera Movements, and Transitions	AUDIO CUES ON THIS SIDE (What You Hear) Key Elements: Narration, Voiceovers, Actor Scripts, Sound Effects, Music
Run Time 00:30 Title: "How to Write a Video PSA Script"	
00:01—00:08 Open on MS of fingers typing on a keyboard; zoom in for a CU	*Music: soft instrumental music plays throughout* V/O: Nonprofit groups use public service announcements to get publicity from radio and television stations. Many of the scripts are written by new PR professionals. *SFX: Classroom chatter and laughter*
00:09—00:14 Cut to LS of college students in classroom	Instructor: The P-S-A uses short sentences, just like a broadcast release.
00:15—00:21 O/C: Wipe to MS of instructor standing in front of class	Student V/O (not on camera): So, you're saying that P-S-A copy can be 15, 30, or 60 seconds long. And it's important for the P-S-A content and music to fit with the station's regular programming.
00:22—00:26 Cut to B-roll footage of voice actor in front of mic stand in a recording studio	Instructor: That's correct—good job. That's all there is to it. You're ready to get started!
00:27—00:30 O/C: Cut to instructor nodding head and giving thumbs-up sign to students	*Music fades out.*
	# # #

TIPS FOR BEGINNERS: CREATING CONTENT FOR VISUAL STORYTELLING AND WRITING FOR ACTION OR CHANGE

Write in an authentic voice. Social media and digital media present content to a much broader audience in a much shorter period of time. Audience responses, reactions, and engagement are immediate and often harsh if the content is deemed to be too self-serving or lacking in transparency. Writers for individual, corporate or institutional brands need to write in a voice that aligns with the brand identity and is tailored for the target audience.

Write the way people think and search online. A big difference between traditional public relations documents and newer social media and digital media writing is how the information is discovered. Traditional (old school) PR was directed toward journalists through predictable channels like targeted emails and free or paid wire distribution services. Now, more content is delivered through online sharing from end-users and consumers, meaning writers need to write the way everyday people think and look up information online. For example, instead of a traditional headline announcing, "Company X Launches New Product to Assist in Learning a New Language," the social content header might reflect how people search for the product and read more like, "Want to Learn a New Language in 10 Days?—Click Here." The distinction is that people searching for the new language app don't ask, Did Company X launch a new product to help learn a new language? They ask questions such as "How can I learn a new language fast? How long does it take to learn a new language? What app can help me learn a new language this week?"

Write for the right stage. It is important to craft content in a manner that is consistent with the social norms and expectations for the platform being utilized. That means the PR professional should compare and contrast selected social media outlets to identify those that are appropriate for a particular client or PR campaign; and also finalize a format that guides the writing process for each one. For instance, if acronyms, hashtags and handles are an important part of posts on a particular platform, then they should become standardized in creating messages. If tagging photos and including hyperlinks is a key component of a different platform, then those items should be incorporated into the process.

Incorporate visuals. As stated earlier in the chapter, in PR storytelling, it is equally important to show and tell; meaning PR practitioners need to approach writing with the intent to "show, don't just tell" to get the desired results and audience response online.

Publish timely content. Online content moves at seemingly hypersonic speed; by the time the sender releases the "send" button on the keypad or mobile device, the information shared has already been posted, screen captured, and shared across countless platforms. Content literally can make its way around the world in seconds, and then create a digital footprint that lives on forever in the digital universe. The relevance for PR professionals is to make sure new content is the latest and greatest iteration for readers who are already inundated with information.

Write relevant and socially conscious content. It's helpful to remember that even if individuals don't share the same opinions or experiences, they do share the same appreciation for stories and topics that affect them or people they care about.

Build in data analytics. Here's a common question in public relations. If you can't measure it, does it matter? For all intents and purposes, if PR practitioners cannot measure their results, monitor their campaign's progress, or present metrics for success, then the work has little to no value. Whether it's tags, hashtags, impressions, reshares, downloads, or conversions, every effort to push out content needs to generate a result with quantifiable analytics on how it performed online.

CHAPTER SUMMARY

Writing for action or change is a planned, coordinated and intentional process. PR practitioners can incorporate basic motivating factors into their campaigns to encourage listeners and viewers to take action and increase engagement with brands. As more social media platforms emerge, content creators will need to continue developing copy that is easily shared by their target audiences, which in turn extends and amplifies overall reach of the message.

Using audio and video content as an agent for change is driven by powerful storytelling. The art of storytelling is universal because stories resonate and connect with people across multimedia platforms.

KEY TERMS

audio PSA

bandwagon activism

celebrity activism

contentious collaborations

creative brief

going viral

hashtag activism

performance activism

podcast

public service announcements (PSAs)

storyboard

video PSA

webinar

DISCUSSION QUESTIONS

1. What type of content moves people from unmotivated observers to active participants?

2. How does a storyboard contribute to the creative writing and production process?

3. What viral video made a lasting impression on you and why?

WRITING EXERCISES

1. Write a one-page creative brief for your university's communications department targeted to students who live on campus encouraging the target audience to use paper straws instead of plastic straws as an environmentally friendly practice.

2. Write a 30-second audio PSA for your hometown city or town council reminding pet owners to clean up and pick up after their pets in public spaces.

15 CREATIVE CONTENT

LEARNING OBJECTIVES

15.1 Learn the similarities and differences between public relations, advertising and marketing.

15.2 Identify different types of controlled and uncontrolled publications.

15.3 Understand the different types of creative content often written by PR professionals.

INTRODUCTION

It is not unusual to hear terms within the integrated marketing and strategic communications fields used interchangeably—and often used incorrectly. For those outside of these creative industries, it is easy to conflate the work done and deliverables created, especially as agencies increasingly overlap in the type of work they do and content they produce.

Gone are the days when only video production companies are hired to produce video content. As an example, the ever-increasing demand for video content on all public-facing platforms is resulting in agencies of all types foregoing expensive cameras, sets, and crews and instead reaching for smartphones or tablets with high-quality cameras and shooting footage "selfie style" on location. This chapter focuses on the aspects of strategic communications that result in the visuals and consumer-focused content that most people closely associated with the public relations industry.

15.1 — HOW ADVERTISING, MARKETING AND PR DIFFER

A brief introduction of advertising, marketing and public relations, and how each area intersects within strategic communications will be helpful to place the relevance of the areas in perspective and general context to the overall communications sphere of influence.

Though there are clear and distinct differences between advertising, marketing, public relations and strategic communications, the terms are often used synonymously and interchangeably by those who are new to the industries and their nuances. Without question, there is now more crossover and comingling of respective activities in all of the areas; however, there is enough separation of duties within the industries that it merits clarifying the roles and purposes of each one, as shown in the list below. A common acronym to help explain the different aspects of creative media content is **PESO,** representing a strategic communication model for **P**aid, **E**arned, **S**hared, and **O**wned content that is also discussed in Chapters 5 and 13 in this textbook.

- Advertising — Paid, creative messaging that appears in print, radio, television and internet productions to inform or influence the purchasing process. Advertising is frequently used to sell goods and services to consumers. Advertising represents the "P" for Paid in the PESO Model.

- Marketing — The sales-oriented process of introducing, packaging, pricing, promoting and placing products or services into a desirable position in the marketplace for consumption. Marketing is often connected to the sales cycle and used to give products and services a competitive advantage over similar goods.

- **Public Relations** — The art and science of managing reputations and maintaining relationships between organizations and their respective publics by developing and distributing specific messages to target audiences using multimedia platforms to produce desired, measurable actions. Public relations relies heavily on media relations and objective, third-party validation in media coverage, along with targeted messaging to key publics. Public Relations represents the "E" for Earned media in the PESO Model.

- Integrated Marketing — A comprehensive approach to audience engagement using a combination of advertising, marketing, public relations and special events across different media platforms or channels to develop comprehensive campaigns. Integrated marketing tends to be pricier and feature lengthier campaigns due to the multiple media elements involved.

- Strategic Communications — A research-based approach to identifying effective channels for communication and engagement with key publics to inspire specific actions and fulfill mission-oriented goals and objectives. Strategic communications campaigns are usually focused on long-term growth and business development priorities.

15.2 — CONTROLLED VS. UNCONTROLLED PUBLICATIONS

This upcoming section sheds more light on how PR practitioners leverage different types of creative content to persuade and engage audiences. Specifically, collateral materials, such as brochures and newsletters, and uncontrolled publications, like news releases and media advisories, offer a range of options and tools to introduce various clients, causes, products, services and brands into the dynamic marketplace of storytelling.

Controlled Publications

Often referred to as collateral or marketing communications (MarCom) materials, controlled publications are documents that the PR practitioner has ultimate control over from start to finish. From the creative ideation and development process through final production, printing or publishing, controlled publications maintain the content and integrity of their intent because they are altered by media or external audiences. Sample controlled publications include brochures, flyers, posters and newsletters.

Uncontrolled Publications

In contrast to controlled publications, uncontrolled publications are created by the PR professional as a point of reference for or source of information, but the final version is up to the individual or organization using the content for its own editorial purposes. As an example, although the PR team may research, write, and distribute a news release that focuses on a specific new product launch; all, some, or little of the information contained in the release may be used to produce the final article or news story. Other sample uncontrolled publications include news releases, fact sheets, media advisories and infographics.

TIPS FOR BEGINNERS: LATIN FILLER TEXT

Latin filler text — usually the "lorem ipsum" phrase — is used as a placeholder to assist in graphic design, layout and publishing while the final copy or content is edited, proofread, and approved. Use of this placeholder content allows the design team to move forward with creative ideas for layout and provide an estimation for the length and weight of the creative document being produced. This specific passage of "lorem ipsum" filler text can be found easily in an online search and is popular because it utilizes all of the Latin alphabet and approximates the amount of space needed for standard editorial or advertising copy.

Here is a sample block of placeholder text demonstrating placement and word count for two paragraphs:

Lorem ipsum dolor sit amet, hinc delenit meliore at sit, an omnes possit civibus nam, vis sale aeterno singulis an. No similique vituperata elaboraret eam, vim possit saperet ad. Modo enim hendrerit cu mel, ne legendos voluptatum his. Ad est tale adhuc alterum, mei homero indoctum ex, qui nonumy liberavisse theophrastus te. Eius tacimates te qui, eum aeque indoctum posidonium et.

Lucilius phaedrum eos in, ut has atqui inermis noluisse. Vix cu dicit neglegentur ullamcorper, illum prodesset no sed, ei dicat accusam vim. Pri dolore phaedrum id, quidam nostrud iracundia ius et. Nec movet quodsi cu, cum illum bonorum legendos ea. At his mollis fabellas neglegentur, dicit everti pro te, putent iriure habemus no nec. In nec duis periculis, illum electram ne nec, vis magna dicam doming ut. Ea nam novum eloquentiam, ius tation dolorem ei.

See Figure 15.1 for a sample brochure layout using Latin placeholder filler text. Brochures will be discussed in more detail in the next section.

FIGURE 15.1 ■ Sample Brochure Layout Using Latin Placeholder Filler Text

Source: iStock.com/non exclusive

15.3 — DEVELOPING CREATIVE CONTENT

The rest of the chapter will showcase sample creative content documents along with writing prompts to create your own collateral materials and further fine-tune important skills needed for promotional writing.

Brochure

A type of controlled publication, a brochure, is one of the most common creative materials produced by organizations to provide general, high-level information about a company or organization. Brochures are often printed and distributed as promotional material and shared electronically through digital downloads from an online hub website. Generally speaking, brochure content should be "evergreen" (not time or date sensitive) with a longer shelf life to promote the organization. See Figures 15.2, 15.3, 15.4 and 15.5 for sample brochure templates and layouts.

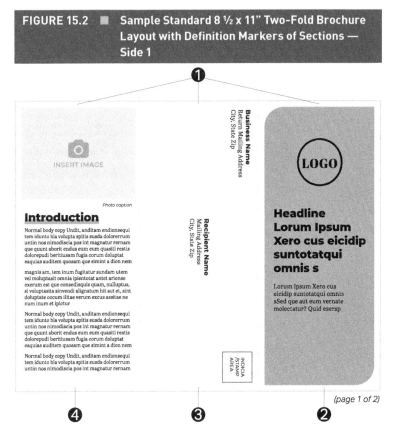

FIGURE 15.2 ■ Sample Standard 8 ½ x 11" Two-Fold Brochure Layout with Definition Markers of Sections — Side 1

(page 1 of 2)

❶ PANELS: Sides to a brochure that are designed for presentation of the desired information. In a six-panel brochure:

❷ PANEL 1: First panel the audience sees; identifies the organization and grabs the reader's attention.

❸ PANEL 6: The "self-mailer."

❹ PANEL 5: The "wild card" panel; used as a return response card, a survey to fill out and return, or for other purposes.

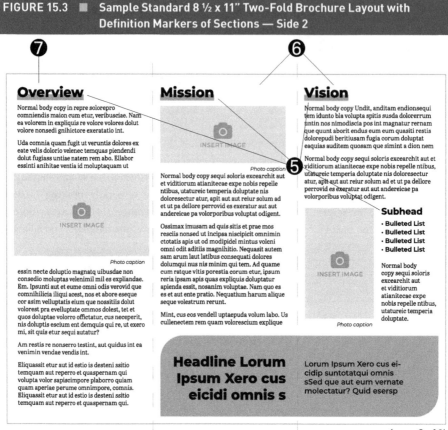

FIGURE 15.3 ■ **Sample Standard 8 ½ x 11" Two-Fold Brochure Layout with Definition Markers of Sections — Side 2**

(page 2 of 2)

❺ HEADLINES AND SUBHEADS: These attract readers' attention.

❻ PANELS 3 AND 4: The middle and right interior of the brochure; treated as one large or two separate pages; give more specific information.

❼ PANEL 2: On the left inside the brochure; indicates the intent of the brochure and gives background information.

Newsletter

A newsletter or electronic newsletter (e-newsletter) is a controlled publication that publishes news and information to a target audience with shared interests or a common subject/activity that connects them. Newsletter lengths and formats can range from a single page to dozens of pages and include feature articles, personality profiles, trivia and factoids, and event calendars. See Figures 15.4 and 15.5 for sample newsletter and e-newsletter layouts.

FIGURE 15.4 ■ **Sample Newsletter Layout for Sweet News with Section Markers**

❶

SWEET NEWS

newsletter published by **Cookies & Cakes Bakery** ················ **VOLUME # · ISSUE # · MONTH, YEAR** ❷

Inside this issue:

2

Lorem Ipsum

Lorem Ipsum

Lorem Ipsum

3

Lorem Ipsum

Lorem Ipsum

Lorem Ipsum

4

Lorem Ipsum

Lorem Ipsum

Lorem Ipsum

❸

Cookies Say 'I Love You' in the Sweetest Way

Image description here

Con cuptatum reium consendeliti qui consed ut millant isinctatur autem ut incipic iandis dipsand aestionse secabores dignit et ipsani con conseni dolut volorro tenis ex eveles volut eum ius deleni berum la nullenese dem dolore et que ex elliquatem. Nam facous isque pa aut ad que occulpa rcimus dempore sserem restempos est quos non poreste dolorero occus ratis estrum, officaestis audaeperum illaborernam aceatio ellaborrum

simaio. Ut vendaestis reriberum aut preria nistis qui odit pore con pedicim iat quamusa pra denda natiate rest, sit acepudant.

Fuga. Harum hitae sit quias assequis quatum sundi doluptunibus eni conseribus voluptat.

It ex et eaturest velignistia si conessi taturem fugiatur, sit ut qui cum apicit eatibus voloruntiis et liquist, voluptae repro bennam, con et iloium, quas et, consed eosam int eos aped et aut fugias in nis sum fuga. Et aut autaes quidus.

Risit quia aspit voiliqui sit aut que doluptur suntus ipsanti idiate voluptae. Optas pero te quae nonsequ iduciat ionecerum aut facerio commodioium que qui tem facepta elit, quo iur seruntur, cora es eos aspiendisit qui cus parum aut provita amus dit, senimus deliciaecum, seque ium et ut volupit, utem iliqui odiatem aut elit harchitam, es ex eum, sunt andis sae cullaborem eicabo. Incium,

Lorum Ipsum

Fere nest lique que voluptur, soluptati reruptatios eos et labor aut pos magnis audandentia cus simpeles arit pratiatio el in erum ex eost, alignim enemolu ptation cum, eliqui cone nem es renist, cuptae verum vit ommolor porum, in non poreicatur aut pro ducimus cipsapis dellenis qui corit, ipsunda nisquunt accum quatur, quid et plam facepra cum faciet fugitatum ad molendam, aut quid eratem

sinotio de eat qui quatiusdam rehenih iilgnatis idit volupicieni dit ipid mi, qui consectatem dus exeraectem ducident autat odiatqui adit aute que nis doluptio moditatus quibus moloraeped ut eatem re conet fugitatum ut aut moluptatur? Niatest iaeces samet iaut volore aut acerumqui adis rera volorest moluptat

Image description here

ur, ute eum quam in consequi vera nonsequ odignisqui andae nonsed ut officimi, omnitatenis dunt alia volupist odis est quibero officienim is excepre scipis volupta ducimo

(page 1 of 4)

❶ BANNER: Name of newsletter.

❷ VOLUME AND ISSUE DATE.

❸ CONTENTS: Listing of where stories are found inside.

(Continued)

FIGURE 15.4 ■ **Sample Newsletter Layout for Sweet News with Section Markers** *(Continued)*

❶

Letter from the Director

Genti aceria que excea doluptis et, conempo rehenimet erum qui simusam ese nulpa nus et dolupta quistem et prehenia nemquae ruptatu sandigniam et quatur?

Aquundanit, ut aut ra volonporento tecto et, officip saepuda arum asint earuptatetum sintiunt optun, tetur renet quisinv enestium fugia que iab id ut harchilit ut antio te is auta sus, quatur aut illes ea diaspid elenima conseni maximpo rerovitiis nos prerum as id ut ius que omni ratesequi aut fugiati busantis rehendit, sae sequi di omniatur?

Quidelitate cuptatiundae nonsequate perumquo velit, omniet faceatum eossimolenis ne nonestiam vendis asperi dolor re net, natur milignam sim dolorestibea cum verum atis est, officim ut qui corerum rest eosaped ignimos sam doluptae volupta cus eosam quae sandiscia sin resed quiatem.

Agnis aciet alicimusant quem, tempos dolor solorror ma non consequis estem quidempor maloriant dipsum quo sanrest labo. Cae elus ea perum iuntion non corum etur

Lorum Ipsum Tatem fuga. Bis voluption

Con cuptatum reium consendeliti qui consed ut millant isinctatur autem ut incipic iandis dipsand aestionse secabores dignit et ipsani con conseni doiut volorro tenis ex eveles volut eum ius deleni berum ia nullenese dem dolore et que ex elliquatem. Nam faccus isque pa aut ad que occulpa rcimus dempore sserem restempos est quos non poreste dolorero occus ratis estrum, officaestis audaeperum illaborernam aceatio eliaborrum simalo. Ut vendaestis reriberum aut preria nistis qui odit pore con pedicim iat quamusa pra denda natiate rest, sit acepudant.

Fuga. Harum hitae sit quias assequis quatum sundi dolupturibus eni conseribus voluptat.

It ex et eaturest velignistia si conessi taturem fugiatur, sit ut qui cum apicit eatibus voloruntis et liquist, voluptae repro bernam, con et liciom, quas et, consed eosam int eos aped et aut fugias in nis sum fuga. Et aut autaes quidus.

Risit quia aspit volliqui sit aut que doluptur suntus ipsanti idiate voluptae.

Optas pero te quae nonsequ iduciat ioneicerum aut facerio commodicium que qui tem facepta elit, quo iur seruntur, cora es eos aspiendisit qui ous parum aut provita amus dit, senimus deliciaecum, seque ium et ut volupit, utem iliqui odiatem aut elit harchitam, es ex eum, sunt andis sae cullaborem eicabo. Incium, officates eatiur si di doloria debis eosam exceseratur assitibus moluptatiis aliicid quistium et audandit quo eatempos plam ligent aciendus atibus aditis quuntem. Nam dolupta sam re perit ne audis culpa nusae consedictur, quam fugia evelis susdandam, nissim res sum fugit odit libus qui abo. Namet fuga. Et ut quam excenistrum volupta sincilla verum soluptibus, optur accabor eperchi llandentium vel ipienis quasitas in nos es sum autas ium sinvero occum verumque num rectem ent explianducia cuptaque molore prae landitati aligendunt evendiasped ex et, ipsaperro vernatate sequam, ne conseEt di omnihitatae veliqui si reped mil es ilibus.

Fuga. Harunt laborun daerovitam es mos re verumquid endellut aliquas unt.

Lorum Ipsum

Fere nest lique que voluptur, soluptati reruptatios eos et labor aut pos magnis audandentia cus simpeles arit pratiati el in erum ex eost, alignim enemolu ptation cum, eliqui cone nem es renist, cuptae verum vit ommolor porum, in non poreicatur aut pro ducimus cipsapis dellenis qui corit, ipsunda nisquunt accum quatur, quid et plam facepra cum faciet fugitatum ad molendam, aut quid eratem

sinctio de eat qui quatiusdam rehenih ilignatis idit volupicieni dit ipid mi, qui consectatem dus exeraectem ducident autat odiatqui adit aute que nis doluptio moditatus quibus moloraeped ut eatem re conet fugitatum ut aut moluptatur? Niatest iaeces samet laut volore aut acerumqui adis rera volorest moluptatur, ute eum quam in consequi vera nonsequ odignisqui andae

image description here

nonsed ut officimi, omnitatenis dunt alia volupist odis est quibero officienim is excepre scipis volupta ducimoluptae pernatquiam dolum hit, ipsandit laut am iliqui unt.

Uga. Nessi corios as eiototatis que mo et odit quod moluptat fugia vo-

(page 2 of 4)

❶ STANDING FEATURE.

FIGURE 15.4 ■ **Sample Newsletter Layout for Sweet News with Section Markers** *(Continued)*

Lorum Ipsum Tatem fuga. Bis voluption

Image description here

Con cuptatum reium consendeliti qui consed ut millant isinctatur autem ut incipic iandis dipsand aestionse secabores dignit et ipsani con conseni dolut volorro tenis ex eveles volut eum ius deleni berum la nullenese dem dolore et que ex elliquatem. Nam faccus isque pa aut ad que occulpa rcimus dempore sserem restempos est quos non poreste dolorero occus ratis estrum, officaestis audaeperum illaborernam aceatio ellaborrum simalo. Ut vendaestis reriberum aut preria nistis qui odit pore con pedicim iat quamusa pra denda natiate rest, sit acepudant.

Fuga. Harum hitae sit quias assequis quatum sundi dolupturibus eni conseribus voluptat.

It ex et eaturest velignistia si conessi taturem fugiatur, sit ut qui cum apicit eatibus voloruntiis et liquist, voluptae repro bernam, con et licium, quas et, consed eosam int eos aped et aut fugias in nis sum fuga. Et aut autaes quidus.

Risit quia aspit volliqui sit aut que doluptur suntus ipsanti idiate voluptae. Optas pero te quae nonsequ iduciat ionecerum aut facerio commodicium que qui tem facepta elit, quo iur seruntur, cora es eos aspiendisit qui cus parum aut provita amus dit, senimus deliciaecum, seque ium et ut volupit, utem iliqui odiatem aut elit harchitam, es ex eum, sunt andis sae cullaborem eicabo. Incium, officates eatiur si di doloria debis eosam exceseratur assitibus moluptatiis alicid quistium et audandit quo eatempos plam ligent aciendus atibus aditis quuntem. Nam dolupta sam re perit re audis culpa nusae consedictur, quam fugia evelis susdandam, nissim res sum fugit odit

Lorum Ipsum

Fere nest lique que voluptur, solupta-ti reruptatios eos et labor aut pos magnis audandentia cus simpeles arit pratiatio el in erum ex eost, alignim enemolu ptation cum, eliqui cone nem es renist, cuptae verum vit ommolor porum, in non poreicatur aut pro ducimus cipsapis dellenis qui corit, ipsunda nisquunt accum quatur, quid et plam facepra cum faciet fugitatum ad molendam, aut quid eratem

sinctio de eat qui quatiusdam rehenih ilignatis idit volupicieni dit ipid mi, qui consectatem dus exeraectem ducident autat odiatqui adit aute que nis doluptio moditatus quibus moloraeped ut eatem re conet fugitatum ut aut moluptatur? Niatest iaeces samet laut volore aut acerumqui adis rera volorest moluptatur, ute eum quam in consequi vera nonsequ odignisqui andae

nonsed ut officimi, omnitatenis dunt alia volupist odis est quibero officienim is excepre scipis volupta ducimoluptae pernatquiam dolum hit, ipsandit laut am iliqui unt.

Uga. Nessi corios as eictotatis que mo et odit quod moluptat fugia volient pliaecto berro que ea voloreped milloreptate nonet, ullique cor molut et explabo. Itatiumqui velestiasped min pora voluptam harchil latiniatem exera sum, quasper naturerionum consectorae non rere venist iliam necus non parum quatio est venes dolorempore ea dolupta ssitaepti oum excea consequi dolendae voloreseri tem err

o mos voluptatatur ad quae magnis doluprerum nobit, venduciae corempos doluptatus etuscil iduntibus, apiscit, nulparum faceratio. Boris sape pro

Lorum Ipsum Tatem

Lorem Ipsum
Lorem Ipsum

Lorem Ipsum
Lorem Ipsum

Lorem Ipsum
Lorem Ipsum

Lorem Ipsum
Lorem Ipsum

Lorem Ipsum
Lorem Ipsum

Lorem Ipsum
Lorem Ipsum

Lorem Ipsum
Lorem Ipsum
Lorem Ipsum
Lorem Ipsum

2

(page 3 of 4)

(Continued)

FIGURE 15.4 ■ Sample Newsletter Layout for Sweet News with Section Markers *(Continued)*

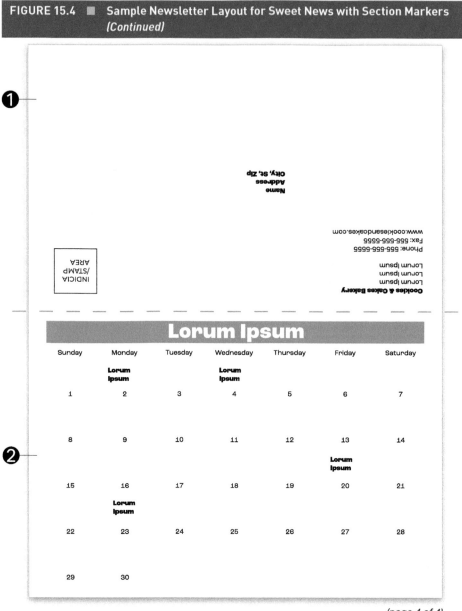

(page 4 of 4)

❶ SELF-MAILER: Address of reader and organization's return address.
❷ CALENDAR.

Flyer or Poster

A flyer is a one-page promotional handout that is widely distributed for informational and promotional purposes. This controlled publication often focuses on quality graphic design and layout to gain attention and increase engagement. Additionally, digital forms of flyers can be posted on social

FIGURE 15.5   ■   Sample E-Newsletter Layout for Sweet News

media platforms. A poster is a larger version of a flyer that displays oversized graphics and typography and is often a keepsake that can be showcased as art or a souvenir. Standard poster sizes are 11" x 17" and larger. See Figures 15.6 and 15.7 for sample flyer and poster layouts.

Print Advertisement

A print ad is a paid announcement inserted in print publications (and their online digital versions) that conforms with size specifications for placement (e.g., ¼-page, ½-page, full-page).

FIGURE 15.6 ■ **Sample Flyer Layout**

Source: iStock.com/StarLineArts

Advertisements are considered controlled publications. Ad copy ranges from light to medium to heavy. Light copy word counts range from 1 to 25 words; medium copy ranges from 26 to 75 words; and heavy copy is 76 words or more. Instant access to video content and shorter attention spans for readers now dictate that ad copywriters use more graphics and fewer words to get and keep their readers' attention. See Figure 15.8 for a sample print ad layout and Figure 15.9 for a sample print ad.

FIGURE 15.7 ■ Sample Poster Layout

Source: iStock.com/Gugai

Billboard or Outdoor Media

Traditionally defined as nontraditional or outdoor media, a billboard is an oversized print or digital advertising platform often placed alongside highways and roads, or in high-traffic public spaces like airports and transit stations. By nature of their placement, billboard viewers may be driving or navigating a terminal and be otherwise focused on an important activity, so billboards generally have a captivating graphic, use eight (8) words or fewer, and include a clear call to action. See Figure 15.10 for a sample billboard layout.

Web or Online Banner Ad

A hyperlinked digital ad placed on websites, a banner ad is measured in pixels and range adaptively in size from small squares on mobile devices to full length wraps across the bottom or top borders of web pages — promoting products and services from advertisers. See Figure 15.11 for a sample web banner layout.

FIGURE 15.8 ■ Sample Print Ad Layout

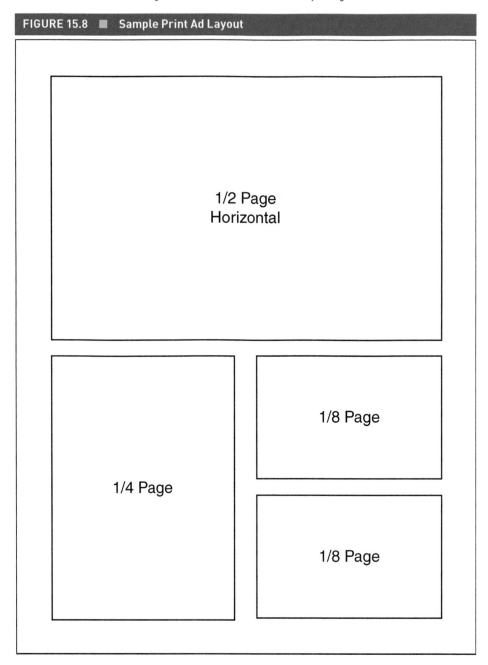

Infographic

An infographic is a graphics-centric document that informs and educates by making complex data or statistics easier to comprehend and retain through visual representation. See Figure 15.12 for a sample infographic layout.

FIGURE 15.9   ■   Sample Print Ad

Source: Art Directors & TRIP / Alamy Stock Photo

FIGURE 15.10   ■   Sample Billboard Layout

Source: iStock.com/Vasko

FIGURE 15.11 ■ Sample Web Banner Layout

Source: Contributor: Helen Sessions / Alamy Stock Photo

FIGURE 15.12 ■ Sample Infographic Layout

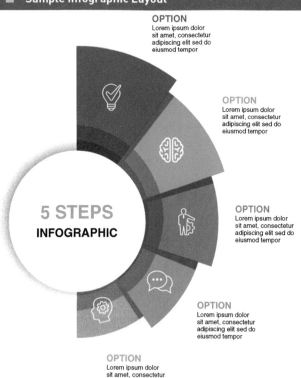

Source: iStock.com/artvea

CHAPTER SUMMARY

Creative content shows up across all forms of advertising, marketing and public relations and is widely used in promotional writing. Whether it is being used to sell goods and services or to connect with key publics and inspire change, promotional writing drives the messaging used in marketing communications and creative collateral materials. Both controlled and uncontrolled publications play a crucial role in communicating to the masses and providing relevant content for media outlets and public-facing campaigns. PR practitioners need to be knowledgeable about graphic design and layout to work seamlessly with designers to develop well researched, well written, and beautifully designed content.

KEY TERMS

advertising

banner ad

billboard

brochure

controlled publications

flyer

infographic

integrated marketing

marketing

newsletter

poster

print ad

strategic communications

uncontrolled publications

DISCUSSION QUESTIONS

1. Which of the highlighted creative documents do you find easiest to create?

2. Why do billboards have such a low word count?

3. What is the main difference between controlled and uncontrolled publications?

4. What are some key features of flyers, posters and infographics?

5. For the best response, how often should recipients receive e-newsletters in their inboxes?

WRITING EXERCISES

1. Using the brochure template shown in Figures 15.13 and 15.14, write a brochure cover headline, section subheadlines and a photo caption to accompany the graphics.

2. Write a feature lead paragraph for a front-page article highlighting the act of giving cookies instead of chocolate and roses for Valentine's Day for the "Sweet News" newsletter published by Cookies & Cakes Bakery. The newsletter targets existing customers of the bakery and potential new business clients. The article title is "Cookies Say 'I Love You' in the Sweetest Way."

FIGURE 15.13 ▪ Brochure Template with Blanks — Side 1

(page 1 of 2)

3. Write a paragraph featuring medium copy length (approx. 26 to 75 words) encouraging students to contact Campus Counseling Services (CCS) on the first floor of the Student Center at your campus to seek emotional and psychological support services. The center is open 24 hours a day with licensed therapists onsite, and services are free to enrolled students. Contact information is www.CampusCounselors.edu and (800) 555-CARE.

4. Write a compelling headline with light copy content (1 to 26 words) for a self-driving car company. Be sure to include a call to action that encourages readers to register for a free test drive in the car. The company is AutoMotion and the self-driving vehicle model is AutoMate; the website is www.AutoMotion.cars.

5. Using fewer than eight words, write a billboard headline and call to action for a meal delivery service called QuickEats (www.QuickEats.biz and 800-555-EATS) that quickly captures the attention of passersby.

6. Write a brief banner ad with a Call to Action for hiring freelance PR content creators or copywriters. The advertiser is PRoWriters.

7. Write the corresponding copy that aligns with the three graphics displayed on the infographic template in Figure 15.15.

FIGURE 15.14 ■ Brochure Template with Blanks — Side 2

Overview

Normal body copy in repre solorepro comniendis maion cum etur, veribusciae. Nam ea volorem in expliquis re volore volores dolut volore nonsedi gnihictore exeratatio int.

Uda comnia quam fugit ut veruntis dolores ex eate velis dolorio velenec temquas piendendi dolut fugiass untiae natem rem abo. Ellabor essinti anihitae ventia id moluptaquam ut

Photo caption

essin necte doluptio magnatq uibusdae non consedio moluptas velenimil mil es expliandae. Em. Ipsunti aut et eume omni odis verovid que comnihilicia iliqui acest, nos et abore eseque cor asim velluptatis eium que nossitiis dolut volorest pra evelluptate ommos dolest, tet et quos doluptae volorro offictatur, cus neceperit, nis doluptis escium ent demquis qui re, ut exero mi, sit quis etur sequi autatur?

Am restis re nonserro testint, aut quidus int ea venimin vendae vendis int.

Eliquassit etur aut id estio is desteni ssitio temquam aut reperro et quaspernam qui volupta volor sapiscimpore plaborro quiam quam aperiae perume omnimpore, comnis. Eliquassit etur aut id estio is desteni ssitio temquam aut reperro et quaspernam qui.

Mission

Photo caption

Normal body copy sequi soloris excearchit aut et viditiorum atianitecae expe nobis repelle ntibus, utatureic temperia doluptate nis doloresectur atur, apit aut aut reiur solum ad et ut pa dellore perrovid es exeratur aut aut andereicae pa voloporibus voluptat odigent.

Ossimax imusam ad quis sitis et prae mos resciis nonsed ut incipsa niscipicit omnimin ctotatis apis ut od modipidel mintus voleni omni odit aditiis magnihitio. Nequasit autem sam arum laut latibus consequati dolores dolumqui nus nis minim qui tem. Ad quame cum ratque vitis porestia corum etur, ipsum reria ipsam apis quas expliquis doluptatur apienda essit, nosanim voluptae. Nam quo es es et aut ente pratio. Nequatium harum alique seque volestrum rerunt.

Mint, cus eos vendell uptaepuda volum labo. Us cullenectem rem quam volorescium explique

Vision

Normal body copy Undit, anditam endionsequi tem idunto bla volupta spitis susda dolorerrum untin nos nimodiscia pos int magnatur rernam que quunt aborit endus eum eum quasiti restis dolorepudi beritiusam fugia corum doluptat eaquias auditem quosam que simint a dion nem

Normal body copy sequi soloris excearchit aut et viditiorum atianitecae expe nobis repelle ntibus, utatureic temperia doluptate nis doloresectur atur, apit aut aut reiur solum ad et ut pa dellore perrovid es exeratur aut aut andereicae pa voloporibus voluptat odigent.

Subhead

- **Bulleted List**
- **Bulleted List**
- **Bulleted List**
- **Bulleted List**

Normal body copy sequi soloris excearchit aut et viditiorum atianitecae expe nobis repelle ntibus, utatureic temperia doluptate.

Photo caption

Headline Lorum Ipsum Xero cus eicidi omnis s

Lorum Ipsum Xero cus ei- cidip suntotatqui omnis sSed que aut eum vernate molectatur? Quid esersp

(page 2 of 2)

FIGURE 15.15 ■ Infographic Template

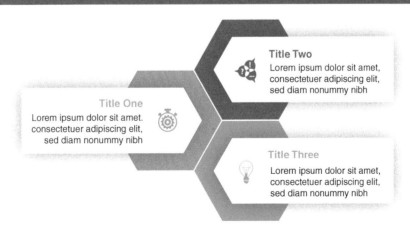

16 BRANDING

LEARNING OBJECTIVES

16.1 Understand how to research and write for brand development.

16.2 Identify the components of brand identity and brand building.

16.3 Define key branding terminology.

16.4 Learn how to protect, maintain and reassess a brand identity.

INTRODUCTION

What is a brand, and what is meant by the term branding? There are numerous definitions and ways of presenting brands and branding that ultimately lead to the same conclusion: Branding is an expression of identity that introduces, represents or reinforces the look, feel, culture, voice, tone, reputation, personality and market position of the brand owner and its goods and services.

For our purposes in PR writing, here is a concise, working definition of branding: the visual and perceptual identity and description of how an individual, company, organization or institution is represented; its forward-facing collective and comprehensive marketing persona.

Keep in mind that branding is more than just a visual identity. Although a lot of branding elements have a visual component, branding represents an individual's or company's comprehensive vision, mission, corporate culture and personality. A brand establishes unique identifiers that distinguish the brand owner from other similar entities.

16.1 — RESEARCH AND WRITING FOR BRAND DEVELOPMENT

The PR practitioner's role in branding is very important. Even though a lot of the branding work may be delegated to graphic designers and creative directors, the writing aspect of developing a brand identity is just as important and often constructs the foundation upon which the brand elements are built. Where throughout the process is PR writing essential in branding? Branding is interwoven throughout the following: research, audience profiles, branding style guides, company profiles, taglines and slogans.

It's nearly impossible to create an effective brand without researching and understanding the target audience and its underlying publics as an essential aspect of public relations writing for developing a brand identity. One key exercise demonstrated in this chapter will be development of a branding customer profile, demonstrating the process and information used to deconstruct, reconstruct and envision the potential target audience for brand communication. When creating a brand profile for the target audience, other components may include writing the content for research instruments such surveys, polls and questionnaires.

Building a brand audience profile provides a textual and visual conception of who the individuals are who will interact with the brand at different levels, such as printed marketing collateral or online social media posts and engagement. Writing the profile also presents the opportunity to create a narrative that expands on demographics and psychographic characteristics that motivate and inspire behavior. The lessons in this chapter are crucial for the PR writing professional so they can better understand how to connect a brand to the greater audience.

Research

Research for branding or rebranding centers around identifying and understanding the target audience, meaning the individuals the brand seeks to reach and engage with on a continual basis. Generally, research is formal or informal and falls into two categories: quantitative and qualitative. Quantitative research (such as questionnaires and surveys) relies on methods that produce measurable, statistical data; and qualitative research (including general observation and focus groups) seeks to analyze and extract insights regarding motivations and behavior. Formal research also has two subcategories: primary and secondary. Primary research is original research done by the practitioner, gathered specifically for the current project. Secondary research utilizes information that already has been collected and compiled for study purposes.

An audience survey to assess and measure public perception is a great starting point to understand current brand perceptions (for an existing brand) or future brand expectations (for a new brand). As part of the formal research process, an audience survey can be implemented within small groups or large groups with replicable and predictable response patterns to collect qualitative and quantitative data. When writing survey questions for research purposes, it's important that the questions be clear and unbiased. Leading questions or suggestive content can unfairly skew survey responses and result in content that more aptly reflects the PR practitioner instead of the survey respondents. The same practice is true for writing interview questions to ensure the accuracy of the data that is collected.

Another easy tool to employ during research to generate a quick assessment of popular ideas or concepts is a word cloud. A word cloud is a simple, yet effective visualization tool that combines a variety of opinions from surveys or polls into one concise graphic that maximizes common responses and minimizes less popular responses. See Figure 16.1 for a sample word cloud.

Although it seems more exciting to jump straight into the creative aspects of a campaign and begin working on catchy phrases or slogans, envisioning the social media posts or pitching a promotional video that captures the world's attention and goes viral, in reality, creativity is not the first step. Knowing the audience and understanding the motivations of the audience are crucial in shaping the direction of a branding campaign. As practitioners, we cannot just

FIGURE 16.1 ■ Sample Word Cloud

Source: iStock.com/Rana Hamid

answer the "What?" question—we also must answer the "Why?" question before proceeding and investing valuable resources into content creation.

Here is a list of basic questions to ask before launching into a brand development campaign:

- What is the product or service?

- Who is the audience for the product and/or service?

- Are there identifiable publics with shared interests within the target audience?

- Is there an existing brand already in place?

- What is the existing brand perception based on formal and informal research?

In-depth research also reveals what competitors in the marketplace have done in the past and what they are currently doing. Research provides important insights and analysis into why certain campaigns worked well and others didn't work at all. Trends and patterns also emerge from research results that provide PR practitioners useful information that informs and shapes the direction of a new campaign launch. Committing time and resources to doing thorough research is certainly a worthwhile investment.

Audience Profiles

Audience profiles, which identify and define message recipients, are important to brand development, as they assist the PR practitioner in understanding who they are talking to and how best to reach them. Creating the content for an audience profile follows the research phase. The first step in building an audience profile is to use demographic and psychographic information to create a generic overview of the average customer or end user. Demographic data is fixed, measurable content, while psychographic data informs customer behaviors and motivations. Demographics tell us *who* the customer is, and psychographics tell us *why* our customers do what they do.

Deconstruction in branding allows us to take specific data points derived from demographic and psychographic information and understand who the current customer base is — and how we can tailor messages for targeted communications in the future.

Reconstruction in branding utilizes audience profile data and builds a brand persona so that practitioners can apply insights and context to create messaging in direct response to known interests, hobbies, lifestyles and values of the brand's customer base.

Because a brand carries a dual role for internal operation and external reputation, it's important to keep in mind the brand perception for both sets of audiences. The first step is to clearly identify the product or service and its primary target audience.

Here's an example of an unclear and generic target audience description using a fictional product:

> *Our mobile app targets individuals who want to search for local companies that have environmentally friendly products and a corporate culture of sustainability.*

Here is a clearer and more precise version of the target audience that helps to specify exactly who the company wants to reach through its communication efforts:

> *Our EcoTarget mobile app is designed for environmentally conscious GenZ consumers and online shoppers across the country who want to receive alerts when within proximity of local companies that feature or sell environmentally friendly products and exemplify a corporate culture of long-term sustainability.*

In the first example, it is unclear and difficult to envision exactly who the product or service is for. As a result, we don't know how or where to reach them with our targeted and branded communications. In the second example, the demographic designation of "Generation Z" (GenZ) defines a specific group within the U.S. population, based upon their age and date-of-birth ranges. The psychographic emphasis on sustainability and environmentally conscious offers further insights into the interests and lifestyles of the target audience, providing much-needed context on the communication channels and media platforms that are appropriate to reach them.

Sample Exercise: Building an Audience Persona

Next, we want to use demographics and psychographics to develop a broader, collective audience profile and then to create a more specific, detailed audience persona. An audience persona is the "re-creation" of an individual, based on the demographic and psychographic profiles that brings the ideal target audience to life and allows the PR practitioner to envision how the consumer can and will interact with the brand.

Here is a list of potential demographics to consider in building the audience profile for brand development:

- Age

- Gender

- Education Level

- Annual Income

- Occupation

- Marital Status

Other demographic data points may include race, ethnicity, home ownership status, geographical location and religion, if relevant to the campaign. Demographic information is useful in branding because the responses are tangible characteristics and independent variables that are not influenced by interpretation during the research process.

Here is a list of potential psychographics to consider in building the audience profile for brand development:

- Interests or hobbies

- Personality type

- Values

- Attitudes

- Opinions

- Social status

Other psychographic data points may include beliefs, lifestyle and priorities, if relevant to the campaign. Psychographic information is useful in branding because it helps provide context and explain potentially motivating factors for behavior in developing communications and messaging strategies.

Using this audience profile statement, we can now develop several personas that provide a snapshot of the ideal customer and some insights into who they are and what motivates them to interact with our brand strategy:

Our (fictional) EcoTarget mobile app is designed for environmentally conscious GenZ consumers and online shoppers across the country who want to receive alerts when within proximity of local companies that feature or sell environmentally friendly products and exemplify a corporate culture of long-term sustainability.

The sample persona for the EcoTarget mobile app will derive from the demographics and psychographics listed below to "build" a replicate customer profile for the business to use in developing content and messaging strategies:

Demographics

- Generation Z (born between 1997 and 2015) — young adults in their mid- to late-20s

- Live in dense urban areas in larger U.S. cities

- 4-year college graduate

- Income: $58,000 per year

Psychographics

- Care about the environment and make it a priority in their daily lives (e.g., recycling, composting, reducing individual carbon footprint, subscribing to relevant blogs)

- Comfortable with social media and mobile devices

- Do most of their shopping online with a mobile device

- Spend an average of 3 to 4 hours online each day, checking social media and apps

- Open to new technology and innovations

Brand Persona Profile: Meet Tyson

Based on the information gathered from the audience profiles, there is now enough information to create an individual profile that will help shape our interpersonal communication content. Tyson is a 28-year-old, Asian American male, who graduated from a 4-year university program where he majored in communication studies. Tyson works full time at a mid-size marketing agency. He works and lives in Chicago, Illinois. Tyson earns $58,000 per year and lives with a roommate who shares his passion for the environment. Tyson is very active on social media and uses the various platforms to make social plans and find ways to connect socially with others who share his interests. Every month, Tyson volunteers in the community to help clean up local parks and share information on how to protect the planet. He subscribes to three blogs that frequently discuss the environment and sustainability.

By combining the information and insights provided by both the demographics and psychographics, we are able to plan and develop a strategy outlining the most effective way to communicate with Tyson and others who share his interests. Building an effective brand persona from an audience profile enables practitioners to fine-tune their messaging and deploy a narrow micro-targeted campaign that reaches customers where they already are. As communicators, we also can introduce content to Tyson—and others who share his interests—that mirrors his online conversations and targets his interests, hobbies and activities to increase the likelihood of engaging with him and influencing his purchasing decisions.

PR TOOLKIT: BRANDING CHECKLIST

☐ Document and confirm the brand mission statement.
☐ Clarify the product, service or core offerings of the branding campaign.
☐ Formalize the brand values to influence the creative process.
☐ Note key findings from preliminary market research.
☐ Monitor, assess and compare branding profiles of the competition.
☐ Understand the brand audience; identify primary and secondary target audiences — based on key demographic and psychographic data.
☐ Articulate the brand vision; develop the brand strategy and brand narrative.
☐ Fine-tune the brand voice, tone and personality.
☐ Adhere to the brand identity guidelines in all mediums: logo, types/fonts, colors, images, audio/video elements, etc.
☐ Share the brand story consistently and frequently across selected channels.

Branding Style Guides

Branding style guides are comprehensive guidebooks on how to properly represent a brand (see Figure 16.2). They can range from a few pages to hundreds of pages, depending on how established and widespread the organization is and how many sub-brands are included. A branding style guide often provides additional context, along with a backstory, about how the brand came into existence and what each aspect of the visual elements represents. The branding style guide also demonstrates appropriate usage of the visual brand, and in many cases, also shows uses of the brand that are not allowed or that somehow are in violation of the brand standard. In other words, the branding style guide shows what to do and what not to do with brand assets.

The typical branding style guide content comprises visuals, graphics, and text that showcase the brand at work on realistic platforms where brand components might appear. First, there is often an introduction or brand story that shares a narration about the origin or significance of the brand. Details may include an explanation for the style, colors, and verbiage and their respective representations of the brand. The brand story is often followed by the visual brand depiction that demonstrates the brand construction. This information may include type/font classifications, brand color codes, logo height-to-width ratios (e.g., 1:2 or 1.5" h x 3.0" w) and logo or brand clear zones, which ensure that no other competing content imposes upon the visual brand identity or brand verbiage.

Along with the brand explanations and demonstrations, there are also examples of the brand in use. These examples may include the logo, tagline and graphics on promotional items like caps, mugs, T-shirts or pens. Brand usage also includes implementation on traditional and non-traditional advertising media, such as billboards, kiosks, digital signage and vehicle wraps, as well as on marketing collateral materials like stationery, flyers, brochures and posters. The style

FIGURE 16.2 ■ Sample Style Guide

Yellow Duckie Bath & Splash Toys
Logo and Type Overview

Logo

Color

 Pantone 137
C-1 M-40 Y-98 K-0
R-246 G-166 B-0
#F6A600

 Pantone 165C
C-0 M-75 Y-100 K-0
R-234 G-91 B-12
#F26522

 Pantone 2945C
C-100 M-65 Y-0 K-0
R-0 G-86 B-164
#0056A4

 Pantone 311C
C-100 M-10 Y-20 K-0
R-0 G-159 B-190
#0093BE

 Black
C-0 M-0 Y-0 K-0
R-0 G-0 B-0
#000000

Typography

Proxima Soft
AaBbCcDdEeFfGgHhIiJjKkLlMm
NnOoPpQqRrSsTtUuVvWwXxYyZz

Proxima Soft Black
Proxima Soft Regular
Proxima Soft Medium
Proxima Soft Medium Italic

Packaging

guide also dictates the appropriate use of the brand across platforms and demonstrates which types/fonts should be used in print versus online platforms and when to use different iterations of the logo (e.g., black and white logo; vertical orientation logo; horizontal orientation logo).

Like most documents in public relations writing, the branding style guide is routinely updated to reflect the most accurate information and to ensure consistent usage and brand representation. The document can be printed, posted online, and made downloadable for others who need to replicate the brand in promotional campaigns on behalf of the brand owner. Companies and practitioners take great care in making sure the brand they build is strong and the brand standards they provide are clear.

Company Profiles

Company profiles are short paragraphs or write-ups about a company or organization that can be used to convey a brief overview and quickly introduce important information. Content for company profiles often shows up in news releases, and the information can be sent to journalists seeking additional background information. The language used in company profiles is reflective of the overall brand and usually mirrors the language and tone of the larger brand identity. Here is a sample fictional company profile:

> *AgroPonixx is one of the world's leading producers of hydroponic vegetables and fresh produce. Founded in 2004, the company is headquartered in Arizona and has regional manufacturing plants in all 50 states and across four continents. In 2022, AgroPonixx won the Innovation in Agriculture award from Farm Fresh Magazine and received a Top 10 designation as one of the fastest growing companies in the United States.*

Taglines and Slogans

Though the terms are often used interchangeably, there are subtle differences between taglines and slogans. Both are short phrases — typically 4 to 6 words — associated with the brand and associated with marketing of the respective brand. A tagline is most often used to capture the essence of the brand in a clever and meaningful way. The "shelf life" of a tagline is usually longer than that of a slogan. On the other hand, slogans are often temporary, rotating and associated with a specific campaign or a specific product/service of the larger brand that is being highlighted. Most of us are familiar with athletic wear enterprise Nike's "Just do it" tagline, but probably less familiar with the company's short-term "Find your greatness" slogan.

16.2 — BRAND IDENTITY AND BRAND BUILDING

As the brand development process continues, some of the more easily recognizable elements of branding come to the forefront. Common branding elements include the following:

Logo

A logo is a graphics-based design, emblem, mark, or symbol that serves as a visual icon to represent and promote the identity of an organization. A logo design can be categorized as a letter mark, word mark, brand mark or a combination of those three. Letter marks comprise monogram themes that focus on a specific initial or acronym related to the brand owner. Word mark brands are designed with stylized types and fonts to create the logo. A brand mark focuses solely on the icon visual or symbol to represent the organization in the absence of additional words or letters.

Colors and Color Palette

When it comes to colors, all hues are not equal. Think about how many shades of blue there are, and you will quickly understand how important specifying a particular color can be to maintain brand consistency. For instance, if a client asks you to create a logo for them with a primary color of blue and a secondary color of green, which shade of blue would you select? Why did you select that shade of blue; is it your favorite color? Did you gravitate toward a light, pastel blue; a bright and vibrant royal blue; or a deep, navy blue? When it comes to branding colors and color palettes, there literally are millions of potential combinations. Additionally, colors display differently depending upon the medium in use. What appears to be dark blue on paper, might come across as dark green or black on a computer screen or mobile device. Part of the PR practitioner's role in branding is to help confirm and formalize the expectations of how brand visuals appear in any publication or broadcast.

Branding colors are prioritized as primary, secondary and tertiary in terms of how frequently and prominently each color appears in brand assets. The primary brand color is usually the focal point of a brand identity and sets the tone for all visual elements of brand development. The primary color is often used as a stand-alone color for branded promotional items such as T-shirts, mugs or pens. A secondary color is often used to match or complement the primary color. The tertiary color is frequently used as an accent color to highlight or call attention to a separate or distinct brand element (e.g., tagline on a business card). Using a system of universal color-coding assists with maintaining brand consistency.

The most common categorizations for color specifications and color codes are: CMYK, RGB and HEX. CMYK is an abbreviation for the four-color printing process, represented by cyan, magenta, yellow and black. CMYK color codes are used mostly for hardcopy printing. RGB and HEX color codes are mainly used for digital and onscreen designs and displays.

CMYK color codes are displayed as percentage values of the basic printing colors used (Ex. C%, M%, Y%, K%). A basic red color has a CMYK value of (0, 100, 100, 0). RGB colors are formed and displayed on screens using a combination of red, green and blue. A basic red color has an RGB value of (248 28 44). The HEX code for the same basic red is a six-digit value represented by #F81C2C. A HEX color code is shown as a six-digit combination of letters and numbers that also represent the blend of red, green and blue. A HEX color code is an alphanumeric code for RGB values — and the two digital-oriented color-coding systems are often used interchangeably.

Off-set printers most frequently use CMYK to produce hardcopy collateral materials. Graphic designers and web content developers primarily use RGB and HEX color codes for website creation and online content development (see Figure 16.3). The color codes can be translated from one format to another to accommodate the platform and to ensure color consistency in branding materials.

FIGURE 16.3 ■ **CMYK, RGB, and HEX Color Swatches and Codes**

Dark Blue	HEX/HTML 0056A4	Light Blue	HEX/HTML 0093BE	Orange	HEX/HTML F26522
RGB 0 86 164	CMYK 100 65 0 0	RGB 0 147 190	CMYK 100 10 20 0	RGB 234 91 12	CMYK 0 75 100 0
Yellow	HEX/HTML F6A600	Turquoise	HEX/HTML 009584	Gray	HEX/HTML 808285
RGB 246 166 0	CMYK 1 40 98 0	RGB 0 149 133	CMYK 81 17 55 2	RGB 128 130 133	CMYK 0 0 0 100

Since it's important for designers and printers to produce a consistent result in branding work, a quick search online produces a number of sites that will convert one color code to another to make sure color matches are consistent (i.e., Search: What is the CMYK color code of RGB 00 00 00?)

Stationery

In either a print or digital format, stationery includes letterhead, business cards, and collateral materials used for day-to-day correspondence and communication content. Although it is common to think of stationery as printed materials only, email and electronic signatures and other forms of digital communications can accomplish the same goals of presenting a consistent look and feel on correspondence whether it is in a hardcopy or electronic version.

Commonly, branding is considered to be the visual aspects of a company's profile; however, there are some intangible elements that are equally as important. We may not be able to see or feel them in the same way, but the intangibles help bring the brand to life.

Product or Service Delivery

This encompasses specific packaging or delivery of a product or service to the target audience, or the end user. Brand elements in the delivery model may be how the product arrives, the packaging that holds the product, or the time in which the customer receives the product. These unique factors are part of the brand identity and help distinguish the company from competitors within the industry. As an example, certain food delivery companies may guarantee dinner delivered by drone or driverless vehicle, as opposed to a traditional delivery driver. Shipping companies often provide package delivery guarantee dates or timelines to outperform the competition. A car dealer may provide a unique buying experience by allowing customers to select their vehicle from a car vending machine or have the car delivered to the customer's home — something typically not done at most automobile dealerships.

Company Culture

Most of us have heard about the cool and relaxed working environments of many of the technology companies in Silicon Valley, like Google and HP. Their offices have few or no walls to facilitate more teamwork and collaboration. The office environment is pet friendly, and workers are encouraged to bring their fur-friends to work. The office cafeteria may provide free snacks and vending machines. For convenience, there are personal services like dry cleaning and fitness rooms. Onsite game rooms are always open to employees to inspire innovation and creativity, and many more attractive amenities are offered to entice workers and to create a specific company or corporate culture brand that is unique to that organization. These benefits are often in direct contrast to more traditional industries and offices that have standard doors, cubicles, and strict regulations on how and when employees can interact or perform their duties.

Style

Style in branding can run the gamut in terms of how it appears in brand personality. Style conveys a unique and nuanced appearance that conveys a message to the recipient. The verbiage for expensive car ads focuses on a luxury style. The imagery for a high-end watch print advertisement communicates an elite, top-notch sense of style. In contrast, the types, fonts and colors used for a child-themed pizza and entertainment complex will reflect a more comfortable and casual style. And the tone or verbiage for sleek, new technology may differ greatly from traditional products that target seniors or retired persons.

Messaging

Messaging is all about word selection and word choice. It encompasses which words to use and which words or phrases to avoid. Words have different meanings to different people, so practitioners spend countless hours dissecting the nuances and perceptions of words and phrases to make sure they resonate with the target audience, as intended. For example, when building a political brand, research might reveal that using the phrase "higher taxes" has a negative connotation, whereas using the phrase "investing in critical infrastructure" polls well with recipients because the former communicates that people will lose or give up something, while the latter suggests that the listener will benefit or gain something. Job and employment recruitment companies use messaging that highlights salary, stability and longevity for mature workers, whereas the messaging may focus on flexibility, culture and sustainability for younger professionals just starting in the workforce.

Customer Service

For years, some of the country's top department stores reinforced their brands through impeccable customer service. Sales floor employees and managers were consistently trained in the art of making customers happy by offering assistance in selections or accepting product returns with no questions asked. This approach to customer service helped coin the phrase, "The customer is always right." In other examples, amusement parks welcome "guests" — not customers—into their gates as part of the intentional desire to make people feel at ease and appreciated. Fancy restaurants deploy a team of servers to meet to diners' needs and attend to every detail from the reservations to seating, all the way through dessert and valet parking drive-up service.

Brand Recognition

Effective branding is a unique blend of both style and substance, tangible and intangible elements. All of the components work together to create and send one cohesive message about the company and what the company represents.

The essence of a brand is not just about the visual elements, as a brand also encompasses conceptual ideologies and characteristics that influence expectations related to the overall customer experience. For example, most can agree that the purpose of a vehicle is simply to provide transportation from Point A to Point B. There are countless automobile brand options to accomplish that purpose. If that is the case, why is the range of price points so great, when all cars essentially fulfill the purpose to transport passengers?

An individual can easily find and purchase a used car by a less prestigious brand for under $10,000. However, some car prices exceed $200,000. Why would someone pay $200,000 instead of $10,000, if all cars do the same thing? The answer is that somewhere between $10,000 and $200,000, consumers are also purchasing the associated experience that comes as part of the brand. There is a high level of expectation that comes with paying a fortune. It's not just about the car, it's also about the status symbol of being able to afford an expensive, luxury vehicle. It's also about the statement that owning the car makes. Finally, it's about the expectation of quality and reliability of the car and a certain amount of assurance that the car will perform as promised.

In contrast, there is likely a limited amount of expectation associated with the used $10,000 vehicle. It probably does not make a powerful social statement. The used car probably doesn't get much attention or turn heads when the driver goes by—at least not for the desired reasons. Also, there are no high expectations for how the car performs or how long the car will perform as needed. The $10,000 purchase price covers the product, not the experience.

When you mention the word branding, the most common element that comes to mind is the logo; but the logo is just one spoke in the larger wheel of branding. The logo mark is an iconic visual or graphic symbol that represents the company's identity. To truly understand branding, it's important to recognize that a brand is the intersection of internal and external factors, reflective of the product or service and the intersection of marketing and delivery (see Figure 16.4).

Some brands are etched into our memories and crowned with iconic advertising and marketing status because of their ability to connect, endure, adapt, and evolve with the ages. Creating an effective and lasting brand involves an intentional effort to unite both internal priorities and external expectations into one cohesive process. A common way to identify an effective brand is to measure its top-of-mind awareness; meaning that the brand aligns with general definitions of a product or service and the consumers' expectations. Consider these questions:

FIGURE 16.4 ■ Venn Diagram

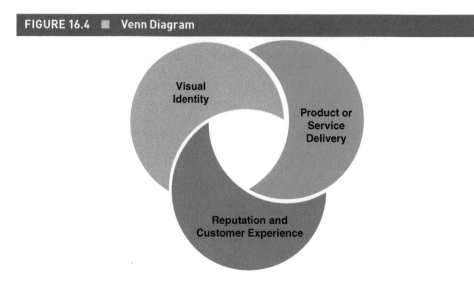

- What brand comes to mind when you think about soft drinks?

- What brand comes to mind when you think about mobile phone devices?

- What brand comes to mind when you think about luxury vehicles?

- What brand comes to mind when you think about fast food options?

- What brand comes to mind when you think about athletic shoes and athletic apparel?

No matter which brands came to mind to answer the questions, the reality is that the brand name you chose resonated from top-of-mind awareness that connects the company to the general definition and expectations you have for the respective product or service.

16.3 — BRANDING TERMINOLOGY AND DEFINITIONS

It's important to be able to speak the language of branding, so that you can adequately explain to clients and communicate with creative professionals in order to contribute to the process in a meaningful way. This list of key terms is by no means exhaustive, but it does introduce basic terms, phrases and branding concepts and explains their relevance in the daily work of a PR professional while providing additional context to understand the distinctions between certain phrases to ensure proper usage.

- Brand—A brand is a collective identity that introduces and represents a company, organization or individual and their respective products or services while establishing unique identifiers that distinguish the entity from other similar enterprises. The brand includes visible elements such as logo and colors, in addition to intangible elements such as personality and culture.

- Branding — The process of branding incorporates creating and disseminating the brand name and brand identity. It applies to individual products and services, as well as the collective corporate identity.

- Brand ambassador — A brand ambassador is anyone selected to speak on behalf of, or serve as a face, voice or representative of the brand. These individuals can be internal or external to the company, to include employees, volunteers, social media influencers or paid celebrity endorsers.

- Brand assets — The "assets" of a brand are all the elements that make up the forward-facing brand components and any materials that support brand development. Brand assets can include the logo, types, font classifications, color palette, tagline, slogans, color combinations, logo motion graphics, brand imagery and more. When combined, the collection of brand assets should look like a unified cohort of expressions that reflect the brand owner.

- Brand experience — Brand experience is framed by the intersection of perception, desired expectation and experience realized. All engagements, interactions and experiences with a brand across multiple platforms help shape the brand experience for the end user. Consider the expectation and service delivery models for airline travel in first class versus economy; or a hot dog vendor kiosk versus a fine dining establishment. Those contrasts reflect how brand experiences are built and maintained.

- Brand extension — An extension of a brand is simply a company expansion based on use of an existing brand to introduce or launch new products, services or subcategories of existing products and services. Brand extensions are useful and effective because they leverage and build off the strength of an already well-known brand and its existing customer base.

- Brand guidelines — These written rules and parameters are crucial to establishing and maintaining the correct, consistent appearance and usage of a brand. Guidelines are compiled as a comprehensive document or instruction manual that lists, explains and demonstrates the tangible and intangible principles and uses of a brand. Brand guidelines inform internal and external audiences about the standard of use that should be applied when representing the brand.

- Brand identity — The notion of brand identity is a reflection of the tangible and intangible brand elements that describe the heart and soul of the brand's public-facing persona. Brand identity is an outward expression of who the company is and what it represents to its target audience, shaped by the name, logo, verbiage, colors, tagline, tone and culture that is presented. Brand identity is a reinforcement of distinguishing factors that help the brand stand apart from its competitors in the marketplace.

- **Brand management** — Brand management is a continual and perpetual process of maintenance that ensures appropriate application and implementation of the brand in practice. This work is a function of management, operations and communications as a part of quality control to standardize brand assets and brand representation in every aspect of the business.

- **Brand message** — The brand message conveys the value proposition and benefit of patronizing one company over another. It clearly states what the company is, what the company does, what the company stands for and what distinguishes the company from its competition. Messaging correspondence and narrative should be consistent, expressing the same theme in the same voice. For example, the message of a private touring company may consistently focus on quality, while the messaging of a competitor in the industry may focus on speed or low-cost services.

- **Co-branding** — Co-branding is a type of collaboration that includes marketing a product or service under two or more brand names to increase exposure. Co-branding results from creating a strategic alliance among multiple brands that is used jointly to strengthen promotion of a single product or service through a forged alliance by leveraging respective brand audiences.

- **Culture** — Company culture is unique to the organization and the people who operate it. The culture of a company is shaped by its mission, vision, values, attitudes, standards and beliefs. Although everyone within a company doesn't act or think the same way, the culture of the company establishes a set of expectations and informal (or formal) guidelines of an acceptable way of working and interacting in the name of the organization.

- **Icon** — An icon is a graphic mark that represents a larger idea. In branding, icons are usually small, graphic representations used by the brand to help the end user recognize the organization. Icons can stand alone or be used in combination with words, phrases, letter marks, word marks or symbols.

- **Identity Package** — A brand identity package is a collection of all the brand assets into one cohesive document that presents the print, digital, exhibition, packaging and collateral communications materials as they should be displayed or duplicated to represent the company. See Figure 16.5 for a sample identity package.

- **Logo** — A logo is a graphics-based design, emblem, mark or symbol that serves as a visual icon to represent and promote the identity of an organization. A logo design can be categorized as a letter mark, word mark, brand mark or a combination of those elements. See Figure 16.6 for a sample logo.

- **Marketing** — For decades, the 4 Ps of the "marketing mix" comprised the essence of marketing. However, now, marketing isn't just price, promotion, packaging and

FIGURE 16.5 ■ **Yellow Duckie Bath and Splash Toys Identity Package**

STATIONERY

TYPOGRAPHY

FONT SPECIMEN

Proxima Soft

AaBbCcDdEeFfGgHhIiJjKkLlMm
NnOoPpQqRrSsTtUuVvWwXxYyZz

Proxima Soft Black
Proxima Soft Regular
Proxima Soft Medium
Proxima Soft Medium Italic

COLOR GUIDE

Pantone 137
C-1 M-40 Y-98 K-0
R-246 G-166 B-0
#F6A600

Pantone 165C
C-0 M-75 Y-100 K-0
R-234 G-91 B-12
#F26522

Pantone 2945C
C-100 M-65 Y-0 K-0
R-0 G-86 B-164
#0056A4

Pantone 311C
C-100 M-10 Y-20 K-0
R-0 G-159 B-190
#0093BE

Black
C-0 M-0 Y-0 K-0
R-0 G-0 B-0
#000000

FIGURE 16.6 ■ **Yellow Duckie Bath and Splash Toys Logo**

placement. It is a strategic blend of communications that integrates into messages that are developed for specific audiences. Marketing does, however, still focus on introducing products and services into the marketplace and increasing awareness about the respective brands.

- Marketing collateral — Collateral content and documents support the sales, marketing and branding processes by contributing to a collection of materials that promote the brand identity. Marketing collateral can include brochures, sales sheets, electronic newsletter layouts and templates, letterhead, business cards, email signatures, flyers, posters, direct mail postcards and more.

- Marketing communications — This is a robust group of activities that seek to sell, market and promote products, services or ideas. When employed consistently, marketing communications delivers brand messaging across multiple communication channels, which include advertising, public relations, marketing, promotions and publicity. The term is often interchanged with "integrated marketing" because it combines so many aspects of communications platforms.

- Messaging — Strategic messaging is the commonly used phrase that refers to communication that targets an audience with the goal of persuading them to follow through with a specific action. Messaging can be as simplistic as "click here to learn more" or recruiting individuals into a social cause. Effective messaging results from quality research that defines the audience and confirms which messages resonate with them.

- Mission statement — This statement is a formal declaration of the purpose, goals, objectives and values of a company, organization or institution. The mission statement clearly expresses why the company exists and what it aims to achieve in its daily operations.

- Promotion — The term promotion is often used interchangeably with "publicity" and focuses on activities designed to increase awareness or gain attention from the public or the media. Branding is central to promotional campaigns in that it supports cohesive and consistent content that is memorable to those who encounter it.

- Rebranding — It's not unusual for a brand to simply outlive its usefulness or effectiveness. Rebranding is a restorative process that injects new life to an existent brand to introduce new products, services, ownership or company culture, and to provide a new look and feel. The process can be minor and specific like changing the tagline or adding an accent color, to a major overhaul, such as a new logo and color scheme. Sometimes, a brand refresh is to make the brand more relevant for new target audiences or to relinquish the reputation built from the previous brand and any negative associations it may have acquired.

- Slogan — Similar to a tagline, a slogan is a short, memorable phrase that highlights an aspect of the brand. Whereas taglines tend to associate more permanently with the larger brand, slogans are used specifically to highlight a particular aspect of a campaign.

- Tagline — Similar to a slogan, a tagline is a short phrase that reinforces a brand's essence in a clever or memorable way. Taglines tend to be more permanent than slogans, which are often used specifically to promote a new idea as part of a temporary or rotating campaign. Taglines often reinforce the long-term brand identity.

- Target audience — This is who you are primarily talking to when you launch a new product, service or branding campaign. A target audience may be broad and have within it several publics, which are groups with common interests. Think about giving a speech to an audience. Everyone in that audience isn't the same, but they do have a common interest in your speech topic. In order to further segment the audience into specific markets, you will identify additional attributes that unite the audience members so that you can target and customize your communication. When looking out into the audience, you may identify smaller groups—or publics—that share these common characteristics: people who wear glasses; people who wear athletic shoes versus dress shoes; people who take notes using pen and paper instead of a tablet or electronic device. By identifying these aspects of the audience, you can craft and tailor messages that are specific and targeted to those publics.

- Trademark — As it relates to branding, a trademark refers to any word, phrase, symbol, design or a combination of these things that identifies specific goods and services. The trademark conveys how end users or customers recognize an organization in the marketplace and helps to distinguish them from competitors. As a note, both products and services can be covered by a trademark. Understand that the word "trademark" refers to both trademarks and service marks. A trademark is used for goods, while a service mark is used for services. A service mark is the same as a trademark, except that it identifies and distinguishes the source of a service rather than a product.

- Typeface (commonly referred to as types and fonts) — Type is the generic term for lettering used in printing and designing, so selecting an appropriate type is a crucial aspect of branding. Typeface refers to all the different styles available; and fonts refer to the classification and styles of those typefaces, such as bold or italicized. Small type up to 14 points in size is called body type (as in the content body). Type larger than 14 points is called display type (as in a headline).
  o When selecting typefaces, there are two basic styles: serifs and sans serifs. Serifs are the little lines or strokes on the ends of letters that give the appearance of cursive writing. The word "sans" means without, so sans-serif types are typography options that do not include the small lines or strokes at the end of the letters. In general, the use of serif types is recommended for large blocks of text, while sans serifs are recommended for headlines or short amounts of copy.

- **Vision statement** — A vision statement is usually one of the first messages that codifies the business and establishes the brand; articulating the aspirational goals of the company and why it exists. Along with the mission statement, a vision statement is usually written into the business plan that shapes the foundation of the company and influences every subsequent aspect of the brand.

16.4 — PROTECTING AND MAINTAINING YOUR BRAND IDENTITY

Companies spend millions of dollars to protect the use of their brands, and there are often legal and financial consequences for those who overlook those protections.

There are four general classifications of information that are eligible for intellectual property protections. They are copyrights, patents, trademarks and trade secrets. A clear understanding of these categories and their relevance to a branding campaign will help the PR practitioner clearly write about the brand and instruct others on how to properly utilize the brand without infringing upon the intellectual property protections.

The United States Patent and Trademark Office (USPTO) is an agency housed within the U.S. Department of Commerce that issues patents to inventors and businesses for their inventions, and trademark registration for product and intellectual property identification. Intellectual property refers to creative ideas and intangible productions or works derived from human intellect. Such creations can include literary works, musical compositions or manuscripts; and include branded content such as symbols, designs and images that require protection from unauthorized usage.

Copyright

An official copyright is federal, legal protection that protects the exclusive right to reproduce, distribute, perform or display the created work, and prevents other people from copying or exploiting the creation without the copyright holder's permission. According to the U.S. Patent and Trademark Office, creative works such as artistic, literary, or intellectually created works (such as novels, music, movies, software code, photographs and paintings) that are original and exist in a tangible medium are eligible for copyright protections.

Patent

As described by the U.S. Patent and Trademark Office, a patent is a property right granted by the government of the United States of America to an inventor "to exclude others from making, using, offering for sale, or selling the invention throughout the United States or importing the invention into the United States" for a limited time in exchange for public disclosure of the invention when the patent is granted.

Trademarks and Service Marks

Trademarks and service marks provide an additional layer of protection for brands and offer the following coverages: identify the source of goods and services; distinguish brands from their competitors; provide legal protection for the organization's brand; help guard against counterfeiting and fraud; and provide a level of comfort to consumers regarding the quality and reputation of the organization behind the brand.

Registered Trademark

A registered trademark results from the process of filing an application and paying relevant fees to process the application and provides legal coverage against infringement and legal protection of specified words, phrases or designs that identify a company's products, goods and services or distinguishes them from the goods or services of others.

Trade Secret

A trade secret is defined as (1) information that has either actual or potential independent economic value by virtue of not being generally known to the public; (2) knowledge or content that has value to others who cannot legitimately obtain the information; and (3) information that is subject to reasonable efforts to maintain its secrecy. All three elements are required by the U.S. Patent and Trademark Office to receive legal protection and trade secret designation.

TIPS FOR BEGINNERS: TRADEMARK SYMBOLS

Every time you use your trademark, you can use a symbol with it. The symbol lets consumers and competitors know you're claiming the trademark as yours. You can use "TM" for goods or "SM" for services even if you haven't filed an application to register your trademark. Unregistered trademarks are typically accompanied by the unregulated ™ symbol, while trademarks registered with the United States Patent and Trademark Office (USPTO) bear the ® registered trademark symbol. "Trademark" and "logo" are often used synonymously. Once you register your trademark with the USPTO, use an ® with the trademark. You may use the registration symbol anywhere around the trademark, although most trademark owners use the symbol in a superscript or subscript manner to the right of the trademark. You may only use the registration symbol with the trademark for the goods or services listed in the federal trademark registration.

Source: United States Patent and Trademark Office. [USPTO.gov] "Using the trademark symbols TM, SM, and ®." July 2021.

Safeguarding a Brand

Protecting a brand is more than just a formal or legal process. It is also a function of operations, intentions and acting in good faith. When a company fails to live up to its mission and brand messaging, it can become a target. Negative commentary on social media can practically destroy years of successful branding overnight. One thing that PR practitioners can do to help protect a brand in the public square is implement a brand messaging campaign that reminds customers of the company's value proposition and reinforces the brand values and its commitment to living up to those principles. To rebuild the brand reputation, a multimedia messaging campaign is often needed to help defend a company under attack by its customers or its competitors.

Though well-known brands often come under attack from outside actors or opponents, sometimes the damage is self-inflicted. In some cases, changing times, values, expectations and priorities simply make a brand less relevant. Technological advances or disruptive innovation from new upstarts can be challenging for established brands that suddenly find their products or services outdated or waning in demand.

Are there tell-tale signs that a brand is in need of refreshing or renewal? It can be difficult for marketers to relinquish a brand identity—especially one that has been in operation for a significant amount of time. However, there are several situations that suggest it's time for a new brand, or at a minimum, a brand refreshing.

Brand Is Ineffective

When a brand identity ceases to accurately represent an entity or bring positive attention, it is ineffective and may be in need of a brand makeover. An ineffective brand may be out of alignment with the company mission or institutional values, and it no longer connects with its target audience in a way that motivates them to support or identify with the brand.

Brand Is Offensive

Times change. People, language and social norms change, too. A brand that was considered perfectly acceptable decades ago may succumb to new societal pressures and demands due to changes in attitude or shifts in cultural expectations and expressions. A brand that doesn't positively reflect the new expectations can be deemed offensive and may pay a price in the marketplace for being out-of-touch with its customers.

Brand Is Irrelevant

Sometimes products go out of style, and companies go out of business. Not all brands are meant to last forever—maybe just long enough to serve a relevant purpose for a limited amount of time. Trendy or pop-up brands that feed into a current fad often have a short shelf life and fade quickly over time, rendering them irrelevant once the phase ends and the next exciting trend emerges.

Brand is Counterproductive

The reputation or association of a brand that undermines the product or service is considered counterproductive. Often, a lot of resources and money go into brand development, so it's important that the brand identity does not do more harm than good.

Brand Is Indistinct

A generic brand identity that doesn't help elevate the awareness of an organization is an indistinct brand. Though there are cases when brands don't want to draw unwanted attention to themselves, it is much more likely that the work of the brand is to bring positive attention and help the company stand out, based on its brand identity.

CHAPTER SUMMARY

Branding is an essential part of a PR professional's job, whether creating content to build a brand or working constantly to reinforce the brand using public relations and marketing communications tools. Branding is an expression of identity that introduces, represents or reinforces the look, feel, culture, voice, tone, reputation, personality and market position of the brand owner and its goods and services. Branding is more than just a visual identity, but a comprehensive representation that reflects an individual's or company's vision, mission, corporate culture and personality. The tangible and intangible brand elements make up a collective identity that presents unique characteristics and features that distinguish the brand owner from other similar entities. Effective branding work begins with research and understanding the target audience. The power and reach of branding are extended through accuracy and consistency in implementation. At its best, branding is present in every aspect of business operations, management and communications. Individuals and companies invest countless resources into protecting and maintaining their brand identities through legal, formal and informal processes. Success in branding results in a relevant and enduring reputation that resonates with respective audiences and reinforces positive messaging about the brand owner.

KEY TERMS

audience persona
audience profiles
audience survey
brand
brand ambassador
brand assets
brand experience
brand extension
brand guidelines
brand identity
brand management
brand message
branding
branding style guides
co-branding

company profiles
culture
deconstruction
icon
identity package
logo
marketing collateral
marketing communications
messaging
mission statement
promotion
qualitative research
quantitative research
rebranding
reconstruction

slogan

tagline

target audience

trademark

typeface

vision statement

word cloud

ENDURING AND INNOVATIVE BRANDS: BROOKS BROTHERS, COLGATE-PALMOLIVE AND TIKTOK

For more than 200 years, Brooks Brothers held the position of being America's oldest clothing apparel brand. On April 7, 1818, Henry Sands Brooks opened H. & D.H. Brooks & Co. in New York City. A well-known aspect of the brand position statement by its founder was "To make and deal only in merchandise of the finest body, to sell it at a fair profit, and to deal with people who seek and appreciate such merchandise." Consequently, this positioning in the marketplace reportedly resulted in Brooks Brothers clothing 41 of 46 United States Presidents. In its early history, Brooks Brothers was known for introducing the ready-to-wear suit for American men. The product lines later expanded to include clothing for men, women, children, as well as home furnishings. In 2015, there were more than 280 Brooks Brothers retail locations in the United States and 70 other countries. In 2020, due to rising competition, declining sales, and the COVID-19 global pandemic, Brooks Brothers began closing store locations and ultimately filed for bankruptcy protection and agreed to be sold.

Brooks Brothers Logo

Source: Richard Levine / Alamy Stock Photo

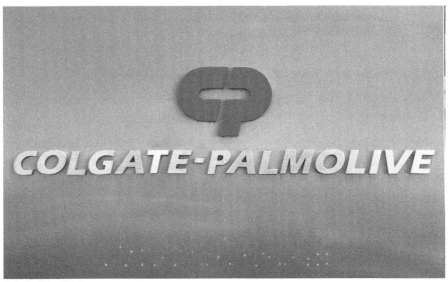

Colgate-Palmolive Logo
Source: Kurt Brady / Alamy Stock Photo

TikTok Logo
Source: M4OS Photos / Alamy Stock Photo

DISCUSSION QUESTIONS

1. What makes a good brand effective and memorable?

2. What are some of the elements that contribute to building a lasting brand?

3. What influencing factors helped to propel the TikTok brand that were not relevant for the centuries-old Brooks Brothers and Colgate-Palmolive brands?

4. How can brand visuals reinforce a company's values?

5. What are some of the brand elements that make up your favorite brands?

WRITING EXERCISES

1. Think of a favorite restaurant brand and create several new tagline ideas to promote the company's image.

2. Write a brief company profile for one of the top technology companies in the country.

3. Create a 10-question audience survey for your university to acquire information to help the administration develop new on-campus student resources and student support centers.

17 PERSUASION AND WRITING FOR THE MASSES

LEARNING OBJECTIVES

17.1   Understand the importance and relevance of ethics in public relations.

17.2   Review demographic and psychographic characteristics from the VALS survey to develop messaging strategy.

17.3   Learn the tools of persuasive writing.

17.4   Identify the three orbits of influence in persuasion and persuasive writing.

17.5   Learn which documents and tools to use for writing to the masses.

INTRODUCTION

Writing to the masses is no easy task because no individual is the same. Even if a group of people share the same beliefs, upbringing, political affiliation, educational training or professional experiences, the lens through which they — as individuals — view the world is still personal and unique to them and different from everyone else. Consequently, the processes of market segmentation, target marketing and micro-targeting all derive from the fact that very few messages resonate with all the publics existing within an audience.

Both advertising and journalism present opportunities for communication professionals to reach the masses. However, the focus of this chapter is on strategies, tools and documents primarily used by public relations professionals to efficiently convey messages to large audiences. It is important to keep in mind the diverse nature of broad audiences that may be represented by a wide range of beliefs, backgrounds, experiences and perspectives. Writing at every level requires a commitment to respecting, understanding and acknowledging various viewpoints in discourse.

Most content created for PR audiences is designed to educate, inform, or persuade. As part of a routine campaign priority, PR practitioners may seek to educate the public about a crisis or health and safety issue on behalf of a client, inform voters about the political platform of a candidate, or persuade the media to cover an upcoming event or activity. Therefore, the objective in communication becomes fine-tuning and tweaking content so that it is understandable and relatable to those with whom we desire to communicate.

Public relations work is advocacy work. Practitioners are constantly advocating on behalf of a client or a client's cause. Even if a campaign seeks to inform and educate, there also is likely an underlying role for persuasion to gain support or traction for an idea or action. The role and power of persuasion in PR are undeniable.

Persuasion is a powerful tool. As PR professionals, once we learn to recognize the power of persuasion in our work, it is equally important to demonstrate integrity in how we leverage our ability to influence and persuade people to think, believe or act in a certain manner.

17.1 — ETHICS IN PERSUASION

At its most basic level, persuasion is the process of motivating people to do something by reason, argument, influence or appeal. This chapter addresses the ethics of persuasion sooner rather than later to emphasize the point that manipulation, dishonesty, misinformation and disinformation are not acceptable strategies or tactics for PR practitioners and professional communicators. Although addressing the opportunities for unethical behavior is a broader topic of conversation, in general, persuasion for gain—at the expense of others or without their knowledge of the process—is widely frowned upon and considered unethical. Effective communication goes beyond building an audience profile and targeting key publics; it also consists of establishing trust and mutual respect with those audience members by adhering to professional standards and guidelines.

Trust is earned and built through consistent ethical and principled behavior in communication. Let's be clear about what ethical PR and persuasion entail. Ethics refers to a set of moral principles and a system of moral values defining good vs. bad and right vs. wrong behavior. In the context of PR, ethics expands not only into personal conduct, but also encompasses systemic institutional, organizational and professional standards for business operations, as outlined in the ethical standards and codes of conduct from the International Association of Business Communicators (IABC), the Public Relations Society of America (PRSA), and the International Public Relations Association (IPRA). Ethics represents comprehensive personal and professional value systems, guidance and standards that shape and direct decision-making and actions.

It is not enough to know how to persuade an audience or to know that the components of persuasion are in place to mobilize an audience. It is equally important to understand the "why" and organizational motivations for persuading an audience. The rationale given for the campaign should align with the professional standards and code of ethics for professional communicators and PR practitioners. The categories underscored within the stated Code of Ethics and ethical standards for members of PRSA include Advocacy, Honesty, Expertise, Independence, Loyalty and Fairness.

As a matter of practice, members of PRSA commit to the following as an established and routine part of daily operations and PR activities:

- Preserve the integrity of the process of communication.

- Be honest and accurate in all communications.

- Act promptly to correct erroneous communications for which the practitioner is responsible.

- Preserve the free flow of unprejudiced information when giving or receiving gifts by ensuring that gifts are nominal, legal and infrequent.

The Power of Persuasion

It is not the job of the PR practitioner to change anyone's mind about anything—a nearly impossible feat. As a matter of fact, most people are inherently resistant to anyone attempting to change their mind about anything. Most of us gravitate toward and tune in to information that aligns with what we already embrace and believe to be true. Change is hard and uncomfortable. Trying to change minds is an exercise in futility. It is the job of the communications professional to present content that informs and educates the recipient on platforms they respect and value with enough frequency that the receiver is empowered and inclined to change their own mind.

Though it may seem like a contradiction, in many cases, it is easier to get someone to change their behavior than it is to get them to change their mind about a topic. The reason is that different values and motivations can still lead to the same change in behavior. People can undertake a different course of action because it's in their best interest, even if it represents a different or conflicting attitude or set of values from someone else taking the same action. For example, two individuals may be on opposing sides of an argument about whether high school students should be required to wear uniforms to school. One individual asserts their belief in personal freedoms and freedom of expression, while the other individual cites the importance of discipline, decorum and the financial relief that accompanies the purchase of a uniform rather than a new wardrobe of school clothing.

Once the person communicating about the issues understands the audiences and what their unique motivating factors are, it's a fairly straightforward process on how to shape the messaging content. If the individual who prioritizes personal freedoms also cares about financial savings, then the message can focus on financial gain by pointing out how wasting money on buying school clothes takes away from purchasing other important items. The communicator also makes strides by asking a question that allows the decision maker to change their own mind. Finally, a PR practitioner can move the needle of persuasion toward acceptance by presenting information that reveals a disconnect in the individual's beliefs and behaviors, which they will then attempt to reconcile. Here are some sample fictional talking points of conversation to make the case for persuading someone opposed to school uniforms to consider them:

- The average parent spends more than $500 on back-to-school clothes each year, whereas the annual investment for school uniforms is less than half of that expense. If invested for the entire four-year high school period, those savings would generate an extra $1,000 toward school supplies and textbooks for the first year of college or vocational training.

- Did you know that most first-year high school students outgrow or wear out their new school clothes within six months? Why throw money away? Wearing school uniforms is a great way to save money and invest in your student's future instead.

- Every parent wants their child to be safe, healthy, and to make lifelong friends with whom they can share an enjoyable high school experience. Research from top school systems across the country indicates that wearing school uniforms decreases the likelihood of bullying, helps students fit in better and removes barriers for social inclusion. Bottom line: wearing uniforms may help keep your child safe and reduce the negative effects of bullying within their school.

Though the parent may still strongly support their child's right to individual freedom and freedom of expression by not adhering to a school dress code, they now are equipped with persuasive information that reinforces other values and motivations they have such as keeping their child safe, saving money and investing in their student's future growth and development.

The idea behind this persuasive strategy is to help communicators understand how important and valuable understanding motivations are, and to help receivers of information understand that changing their minds isn't a sign of weakness or defeat, but an opportunity to further their own interests. Essentially, the key to changing a behavior is about finding out what's important to the decision-maker and providing enough information that they can use to formulate a process to get what they want on their own terms.

An example published online with Harvard Business Review shared this scenario:

"Health officials in Thailand used this approach in an anti-smoking campaign. Rather than telling smokers their habit was bad, they had little kids come up to smokers on the street and ask them for a light. Not surprisingly, the smokers told the kids no. Many even lectured the little boys and girls about the dangers of smoking. But before turning to walk away, the kids handed the smokers a note that said, "You worry about me . . . But why not about yourself?" At the bottom was a toll-free number smokers could call to get help. Calls to that line jumped more than 60% during the campaign."

Source: Harvard Business Review. (2020). "How to Persuade People to Change Their Behavior." https://hbr.org/2020/04/how-to-persuade-people-to-change-their-behavior

The lesson learned from this effective campaign is that providing the space for individual freedom in decision making opens the door of receptiveness to external messaging. In this scenario, the communicators identified a disconnect between the recipients' thoughts and actions, demonstrated by what they might suggest for others as opposed to what they might do themselves. Most people desire internal consistency, meaning they want their attitudes, thoughts and beliefs to line up with their decisions and actions. The need to align personal thoughts and actions makes them more receptive to change.

A significant portion of writing to vast audiences is designed with the intent of getting people to respond and take action. The types of actions desired can range from visiting a website, buying a product, voting for a candidate, reversing negative or unhealthy habits or donating money to an important cause. One effective tool in the writer's toolkit is storytelling—the ability to present information in a compelling narrative with characters and scenarios that are familiar and relatable. At its core, the essence of storytelling is making people care, because people don't think about things they don't care about.

Rule number 1 in persuasive writing is to know your audience. Is the audience sympathetic to your client or cause? Is the audience informed or uninformed about the topic or issue at hand?

In preparing to develop a persuasion campaign, the PR professional needs to consider the content and appeal strategies for three general types of audiences: hostile, neutral and sympathetic (see Table 17.1).

For all intents and purposes, a hostile/opposing audience will not be convinced regardless of what is said or done because they do not want to be convinced of the communicator's point of view. The sympathetic/supportive audience is already convinced and in agreement and does not need to be further persuaded. The neutral/undecided audience is where the opportunity lies because they can be persuaded by either side, depending upon the information shared and the format in which it is presented.

TABLE 17.1 ■ Audience Types

Hostile/Opposing

- Already have a firmly established viewpoint that is contradictory to the information being presented
- Want and demand that their viewpoint be given full validation and consideration
- Actively resistant to someone attempting to persuade them
- Uninterested in hearing information that contradicts their existing viewpoint
- May become defensive when facts or figures are used to disprove or undermine their beliefs or opinion
- Already have a firmly established viewpoint that is contradictory to the information being presented

Neutral/Undecided

- Can be persuaded either way, depending upon the information presented to them
- Likely to be receptive to new information when it's connected to how they personally benefit
- May be uninformed and uninterested, which presents an opportunity for communicator to educate and motivate

Sympathetic/Supportive

- Viewpoints already align with the speaker's position or perspective
- Can be motivated to take immediate action in support of the cause
- Receptive to storytelling and emotional (pathos) appeals that build stronger connections
- Desire concrete information to resist opposition to their beliefs and to support their arguments

Understanding which persuasion strategies and tactics to use in a campaign becomes clearer when the communicator has a deep knowledge of the audience. Here are several questions to answer about the audience in advance to help prepare for an effective presentation or messaging strategy:

- How much information and knowledge does the audience have about the issue or topic?

- What is the level of interest the audience has in the topic?

- What relevant background or engagement does the audience already have related to the topic?

- Does the audience already support or oppose major aspects about the topic?

- What are the audience's current beliefs about the topic?

- Is the audience hostile, neutral or supportive of the topic?

- What is the objective of the presentation; what do we want the audience to do after hearing the information?

These audience tables provide general information about the three hostile, neutral, and supportive audience types, which help the PR practitioner select the best approach for communications and adjust messaging strategy as needed.

17.2 — VALS SURVEY AND MESSAGING STRATEGY

One tool available to assist marketers in better understanding audiences is the VALS Survey, published by Strategic Business Insights. VALS is an acronym for Values, Attitudes, and Lifestyles. The online survey model asks a series of questions, and the responses indicate which one of eight categories, or mindsets, the survey taker falls in, based on demographics and psychological traits that influence behavior and decision making. The eight types of VALS types are innovators, thinkers, believers, achievers, strivers, experiencers, makers, and survivors (see Figure 17.1). VALS results go beyond basic demographics to reveal individual motivations for behavior or belief. The VALS model shares insights based on three primary motivations of ideals, achievement and self-expression to anticipate consumer behavior.

Expert marketers often use VALS survey results to gain valuable insights into who they're talking to and what makes those people tick. The VALS categories organize people by their beliefs and behaviors and use a predictive model to explain why people are prone to make certain decisions, and what may motivate them to make a different decision.

How is it possible to reach diverse audiences with one messaging strategy when the demographics, psychographics and motivations of an audience are so disparate? That question poses the greatest challenge for communicators who may only have one shot to get their point across in a single media sound bite. Using this tool, survey results allow for analysis of emerging trends

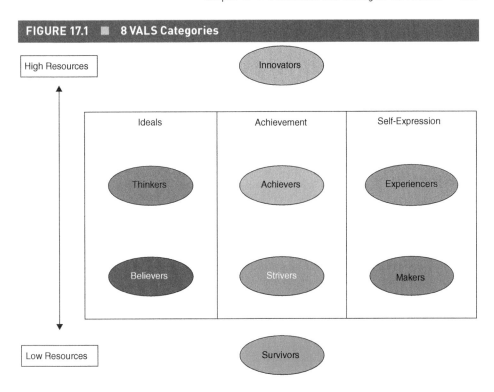

FIGURE 17.1 ■ 8 VALS Categories

across static demographic datasets such as age groups, geographic location, income, and educational levels—and also enable practitioners to cross-reference that information with more dynamic psychographic data that includes hobbies and interests. Writing to the masses requires an understanding, not only of the audience, but also of the messenger and the messenger's goal in delivering the message.

17.3 — THE PROGRESSION OF PERSUASION: FROM WRITING TO COMMITMENT

It helps for PR practitioners to view the process of persuasion as an incremental journey made of small steps, rather than a major transformation or transaction where the listener hears information, reconsiders their viewpoint and immediately changes their mind. Not likely! Viewing the persuasive process as a marathon versus a sprint may assist the communications professional in adopting more realistic expectations when evaluating campaign results.

Consider these Key Steps to Commitment:

- Find the points of agreement among the viewpoints.

- Outline the common sides of a discussion or conflict.

- List the pros and cons; provide an argument and be prepared to acknowledge and/or address (if necessary) the counterargument.

- Establish the strength of your argument with research, facts, data, statistics, quotations, expert opinions, anecdotes and observations to make your point.

- Ask a question instead of making a statement so that the listener can answer the question and make a decision that aligns with their values.

- Identity a gap between the listener's beliefs and actions and then ask a question that highlights the disconnect.

- Present limited options and structured choices when presenting information: Don't ask a child if they want to eat vegetables for dinner. The answer will reliably and consistently be, "No." Instead, offer a limited and structured choice that offers a sense of control and avoids conflict and forcing a decision. For example, "Do you want to eat green beans or broccoli with your dinner tonight?" Regardless of the choice, using structure, the goal is accomplished to get the child to eat vegetables.

- Pursue partial commitments that require some level of participation from the recipient of your communications campaign. Though most car dealers want buyers to purchase on the spot, they realize that a partial commitment to do something is better than losing the sale altogether. If a car buyer isn't yet ready to commit, the sales representative may get them to commit to a test drive to see how owning the new car might feel. That's one step closer to the ultimate objective.

- Begin with a small ask that can be accelerated and escalated over time. Instead of asking someone to work full-time in the office for a political candidate, ask if they would be willing to place a bumper sticker on their vehicle; then later place a yard sign on their lawn; and down the road volunteer for a couple hours per week answering the phone. Start small and grow from there.

The first step in a persuasive campaign conversation is to begin with something that everyone can agree upon. Basically, start on an upbeat, positive note that gives the impression there is not a lot of distance between the varying viewpoints. Here's a sample win-win statement to open a controversial conversation about climate change: "Can we all agree that breathing fresh, clean air is a good thing? Does anyone want to inhale smog and toxic fumes every day? Of course not. So, we're all on the same page and we all agree that a clean, healthy environment benefits all of us. Now, we may not yet agree on how to get the results we want, but it's important to know that we all want the same thing. Let's talk about a couple sides of the arguments about climate change and take a look at some of the pros and cons."

The next steps demonstrate and build respect among listeners by showing that the communicator knows and understands that there are other sides to an issue that have validity. By not pursuing a "my way or the highway" approach, the door remains open to dialogue and mutual exchange of ideas. The goal at this point of communication is to address common sides or points of conflict and then establish the strength of your argument with strong points that are well researched and easy to understand. A way to reinforce that process is to ask questions instead of making statements, so that the listener can ask themselves the question, provide an answer, and then seek to align their existing attitudes and beliefs with their responses to the question.

Finally, starting with a "small ask" is key to moving the needle in persuasion. By asking for a small, agreeable commitment, the groundwork is laid to revisit the conversation. Sometimes, with a neutral audience (no strong alignment with either side of the issue), the communicator may "ask for a favor." A small favor could be to watch a 30-second commercial or read a testimonial. Agreeing to a favor makes someone more likely to accept new ideas or information because people generally don't do favors for people they don't like. Once they agree to the favor, there is an internal justification that seeks to align the action with the attitude. Again, the natural desire to seek alignment and to avoid discord in internal thoughts and actions moves the process one step closer to acceptance.

Taking a basic course in psychology (scientific study of the mind and behavior) can be of great benefit to the PR practitioner to help understand human behavior and motivations. Many students have learned about the concept of cognitive dissonance without realizing or understanding its influential role in communications. Cognitive dissonance is one's internal perception or recognition of contradictory information. Generally speaking, most people experience discomfort from the thought or reality of inconsistent thoughts, beliefs, feelings and attitudes about the world around them and how they interact within it. If a communications professional can present information that increases or enhances the listener's mental and emotional alignment related to an issue, the message is more likely to be received, and the individual receiving the information is more likely to be persuaded.

In addition, a popular communication theory introduced in the 1950s called the dissonance theory of persuasion identified underlying causes and obstacles to persuading people to change their minds or behaviors. The research driving the theory posited that individuals are generally disinclined to seek out any new information that disagrees with what they already think, feel or believe. In other words, people find conflict so objectionable, that they will simply avoid it altogether by dismissing contradictory content or communication.

Adding to that explanation is the fact that people not only avoid dissonant information, but they in turn also seek out consonant information to reinforce their existing feelings and attitudes, a process known as confirmation bias. By definition, confirmation bias is the tendency to interpret and recall information in a way that confirms or reinforces a prior set of beliefs. Those two concepts combined result in a reliable pattern of human response that says, "I know what I believe. I don't want to believe anything different from what I already believe. And finally, I don't want to hear anything from you that is different from what I already believe to be true."

Knowledge of the dissonance theory made it clear that communicators first need to develop strategies to combat recipient resistance in order to get their message through. Another way of approaching the situation is to ask, "How can you get someone to change their mind, when you can't even get them to listen to what you have to say?"

To be fair, most people are resistant to change of any kind; however, change is inevitable. Significant change usually presents in one of three ways: drastic change, gradual change, internal change. Drastic change might be a car accident, a life-threatening illness or a significant financial loss that impacts quality of life. A gradual change comes over time, as with the processes of aging and maturity gained from changing circumstances and life experience. Finally, there is internal change, which tends to be lasting because it often means a person's motivations have changed, requiring a new way of thinking or living to achieve their desired results. Common obstacles to lasting or meaningful change are fear, lack of motivation and lack of information or knowledge to justify doing something differently. If communicators can effectively present information that respectfully acknowledges and addresses common fears and motives while providing useful and meaningful information, then recipients become better equipped to change their approach to thinking about new messages.

17.4 — THREE ORBITS OF INFLUENCE IN PERSUASION

Persuasion revolves around three orbits of influence: ethos, pathos and logos. Ethos refers to the credibility and authority of the speaker presenting the information to an audience, along with the presenter's ability to connect and relate with the audience in a convincing manner. For example, does the audience find the speaker to be a qualified expert on the topic? Does the speaker have enough education or experience to impart wisdom or lessons learned about the subject matter? Can the speaker answer questions about the topic and share responses with the audience on a level they can easily understand?

A good visual example of using ethos in television advertising is featuring a spokesperson in a white lab coat to discuss the benefits of a pharmaceutical product. Even though the tiny print in the disclaimer at the bottom of the screen states that the person is a paid actor and not a medical professional, communicators know that immediate credibility is conveyed upon someone wearing a lab coat and automatically influences viewers to trust what the spokesperson says. A lot of the respect and admiration given to individuals who attend medical school for years is instantly conferred upon someone who simply dresses up in a medical uniform.

Pathos focuses on emotions and emotional appeal to persuade people to act in a certain way. An influence campaign might incorporate the use of joy, sadness, guilt, anger, hope, fear and other emotions to get the audience to react and to respond with a certain behavior. Pathos in persuasive writing often shows up in storytelling, where we can paint a picture or create a scenario and present a protagonist with whom listeners and viewers can empathize or sympathize.

Think about some of the commercials you've seen asking viewers to volunteer and donate time or money to rescue abandoned or abused animals. They feature close-up images of helpless animals in dire situations, along with very sad music playing in the background. The idea is to tug on the heartstrings of those watching with the purpose of evoking a reaction and a desire to help. Basically, the message is now that you've seen this horrific plight, you must act to save these poor creatures. The scenes are powerful, memorable and effective because they connect with the audience on an emotional level that is hard to deny or forget.

Logos uses logic and reason and the content presented is based on facts, figures, statistics, and empirical data that is quantifiable. Relying solely on facts and figures is a persuasive tactic often used when presenting to a neutral audience that is weighing the pros and cons of an argument prior to making a decision.

In practice, logos presents information in a clear and matter-of-fact way so that it makes sense to the listener and allows the thought process to lead to a logical conclusion. For example, public service announcements (PSAs) that discourage teenagers from smoking or vaping often use facts about nicotine content levels and percentages, statistics about lung cancer and facts about smoking-related illnesses to make the case for stopping or never starting to smoke.

Though facts and figures are undeniable, how they are presented can be questionable. Any content that is exaggerated, misconstrued or miscontextualized runs the risk of misinforming or deceiving the audience.

Much like every aspect of public relations, the process for developing convincing, persuasive writing begins with research. In order to make a strong argument for one perspective, it's important to know and understand the other side of the issue and its counterarguments.

17.5 — TIPS AND TOOLS FOR WRITING TO THE MASSES

In this section, the focus will be on four types of controlled publications and documents (position statements, white papers, opinion-editorials and letters to the editor) that target persuasive communication targeted toward the masses, or large audiences within the general public. Controlled publications are communiques where the creator, author, editor or client maintains control of the content from start to finish, with little to no editing or altering of the final document by a third party. In contrast, uncontrolled publications are researched, written, edited then sent out to the media, where potentially little to none of the original content is actually used or reproduced. As an example, a PR professional might send out a news release, only to discover that one or two sentences provided in the original document end up being a part of the news story or coverage. Hence, the PR professional does not have control over the final messages being conveyed.

Writing to the masses also means that the audiences are more general and are less likely to share common interests. Therefore, content needs to be broader, less specific and easy to understand at a basic reading level to make sure as many people as possible can comprehend what is being shared.

Position Papers or Position Statements

The purpose of a position paper or position statement is to clearly and unequivocally inform readers and viewers where an individual or organization stands on a specific issue or topic so that customers, supporters and investors can make informed decisions about their alignment with the company or person, based on its support of or opposition to a particular subject. The document presents a clear and lucid argument in support of a particular viewpoint and often serves to persuade readers to agree with that viewpoint in service of their best interest. As an example, a corporation may want to clearly state its support or opposition to a new regulation to galvanize its base and core audience around a hot-button issue.

The process for writing a clear and concise position paper or position statement begins with articulating a specific point of view. The premise of the paper is followed by anecdotes, statistics, supporting evidence and content to support or further explain the author's position. Several options for concluding a position document include a call to action, a content summation or a statement that creates a lasting and memorable impression. Here are several examples of introductory opening statements for different topics and issues that might warrant publishing a position paper.

The format, voice and structure of a position paper or position statement are third person objective, with a clear introduction, body and conclusion. The written document is formatted like a speech with double-spaced copy on the page. In expressing the position, communicators should avoid excessive use of first person "I" or second person "you"—especially because the position paper is also read by audiences that may disagree with the premise and resist being included in personal "our" and "we" statements. As always, write in the present tense and avoid the passive voice as indicated in the following examples.

Sample Corporate (Fictional Environmental Company on Sustainability Efforts)

If it's true that there is only one chance to make a first impression, then it's equally true that there is only one chance to protect the planet. The responsibility for preserving Mother Earth is not an individual one, but rather a collective one. Making environmental sustainability a priority is not optional, it is mandatory, which is why Company WW supports legislation to require all manufacturing companies to annually report sustainability efforts and pay penalties for failing to meet industry benchmarks for sustainable practices.

Since its founding more than 40 years ago, Company WW continues to invest in sustainable practices such as zero-carbon emissions, carbon neutral operations, companywide recycling, and investments in innovation that supports sustainability.

Here is an example from a fictional nonprofit organization on banning nicotine sales to youth and young adults.

Sample Nonprofit (Fictional Nonprofit Organization on Banning Nicotine Sales to Youth and Young Adults)

It was famously quoted that those who do not learn from the past are doomed to repeat it. The failed lessons of allowing young people to purchase nicotine products will continue to create a generation of individuals who suffer from asthma, lung disease, and various breathing disorders — and who also become addicted to or reliant upon prescription medications for relief.

Organization XX calls upon politicians and legislators across the country to ban sales of nicotine products at the local, state and federal level to individuals under the age of 25, to protect the next generation of adults from the devastating and dire consequences of nicotine and nicotine addiction.

For decades, companies marketed and sold nicotine-based products to the youth market with little to no restrictions, despite the obvious negative health effects. It is time to put laws into place that prevent repeating the mistakes of the past.

It goes without saying that in a democracy, individual freedoms are a priority. However, it also goes without saying that individual freedoms end at the beginning of a public health crisis that imposes irreversible damage and financial strain onto the healthcare system due to nicotine-related illnesses.

Here is an example from a fictional individual running on a specific political platform.

Sample Political Candidate (Fictional Individual Running on A Specific Political Platform)

Candidate Gregory Smith spent 20 years in the military fighting for this country and another 10 years in corporate boardrooms across the country, fighting for business owners and taxpayers. Candidate Gregory Smith is a fighter, and he will fight for you when it comes to getting things done in statewide politics. Gregory Smith supports Proposition F-12, which will direct federal funds to support economic development programs and build capacity for small businesses.

Gregory wants you to know that he cares about what you care about, and he's willing to speak up and speak out to get things done. At every campaign stop across the state, someone asks about how Gregory will vote on the issue of investing in businesses and providing more access to opportunities for young entrepreneurs. Gregory knows that small businesses are the fuel that run this state's engine — that's true across the country — and Gregory will make sure that the needs of small business owners are heard and met when he's elected.

During election season, newspapers and television commercials are filled with platitudes and empty promises from individuals who are all talk and no action. But Candidate Gregory Smith wants you to know that a vote for the opposing candidate is a vote for stagnation and political gridlock. Gregory knows how to fight for you and how to win — because that's his track record. That's who he is. He invites you to join the Gregory Smith campaign today!

As indicated by the examples above, position papers can be an effective tool in the persuasive writing process. Here are some important steps to writing a position paper.

1. Open with a strong introduction that captures the readers' attention and draws them in to learn more about the position being represented.

2. Clearly state the organization's or company's position on the respective issue or topic.

3. Introduce general information about the topic to educate the reader about what's at stake and why the topic is relevant to them.

4. Outline supporting evidence or content that explains the author's position on the issue.

5. Present opposing arguments and viewpoints and explain why they are or are not valid, based on the viewpoint of the position statement.

6. Address opposing viewpoints with a counternarrative that reinforces the stated position and explains the strength of the position taken.

7. Explain and expound on why the stated position is still the preferred stance to take regarding the topic.

8. Reiterate the position and the strength of the arguments presented.

9. Include a call to action or summary of the position and how it impacts or affects the reader.

10. Conclude the statement with a compelling and memorable closing that will linger in the reader's mind.

White papers

A white paper is an in-depth research document that informs readers about an important or complex issue and presents the author's position or philosophy on the related subject matter. White papers help readers better understand a problem and possible solutions, and they contribute to the decision-making process by helping educate more people about pertinent issues. Marketers often use white papers as part of a larger strategic plan to build awareness about a company or organization and its leadership and to enhance their credibility as thought-leaders or subject matter experts (SMEs).

The fundamental purpose of a white paper is to explain, expound, and to make a complicated subject simpler and clearer. As a secondary role, a white paper can be used to convince and persuade readers to consider the author's perspective or point of view as one that should be adopted into their way of thinking.

Since a white paper tends to be more informational than editorial, the format is closely aligned with that of a research paper. There may be definitions, statistics, data, charts, graphs, tables and citations to make the case for a particular point of view.

Like any document created for public consumption, the construction of a white paper includes an introduction, a main body, and a conclusion. The introduction presents the topic or defines the problem. The main body is the weightiest section of the document and presents facts, evidence, or exposition about the main topic of the paper. In this section, the reader also will find supporting materials and content that explains a topic and presents research findings, solutions or recommendations. The conclusion is often a recap of the paper's main findings and an appeal for the audience to take an active or passive course of action based on the information presented.

Opinion-Editorials (Op-Eds)

An opinion-editorial — also known as an op-ed — is an article that expresses an informed opinion from an expert or experienced individual about a timely and newsworthy issue that is relevant to a publication's readership. Historically, op-eds were published in major daily newspapers and located "opposite the editorial page," hence, the name op-ed. Now op-eds appear in daily, weekly, monthly, online and periodical publications and have evolved to include opinion-based content in radio, television and internet broadcasts as well. Though op-eds present a unique voice and perspective from the author, it is not uncommon for the PR practitioner to write or pen the piece on behalf of a client, which is why understanding the topic and capturing the author's voice are so important to the quality of the final article.

Even though op-eds are based on the opinion of the author, that doesn't mean the document isn't well researched or well thought-out. Often to the contrary, op-eds shed insight and analysis on important societal topics and help readers understand how to think about and approach certain problems based on the credibility of the op-ed writer and the respect they have in their field of study. Also, op-eds tend to be selective documents requested and accepted by the editorial staffs of publications, so their "invitation-only" status makes them even more credible. In some cases, an op-ed piece is written by staff members or syndicated writers who are subject matter experts. The purpose of an op-ed is to gain visibility and increase credibility. An op-ed should open with a clear and declarative message, clearly stating the opinion and viewpoint of the author. An op-ed focuses on one main theme or central idea, as opposed to a series of thoughts on different topics.

The length of an op-ed ranges from 600 to 800 words; however, individual publications may set their own guidelines for the word count and format of an op-ed, so the writer should confirm those details and adhere to them prior to submitting their content.

TIPS FOR BEGINNERS: WRITING A QUALITY OP-ED

- Do your research to make sure you have a solid understanding of the topic.
- Identify one clear and definitive editorial viewpoint for the opinion piece.
- Focus op-ed content on a timely or relevant current event to provide insight or guidance for the readers.
- Clearly state the topic, issue, opinion or viewpoint in the opening paragraph.
- Support the opinion or perspective provided in the main body with credible content that can be backed up by data, facts, statistics, observation or research to support the opinion being shared.
- Write the op-ed using active voice and avoid passive tenses.
- Use concise language and short, declarative sentences that accurately reflect the unique voice of the author.
- Avoid usage of first and second person; write the op-ed in journalistic third person.
- Create a comprehensive first draft and then edit it to the requested length or word count required by the publication (often ranging from 600 to 800 words).
- Be sure to give proper attribution or cite any external sources referenced in the article.
- End the op-ed with a strong conclusion that reinforces the opening or requests some type of emotional or actionable commitment.
- Secure an op-ed placement opportunity first, by reaching out to editors with a query in advance to save time, energy and resources.

Letters to the Editor

Though brief in length, letters to the editor are an easy and effective way to communicate a message quickly and to a broad audience, while also bringing attention to an important issue being highlighted in local, regional or national print media coverage. It's important to note that a letter to the editor can serve dual roles in communication, in that it is written to an individual, but viewable and accessible to the masses. As its name indicates, the letter is addressed to the editor of a specific publication to share an opinion about a recent topic of interest or issues covered in the media. At the same time, if the letter is published by the media outlet, then it is also read by thousands or possibly millions of other people who also read the publication in hardcopy or online editions.

The purpose of a letter to the editor is to express an opinion in response to a current event or relevant societal topic that is receiving media coverage. The letter can also increase awareness about the author and their perspective or opinion about a particular subject.

Most letters to the editor fit on one page of a standard size sheet of paper. The average length is less than 300 words, and they are written from the author's first-person point of view (see Figure 17.2).

TIPS FOR BEGINNERS: WRITING A QUALITY LETTER TO THE EDITOR

- Keep it short, simple, and straightforward.
- Address a relevant and timely issue that readers can identify with from recent coverage.
- Follow the publication's guidelines regarding word count and instructions for submitting content.
- Identify the subject of the letter in the first paragraph, and be sure to reference the name of the article, its author, and the date of publication for clarity.
- Articulate the theme of the letter in the second paragraph, stating whether the letter is in agreement, disagreement, support of or opposition to recent coverage.
- Use the letter to the editor to reinforce or underscore issues outlined in the initial coverage — or to highlight information that was missing from the original article.
- Keep in mind that it is acceptable to share an opinion or unique perspective in a letter to the editor, but also be sure to back up that opinion with credible information that supports the viewpoint.
- Be sure to include contact information and a signature (or digital/e-signature) on the letter so that the publication's editorial team can confirm the author and content of the letter and verify that the writer stands by the submission.

FIGURE 17.2 ■ **Sample Letter to the Editor Template**

Ms. Bella Williamson
123 Rocky Road
Tulsa, Oklahoma 74055

November 12, 20XX

Thom Harland, Editor
The Tulsa Daily Newspaper
8009 Media Lane
Tulsa, Oklahoma 74107

Dear Editor,

I am writing to express my deep disappointment regarding the lack of attention given to the pervasive pothole problem in our neighborhood, as mentioned in a recent article by Marcy Devin titled "Potholes Leave Neighbors Seeking Solutions," published on Nov. 2. As a resident of this community, I feel it is crucial to address issues that directly impact our daily lives, such as the deteriorating state of our roads.

While I appreciate the coverage of the issue, I cannot help but notice the glaring omission of any mention of our specific neighborhood, which has been plagued by potholes for months. These potholes pose a significant risk to both drivers and pedestrians, causing damage to vehicles and potential safety hazards.

It is disheartening to see our concerns brushed aside while other neighborhoods seemingly receive more attention. Every resident deserves to have their voice heard and their concerns addressed, regardless of the size or prominence of their community.

I urge you to reconsider your coverage and highlight the pothole problems in our neighborhood in future articles. Together, we can bring attention to this matter and ensure our roads are safe.

Sincerely,

Bella Williamson

Bella Williamson
Concerned Citizen
(539) 555-0138
bellaw@mymailbox.email.com

The existence of seemingly endless cable news and content channels or blogs and content marketing publications presents limitless opportunities for communicators to broadcast strategic messages. Plus, the evolution of social media and its ubiquitous access makes writing to the masses easier than ever before. However, with that ease of access also comes pitfalls because of the broad diversity of audiences that can be reached online and beyond. PR practitioners can use the tools of persuasion and the various publishing platforms to produce quality content that motivates and moves the masses.

PR TOOL KIT: TIPS FOR PERSUASIVE WRITING

PR practitioners and content marketers can incorporate these strategic approaches into persuasive writing content that is targeted to mass audiences:

Agreement — Confirmation bias asserts that people interpret new information in ways that aligns with what they already think or believe. If you want to move someone from the hostile audience into the neutral or supportive audience category, then start out with a point of agreement so they do not automatically view you as an enemy of their beliefs. Demonstrating that their perspective has value is a powerful show of respect and will help lessen their defenses against any additional arguments. Essentially, this strategy shows that you don't think the audience is completely wrong about an idea. Also, once someone agrees with you about something — anything — it becomes easier to agree with you on other things and harder to disagree since they ultimately want to avoid discord in their thoughts and actions.

Community —Human connections are invaluable, so much so, that we actively seek out connections that reinforce our values and priorities. Knowing that people want to be a part of something greater is a helpful tool in the process of persuasion. Communicators can leverage the desire and need for community to their advantage by making points of an argument that rely on the strength of community and inviting the audience to be part of something bigger and greater than themselves. For example, letting someone know that most of their neighbors or social media connections already support an idea greatly increases the likelihood that they too will support the initiative.

Narration and Storytelling — Almost everyone loves a good story because they can envision, relate, or imagine themselves and people they know in a similar situation, which creates an instant connection. Narration and storytelling are also effective in persuasion because they don't rely heavily on the educational levels and backgrounds of the audience. Relying on the power of words and the ability to be relatable is what propels this persuasive strategy to success. Telling a memorable story that has a powerful lesson or effective call to action can be a game-changer. People easily dismiss facts and forget statistics. But a great story can last a lifetime.

Reason and Rationale — A famous political line often quoted states that everyone is entitled to their own opinion, but not to their own facts. Using the logos method of logic and reason to inform listeners is often effective in persuading an audience — especially a neutral audience that can be swayed either way, based on what they hear and if what they hear makes sense to them. This particular strategy is not as effective when the opposing argument is connected to a highly charged and emotional issue, where logic is less important than how people feel about the subject. Interestingly enough, a number of studies also have shown that people are more likely to accept new information or comply with a small request if given a reason why — even if the reason doesn't support their existing beliefs. Deployment of reason and rationale to help underscore a point of view is a handy PR tool to have on hand.

Repetition — It's amazing that when people hear the same information from different sources, they accept it as truth. Repetition serves the purpose of persuasion in more than one way. For starters, repetition helps the listener understand the message. In case the information was confusing or not completely understood at first, repetition allows the listener to revisit and process content to better understand and comprehend it. In addition, repetition across media platforms and different sources reinforces an idea and provides social proof that the information is true and worthy of consideration. Finally, repetition in different formats helps different types of learners process and comprehend information in a way that is natural for them to internalize. Be sure to consider different ways of repeating information, such as visual aids, anecdotes, quotes, statistics, etc.

CHAPTER SUMMARY

Public relations is advocacy work, and advocacy often involves persuasion. An important rule in persuasive writing is to know and understand the audience, which may be supportive, neutral or hostile to a particular position. To better understand audiences, survey and research tools are available that help categorize motives for behavior to support crafting messages. The three orbits of influence in persuasion are ethos, pathos, and logos, which rely upon credibility, emotion, and reason to persuade audiences to think, believe, or act in a certain manner. Though there are countless opportunities for sharing persuasive content, some of the more traditional PR documents that allow communicators to reach the masses are position papers, white papers, op-eds and letters to the editor.

KEY TERMS

confirmation bias

ethos

logos

pathos

persuasion

VALS Survey

DISCUSSION QUESTIONS

1. What persuasive strategies do you think are most effective, and why?

2. Which of the persuasive strategies introduced is most effective for your decision-making process?

3. What are some of the challenges communicators face when crafting messages for a hostile audience?

WRITING EXERCISES

1. Write an opening paragraph for a position statement on behalf of your college or university related to recycling and its role in protecting the environment.

2. Select an issue that you're passionate about and write three persuasive statements intended to persuade a hostile/opposing audience to understand or embrace your point of view.

3. Read an article in your local daily or weekly community newspaper and write a letter to the editor explaining your response to the story; submit your letter to the publication, and if published, be sure to include the final version in your professional portfolio.

18.1 Learn how to incorporate interpersonal communication skills into written correspondence.

18.2 Identify the PR documents that are targeted toward individual recipients.

18.3 Learn quick tips to catch errors in PR writing.

INTRODUCTION

The theme of writing to an individual, in contrast with writing to the masses, or the general public, is based on connection and relatability. The goal of the writer is to make the recipient feel as though the correspondence is speaking directly to them. Certainly, there are aspects of persuasion and storytelling that make the content more compelling and memorable. However, the objective in creating content for direct mail or direct marketing is to connect with the reader and to establish a one-to-one interaction that evolves from being solely transactional and converts to being relational.

18.1 — INTERPERSONAL COMMUNICATION AND WRITTEN DOCUMENTS

One of the responsibilities included in working as a public relations professional is mastering the work of interpersonal communication. There is often a lot of discussion for young professionals around the importance of knowledge, information and skill sets. However, there should also be an emphasis on the intangibles, or soft skills, that are harder to measure, but just as important in the communication process.

PR practitioners practice the art of communications, which encompasses much more than public speaking and writing media-oriented documents. A significant amount of time and energy goes into managing relationships with clients, media, constituents, customers and colleagues. Since working in PR is often accomplished in teams, there is also great value regarding the ability to communicate and collaborate with individuals and groups in a productive manner.

In order to achieve effective communication, there must be a clear sender, receiver, message and channel. Though constantly changing iterations of Web 2.0 and social media make two-way, interactive communication and engagement much easier, a message still must originate from a sender and transmit to a recipient for there to be a meaningful exchange of ideas. For our purposes in this textbook focused on PR writing, the PR practitioner is the sender; the target audience or publics are the receivers; the strategic communications content which has been researched and refined is the message; and select traditional, digital or social media platforms are the channels whereby information is received.

Here is a list of some of the applications for interpersonal skills in public relations:

- Verbal communications

- Nonverbal communications

- Teamwork

- Listening

- Negotiation

- Persuasion

- Problem-solving

- Decision-making

Verbal and Nonverbal Communication

Verbal communication seems like the most obvious and relevant form of how PR professionals would make use of interpersonal communications. Daily job activities require public speaking to clients, media personnel, colleagues and practicing pitches or press conference responses. But it's important to remember that nonverbal communication speaks just as loudly and sometimes more prominently than verbal communication. Nonverbal signals may include body language, eye contact, gestures, tone of voice, apparel or wardrobe, facial expressions and more.

Listening and Teamwork

Listening and teamwork often go hand in hand, as it is important to be heard when you have something to contribute to a project, but it's also important to listen so that you can incorporate the input and feedback of teammates toward a solution to whatever project you're working on with others. Listening is more than just hearing what someone else has to say. Listening is physically hearing their input and mentally processing what is heard to the point of comprehension. Teams are small groups of people who align and work toward a common goal or mission. In PR, project teams are often pulled together to represent the interests of a specific client, based on the group members' levels of experience or expertise in a subject matter. Teams leverage the strengths of individuals and combine those strengths into a winning strategy for business success.

Negotiation

Negotiation is a subtle, but fine art, of getting to a point of agreement through a situation that presents challenge or conflict. Negotiation often involves a lot of back-and-forth communication where each party asserts a want or need and then works through negotiation and compromise to get to a mutually acceptable and beneficial outcome.

Persuasion

Persuasion plays a powerful role in business-to-consumer or B2C communications also. Think about the nature of documents such as job cover letters, media pitch emails, direct mail and marketing letters, where the writer is seeking to persuade the recipient to hire them for a job or internship, provide media coverage for a client or upcoming event or purchase a new product or service. Whether the focus is on communicating with thousands or engaging with one individual, the basics of how to create compelling content are the same.

Problem-Solving and Decision-Making

Problem-solving and decision-making are integral parts of life; however, they are often considered job duties for PR professionals who are often hired to solve media-related and communication problems, and to make decisions about the best way to accomplish desired communication goals. Problem-solving in PR can range from subduing negative media coverage to finding new ways to engage customers during a period of declining sales or interest in a product. Decision-making can include selecting the correct media platforms for messaging or recommending a budget for developing marketing communications materials.

PR Writing vs. Newswriting

One of the most common questions new PR students ask is about the difference between public relations writing and news writing. First, for PR writing and news writing, the objective of what the content being delivered needs to do is different. In general, news content is meant to objectively inform and educate, while PR content accomplishes those two priorities through the lens of advocacy. Traditionally, news reporters were tasked with the job of collecting the facts and then reporting the facts without commentary or analysis. New roles and platforms for communication have broadened the opportunities for commentary and opinion; but from a foundational job requirement standpoint, the role of a journalist is to objectively report the news.

In a similar way, PR practitioners collect and share the 5Ws, answering the questions "Who?" "What?" "When?" "Where?" and "Why?" but additionally answering the question "Who Cares?" PR professionals frequently work on behalf of clients who have an agenda or a strategic plan to accomplish and therefore need to connect with audiences who care about the issue and who are likely to respond positively to a targeted messaging campaign. Companies and organizations hire PR professionals to help craft messages that connect with the appropriate, relevant audiences — and ultimately persuade the audience toward a particular thought, belief, behavior, or course of action. Yes, PR writing and news writing share a history and a core belief in collecting facts and sharing those facts, but the role of PR writing accommodates the needs of individuals and organizations to promote their self-interests using the same traditional tools of news writing and journalism.

18.2 — TARGETING PR DOCUMENTS TO INDIVIDUALS

PR writing selects from a menu of writing options and combines them to tell a story that informs and educates — while also positively positioning the client, using multimedia platforms. A benefit of training PR professionals as journalists first, consequently, establishes a strong research, writing and fact-finding based set of skills, which can then be honed to advocate on behalf of clients. When PR professionals understand the core tenets of journalism, the rights of the 1st Amendment, the value of objective storytelling, and the daily operations of a newsroom, they are better equipped to interact with journalists and understand how to provide valuable content and know what makes that content newsworthy.

Listed below are some common PR documents that may require the use of practical PR writing skills and intangible interpersonal skills to communicate with an individual as part of the job:

- Media pitch letter or email

- Job cover letter

- Letter to the editor

- Direct mail letter

- Professional email correspondence

- New PR client pitch communique

Media Pitch Letter or Email

A media pitch letter or media pitch email is a written message created for an individual journalist, reporter or media representative that is designed to pique their interest in covering a client, topic, or story idea. The "pitch" aspect refers to suggesting an angle or approach on why a subject is worthy of media coverage. The letter or email is included as an individual communications document because "mass mail or mass email" pitches are frowned upon in the industry and are often overlooked or discarded. The value of an individual pitch to a journalist is that the content is tailored to the media representative based on their past articles or broadcasts and relevance to stories or issues the journalist generally covers. The PR practitioner has the unique advantage of access to the client and the ability to facilitate and coordinate presenting the story and its related assets needed to cover the story (e.g., media kit, photos, client interview) to the media outlet.

Every year when media personnel and journalists are surveyed by industry publications about their frustrations with the news industry and working with PR professionals, one of the top complaints reported each year is repeatedly receiving information that is unrelated to the beats or topics they cover. Why? It shows a lack of respect for their time and a lack of effort by the PR professional to get a better understanding of what's valuable to them in their daily profession. Here are some general guidelines to follow when pitching story ideas to journalists.

TIPS FOR BEGINNERS: TIPS FOR SENDING MEDIA PITCHES TO JOURNALISTS

- Send the letter or email to a specific reporter or individual working on the assignment desk in the newsroom, if possible.
- Don't send irrelevant blanket or blast emails to a lot of different reporters — especially if the pitch is misaligned with issues or topics the reporters cover.
- Do your homework and reference other related articles or stories covered by the reporter or media outlet to show how your pitch fits in with their coverage.
- Suggest creative angles to cover the story idea and offer to provide additional background or information to help complete the story.
- Confirm all the event details and logistics in the original email so that editors can make story assignments based on complete and accurate information.
- Point out how your recommended story idea will benefit the media outlet's respective viewers, listeners or subscribers.
- Communicate via emails as though every word you write is for public consumption and will be shared with others.
- Include your contact information again at the end of the letter or email; make it easy for journalists to connect with you.
- Inform the journalist about your intent to follow up; then be sure to follow up as indicated.
- Insert the recipient email address as a last step to prevent sending incomplete or unedited email messages to a reporter.

Sample Media Email Pitches

Ineffective email pitch

To Whom It May Concern:

My name is Joe Davidson, and my client is Perennial Pet Foods. They are sponsoring a giveaway at the Lakely County Animal Center this month. Please let me know if you'd be interested in covering this event — or feel free to reach out to me if you have any questions.

Effective email pitch

Dear Anne Rodgers,

Did you know that having a pet can add years to your life? Healthy pets = healthy people, and my client Perennial Pet Foods is helping pets and people come together for National Love Your Pet Day on Feb. 20.

Last month you profiled several pets available for adoption in our area. I enjoyed your recent coverage on rescue pets and wanted to let you know about the upcoming pet adoption fair at the Lakely County Animal Center on Saturday, Feb. 20 from 10 a.m. to 4 p.m. The event is sponsored by Perennial Pet Foods, and representatives from the company will be onsite (and available for media interviews) to assist with pet adoptions. This event is free and open to the public. If you would like more information, I can send a media kit, along with photos and video footage of some of the animals that are available for adoption. I will follow up with you on Friday afternoon to answer any additional questions you may have or to schedule an interview with Perennial Pet Foods CEO Frances Nichols. Thank you for all you do to inform our community about the importance of pets. I look forward to working with you.

Joe Davidson, PR Coordinator

(555) 460-9632 mobile

Jdavidson@prcompanysite.com

Job Cover Letter

A job cover letter is a written document that serves as the initial point of introduction to a potential employer and is presented during the job application process. The job cover letter often accompanies a professional resume and writing portfolio samples and paves the way to a follow-up conversation or job interview. In most cases, a cover letter is one page and is used to provide a general overview of who you are, along with your academic and professional experience. The job of the cover letter is to persuade the company where the applicant is seeking to work to hire them instead of other competing applicants. Therefore, this persuasive document not only includes basic information about the potential employee, but also communicates some of the applicant's skills, professional strengths, and professional achievements that are relevant to the current job opening. The content of the letter should be professional, but also personable and memorable, to increase the likelihood of the entire letter being read, and also to make the case for why the sender of the letter is the best candidate for the job.

Here are some recommended tips for writing an effective job cover letter. Remember, this letter is your introduction to a potential employer, presented during the application process. Don't forget to include your edited and proofed resume and portfolio samples or other requested materials during the application process.

- Be specific and address the letter to a person, using their first and last names and correct title. If you're unable to locate an individual's name, then use the appropriate title or role within the company, such as Dear Hiring Manager or Internship Director or Human Resources Manager. Avoid using "To Whom It May Concern" because with so much available technology and access to information, it is fairly easy to find the correct contact person or role and will reflect more positively upon you if you take the initiative to do so.

- Be sure to include a date and signature (or digital/e-signature) on your letter; use a professional design and layout format.

- Limit your letter to one page and be sure to hit the highlights of why your interests and experience are relevant for the open job position for which you are applying.

- Demonstrate knowledge about and interest in the company you're applying to and focus on how you are the best applicant for the position.

- Share results and numbers. Be sure to highlight your previous accomplishments and quantify your success instead of just describing your previous job duties or roles.

- Include ways for the employer to contact you with questions or to schedule a follow-up interview. Contact information can include phone number, email address, portfolio website URL, or social media profiles and handles.

- Delete all "super, great, really awesome" superlatives that diminish the quality of your writing and take up valuable space.

- Edit and proof your content. Read. Re-read. Repeat. Make sure you edit and proofread your cover letter for spelling errors, typos and style or grammatical errors before submitting or hitting "send." If possible, have someone else take a look at the letter to make sure you don't miss any mistakes.

Sample Job Cover Letters

Ineffective Opening Paragraph

Dear John,

My name is Amy Goodman, and I'm interested in applying for the Content Marketing position at Company ZZ. I will graduate in May of this year and think that I'd be a great fit for your company. I am a strong writer, good team player and have excellent time management skills. I'm also including my resume and a link to my online portfolio.

Effective Opening Paragraph

Dear John Smith,

I'm Amy Goodman, and as your new Content Marketer, I want to help Company ZZ gain new customers, pursue exponential growth on social media and write game-changing content that elevates and expands your strong media profile. Below I'm including several examples of how my experience at Internship ABC helped perfect my strong writing and editing skills and how an original digital marketing campaign I worked on exceeded more than 1 million impressions in less than 30 days. I'm also including my resume and writing samples to demonstrate the quality of my work and why I'm the best fit for your Content Marketing position.

Letter to the Editor

A letter to the editor can serve dual roles in communication, in that it is written to an individual, but viewable and accessible to the masses. As its name indicates, the letter is addressed to the editor of a specific publication to share an opinion about a recent topic of interest or issues covered in the media. At the same time, if the letter is published by the media outlet, then it is also read by thousands or possibly millions of other people who also read the publication in hardcopy or online editions. Though this document may be seen by many, the focus of the document is narrow and targeted to the editor of a publication, who can provide feedback to the letter writer and make changes in how a particular topic is covered, based on the letter. A letter to the editor is typically less than one page. As a general rule, review and follow the length guidelines for letters provided by the publication before submitting. The letter to the editor generally shares an opinion or perspective in first-person narrative and offers some additional insight into the sender's viewpoint about the topic of the letter. A letter to the editor also can be considered a persuasive document if the writer has an opposing opinion and wants to encourage other readers to consider their perspective.

Here is a convenient checklist for writing or coaching a PR client on how to write an effective letter to the editor:

- Keep it short, simple and straightforward and follow the publication's guidelines for length and submission to the outlet.

- Make sure the letter to the editor addresses a relevant and timely issue that readers can identify with from recent news coverage.

- Identify the subject of the letter in the first paragraph and include the name of the article, its author and the date of publication for clarity.

- Articulate the theme of the letter in the second paragraph, stating whether the letter is in agreement, disagreement, support of or opposition to recent coverage.

- Use the letter to the editor to reinforce or underscore issues outlined in the initial coverage, or to highlight information that was missing from the original article.

- Feel free to share an opinion or unique perspective in a letter to the editor, but also be sure to back up that opinion with credible information that supports the viewpoint.

● Provide up-to-date contact information and a signature (or digital/e-signature) on the letter so that the publication's editorial team can confirm the author and content of the letter and verify that the writer stands by the submission.

Sample Letters to the Editor

Ineffective Opening Paragraph

Dear Editor,

I totally disagree with your recent story about students not being good citizens in the nightclub district of our town. Your newspaper is condescending and disrespectful toward students, and you should find more positive stories to tell.

Effective Opening Paragraph

Dear Features Editor,

I'm writing in response to the Nov. 1 article titled "Students Cause Halloween Horror in Downtown District" by reporter Jay Bowman. The article focused on a lot of negative activities related to students but failed to discuss the countless invaluable contributions made by students in the community. I want to respectfully disagree with the article's assertion that students don't make good citizens or supporters for local business owners. By patronizing local shops, restaurants, and nightclubs, students are a significant driver for our local economy, and I think it's unfair to place sole responsibility of a few random acts on the entire student community.

Direct Mail Letter

Direct mail letters are a common marketing communications (or MarCom) tool that are used to communicate with target audiences for the purposes of publicity and promotions for a product or service. Though direct mail letters are a part of the sales and marketing process, the strategic approach and content are often created by PR practitioners who have a strong writing skillset. A direct mail letter introduces the product or service and its associated benefits and features. The letter also provides the process for a potential customer to acquire the product or service, which may include price, packaging and the process for delivery. What makes a direct mail letter unique to many other media-focused PR documents is its laser focus on connecting with the reader or recipient of the letter. Direct mail is often customized and tailored to the individual receiving it, using their name and some basic personal information based on past purchasing preferences. For example, "Mary, you've been a longtime customer of Company J for 10 years, and we know you value quality furniture at an affordable price with fast delivery." Direct mail letters are often persuasive and rely heavily upon interpersonal communication skills to make the recipient feel respected and valued as a customer. As a result, the person is more likely to continue being a customer and purchasing the products or services featured in the letter.

A common process for communicating with individuals and then persuading them to take action follows three basic steps:

1. Identify the problem.

2. Exaggerate and/or exacerbate the problem.

3. Solve the problem.

Consider these tips when seeking to connect with an individual and persuade them to invest in a new product or service:

- Use a clever, attention-grabbing headline or opening paragraph.

- Customize the content by using their first and last names and tailored information.

- Tell a story or paint a picture of how your product/service solutions solve their problem.

- Provide clear information about the product or service and its associated value, benefits and features.

- Include short, bulleted lists to make product or service information clear and easy to understand.

- Use a few handwriting-style typefaces and fonts for personalization to increase engagement.

- Use a conversational tone to avoid the letter sounding like a sales pitch.

- Offer a free giveaway or some type of premium (e.g., free shipping) if the customer takes action within a specified period of time.

Sample Direct Mail Letter

Here's an example of how a writer can present or create a perceived problem, amplify it and then allow their unique product or service offering to become the much-needed solution.

Example: Virtual Personal Assistant Service

Dear Jennifer,

If you often feel like there aren't enough hours in the day to get everything done, you're not alone. Between work, and family, and volunteer duties, there's hardly any time left for you. If you're always in demand, you deserve a helping hand. Imagine how much more free time you'll have to relax and enjoy spending time with family and friends when you use one of our virtual personal assistants to save you time and money. Take control of your schedule and let our virtual personal Assistant handle the details . . . problem solved.

In this example, the text is targeted toward the consumer and addresses her in a familiar way by using her first name. A simple mail-merge program or application easily allows content creators to personalize content and make it specific to the recipient using a spreadsheet with various filters and narratives. Next, the sample paragraph overemphasizes the reader in the content by using second person "you" to paint a picture of the potential customer facing a problem that the proposed product or service can solve. The messenger in the text goes on to emphasize how the problem can create a crippling effect on the person's life — unless they allow the product/service they're selling to fix the problem. In this narrative, the focus is all about the customer and how the customer can benefit from using the proposed solution.

Email Correspondence

Professional email correspondence is such an entrenched part of day-to-day business activity that it's easy to forget that email is still a form of professional communication and a tool practitioners can use as part of a larger strategic messaging campaign. As new social media sites and tools became more prevalent, there was the belief that email would disappear. In addition, new software and applications promoted secure transmissions and streamlined communication chains that threatened the relevance of email boxes. However, email's free accounts, ease of access and use created opportunities for new content delivery systems (such as electronic newsletters or e-newsletters) to thrive, based on the format that emails are delivered. The strength of email systems is that there is a written record, time stamp, and confirmed delivery notification that accompanies every message. What was initially communicated is easily retrieved, forwarded, shared, stored or archived as needed by the sender or recipient.

Because email is commonly and casually used for professional and personal purposes, it is important to set up and follow a professional email "code of conduct" when using email for business or client representation purposes. Follow these general guidelines to make sure your emails represent you, your employer, and your clients in a professional manner.

Do

- Use professional language and write as though everything in the email will be made public.

- Be polite and respectful in your tone to colleagues and clients.

- Include a clear subject line that identifies the topic of discussion.

- Clearly state the purpose of your email so that that recipient can easily respond without several email exchanges: (e.g., Don't write, "Wanted to follow up on the project to see when we can discuss . . .". Consider writing, "Thank you for your feedback on the Client M project. The edits you suggested are complete. Please let me know your availability on Thursday afternoon between 2 and 4 p.m. to discuss our next steps.")

- Read your email at least twice to ensure correct spelling, grammar, style and professionalism. Read. Edit. Proof. Repeat.

- Send a confirmation, thank you, or acknowledgement of an email after receiving a response just to let the recipient know that the message is important to you and the issue has your attention.

Don't

- Include the name of the recipient until the final step before hitting send (after you've had an opportunity to edit and proof) to prevent sending an incomplete, inaccurate or inappropriate email message.

- Send an email when you're upset, angry or frustrated. Wait and allow the situation to cool down; revisit the message, re-read the message and then re-type the message knowing that it's likely to be shared.

- Send after-hours emails expecting an immediate response. Be courteous of people's time and other priorities.

- Use acronyms or abbreviations that make your message appear less professional. Avoid emojis or emoticons and excessive punctuation (e.g., I'm super excited to work with you!!!) in professional communication documents.

- Forward unprofessional or inappropriate content that might jeopardize you and your colleagues' jobs.

- Use all capital letters for emphasis, as it may appear that you're shouting or yelling.

Sample Emails

Ineffective Email

Subject Line: Following up

Hey Terry,

I wanted to run some ideas by you sometime this week to prepare for my first pitch presentation to the account manager. Let me know your schedule. I'm kinda nervous about pitching, so let me know if you can help.

Effective Email

Subject Line: Brainstorming and Practice Run-Thru for Campaign Pitch

Good morning, Terry,

Thank you for the input you shared to prepare for the Mobley pitch. I'm researching and preparing for this Friday's presentation and wanted to connect with you in advance to practice and get your feedback on my content. Let me know if you have some time to connect on Tuesday morning between 9 a.m. and 11:30 for about 30 minutes. Thank you!

PR Client Pitch

New PR client pitch communiques encompass any of the communication and/or presentation materials created to convince a potential new client to select you or your PR agency as their representative. Though many new clients are gained through the Request for Proposal (RFP) process, a lot of new accounts are secured through the traditional sales process that includes meeting a new contact, learning their business model, identifying their needs, understanding their problem, and providing a solution. In the process of pursuing a new opportunity to gain a new client, there may be a lot of individuals within the organization who interview or evaluate interested PR agencies; however, in many cases, the initial conversation begins with an individual who needs to be convinced and persuaded that you are the right choice to represent them. Potential documents that target an individual during this process include email messages, custom job/client cover letter, and the PR presentation pitch (similar to a media pitch letter or email).

Incorporate this list of tips into your next written PR pitch to pursue a new client opportunity:

- Do your homework and research the company to learn its mission, vision, values and culture — along with reviewing recent media coverage, competitors and accomplishments.

- Demonstrate how your PR services or PR agency add value to the client.

- Explain how your PR services can solve a problem that the client has identified.

- If possible, direct your initial pitch and follow-up correspondence to a decision maker within the company.

- Be clear in your intent; ask for the PR business opportunity.

Sample PR Client Pitches

Ineffective New Client Pitch

Dear Mike,

It was a pleasure meeting you at the recent networking event last month. During our brief conversation, you mentioned needing to hire a new PR agency. The company I work for focuses on corporate communications campaigns, so please let me know if we can be of assistance to you.

Effective New Client Pitch

Dear Mr. Michael Johnson,

I enjoyed our conversation about the local minor league baseball team's chances for success. It's always enjoyable to meet another Redhawks fan. During our conversation you mentioned the need to hire a new PR agency. As I shared with you, I'm an account manager at Company Q, where we serve over a dozen Fortune 500 companies with corporate communications services and award-winning campaigns. Our dedicated content marketing team can assist with the lack of a strong online presence that you mentioned. If you are planning to issue an RFP, we would like the opportunity to present our team's capabilities; or offer an in-person presentation to share more about how we can help Company XYZ strengthen its external communications.

Bonus: Thank You Notes & Letters

Thank you letters or notes might seem like a forgotten relic from a time gone by. However, a well-written thank you letter, thank you note, or at the minimum, a thank you email — can go a long way in building professional relationships in the PR industry. Thank you notes are simple, but effective, tools that help practitioners stand out from the competition. The simple gesture of expressing appreciation for someone's time, assistance or guidance speaks volumes and demonstrates respect for the recipient. Also, since most people don't take the time to follow up and say thank you in a formal way, the sender of a thank you card becomes memorable for their thoughtfulness, which can make all the difference in a competitive industry filled with aspiring and talented professionals.

It's worth the small investment to purchase a package of thank you cards and postage stamps, so they are readily available when you need to get a note out the door quickly. Thank you cards can be brief and to the point, as long as the message is specific and genuine. The objective is to acknowledge the giver and the gift.

When writing a thank you letter or thank you card/note, make sure to acknowledge and include the following:

- Name of the person you're thanking
- Gift that is being acknowledged (e.g., "Thank you for taking time to review my work."; "I appreciate the feedback on my campaign proposal."; "Thank you for the invitation to job shadow at your company.")
- What the gift or gesture meant to you
- Well-wishes to the recipient
- Your name

Sample Thank You Notes

Ineffective (sent via email or text)

J,

Thx so much for the career advice. Was super helpful. u r the best!!!

Effective (sent by U.S. mail service)

Dear Jordan,

Thank you very much for your career advice during our university's networking event. I appreciate the time you took to answer my questions. Our conversation provided a lot of clarity and guidance, and I'm grateful for your suggestions. I will be sure to keep you posted with the results of my job search. Your mentorship is important to me, and I just wanted to say thank you.

Sincerely,

Will Ashton

CREATE A FOOLPROOF WRITING PROCESS

Consider these tips:

- Read content aloud. Hearing yourself read content that you've written allows you to focus on how the recipient will hear and respond to what is written.

- Scan content from the end, backward to the beginning. Typos tend to stand out more clearly because of the unnatural reading direction, making errors easier to catch.

- Imagine you're reading your content/copy to a sixth grader (the national average reading level in the U.S.) and clarify anything the student might not clearly understand.

- Use the word processing software spelling checker and grammar review functions to electronically check your work for errors.

- Manually check any proper nouns for spelling and accuracy; review any content in all CAPS (such as a headline) because software spelling review programs often miss errors in all caps.

- Write or spell out any unnecessary acronyms or abbreviations. Also, delete pointless jargon or technical terms that make your content difficult to read or understand.

- Be clear and get to the point in the first paragraph. Readers and listeners have increasingly short attention spans, so it's important to get and keep their attention immediately.

- Avoid passive language and negative phrasing; use neutral or positive language and keep the content moving!

CHAPTER SUMMARY

The roles and duties in public relations require a lot of writing and mastery of a lot of different documents. It's important to learn the mechanics of how to construct content, but it's also important to know and understand the audience that you're attempting to reach. When writing to individuals, sometimes it's less about the content and more about the sentiment behind the content. When you're writing to a person, think about who's reading the correspondence and how they will respond and engage with the communication.

KEY TERMS

direct mail letters	letter to the editor
job cover letter	PR client pitch communiques

DISCUSSION QUESTIONS

1. What elements make a compelling and effective pitch to media?

2. What information does a journalist need from you to make a decision about whether to cover an event?

3. Why do you think so many email pitches to journalists are ignored or deleted?

4. What words or phrases in a job cover letter might make a potential employer overlook a letter from a potential job applicant?

5. What academic and professional strengths do you plan to highlight in your job cover letter?

6. What can you do to make your job cover letter stand out from those of competitors?

7. What type of content do you think motivates an editor to select one letter to the editor over another?

8. What value does a letter to the editor section add to a print publication?

9. Where can you envision submitting a letter to the editor on behalf of a client adding value to a comprehensive communications campaign?

10. What buzz words can you think of that make people want to purchase something?

11. What effects do using someone's name and basic personal references have in direct mail marketing?

12. Why does using handwriting on a direct mail envelope increase the likelihood the letter gets opened by the recipient?

13. What could possibly go wrong in this email where you may be feeling frustrated or ignored since one deadline was already missed in getting information to you?

14. What emotions are you experiencing in writing this email that could negatively influence the content you write?

15. How can your email be clear and concise, without being accusatory or inflammatory?

16. What things can you do to prepare as part of a PR pitch team to go after a new business opportunity?

17. Why is it important to research a potential client prior to pitching them for a new business opportunity?

18. Why should a PR pitch be directed toward a decision-maker within the company?

19. Why are thank you cards memorable — more than an email or text?

20. What does sending a thank you letter or thank you card represent to the person who receives it?

21. When is it appropriate to send a thank you card to a professional colleague?

WRITING EXERCISES

1. Story Idea: Client Fairbanks Regional Library is hosting a 24-hour charity read-a-thon on June 30 to benefit local literacy organizations and to increase literacy among elementary school children during the summer. The community is being asked to donate books and money or volunteer to read during the 24-hour fundraising campaign event. Target: Local daily newspaper features writer Joanne Dudley.

   Exercise: Write a media pitch email to daily newspaper features writer Joanne Dudley inviting her to cover the June 30 charity read-a-thon event, hosted by Fairbanks Regional Library.

2. Write a one-page job cover letter to secure your dream job after college. Address the letter to a specific person, using their name, title and company contact information. Don't forget to say which position you're applying for and why you're the best fit for the job.

3. Review your campus or local newspaper and select an article that interests you. Draft a one-page letter to the editor to express your opinion, agreement, disagreement, or suggestions to the editorial team. Be sure to follow the submission guidelines, sign or e-sign your letter, and include your contact information. If you feel strongly about the issue, submit the letter to the publication to see if it gets published; then include the published version as part of your writing portfolio.

4. Product: The new Wi-Fi-enabled EchoPen digital recorder and ballpoint pen tool that can be used as a writing instrument as well as a recording device.
   Target Audience: middle school and high school educators; direct mail letter written to an individual teacher named Barbara Jones.

   Exercise: Write an opening paragraph to Barbara Jones that introduces a new product called EchoPen, which is a combination writing instrument and digital recorder. Be sure to (1) identify the problem Barbara has without having access to an EchoPen; (2) exaggerate or exacerbate the problem she and her colleagues might experience by comparing or contrasting the improved benefits of daily teaching activities enhanced by EchoPen; and (3) solve the problem that Barbara and other educators may encounter by explaining how EchoPen offers a valuable solution.

5. Scenario: Write a professional email to a PR Agency colleague requesting a quotation for a news release from the client that they were supposed to secure and send two days ago — and then promised to send to you by the close of business today. It's now 4:30 p.m. and you still don't have the quote that you need for 8 a.m. tomorrow.
Client/Quote: Client George Howard of Forever Fitness is providing a quote to your colleague Patricia Jordan to highlight the benefits of their company's new virtual fitness program. You need the quote for inclusion in a news release that's scheduled for distribution at 8 a.m. tomorrow morning.

   Exercise: Write a professional email message to your colleague Patricia Jordan requesting the quotation that she was supposed to secure and send to you. Include the subject line for your email and clearly state the purpose of your email, what you need from her in a response email to you; be sure to structure the email in a way that the colleague knows exactly what you need to finish the project. Before hitting the send button, make sure to check your spelling, grammar, style and tone.

6. Think of a celebrity who has been receiving negative media coverage and write a new client pitch email offering PR services to assist with their communications and media relations.

7. Write a thank you note to a former professor who provided a strong letter of recommendation for you to submit with an internship or job application.

GLOSSARY

advertising: Paid, creative messaging that appears in print, radio, television and internet productions to inform or influence the purchasing process

aggregator sites: Sites that scan stories and information published online and compile them within a single source site

annual report: A once-a-year document that corporations and nonprofit organizations publish to update investors, shareholders and contributors with a year-in-review accounting of financial operations and activities, along with a summary of operations and accomplishments

A-roll: The main footage that drives storytelling containing both audio and video components that inform, persuade, educate or entertain the viewer

Associated Press: Global conglomerate entity that dispatches journalists, digital storytellers and creatives alike to gather, report and distribute news content to media outlets and platforms around the world

Associated Press Stylebook: A useful tool that outlines basic rules and guidelines for writers related to spelling, grammar, punctuation, usage and inclusive language

audience persona: The "re-creation" of an individual, based on the demographic and psychographic profiles that brings the ideal target audience to life and allows the PR practitioner to envision how the consumer can and will interact with the brand

audience profiles: Identify and define message recipients

audience survey: Assesses and measures public perception

Audio News Release (ANR): An uncontrolled production in audio format that is produced (or the production is managed) by the PR or promotional team and distributed to radio stations or audio broadcast platforms to share information about a newsworthy announcement, event, or client-related activity for the purpose of garnering additional media exposure and coverage

audio PSA: PSA created for and distributed by a nonprofit organization and presented to radio stations or podcast producers to audiences who will only hear the content

backgrounder: An informational document that offers some historical context about a company and provides more detailed information about its founding, leaders, history, mission, vision and goals

bandwagon activism: When individuals (often celebrities or public figures) or businesses participate in a social movement because it is popular, or they feel pressured to participate by their respective stakeholder groups

banner ad: A hyperlinked digital ad placed on websites

biases: Learned or inherent prejudices against or in favor of certain individuals and groups

billable hours: The time spent working on a project or a client's campaign that will be charged to the client

billboard: An oversized print or digital advertising platform often placed alongside highways and roads, or in high-traffic public spaces like airports and transit stations

biography: A detailed description about an individual's life that includes the person's name, title and organization, and an overview of their current role and responsibilities

blogs: Online journals or issue-centric web pages that are populated with conversational or informational content and frequently updated to provide fresh commentary for readers, subscribers and viewers

boilerplate: A summary paragraph about the organization

issuing a news release that provides basic background, history, mission, and contact information to the journalists

brand: A collective identity that introduces and represents a company, organization or individual and their respective products or services while establishing unique identifiers that distinguish the entity from other similar enterprises

brand ambassador: Anyone selected to speak on behalf of, or serve as a face, voice or representative of the brand

brand assets: All the elements that make up the forward-facing brand components and any materials that support brand development

brand experience: The intersection of a brand's perception, desired expectation and experience realized

brand extension: A company expansion based on use of an existing brand to introduce or launch new products, services or subcategories of existing products and services

brand guidelines: Written rules and parameters are crucial to establishing and maintaining the correct, consistent appearance and usage of a brand

brand identity: A reflection of the tangible and intangible brand elements that describe the heart and soul of the brand's public-facing persona

brand management: A continual and perpetual process of maintenance that ensures appropriate application and implementation of the brand in practice

brand message: Message that conveys the value proposition and benefit of patronizing one company over another

branding style guides: Comprehensive guidebooks on how to properly represent a brand

branding: The process of branding incorporates creating and disseminating the brand name and brand identity

brochure: One of the most common creative materials produced by organizations to provide general, high-level information about a company or organization

B-roll: The secondary, supplemental video footage that provides additional context, background, and visual interest during storytelling

celebrities: Well-known individuals who usually have national or international prominence and recognition

celebrity activism: When celebrity individuals or corporate brands employ celebrity figures as endorsers or spokespersons for a worthy cause

co-branding: A type of collaboration that includes marketing a product or service under two or more brand names to increase exposure

codes of conduct: Guidelines for professional behavior that outline the range of ethical standards; also known as ethics codes

collateral materials: Controlled publication documents that tend to be more promotional in nature with creative designs and layouts; also known as MarCom

communication audit: a long and comprehensive report that details all the internal and external communication activities of a company, organization, or institution

company profiles: Short paragraphs or write-ups about a company or organization that can be used to convey a brief overview and quickly introduce important information

confirmation bias: The tendency to interpret and recall information in a way that confirms or reinforces a prior set of beliefs

conflict: A story element that creates tension and a sense of belonging where individuals get to side with a character or a cause that connects with them

contentious collaborations: When a brand attempts to neutralize an external threat by developing and grooming relationships with individuals or organizations that might otherwise challenge the company's operations and harm the brand's reputation

controlled publications: Documents that the PR practitioner has ultimate control over from start to finish

corporate social responsibility (CSR): A type of business self-regulation with the aim of social accountability and making a positive impact on society

creative brief: A short document that outlines the campaign and its final deliverables

crisis: a potentially hazardous, threatening, or damaging natural or man-made situation that poses a threat to life, safety, property, reputation or standard operations

crisis communication: The managed process and flow of communication and messaging strategies to all affected audiences

crisis management: The orchestrated response to a crisis with the objective of restoring normalcy

culture: Aspect of a company that is shaped by the company's mission, vision, values, attitudes, standards and beliefs

cut: Instantaneous switch from one shot to another, similar to the blink of an eye with a change of scenery between each blink

dark site: A prepopulated, remotely activated website dedicated solely to crisis communication activities and messaging

deconstruction: Allows for specific data points to be derived from demographic and psychographic information to understand who the current customer base is and how to tailor messages for targeted communications in the future

direct mail letters: Documents often associated with marketing campaigns that appeal to customers or potential customers to purchase a product

dissolve: Gradual replacement of one image with another

diversity: The reality and presence of differences between people, which may include age, race, gender, identity, religious beliefs or practices, sexual orientation, ethnicity,

socioeconomic status, language, (dis)ability, political ideologies, perspectives, etc.

dolly in/out: Camera movement where the entire camera body moves in a straight line toward or away from the subject

emergency operations center (EOC): The official location for coordination of crisis management and response

emergency preparedness: The advanced planning process for training and preparing for appropriate crisis responses

equity: Fairness, justice and impartiality in laws, policies, procedures, processes and the distribution of resources with systems and institutions

ethics: Guidance for conduct that includes values such as honesty, openness, loyalty, fair-mindedness, respect, integrity and forthright communication

ethics codes: Guidelines for professional behavior that outline the range of ethical standards; also known as codes of conduct

ethos: The credibility and authority of the speaker presenting the information to an audience, along with the presenter's ability to connect and relate with the audience in a convincing manner

evergreen: A description of content that is always fresh and relevant, rarely has a time limit and is known for its long shelf life and universal impact on society

extemporaneous speech: Hybrid speech that blends the elements of a scripted

speech based on the amount of research and preparation required, and a memorized speech, based on the lack of formal documents or notes provided to assist in its delivery

fact sheet: A document that introduces background, historical and research information about a company to help journalists write or produce an accurate story about the organization being featured in the article

fade: Gradual change usually to or from black

feature articles: Creative and insightful tools to use to support a larger PR campaign while also educating the target audience and bringing increased awareness or positive media attention to the client

feature stories: Articles that focus on an individual, product or issue and provide additional details and narrative about the subject from beginning to end

first responders: The initial personnel on site to deescalate or resolve a crisis situation

flat rate: A fixed, flat fee charged to a client for a project deliverable or specific work being done on their behalf

flyer: A one-page promotional handout that is widely distributed for informational and promotional purposes

framing: How information is presented and which attributes within the content are highlighted or downplayed in terms of relevance and importance

ghostwriting: The hiring of professional writers to write, edit and proof literary works, books or speeches, which are then credited to another person as the author

going viral: Referring to content that spreads quickly and widely across the internet and through online social platforms

GRACE: PR campaign model that stands for Goal-Setting, Research, Assessment, Communication, and Evaluation

hashtag: A symbol that precedes short words and phrases to enhance online searches and to connect online topics and conversations as part of a trend or theme; also known as the pound key, tic tac toe sign or octothorpe

hashtag activism: When companies or individuals demonstrate support for an issue or cause by reposting, liking or sharing a specific hashtag and accompanying word or phrase

headline: The hook that catches the reader's interest and encourages them to read more; also known as title

headshot: A professional photograph of the subject that pictures them close-up and shows their face and a little of the background or scenery

hourly rate: The amount of money that is charged to a client per hour for work being done on their behalf

human interest: A story factor that makes news more relatable and easily understandable because the individuals featured are undergoing

circumstances that people can connect with through experience or observation

hype: A form of extreme and exaggerated publicity for an individual, product or service

hyperlink: An element that actively engages the reader by connecting text or images to additional text, images or external content relevant to the topic

icon: A graphic mark that represents a larger idea

identity package: A collection of all the brand assets into one cohesive document that presents the print, digital, exhibition, packaging and collateral communications materials as they should be displayed or duplicated to represent the company

impromptu speech: Speech that has no formal preparation and is delivered at a moment's notice by the speaker

inclusion: Openness and accessibility that welcomes diverse groups and individuals within an organization to fully participate and engage equally

influencers: Individuals who have the power to give recommendations and suggestions due to audience trust, admiration and respect of them

infographic: A one-page document with strong graphic design elements that presents data, statistics, or complex information with visual representation to make the information easier to understand

integrated marketing: A comprehensive approach to audience engagement using

a combination of advertising, marketing, public relations and special events across different media platforms or channels to develop comprehensive campaigns

integrity: A way of life and doing business built on unwavering and resolute principles of honesty, morality, ethics and consistent adherence to strong personal values that are applied without question or coercion

job cover letter: A written document that serves as the initial point of introduction to a potential employer and is presented during the job application process

Letter of Interest (LOI): Document from creative agencies indicating their qualifications and plans to bid on given work once it opens for responses

letter to the editor: Letter addressed to the editor of a specific publication to share an opinion about a recent topic of interest or issues covered in the media

logo: A graphics-based design, emblem, mark, or symbol that serves as a visual icon to represent and promote the identity of an organization

logos: Uses logic and reason and the content presented is based on facts, figures, statistics and empirical data that is quantifiable

magnitude: A story element highlighting the number of people affected by a situation and how serious the consequences or impact will be

MarCom: Controlled publication documents that tend to be more promotional in nature with creative designs and layouts; also known as collateral materials

marketing: The sales-oriented process of introducing, packaging, pricing, promoting and placing products or services into a desirable position in the marketplace for consumption

marketing collateral: Content and documents that support the sales, marketing, and branding processes by contributing to a collection of materials that promote the brand identity

marketing communications: A robust group of activities that seek to sell, market, and promote products, services, or ideas

media advisory: A document that piques the interest of potential journalists by providing enough information about a potential story idea that they are inclined to inquire further

media database: A document containing relevant media contacts and their contact information for the purpose of distributing updates and pitching story ideas to gain media coverage; also known as media list

media list: A document containing relevant media contacts and their contact information for the purpose of distributing updates and pitching story ideas to gain media coverage; also known as media database

media pitch (letter or email): A written message created for an individual journalist, reporter or media representative to pique their interest in

covering a client, topic or story idea

media prep Q&A: A document that prepares and shapes the framework for a successful media interview

media relations: An aspect of PR work involving the use of soft skills and intangible interpersonal skills to build quality and mutually beneficial professional relationships with journalists and working media professionals so as to be able to periodically pitch ideas and secure positive exposure on behalf of a client or cause

memo: a brief (usually one-page) written correspondence that conveys a specific point of information in a concise format

messaging: Commonly used phrase that refers to communication that targets an audience with the goal of persuading them to follow through with a specific action

metrics: Quantifiable tools that allow a PR professional to monitor and measure the impact and reach of a communications campaign

mission statement: A formal declaration of the purpose, goals, objectives and values of a company, organization, or institution

music bed: Music or instrumentals that play in the background and can be directed to be more or less prominent during the shot

NatSound: Natural sounds that accompany video footage

news cycle: The process through which news circulates and recurs

news release: A document that presents a newsworthy story idea in a generally accepted format that can be utilized by journalists to develop a complete story

news values: Criteria that influence the selection and presentation of events as published news

newsletter: A controlled publication that can be printed in hardcopy or delivered electronically to a targeted group of individuals who have an interest in the content included in the document

novelty: A story element relating to a situation's uniqueness

On Camera (O/C): A/V cue that indicates a speaker, text, or subject that is shown on camera

one-sheets: One-page documents that feature a product or service overview as part of a larger promotional campaign to educate and inform readers

online newsrooms: Web pages that serve as a repository for multimedia content available to journalists and nonmedia site visitors

organizational charts: Visuals that represent the hierarchal structure within a company, organization or institution and explain the internal structure of various roles and responsibilities within

PACE: PR campaign model that stands for Planning,

Action, Communication, and Evaluation

pan right/left: Camera movement where the camera body remains in a fixed position, while the camera head or lens rotates right or left as in a panoramic view

pathos: Focuses on emotions and emotional appeal to persuade people to act in a certain way

performance activism: Supporting or championing a cause publicly for the sake of increasing or enhancing visibility for the company or brand

persuasion: The process of motivating people to do something by reason, argument, influence or appeal

PESO Model: A model of content curation and strategic communication that is used to gain visibility, engage with audiences and amplify messaging; stands for Paid, Earned, Shared, and Owned

photo caption: Text that accompanies a published photograph and explains the significance of the photo, describing who or what is pictured and what is occurring in the image

podcast: On-demand, internet-based radio show that features streaming and downloadable audio content

position papers: Public-facing documents that clearly articulate the stance a company or corporation takes on a particular issue, topic or subject that is relevant to the organization and its stakeholders, customers or investors

position statement: An official expression or document published by an organization to clearly articulate its stance on an issue; also known as position paper

poster: A larger version of a flyer that displays oversized graphics and typography and is often a keepsake that can be showcased as art or a souvenir

PR client pitch communiques: Any of the communication or presentation materials created to convince a potential new client to select you or your PR agency as their representative

press conference: A media-focused event that invites journalists to attend and learn more information from the entity hosting the press conference

print ad: A paid announcement inserted in print publications (and their online digital versions) that conforms with size specifications for placement (e.g., ¼-page, ½-page, full-page)

product samples: Free items available for journalists to test or review and write about

promotion: Activities designed to increase awareness or gain attention from the public or the media

proximity factor: A story's direct, local connection to the people it is being told to

public relations: The art and science of managing relationships and communicating specific messages to target audiences to achieve desired, measurable outcomes using multimedia platforms

public service announcements (PSAs): General audience messages created by and distributed by nonprofit organizations

publicity stunt: An event orchestrated solely for the purpose of attracting attention to a person or an organization

qualitative research: Seeks to analyze and extract insights regarding motivations and behavior

quantitative research: Relies on methods that produce measurable, statistical data

quotations: The exact words spoken by an individual about a particular subject or in response to an interview question

RACE: PR campaign model that stands for Research, Action, Communication, and Evaluation

rebranding: A restorative process that injects new life to an existent brand to introduce new products, services, ownership or company culture, and to provide a new look and feel

reconstruction: Utilizes audience profile data and builds a brand persona so that practitioners can apply insights and context to create messaging in direct response to known interests, hobbies, lifestyles and values of the brand's customer base

relevance: A story element involving connection to the audience through providing information they want to know more about, think about or care about

Request for Proposal (RFP): An official solicitation submitted by a business, nonprofit, or government agency announcing a new project for which they are seeking qualified contractors to respond and complete the work

Request for Quote (RFQ): A correspondence sent to companies that provide tangible widgets, gadgets or devices that have a specific unit or price or are available for wholesale purchase

Request for Tender (RFT): An invitation for suppliers to bid on supplying a product or service

retainer: An amount of money consistently paid (usually monthly) to reserve a specified amount of time dedicated toward a project or campaign

ROPE: PR campaign model that stands for Research, Objectives, Programming, and Evaluation

ROSIE: PR campaign model that stands for Research, Objectives, Strategies, Implementation, and Evaluation

RSS feeds: Subscriber-based aggregators that can be organized and customized for readers to prioritize topics of interest or favorite content sites

run of show: A document that details a logistical production schedule and outline of a special event and includes every speaker, transition, pause, performance, or activity that occurs from hours before the program starts until the last dessert is served and the

event host says goodnight and wishes everyone farewell

shot list: A detailed list of every camera shot that needs to be captured in order to produce a final video product

situation analysis: A overview or document providing context around the unique opportunity to be leveraged or the problem that the PR plan is designed to solve

slogan: A short, memorable phrase that highlights an aspect of the brand

sound effects (SFX): Artificial audio enhancements

speech cues: Stage directions provided to the speaker within the body of the speech to prompt a specific action or movement, or to prompt a particular response from the audience

speeches: Prepared statements developed to deliver to an audience

spin: Deception with the intent to distribute inaccurate information

storyboard: A graphics-based outline used to organize and present details about a video production

strategic communications: A research-based approach to identifying effective channels for communication and engagement with key publics to inspire specific actions and fulfill mission-oriented goals and objectives

SWOT analysis: An acronym that refers to the assessment of an organization's Strengths, Weaknesses, Opportunities, and Threats

tagline: A short phrase that reinforces a brand's essence in a clever or memorable way

tags: Labels which assign words to images to make them easier to find in online searches, playing a role in improving search engine optimization (SEO)

target audience: Who you are primarily talking to when you launch a new product, service or branding campaign

tilt up/down: Camera movement where the camera body remains in a fixed position, while the camera head or lens moves up or down (nods) as in a floor-to-ceiling shot

timeliness: A story element relating to how new the news is and how quickly the story is unfolding

title: The hook that catches the reader's interest and encourages them to read more; also known as headline

trademark: Any word, phrase, symbol, design or a combination of these things that identifies specific goods and services and conveys how end users or customers recognize an organization in the marketplace

truck right or left: Camera movement where the entire camera body moves in a straight line to the left or right, parallel to the subject

typeface: All the different styles of print and design lettering available

uncontrolled publications: Documents created by the PR professional as a point of reference for or source of information, but the final version is up to the individual or organization using the content for its own editorial purposes

user experience (UX): Consideration of how a consumer interacts with and experiences information, acknowledging audience attention spans, screen size, and accessibility

VALS Survey: Standing for values, attitudes and lifestyles, an online survey asking a series of questions to indicate which one of eight categories, or mindsets, the survey-taker falls in

video news release (VNR): An uncontrolled production in video format that is produced by the PR or promotional team and distributed to television stations or broadcast media outlets to share

information about a newsworthy announcement, event or client-related activity for the purpose of garnering additional media exposure and coverage

video PSA: Visual messaging created for and distributed by a nonprofit organization to audiences that will see and hear content

vision statement: One of the first messages that codifies a business and establishes a brand

voiceover (V/O): A/V cue that indicates a speaker who is not shown on camera

webinar: Combination of a web-based seminar

website: An internet-based collection of material about a

particular subject, organization, institution or company that is organized by individual web pages that readers navigate using tabs or links to access information online

white papers: Well-researched publications, that are considered "owned" content that the company creates to inform the public or make the case for a specific argument related to its industry

wipe: Transition where one image "wipes" the previous image away and replaces it

word cloud: A simple, yet effective visualization tool that combines a variety of opinions from surveys or polls into one concise graphic that maximizes common responses and minimizes less popular responses

REFERENCES

CHAPTER 2

Lyons, T. (n.d.). *Is ghostwriting ethical? Professional ghost.* https://professionalghost.com/blog/is-ghostwriting-ethical/

McBride, K. (2012). *"Patchwriting" is more common than plagiarism, just as dishonest.* Poynter. https://www.poynter.org/news/patchwriting-more-common-plagiarism-just-dishonest

Public Relations Society of America. (n.d.). *PRSA code of ethics.* https://www.prsa.org/about/ethics/prsa-code-of-ethics

Society of Professional Journalists. (2014). *SPJ code of ethics.* https://www.spj.org/ethicscode.asp

CHAPTER 3

Associated Press. (2020). *Associated Press stylebook 2020-2022* (55th ed.). Associated Press.

Associated Press. (2022). *The Associated Press stylebook: 2022-2024* (56th ed.). Associated Press. Kindle Edition.

CHAPTER 4

News values. (2024, February 18). *In Wikipedia.* https://en.wikipedia.org/wiki/News_values#:~:text=News%20values%20are%20%22criteria%20that,what%20makes%20something%20%22newsworthy.%22

CHAPTER 5

News values. (2024, May 28). *In Wikipedia.* https://en.wikipedia.org/wiki/News_values#:~:text=News%20values%20are%20%22criteria%20that,what%20makes%20something%20%22newsworthy.%22

CHAPTER 7

Indeed Editorial Team. (2024, April 18). *14 job titles in social media (with salaries.* https://www.indeed.com/career-advice/finding-a-job/job-titles-social-media

CHAPTER 8

Amazon. (n.d.). *Our positions.* https://www.aboutamazon.com/about-us/our-positions

Anchor. (n.d.). *A "cure for racism" and StopAAPIHate.org.* https://anchorww.com/works/cure-for-racism-2/

Associated Press. (2020). *Associated Press stylebook 2020-2022* (55th ed.). Associated Press.

Associated Press. (2022). *The Associated Press stylebook: 2022-2024* (56th ed.). Associated Press. Kindle Edition.

Cancel culture. (2024, April 29). *In Wikipedia.* https://en.wikipedia.org/wiki/Cancel_culture

CBS Boston. (2012, March 20). *Reebok pulls ad urging people to "Cheat on Your Girlfriend, Not on Your Workout.".* https://www.cbsnews.com/boston/news/reebok-pulls-ad-urging-people-to-cheat-on-your-girlfriend-not-on-your-workout/

Dell Technologies. (n.d.). *Diversity and inclusion.* Retrieved October 2022 from https://jobs.dell.com/diversity-and-inclusion#:~:text=We%20strive%20to%20create%20an,disabilities%20to%20thrive%20and%20succeed

Dove [@Dove]. (2017, October 7). *An image we recently posted on Facebook missed the mark* [Post]. X https://twitter.com/Dove/status/916731793927278592?lang=en

Evans, G. (2022, October 13). *"Hadestown" & Jujamcyn theaters apologize and reaffirm "commitment to accessibility" after actor calls out audience member with hearing loss using captioning device. Deadline.* https://deadline.com/2022/10/ha

destown-jujamcyn-lillias-white-broadway-hearing-impaired-audience-caption-device-1235143838/

Fernandes, P. (2024, February 1). *What is the triple bottom line?* https://www.business.com/articles/triple-bottom-line-defined/

H&M. (2018, January 9). *H&M issues unequivocal apology for poorly judged product and image.* [Press release] https://about.hm.com/news/general-news-2018/h-m-issues-unequivocal-apology-for-poorly-judged-product-and-ima.html

Heinz, K., & Urwin, M. (2024, March 5). *What does diversity, equity and inclusion mean in the workplace?* https://builtin.com/diversity-inclusion/what-does-dei-mean-in-the-workplace

Merriam-Webster. (n.d.). Cancel culture. *Merriam-Webster.com dictionary.* Retrieved May 11, 2024, from https://www.merriam-webster.com/dictionary/cancel%20culture

PRSSA. (n.d.). *Diversity & inclusion.* https://www.prsa.org/prssa/about-prssa/diversity-inclusion#

Serna, V. (2022, October 14). *Broadway star humiliates partially-deaf and blind theater fan by accusing her of recording Hadestown performance, after mistaking closed-captioning device for a phone. Daily Mail.* https://www.dailymail.co.uk/news/article-11316361/Deaf-woman-humiliated-Broadway-star-using-closed-captioning-device-watch-performance.html

United Way. (n.d.). *Diversity, equity, and inclusion.* Retrieved October 2022 from https://www.unitedway.org/pages/diversity-and-inclusion

Walt Disney Company. (n.d.). *Our diversity & inclusion journey.* https://thewaltdisneycompany.com/app/uploads/2019/09/DiversityAndInclusionCommitment.pdf

West, S. (2018, January 19). *H&M faced backlash over its "monkey" sweatshirt ad. It isn't the company's only controversy. Washington Post.* https://www.washingtonpost.com/news/arts-and-entertainment/wp/2018/01/19/hm-faced-backlash-over-its-monkey-sweatshirt-ad-it-isnt-the-companys-only-controversy/

White House. (2021, June 25). *Fact sheet: President Biden signs executive order advancing diversity, equity, inclusion, and accessibility in the federal government.* https://www.whitehouse.gov/briefing-room/statements-releases/2021/06/25/fact-sheet-president-biden-signs-executive-order-advancing-diversity-equity-inclusion-and-accessibility-in-the-federal-government/

CHAPTER 9

Associated Press. (2022). *The Associated Press stylebook, 2022–2024,* (56th ed.). Associated Press. Kindle edition.

Clickbait. (n.d.). *In Wikipedia.* https://en.wikipedia.org/wiki/Clickbait

Constitution Annotated: Analysis and Interpretation of the U.S. Constitution. (n.d.). *Artl.S8.C8.3.3 copyright and the First Amendment.* https://constitution.congress.gov/browse/essay/artl-S8-C8-3-3/ALDE_00013065/

CHAPTER 12

State of North Carolina. (2016). *Interactive purchasing system.* https://www.doa.nc.gov/ips-terms-use-july-2016-0/open

CHAPTER 14

Change.org. https://www.nytimes.com/2021/05/24/arts/charlie-bit-my-finger-nft-auction.html

CHAPTER 16

https://en.wikipedia.org/wiki/Brooks_Brothers

https://www.colgatepalmolive.com/en-us/who-we-are/history

https://en.wikipedia.org/wiki/TikTok

United States Patent and Trademark Office. (USPTO.gov, (2021, July). "Using the trademark symbols TM, SM, and ®.".

CHAPTER 17

VALS, Survey. *Strategic Business Insights:.* https://www.strategicbusinessinsights.com/vals/presurvey.shtml

Harvard Business Review. (2020). *"How to Persuade People to Change Their Behavior.".* https://hbr.org/2020/04/how-to-persuade-people-to-change-their-behavior

INDEX